STUDIES IN EVANGELICAL HISTORY AND THOUGHT

James Denney (1856–1917)

An Intellectual and Contextual Biography

James Denney
from W.R. Nicoll, *Letters of Principal James Denney to W. Robertson Nicoll*
(London: Hodder & Stoughton, 1920)

STUDIES IN EVANGELICAL HISTORY AND THOUGHT

James Denney (1856–1917)

An Intellectual and Contextual Biography

James M. Gordon

Foreword by I. Howard Marshall

Copyright © James M. Gordon 2006

First published 2006 by Paternoster

Paternoster is an imprint of Authentic Media
PO Box 6326, Bletchley, Milton Keynes, MK1 9GG

authenticmedia.co.uk

The right of James M. Gordon to be identified as the Author of this Work
has been asserted by him in accordance with the Copyright, Designs
and Patents Act 1988

All rights reserved. No part of this publication may be reproduced, stored in a retrieval system, or transmitted in any form by any means, electronic, mechanical, photocopying, recording or otherwise, without the prior permission of the publisher or a license permitting restricted copying. In the UK such licenses are issued by the Copyright Licensing Agency, Barnard's Inn, 86 Fetter Lane, London, EC4A 1EN

British Library Cataloguing in Publication Data
A catalogue record for this book is available from the British Library

ISBN 978–1–84227–399–9

Typeset by A.R. Cross
Printed and bound by Lightning Source

Series Preface

The Evangelical movement has been marked by its union of four emphases: on the Bible, on the cross of Christ, on conversion as the entry to the Christian life and on the responsibility of the believer to be active. The present series is designed to publish scholarly studies of any aspect of this movement in Britain or overseas. Its volumes include social analysis as well as exploration of Evangelical ideas. The books in the series consider aspects of the movement shaped by the Evangelical Revival of the eighteenth century, when the impetus to mission began to turn the popular Protestantism of the British Isles and North America into a global phenomenon. The series aims to reap some of the rich harvest of academic research about those who, over the centuries, have believed that they had a gospel to tell to the nations.

Series Editors

David Bebbington, Professor of History, University of Stirling, Stirling, Scotland, UK

John H.Y. Briggs, Senior Research Fellow in Ecclesiastical History and Director of the Centre for Baptist History and Heritage, Regent's Park College, Oxford, UK

Timothy Larsen, Associate Professor of Theology, Wheaton College, Illinois, USA

Mark A. Noll, McManis Professor of Christian Thought, Wheaton College, Wheaton, Illinois, USA

Ian M. Randall, Deputy Principal and Lecturer in Church History and Spirituality, Spurgeon's College, London, UK, and a Senior Research Fellow, International Baptist Theological Seminary, Prague, Czech Republic

*To Sheila,
with thanks*

Contents

Foreword
I. Howard Marshall xiii

Preface xv

Abbreviations xix

Chapter 1
Introduction 1
Principal Denney's Papers 2
Intellectual Biography and Contextual Theology 6
The Making of a Mind 9

Chapter 2
Early Years in Greenock, 1856-1874 12
'My father was a working man' 13
'The Covenants were magnificent [but] not destined to be
indispensable' 17
'Particular churches with their specific polities' 20
'I speak of the things…touching the king' 24
'I feel mad at the cheek of the Pope!' 25
'The Sabbath – gift to man' 28
'The good Rhine wine' 30
Missionary Investment 32
'A widespread relish for the free handling of sacred things' 35
'A Bible centred, ethically stringent Presbyterian evangelicalism' 38

Chapter 3
The University Years, 1874-1879 40
University Education in Nineteenth Century Scotland 41
'Entering into the mind of men eminent in thought and in
power of expression' 46
'He who will not reason is a bigot; he who cannot is a fool;
he who dare not is a slave!' 49
Scottish Phliosophy: 'To make experience intelligible' 50
'The world is a rational and intelligible system' 57
'The absolute significance of Christ' 61

New and Disturbing Ideas 67

Chapter 4
College Years, 1879-1883 ....**70**
The Free Church College, Glasgow...71
The Robertson Smith Affair...72
'Men full of the new learning of the times, and not afraid of it' 74
'He helped to win intelligent acceptance of this truth' 77
'The authority of Scripture independent of criticism'..........................80
'We also adopt the rationalistic principle' 83
'Christianity is essentially a historical religion' 85
'To look on Him with open face' 86
'A light, a challenge, an enigma, a reflection of his Master' 91
'Not anything that he said so much as what he did not say' 95

Chapter 5
Hill Street and Broughty Ferry, 1883-1897 ....**99**
'Some good must come from these meetings' 100
Theological Content..104
Contextual References...107
Homiletic Technique...109
Dundee's Country House...112
'They had for one another a mutual passion' 114
'A confession the utterance of which touches the conscience'............117
'Laboriousness as love's characteristic' 121
'Lots of good people, and an extraordinary mass of indifference'.....123
'One coherent intellectual whole' 125
'One who gladly acknowledges a great debt to the person
from whom he dissents'...128
'What I have learned among you'...132

Chapter 6
The Glasgow Years, 1897-1907 ....**135**
'He was nothing if not a biblical theologian' 137
'The ninth lecture excited considerable discussion' 140
'The most stupendous example on record of lying for God' 143
'There is an inexhaustible truth in trying to understand Christ'..........148
'Sensitive to all the intellectual influences which breathe
around him' 150
'Do what you can, or get the chance of doing' 152
'I hope we are not in for a time of panic, or of apathy either'...........154

The Death of Christ 159
The Atonement and the Modern Mind 162
'In the shadow of his sorrow' 166

Chapter 7
The Glasgow Years, 1907-1917 .... **169**
The Christian Attitude to Christ 171
'The burden of the accumulated traditions of past generations' 173
'The symbol of the church's unity' 176
'Christian doctrines justified by their moral results' 179
'The Spirit of liberty, justice, generosity, and mercy' 181
'To legislate is to take the sword' 184
'Thae Unfidel Suffragettes' 187
'They freely recognised each other's Christianity' 189
'Spiritual freedom is an important principle' 191
War and the Fear of God 196
The Christian Doctrine of Reconciliation 202

Chapter 8
Conclusion **209**
Successor to Rainy - Colleague to Whyte 209
'Loyalty to truth and obedience to that same truth' 212
'True ideas on the authority of Scripture' 215
'Not Bethlehem, but Calvary is the focus of revelation' 220
'We may think of the love of God as becoming transcendently
or inconceivably loving' 224
'Christ at the heart of everything' 227

Appendix 1
Chronology of Early Sermons **233**

Appendix 2
Lecture IX Holy Scripture **237**

Appendix 3
Text of Letter from Denney to W. R. Nicoll **254**

Appendix 4
The Late Dr. Denney **257**

Bibliography **259**

General Index **283**

Foreword

I remember chatting with a friend years ago who was a fan of James Denney and told me that he possessed various of his books including his exposition of 1 Corinthians. I replied by saying that I did not think that Denney had written on 1 Corinthians—2 Corinthians yes, but 1 Corinthians no—and he must be confusing the two. But he persisted and said that he would show me it when we reached his home. Sure enough he burrowed into his shelves and produced a book whose cover clearly indicated that it was on 1 Corinthians and by James Denney. I was flabbergasted, but I opened up the book to see what treasure I had been unaware of. And there on the title page it said 1 Corinthians—by Marcus Dods; somehow my friend had never opened it at that point. 'Well', he said, 'I must confess that I didn't think it was up to the standard of Denney's 2 Corinthians!'. No such disappointment has come the way of Jim Gordon. On the contrary, he has had the remarkable experience of considering a possible topic for a thesis and then being told that there were untold treasures available, an archive of unpublished and unexplored MSS by Denney held in New College Library. (They include, incidentally, a set of sermons by Denney on 1 Corinthians comparable to his series on 2 Corinthians!) No student could have had a better reason for a fresh assessment of a distinguished scholar. But what we have here is not just a tour through this new material and a new analysis based upon it. We also have a much more thorough effort than anything previously done to set Denney into the context in which he lived, both as a pastor and preacher and also as a scholar and churchman.

Denney has a key role in evangelical theology with his powerful exposition of an understanding of the death of Christ that has come to be called 'penal substitution' (although he himself was reluctant to use that phrase). To be sure, when his major work on *The Death of Christ* was republished in a modern edition in 1951, the editor and publishers saw fit to prune it of material that was of little contemporary interest but also showed that the author's critical position was not as acceptable to them as his theology: the famous (and somewhat unjust) quip that 'Saint Paul was inspired, but the author of [the Pastoral] Epistles is sometimes only orthodox' was quietly purged. Denney was a practitioner of biblical criticism, 'believing criticism' as it was called. He was a figure of some controversy in his own time. Nevertheless, his criticism was positive and defensive: his Jesus and the gospel was a powerful defence of the historicity of the Jesus of the Gospels (including his resurrection) against the negative evaluation of the liberalism of his day. Moreover, the warmth and passion with which he reverently explored the death of Christ turns his scholarly books into devotional nourishment of the finest quality. O for more preaching today on the level of Denney's sermons on 2 Corinthians!

It is the merit of this new book that it gives us an honest evaluation of the man that recognises his worth without turning a blind eye to his complexity. Here is a clear and compelling account of a remarkable theologian whose theology was utterly christocentric and for whom 'not Bethlehem but Calvary' was 'the focus of revelation'.

I. Howard Marshall.
November 2005

Preface

My first encounter with James Denney was when, as a recently converted eighteen year old with minimal theological awareness, I was given a book by my uncle, who had long ago lost interest in the book's subject. It was entitled *The Atonement and the Modern Mind*; I never read it. Ten years later, as a young minister, I bought a second-hand copy of J. Randolph Taylor's fine study of Denney, *God Loves Like That!*. In it I encountered a mind characterised by intellectual intensity and spiritual integrity. In Denney's own words, to read him at his best was to 'hear the plunge of lead in fathomless waters.'

Since then, throughout my own intellectual pilgrimage, Denney has been an ever present companion. He has served as an evangelical corrective for my preaching, an intellectually combative and rhetorically persuasive apologist for the New Testament Gospel of Christ crucified and risen, and therefore a regular source of spiritual strengthening and pastoral affirmation. When an opportunity came in 2001 for me to step aside from pastoral ministry for a while, and pursue doctoral studies, it did not occur to me to choose Denney as the subject. That is, until a conversation with Professor David Fergusson, Professor of Divinity at the University of Edinburgh. I learned that a large collection of Denney's unpublished papers had been deposited at New College Edinburgh some years earlier, and that they were as yet unexplored. A quick perusal revealed that they represented an important and entirely new source of primary theological evidence. The result was my three year immersion in the life and times, and the theology and thought, of one of Scotland's most significant yet increasingly neglected theologians.

The present volume, emerging from that study, is an intellectual and contextual biography of James Denney. As biography it has a narrative structure, but since the aim is primarily a contextual study of Denney's mind, particular emphasis is given to the development of ideas. Since intellectual commitments emerge from a person's interaction with the changing context of their life and times, attention has been paid to the personal, intellectual, social, historical and religious environment which influenced Denney's thought and set the priorities of his theological agenda. The book is not a study from a single perspective such as systematic theology or church history. It traces the history of a mind, in the context of a life, with the aim of identifying and describing Denney's mental landscape, mapping his intellectual journey and exploring the distinctives of his thought.

The materials consulted include the published corpus of Denney's work, particularly his major monographs, scholarly articles and more popular journalism. Extensive use has also been made of the large collection of Denney's unpublished manuscripts deposited in New College. Where possible both published and unpublished work have been placed in the context and chronology of Denney's life and used to shed light on the changes and continuities of his thought.

A brief Introduction describes the provenance of Denney's unpublished papers, indicating their significance as a primary source for understanding his thought. Chapter one describes his early years, from 1856-74, spent in Greenock within the Reformed Presbyterian Church. His education at Glasgow University and Glasgow Free College spanning 1874-83, are then examined in chapters two and three, paying special attention to teachers and movements of thought impinging on Denney's intellectual development. The impact of thirteen years of ministry, 1883-97, two in the Gallowgate, Glasgow, and eleven in Broughty Ferry, is evaluated in chapter four. Twenty years spent at Glasgow College represent a time of maturing thought and growing influence. These years are considered in chapters five, (1897-1907) and six (1907-17), and Denney's major theological commitments and ideas set within the narrative and context of his life.

From this nexus of influences and experiences, major themes emerge, not only as intellectual constructs, but as personal theological and spiritual commitments. These include the nature and authority of Scripture, the Christian's claim to intellectual and spiritual freedom, the necessity of atonement, and the centrality and finality of Jesus. By supplementing published with unpublished material, and reading his work in the context of his life, Denney's thought is shown to be dynamic and progressive, yet characterised by a changing continuity.

A change of plans meant the original intention of taking time out of ministry to pursue post-graduate study did not happen. For the first eighteen months of my research I was part-time minister at Stonehaven Baptist Church. The balance of the work was completed over the next two years during a hectic transition from pastoral ministry to the academic environment of the Scottish Baptist College. I wish to express my gratitude to my two supervisors, Professor David Fergusson and Professor Stewart J. Brown, both of New College Edinburgh. They provided advice, support, theological stimulus, historical perspective, and much enjoyable conversation about that galaxy of scholars which shone in the Free Church College and later the United Free Church College, Glasgow, from around 1870 to 1917; they included A.B. Bruce, Henry Drummond, James Orr, T. M. Lindsay, George Adam Smith, and of course, James Denney.

Generous support was provided by a number of Trusts, whose underwriting of post graduate study helps remove from aspiring scholars a major disincentive to research in these days of cutbacks, short term economies and fee inflation – the financial cost! I wish to acknowledge generous help from The Andrew Carnegie Trust whose grant covered the cost of regular travel from Aberdeen to Edinburgh to consult the Denney papers. The Whitefield Institute supported my research with a substantial grant over the time of my research, and even in times of difficult circumstances and reduced resources, kept faith with their commitment to their grantees. The Hope Trust in Edinburgh gave further financial support throughout my studies, including a final and substantial grant towards the balance of academic fees. Financial help with the cost of preparation for publication was kindly granted by The Drummond Trust, 3 Pitt Terrace, Stirling. These are formal acknowledgements required by beneficiaries, and I gladly include them on that basis. However they also represent my genuine personal gratitude to the various groups of Trustees, and my appreciation of the foresight of those whose legacy is the encouragement of theological research and scholarship.

The staff at New College Library have at all times been courteous, understanding, generous in access to their remarkable special collections, good-humoured when requests meant another journey to the basement, interested in the personal progress of toiling post grads, and as a staff one of the University's most effective public relations resources! Eileen Dickson, now retired Librarian, and Sheila Dunn, were especially understanding and helpful, managing a valuable collection without making access more hassle than it needs to be for the protection of the holdings. One of Denney's manuscripts, DEN09-17, entitled "Lecture IX Holy Scripture", this appears as Appendix 2, and is of particular significance for the light it throws on the evolution of Denney's doctrine of scripture. It is reproduced by permission of Edinburgh University Library, New College Library Special Collections.

I am also grateful to the University of Aberdeen Library and Special Collections, and to the family of Sir William Robertson Nicoll for permission granted to publish a letter from Denney to Nicoll, (MS3518/27/10/James Denney/2 April 1901). This appears as Appendix 3, its significance being that it sheds an interesting light on Denney's teacher, Professor A. B. Bruce. The staff at the libraries of the University of Glasgow, Dundee Central Library, The National Library of Scotland, and The National Archives of Scotland have also helped me at various stages in my research.

My wife Sheila pushed me towards doctoral studies and supported me during them, just as she did thirty years earlier when, as a newly qualified teacher, she married a theological student. Together we have shared in a partnership of marriage and ministry, two forms of covenant commitment that combine faith, fun and fulfilment. The book is dedicated to Sheila, in gratitude for her love and friendship.

Abbreviations

Atonement	*The Atonement and the Modern Mind*
BFER	*British and Foreign Evangelical Review*
BW	*The British Weekly*
Church	*The Church and the Kingdom*
Corinthians	*The Second Epistle to the Corinthians*
CWP	*Christian World Pulpit*
Death	*The Death of Christ*
DNB, 1912-1921	*Dictionary of National Biography, 1912-1921*
DSCHT	*Dictionary of Scottish Church History and Theology*
EB	*Encyclopaedia Britannica*, (11th ed.), (New York: 1911)
ExpT	*Expository Times*
Exp	*The Expositor*
Jesus	*Jesus and the Gospel*
LFF	*Letters of Principal James Denney to His family and Friends*
LWRN	*Letters of Principal James Denney to W. Robertson Nicoll, 1893-1917*
Natural Law	*Natural Law in the Spiritual World, by a Brother of the Natural Man*
PGAFCS	*Proceedings of the General Assembly of the Free Church of Scotland*
PGAUFCS	*Proceedings of the General Assembly of the United Free Church of Scotland*
Principal Denney	John Randolph Taylor, 'Principal James Denney: A Survey of his Life and Work and a Critical Analysis and Appraisal of His Contribution to the Field of Biblical Theology', (Aberdeen PhD, 1956)
RSCHS	*Records of the Scottish Church History Society*
Reconciliation	*The Christian Doctrine of Reconciliation*
RPM	*The Reformed Presbyterian Magazine*
Studies	*Studies in Theology*
Thessalonians	*The Epistles to the Thessalonians*
UFCM	*United Free Church Magazine*
UM	*Union Magazine*
War	*War and the Fear of God*
Way	*The Way Everlasting*

Full publication details of books are given in the Bibliography.

CHAPTER 1

Introduction

In the will of Principal James Denney, dated 9 March 1909, witnessed by Professors George Adam Smith and James Orr, one clause is of particular interest. 'The household furniture, books, pictures, silver plate and plated articles, clothes, and in general the whole moveable effects' were to be left to his housekeeper and sister-in-law, Miss Marion Brown. But with one exception. The copyright and royalties of his writings were to belong to the Free Church College, Glasgow, 'not including any manuscripts that may be left by me, and I direct specially that no such manuscripts shall be printed either by my trustees or residuary legatees.'[1] Writing three weeks later to his friend William Robertson Nicoll, editor of the *British Weekly*, on March 30, 1909, he expressed the wish that none of his manuscripts should be published posthumously. 'There is a great difference', Denney explained, '- at least for me - between a MS. from which I can lecture and preach, and one which I could send to the printer: and we have had recent enough examples of what can be done in the way of injustice to the departed.'[2]

The moratorium Denney imposed on posthumous publication of his manuscripts was apparently observed since, apart from *The Christian Doctrine of Reconciliation*,[3] no further work of Denney's has been published since his death in June, 1917. Students of Denney have worked within the known corpus of published material, in itself a sizeable legacy.[4] But given Denney's popularity as a preacher, his fecundity as a writer, and his passionate commitment to theological education and the elucidation of the faith, it was likely he would leave a substantial body of unpublished material, and that he would take precautions to safeguard his posthumous literary reputation. In October 1918, the Court of Session decided that legal title to a large collection of manuscripts found in

---

[1] Record of the will of Professor James Denney, SC 36/51/176, 452-5.

[2] William Robertson Nicoll, *Letters of Principal James Denney to W. Robertson Nicoll*, (London: Hodder & Stoughton, 1920), 135. Hereafter abbreviated to *LWRN*.

[3] This had been specifically excepted, and Hodder and Stoughton paid £50 to the estate for the manuscript. Record of Inventory, SC 36/48/278, 701-2.

[4] Marshall Mikolaski and especially J. R Taylor carried out substantial studies of Denney's thought with no knowledge of the existence of unpublished material. See Bibliography for details.

Denney's home, fell in favour of the trustees and residuary legatees, and not his sister-in-law and housekeeper, Miss Marion Brown.[5]

Principal Denney's Papers

In 1973 a large collection of manuscript papers was acquired by Clive Rawlins, second-hand book dealer, and biographer of William Barclay. They were amongst materials being cleared from the tower of Trinity College, Glasgow, when it merged with the University of Glasgow Faculty of Divinity.[6] They were subsequently confirmed as Denney's unpublished manuscripts and later donated by Rawlins to New College Library, Edinburgh, in April 1987. They were painstakingly sorted and classified into several distinct categories by Dr Ian Moir. The inventory details each item, of which there are over 1,200, including sermons, theological papers, lectures, lecture notebooks, early essays, student notebooks, and other miscellaneous items.[7]

These papers represent an entirely new layer of evidence, awaiting excavation by students of Denney's work. The present study aims to place the main elements of Denney's thought within the intellectual, theological, historical and personal context of his life, using material from the entire corpus, published and unpublished. Systematic concerns will be addressed primarily as they shed light on the developing thought and life narrative, bearing in mind that Denney himself attempted no systematic presentation of his overall theological position. The study is not a comprehensive systematic presentation of Denney's theology, but a biography of the mind which produced it.

The limitations of a posthumously constructed system, which categorises and arranges a theologian's thought under widely recognised theological loci, are particularly evident when applied to intellectual and contextual biography. Understanding a person's thought requires a more dynamic and open process, portraying the living development of a mind responsive to contextual influences, alert to intellectual stimuli which push thought in new directions, enjoying and even exploiting personal relationships with intellectual mentors, and reacting to life-changing experiences which compel fresh thinking and create new perspectives. The intellectual biographer, tracing the inner journey of another mind, requires the travel-writer's eye for detail, observing the changing features of the inner landscape, as they are affected by the circumstances of the outer journey. The unpublished papers provide new, significant material

---

[5] 'Principal Denney's Papers', *Glasgow Herald*, 28 October 1918, 3c.
[6] Information supplied by Clive Rawlins.
[7] New College Library Committee Minutes, 1987.

for a more nuanced understanding of Denney the man, and his intellectual pilgrimage.

The sermons are arranged in biblical order, the majority undated. Those Denney dated are mostly from his years as a minister, 1883-1897.[8] Since Denney claimed he burned most of his sermons on leaving Broughty Ferry, the majority of those surviving and undated are most likely to be post 1897. Nevertheless as will become apparent, a significant number from his time as mission-worker in East Hill Street, Glasgow, and from East Free Church, Broughty Ferry, survived the flames. Where no date is given, which is true of most of the sermons and many of the most important theological papers, some can be dated by internal evidence. This requires detection and conjecture, and while in some cases the date can be fixed with reasonable confidence, in others conclusions remain at best tentative. Establishing the original *Sitz im Leben* of documents often reveals something of the author's intentions, interests, and convictions at a particular time, enabling more precise interpretation within the overall context of the author's developing thought.

Sometimes an identifiable bibliographic reference in a paper has provided a fixed point, indicating an earliest possible date. In a paper on gospel criticism, a reference to Schweitzer's *The Quest for the Historical Jesus* suggests a date of at least 1910 if the reference is to the English translation, which Denney reviewed for the *British Weekly*. However if, as is likely, Denney read it in German, that might push the possible date back to 1905.[9]

Occasion of delivery can also provide an indication of date. For example Denney was a founding member of the Glasgow United Free Office-Bearers Association. A paper he delivered to the denominational office-bearers on biblical criticism and the Church could most likely be dated around 1902.[10] Combined with the title, subject matter, and several specific expressions of concern about the wider implications for the new United Free Church if it reacted negatively and with haste in silencing the voice of critical scholarship, the paper could plausibly be placed in the specific context of the threatened heresy trial concerning George Adam Smith in 1901-2.

Local internal references sometimes allow partial reconstruction of context. 'Preaching and Christian Ethics', refers to the working conditions of women weavers in Dundee, and mentions a recent miner's strike, suggesting a date around 1895, before Denney left Broughty Ferry.[11] The paper, 'Some Impressions of America', refers to a crisis the previous year between Russia and Japan in which the President of the

---

[8] See Appendix 1.
[9] DEN08-05, 'Present and Future in the Gospels'.
[10] 'Christian Faith and the Criticism of the Bible', DEN09-07.
[11] DEN09-21.

United States intervened at the highest diplomatic level. This places the paper in 1906, the year after the threatened war between Russia and Japan when Theodore Roosevelt was awarded the Nobel Peace Prize, and after Denney and his wife's trip in 1905.[12]

Almost invariably in serious theological papers, Denney used other theologians as conversation partners. In three lectures on 'The Atonement'[13] he referred only to his own *The Death of Christ*.[14] Further, he explicitly promised, 'I shall try to avoid as far as possible all technical or difficult language.' While Denney would have made no such concessions to divinity students, addressing the Glasgow School for Christian Workers,[15] his approach would probably be more accessible and less technical. Alternatively, though less likely, one or all three of the lectures were delivered to the St Ninian's Society in Glasgow in 1908.[16] Intriguingly, they contain substantial passages of text reproduced verbatim in his last book *The Christian Doctrine of Reconciliation*. Whatever their earlier provenance, Denney thought some of the content sufficiently represented his mind to lift them into the manuscript of the Cunningham Lectures around 1917.

In a study exploring intellectual development, establishing the chronological context of key papers provides an important point of reference. There have been several occasions in this study when, frustratingly, only the most tentative suggestion could be made. 'Philosophy and the New Testament'[17] is important first as a text in which Denney expounded the absolute significance of Christ, a theme increasingly foundational to his theology from its first articulation in 1894 in *Studies in Theology*. Secondly, because in it he is unmistakably rebutting the metaphysical and religious pretensions of Hegelian-inspired Idealism as mediated through his former teacher, Edward Caird.

The manuscript itself is singularly unhelpful in the attempt to establish a firm original date and occasion. Possible clues include interaction with recent scholarship on the Logos, Philo and the Stoics, a pervasive and developed emphasis on reconciliation as a central NT theme, a substantial section on missions and the larger hope, pointed criticism of the Idealist interpretation of history and by contrast a lyrical exposition of the exalted Christ, and a description of the audience as 'a philosophical society'.

---

[12] DEN10-10.

[13] DEN09-11 to DEN09-13.

[14] Published in 1902, and reissued in 1911.

[15] A lay training initiative in which Orr and Denney were heavily involved.

[16] *The Glasgow Herald*, 23 January 1908, 13d, reports on Denney's Atonement lecture as part of a series.

[17] DEN08-10.

Caird in his 1904 Gifford lectures *The Evolution of Theology in the Greek Philosophers*, vol. ii, devoted significant attention to the Logos concept. The History of Religions school, on the ascendant at the turn of the century, linked the idea with current enquiry into the Graeco-Roman background of the New Testament. Reconciliation as Denney's preferred metaphor for the atonement post-dates *The Death of Christ*, 1902. Denney spoke at the 1910 Edinburgh Missionary Conference, and a number of other significant missionary sermons and addresses date from his last ten years. Several other references critical of Idealist philosophy, are evident in his writing during the Glasgow teaching years, and it is in his later writings that the exalted Christ is most pervasively presented. It has not been possible to identify the philosophical society in question. A plausible if uncertain date might be the last decade of his life.

Despite such frustrations, a number of significant unpublished theological papers can be dated and set in context, where internal evidence and content coincide with known external circumstances. These will be introduced at key points where they provide significant insight into Denney's developing thought, or clarify events and circumstances in which he was involved.

For twenty five years from around 1890, Denney was a regular contributor to the *British Weekly*. Under Nicoll's editorship this Christian broadsheet reflected the interests and values of literate, liberal (in both the political and theological sense) Christian thought during the late Victorian and into the Edwardian period. It was interdenominational, included news and informed comment on the issues of the day, church and secular, and had a large enough circulation to make it a significant organ of Christian opinion. The contributions Denney made represent a sizeable corpus of his most accessible work, the lucid writing of a journalist theologian. The *British Weekly* was by no means a lightweight publication; it was a newspaper, with an editor instinctively aware of the kind of writing that attracted and retained a loyal readership.[18]

The end result of this collaboration is an extensive deposit of Denney's thought and opinion on a miscellany of issues. Leading articles on biblical criticism, the Church, social comment, changing theological fashions, many of them based on extensive review and critique of current theological literature, regularly appeared from 1894-1917. In the present study, these articles represent an important chronological account of Denney's interests and opinions, and where relevant they have been exploited as sources illustrating Denney's views. They also provided Denney with a wide audience, and regular opportunity to disseminate the

---

[18] T. H. Darlow, *William Robertson Nicoll. Life and Letters*. (London: Hodder & Stoughton, 1925). See 67-82, for an account of the *British Weekly*.

thinking of an independent and cultured Christian mind on a host of subjects, from the incidental to the fundamental.[19]

The collaboration with Nicoll extended to the more theologically sophisticated *Expositor*, to which Denney contributed from 1893-1915. The most significant series was in 1901, on 'The Theology of Romans', a major collection of articles never published in book form. Most other contributions were occasional, and often written to help Nicoll maintain continuity of quality copy. The volume containing Denney's letters to Nicoll refers frequently to his editorial demands, and Denney's readiness to respond.

Apart from dictionary articles, sermons printed in the *Christian World Pulpit* and some contributions to his own denomination's *Union Magazine*, almost all of Denney's periodical writing appears in these two journals. Further, apart from his first anonymously published pamphlet, a broadside aimed at Henry Drummond, Denney's books were all published by Hodder and Stoughton, where again, the ubiquitous Nicoll was a major influence in editorial and commissioning decisions. Two volumes of edited letters and sixteen volumes of biblical exegesis, theological reflection and pastoral comment, complete the catalogue of Denney's publications.

Intellectual Biography and Contextual Theology

The corpus of published work available for a study of Denney is therefore substantial and accessible, and it was thoroughly sifted by John Randolph Taylor in his 1956 thesis.[20] Taylor's work attempted a comprehensive synthesis of Denney's thought, gathered around key theological motifs. These were expounded with an appreciative and engaging attention to the whole corpus, but largely innocent of serious critical comment. The introductory chapter setting the context is a brief resume of 'A Century of Theology'.[21] Denney's life is then covered by a sparse summary of biographical details and personal appreciations, followed by a larger section on 'His Mind and Personality'. Much material is gathered together here, including the surviving oral tradition

---

[19] J. R. Taylor in his 1956 Aberdeen PhD thesis, 'Principal James Denney. A Survey of His Life and Work and a Critical Analysis and Appraisal of his Contribution to the Field of Biblical Theology', was right to warn against trying to attribute unsigned leading articles on the basis of style or criticism. See p. 168. That Denney regularly provided Nicoll with solicited copy, certainly makes it possible, if not likely, that many of his contributions were anonymous and used to meet remorseless weekly deadlines.

[20] I note here my personal debt to Taylor. The book based on his thesis, *God Loves Like That!*, first alerted me to the importance of Denney as an attractive and independent voice in Scottish theology.

[21] Taylor, *Principal Denney*, 1-17.

of some whom Denney had known and taught.²² Denney was portrayed as Christian, evangelist, scholar, humanist, human, realist, and stylist, and each of these characteristics documented from oral and published testimony of those who knew him. It is a valuable repository of biographical material, painstakingly assembled. But there is little attempt to contextualise Denney's thought, or to trace the influences, events and movements, which shaped and determined the form and content of Denney's intellectual and theological development, creating just such a mind and personality.

However in fairness to Taylor, two points should be mentioned. Denney's unpublished papers were unearthed long after Taylor's work was done. Access to them may have changed his approach, or qualified some of his judgements. For example, the large collection of sermons provides ample material for a comprehensive study of Denney's homiletics. Taylor relied almost entirely on Denney's volume of sermons, *The Way Everlasting*, and several others published in the *British Weekly*, for his portrayal of the style and content of Denney's preaching. By contrast now, the large holding of sermons, lecture notes of what he taught his classes on the New Testament, coupled with published and unpublished papers on criticism and the biblical text, make an illuminating study of Denney's hermeneutics, while the sermons demonstrate how believing criticism could be effectively preached.

Secondly, Taylor was writing at the height of the biblical theology movement in the 1950's. The rendering of the biblical text into an organised theological scheme, often under a central motif, was an attractive and vitalising process in the biblical studies of his day. Scholars such as Eichrodt and Von Rad in the Old Testament, Dibelius and Bultmann in the New Testament, had given impetus and authority to the movement. Exegesis and experience were the rooting soil out of which new systematic reconstructions of biblical thought were expected to grow. It is no surprise that Taylor's work attempted the same systematic reconstruction and re-appropriation of Denney's theology.

The result, however, is not a study of the mind of Denney, its background, context and development. It is one person's rendering of 'Denney's theology', into an organised system under a selection of theological loci. Granted, in Taylor's day there was less interest in contextualising theology, emphasis being laid more on systematic exposition. But the result is that Taylor's study conveys little sense of the person, the life experience, the spiritual history, the specific, local, personal details of Denney's life, or of those hidden springs of motive and relationship that have decisive influence on both what and how a person thinks. It is this living context that is being sought in this study, as

---

²² Taylor, *Principal Denney*, 18-54, and 55-98.

a way of understanding, critically and appreciatively, what, how, and why Denney thought and theologised as he did.

So while Taylor sought to expound Denney's thought by an examination of his published work, significant questions remained unasked about the personal life and intellectual development of the writer. What then, can be learned, from a study of his life and times, about the mind and personality of Denney? Why did he think as he did? Who amongst the personalities and movements of his times shaped his mind? What can be learned about the thinker, that enables a better understanding of his thought? What was he reacting against, to whom was he responding? What light do Denney's life circumstances, personal experience, and his own spiritual and intellectual history, shed on the major themes of his thought? As one who laid decisive weight on human experience as an interpretive category, surely Denney's own experience, both outward circumstances and inner journey, constitutes essential context for the exegesis of his thought?

Even allowing for the influence of the biblical theology movement on Taylor's approach, and for the fact that he did not have access to Denney's unpublished papers, it remains true that the absence of attention to context and background resulted in a static, systematised study that failed to accommodate change and development in Denney's thought, or to identify and exploit critical incidents and decisive influences in the interpretation of his theology. The major weakness of any treatment that amasses all that an author ever said on a subject, and systematises the results without reference to context, is that it flattens the intellectual topography of ideas, making it impossible to appreciate the contours, scale and perspective which indicate how the landscape took shape, and what it looks like now. Such contextual and critical analysis is essential to provide nuance and texture to Denney's theology, and to present his thought as a living process that emerged from his own unique life experience.

In the case of Denney, reducing his thought to a systematic but decontextualised reconstruction obscures the dominance in his theological methodology of a dynamic view of the Bible as historically conditioned text, yet primary means of grace, through which an infallible gospel is brought home to mind and heart by the inner testimony of the Holy Spirit. The co-existence in the one mind of a progressive view of the nature of the Bible's inspiration and authority, and a more conservative view of the atonement constructed from critical exegesis of the New Testament, raises intriguing and crucial questions not only about Denney's theology, but about the personal spiritual and intellectual experience which inspired it. Attention to context will significantly clarify this and other questions.

Introduction

The Making of a Mind

The Reformed Presbyterian Church was, till the Union with the Free Church of Scotland in 1876, the church context within which Denney's spiritual experience was first moulded. These years were naturally and inevitably formative, instilling an indelible seriousness about spiritual and theological matters. It will be important therefore, in the first chapter, to gauge the immediate impact, and assess the lasting influence of these years, on the mind of one who grew up in Greenock, in a small, tightly-knit community of militant Presbyterianism.

His years at Glasgow University, 1874-1879, and then at the Free Church College Glasgow, 1879-83, were arguably the most formative years of his life. They represent key periods in the intellectual biography of a man who came to believe the life of the mind is answerable to the imperative of truth, and who was motivated by a conception of reality in which theological verity is freighted with moral and existential significance. Nine years of higher education decisively shaped intellectual values and forms of thought, as they were imbibed by an intelligent, religiously earnest student, exposed to some of the most acute minds of his generation.

The lasting influence of the teachers he encountered at Glasgow University, the wider context of religious thought and theological emphasis mediated through the teachers in the Free Church College, Glasgow, will therefore be explored in chapters two and three respectively, placing the mature Denney's thought within a credible historical and intellectual context. Aspects of his thought such as the constructs of argumentation, the principles of valid intellectual enquiry, the relations of truth and knowledge, the tension between traditional doctrine and personal experience, the moral and spiritual compulsion to seek the truth, and the concurrent principle of intellectual liberty to do so within the Christian Church, these were amongst the educational and epistemological principles instilled in Denney before he ever put pen to paper in published theological writing. Their impact on his theology was both inevitable and decisive. The first three chapters will therefore give detailed consideration to these years, representing half of his lifetime, spent in a family loyal to the Reformed Presbyterian Church, then at Glasgow University as an arts student, followed by four years in the Free Church College, Glasgow.

From 1883 when Denney was appointed Missioner in East Hill Street Glasgow, until 1897 when he left East Free Church, Broughty Ferry, on his appointment as lecturer in Glasgow, Denney was a parish minister in the Free Church of Scotland. Much now considered characteristic of Denney's theological style, was initially formed within the context of a Reformed pastoral and preaching ministry. Experience in ministry also offers the best explanation for the pastoral and apologetic concern that informs his writing and public speaking when addressing the faith-disturbing intellectual challenges faced by ordinary Christians in a rapidly changing world.

For Denney, the plea for intellectual liberty, within the constraints of personal experience of Christ and confessed loyalty to Him, was a matter of pastoral and apologetic urgency. Given the soul's loyalty to Christ, the importance of handling truth with integrity and therefore of intellectual liberty in articulating the dogmatic core of the Christian Faith, was a primary and constant principle in Denney's own intellectual life as a Christian, and one which, as Christian pastor and scholar, he argued was the right of each Christian. Its first full articulation was in the sermons and lectures delivered while still a pastor at Broughty Ferry. The significance of these years will be explored in chapter four, tracing the influence of pastoral experience on his overall development as a person.

Denney's thought reached full maturity during the twenty years he spent as a theological teacher in Glasgow, and chapters five and six are devoted to these two decades. His major theological publications began with *Studies in Theology*, 1894, culminating in *The Christian Doctrine of Reconciliation*, published posthumously in 1917. His increasing stature within and beyond his Church made him an important voice, respected by opponents and supporters. Major changes in the ecclesiastical landscape and in the intellectual climate invest these years with unusual importance in mapping Denney's mental topography. They were years in which fulfilment mixed with sadness, beginning with the uncritical optimism of a new century and finishing with the shattering realities of the Great War, and in between, the sudden death of his wife.

They were also years of theological adjustment for Denney and the wider church, of realignment amongst the Presbyterian denominations, and when questions of social reform were being asked with increasing urgency. Denney engaged with a wide range of these issues. Based in Glasgow, the main centre of industrial, commercial and social development, Denney, who preached out in the churches most Sundays, was a scholar preacher who remained in touch with the life of people inside and outside the churches. It is to be expected then, that the Glasgow years provide a rich context out of which some of Denney's most important thought developed, and within which his theological pilgrimage can be more sympathetically understood as the dynamic process it undoubtedly was.

A concluding chapter will indicate the decisive and defining themes which emerge from the study, and which together demonstrate what was distinctive in Denney's mind, what he thought, why he thought as he did, and the profound connections between theological articulation, spiritual experience and human personality. By following his intellectual journey, paying close attention to context, his theological significance can be better understood and his legacy more fully appreciated.

When Denney died, the shock was felt throughout the Church, many witnessing both to the enrichment his presence had brought, and to the sense of diminishment his removal by death created. A perusal of obituaries is not in itself the most objective measure of a person's character or significance for their times. The appreciation incorporated into the Minute Book of Broughty Ferry East United Free Church, following Denney's death, is an account of Denney as he was loved by the one congregation where he was best known.[23] It bears out the epigraph on the College memorial plaque, 'a man of God to whom many owed their souls'.[24]

Of all the reasons given in the predictable rhetoric of obituary notices, informing the world why Denney was all but indispensable and certainly irreplaceable in the lives of those who knew him, being Denney, the verdict of his College was the only one he would not have dared contradict. The cure of souls, by bringing people into contact with the reconciling power of God in Christ, was the chief end of his life. Passionate, intense preaching among the churches, intellectually stretching lectures to generations of students, the adventurous combination of intellectual liberty and soul loyalty to Christ that informed his scholarship, and the range of responsibilities he accepted in the service of the Church, constitute the outward evidence that he lived to expound and embody the visionary imperative of his apostolic mentor:

> If anyone is in Christ he is a new creation; the old has gone, the new has come. All this is from God who reconciled us to himself through Christ and gave us the ministry of reconciliation: God was reconciling the world to himself in Christ, not counting men's sins against them. And he has committed to us the ministry of reconciliation. We are therefore Christ's ambassadors, as though God were making his appeal through us. We implore you on Christ's behalf: Be reconciled to God.[25]

---

[23] Appendix 4.
[24] Quoted in Taylor, *God Loves Like That!*, 189.
[25] 2 Cor. 5.17-21.

CHAPTER 2

Early Years in Greenock, 1856-1874

On 25 June 1879 James Denney wrote to his parents from Dresden. A telling extract from this early correspondence with his family is included in a volume of letters published in 1921.[1] That the letter was written from Germany, by a twenty-three year-old Scot, who had several months earlier graduated from the University of Glasgow with First Class Honours in Classics and Philosophy, and who was now pursuing his studies in German, Greek, Hebrew and philosophy,[2] would of itself have been unremarkable. By 1879 Germany was seen as an indispensable source of learning for those who wanted to be at the cutting-edge of scholarship, and many aspiring scholars spent time there.

However, of the six letters which James Moffatt included in the volume, that of 25 June lacks the light-hearted optimism of the others. The full extract is instructive for the light it throws on the concerns of a young intelligent man, brought up in a working class home in Greenock, whose spiritual formation had taken place within two of the stricter strands of Scottish Presbyterianism, the Reformed Presbyterian and the Free Church of Scotland, and who was now considering application as a candidate for the ministry of the Free Church of Scotland.

> Ministers are having great times and doing great doings in Scotland just now; it is almost enough to frighten an amiable and peaceably disposed person like me from the prospect of their fellowship. But perhaps I should not say that I won't be a minister, till I see whether they will have me or not; and, to tell the truth, I am afraid the very reverend the Presbytery of Greenock will be trying me in their Hebrew scales and finding me wanting, unless some miracle happens. But if the Free Church or any other Church thinks that the orthodoxy of its students can be secured in this way, or that anything at all can be secured by making it impossible for its students to hear from their professors what it is impossible for the students to be students and not hear of somehow or other, then it is mightily mistaken.[3]

The great times and great doings refer to two theological controversies which were coming to boiling point in Scotland in 1879 and which would

---

[1] James Moffatt, (ed.), *Letters of Principal James Denney to His Family and Friends*, (London: Hodder & Stoughton, 1921), 4. Hereafter abbreviated to *LFF*.
[2] Ibid., 2, 8.
[3] Ibid., 4.

culminate in the deposition of the Rev. David Macrae from his ministry in Gourock United Presbyterian Church on 22nd July 1879,[4] and in the removal of William Robertson Smith from his lectureship in the Free Church College, Aberdeen, in May 1881. The impact of these disciplinary proceedings clearly raised doubts in Denney's mind about his own acceptability as a candidate for the ministry. His uncertainty about 'whether they will have me or not', the question mark he places over 'whether the Presbytery of Greenock will be trying me in their Hebrew scales and finding me wanting', and his obvious disagreement with the silencing of teachers as a way of securing the orthodoxy of ministerial students, indicate his personal unease at events unfolding in Scotland.

The last sentence about the Free Church is outspoken, but its complicated syntax points to underlying tensions raised to the surface of Denney's mind by these controversies, as he struggled to think through and articulate to his parents why he thought the Church 'mightily mistaken' in its repressive approach to the critical thought of the 'modern mind'. That unease, tempered as it was by his disclaimer that 'it is almost enough to frighten an amiable and peaceably disposed person' like himself, reveals an early resistance to forms of control, exercised for spiritual purposes over the intellect and conscience of those charged by the church to seek and teach the truth of the Christian faith.

The letter is therefore a revealing glimpse into the mind of James Denney at one of the hinge points in his life. The reasons for his apprehension, and why he looked forward to beginning study for ministry with a mixture of nervousness and anticipation, are best approached by examining the various experiences, influences, and circumstances that together form the context in which Denney's mind had developed.

'My father was a working man'

James Denney was born in Paisley, on 5 February, 1856.[5] Four months later the family moved to Greenock. His father, a joiner, was joint founder and proprietor of a small business, Crawford and Denney.[6] More than half a century later Denney expressed pride in his father's working-class

---

[4] Andrew L. Drummond and James Bulloch, *The Church in Late Victorian Scotland 1874-1900*, (Edinburgh: St Andrew Press, 1978), 32-4.

[5] In 1881 Denney aged 25 was the oldest of five children. At the time of the 1881 Census he had two sisters (aged 23 and 20), and two brothers (aged 16 and 13). Census Report, volume 564-3, C.D. Rom, Enum Dist, 32, 37.

[6] Census details in 1881 give John Denney's occupation as 'Master Joiner Employing 8 Men & 3 Boys.' Ibid.

roots, and a reluctant but honest recognition of his own upward mobility over the years:

> One of the things that has never been out of my mind since I went to Broughty Ferry and got £400 a year, is that my father worked from six in the morning till six at night, and often longer, from the time he was twelve till he died at seventy two, never had a month's holiday in his life, and never made a seventh or an eighth of my income, though he was in every sense of the term as good a man as I am.[7]

Denney's view of his own background, and of his father's social status, emerges again in later life in a discussion about the church's need to pay attention to 'the opinion of the artisans in the Church.' Here again, he is protective of the self-respect and equal value of people like his father, showing impatience with artificial distinctions which betray 'a lot of subconscious patronage'.

> My father was a working man, and while no man could have been freer from any kind of self assertion, I am certain it would have seemed very queer to him to be regarded *in the Church* as belonging to a particular class which had to be recognised in some particular way. With all our faults, the self-respecting working man can keep his self-respect, and be at home in our Church as completely, I believe, as in the apostolic age. I had rich merchants, secretaries of financial companies, schoolmasters, shopkeepers, tradesmen and coachmen in my session, and we were as true a brotherhood in Christ as a minister could wish to have part in. There is no need that a different degree of education should separate men, and I am quite certain that decent working people are proud to think their minister is a thoroughly equipped man, and like him the better and not the worse for it.[8]

Defensive of his own roots, proud of his father's contribution *as a working man* to the life of the church, impatient with any suggestion that education need create social barriers, alert to the 'subconscious patronage' that underlies well-meaning strategies to make the church more relevant to particular classes, Denney was speaking out of his own experience. Raised himself in a working class home, his father was precisely one of those 'decent working people' who valued education and therefore sent his oldest son to the Highlanders Academy in Greenock.

In the 1840's the high fees charged by private instructors was such a severe disincentive that only one in thirteen of Greenock's inhabitants pursued a basic education.[9] Originally intended as a school for the

---

[7] LWRN, 239. See also *LFF* 12, on Denney's father's workload.

[8] Ibid., 107-8

[9] *New Statistical Account of Scotland*, vol. VII, (Edinburgh, 1845), 465. High fees were recorded as 'a serious obstacle in the way of a working man's obtaining the

children of Highlanders, in Denney's time the Highlanders Academy still gave them preference if spaces were scarce. It was built partly by public subscription and partly by Government grant, the ground generously provided at the lowest possible feu duty. The school had two apartments and two masters, an infant and a juvenile section. It had a large playground, and was 'liberally furnished' with 'the usual apparatus'. It employed highly qualified teachers and attracted the children of 'families in the middle ranks'. The Statistical Account reported modestly that 'ordinary acquirements of reading, writing etc. may be had at a comparatively moderate rate.' For several years Denney became a pupil teacher in the school, and may have considered school teaching as a career.[10]

From around the time John Denney arrived in Greenock, and on to the end of the century, the town was the centre of vigorous industrial development. 'During the years from 1875 to 1914 there was considerable development of the shipbuilding industry in Greenock. Tonnage figures had increased to 20,000 tons by 1876 and 52,744 tons by 1882. The total tonnage of sailing vessels registered as belonging to Greenock increased from 29,054 tons in 1825 to 168,644 tons in 1881. The total tonnage of steamers rose from 2,012 tons in 1853 to 50,572 tons in 1881. The number of harbours in the town stood testimony to Greenock's importance as a major world port.'[11] By the early 1880's a wide range of manufacturing companies had been established in the town and surrounding area. There were 'sail cloth factories, sail-making establishments, rope works, woollen factories, a flax mill, and a paper mill. There were also sawmills, grain mills, a large cooper work, a distillery, breweries, soap and candle works, a pottery, a straw hat manufacturer, and chemical work.'[12]

In 1860, James Wallace M.D., a young Greenock doctor published a pamphlet entitled *Observations on the Causes of the great Mortality in Greenock, particularly among Children*.[13] The Greenock Master of

---

unspeakable blessings of an elementary education to a numerous family.' Information in this paragraph comes from this source.

[10] *LWRN*, xiii. See also T. H. Walker, *Principal James Denney D.D., A Memoir and a Tribute*, (London: Marshall, 1918), 18-22, 25. This volume is hagiographic and factually unreliable as Taylor pointed out in *Principal James Denney*, 22-3.

[11] Information from *Greenock-town.co.uk/history.html*. Consulted on 16 April 2001.

[12] Ibid.

[13] Craig Pritchett, *Greenock. Housing, Health and Social Conditions 1860-1885*, (Greenock: Local History Archives Project, 1978), 1. This slim volume collects newspaper extract material from *The Greenock Telegraph* and *The Greenock Advertiser* relating to social conditions in Greenock during most of the period Denney lived there. The disease potential of social deprivation in Greenock is confirmed by the entry in *The Third Statistical Account*, where the role of Dr Wallace in drawing attention to them is

Works, Mr. William Allison published in the same year his *Report on the Sanitary Conditions of Greenock*.[14] It deals with improvements to sewage disposal, refuse collection, the creation of two public parks, and an improved transport system enabling the transport of cheap coal, 'an essential article of comfort, to the end of nearly every street.' In addition because 30,000 of the population carried water from wells at least 100 yards from their homes, which were usually tenement accommodation with several flights of stairs, water was not used in the quantities required 'to further the ends of cleanliness and health'. The answer was to be the creation of a new reservoir with '20 acres of water, 20 feet deep'.[15]

This ambitious report included further short and medium term goals. Proposals included requiring proprietors of tenements to put a branch drain into the main sewer, building a new animal slaughterhouse on the outskirts of the town, paving streets and lanes to remove breeding grounds of infection, building 'public conveniences...for the male portion of the population', closing overcrowded graveyards, and building a new hospital for infectious diseases such as scarletina, measles and smallpox. This forward-looking plan would take years to fulfil, but it indicates the scale of social problems in a town where provisions of housing and public health measures struggled to keep pace with industrial development. These reports by a local doctor and the Master of Works addressed matters of life and death importance for parents like the Denneys whose children were born in 1856, 1858, 1861, 1865 and 1868. At the time of the *Report on the Sanitary Conditions of Greenock*, Elizabeth Denney was expecting a third child, making a total of three children under the age of five.

The year their fourth child was born there was an outbreak of typhus in Greenock serious enough to warrant a Government commissioned report. Dr Buchanan's report made worrying reading for parents of young children. 'Of the eight principal towns of Scotland, whose mortality is examined by the Registrar General in his monthly reports, Greenock is the one which has the highest general mortality...The excessive mortality is largely due to the deaths of children, who are produced in Greenock in remarkable numbers, the birth rate actually reaching 52 per thousand in 1864.'[16] Contagious disease and unhygienic living conditions due to overcrowding were blamed as primary causes. Amongst the recommendations were the closing of houses deemed unfit

---

given honourable mention. *Third Statistical Account of Scotland. County of Renfrew*, H. A. Moisley and A. G. Thain (eds.), and A. C. Somerville (ed.), *County of Bute*, (Glasgow: Collins, 1962), 165 .

[14] Pritchett, *Greenock*, 5.

[15] Ibid., 6.

[16] Pritchett, *Greenock*, 17. The death rate was 41 per thousand in the same year, a net population increase of over 500 despite the high mortality rate.

for human habitation, the enforcing of the Nuisance Removal Act to deal with overcrowding and a minimum width for new streets and spaces between houses.[17]

Fifteen years later another of Denney's letters from Dresden in 1879 refers to the benefits for his own family of recent improvements in social conditions in Greenock. A letter from his father had updated him on local happenings around Greenock. 'It made me wish I was at home, for one thing, to see the new house; I will be quite a prince in my own right when I live in a room with a fender and carpet in it.'[18] The new house was in South Street, part of a newer housing development near Caddle Hill.[19] The Scottish Census of 1861 had generated housing statistics which pointed to massive overcrowding. Of the 666,786 families in Scotland, 226,723, (34%) lived in one room and 246,601, (37%) occupied houses consisting of two rooms. The 1881 Census showed things had improved, concluding that 'the house accommodation of the people of Scotland has been greatly improved.... While in 1871 one family in every three had only one room for its habitation, the proportion in 1881 was one in every four.'[20] John Denney's family were clearly benefiting from the changes in Greenock between the early 1860s and 1879.[21]

'The Covenants were magnificent [but] not destined to be indispensable'

The industrial and commercial diversity of Greenock was mirrored in the town's religious diversity. Of the various Presbyterian options available, John Denney and his family joined the Reformed Presbyterian Church. This small branch of radical Scottish Presbyterianism traces its history

---

[17] Ibid., 21, 24. Overcrowding presented an almost overwhelming challenge to civic authorities in the second half of the nineteenth century. In 1858, almost contemporary with the Greenock reports quoted, and three years prior to the 1861 census which revealed the full extent of the problem, the *Reformed Presbyterian Magazine* carried a brief article on 'The Crowded State of the Population in Large Towns.' in its 'Notes on Public Affairs' section. It provided the kind of anecdotal evidence that would be confirmed by statistics in the Census. 'One common stair at the bottom of a long close, not far from the Cross, leads to seventy nine apartments, furnishing accommodation two hundred and forty four human beings, of whom one hundred and twelve are children, and is the only means of communication with the close. There is no water in any of the houses, and, consequently, none of the conveniences which water secures.' *Reformed Presbyterian Magazine*, 1858, 379. All further references abbreviated to *RPM*.

[18] *LFF*, 3.

[19] The address in the 1881 Census was 32 South Street.

[20] Pritchett, *Greenock*, 4.

[21] *The Third Statistical Account, Renfrew* confirms that after the 1876 Housing Act new improved housing was built to the south and east 'for working men and artisans', 155.

back to the Covenanters and their successors who wanted nothing to do with the Revolution settlement of 1690. They 'asserted the *jus divinum* of a free, Presbyterian and Reformed Church in a covenanted nation which acknowledged the kingship of Jesus Christ.'[22] By 1863 there were six Presbyteries with forty six congregations and around 6,700 communicants.[23]

The lengths Reformed Presbyterians were prepared to go to distance themselves from secular and state affairs explains their being described as 'the extreme Calvinist conscience of all Scottish Presbyterianism.'[24] The tensions created by such principled opposition to the prevailing governments, in an increasingly democratic world, were made more acute with the coming of the 1832 Reform Act. The Act enfranchised some members, but in line with the principle of non involvement with a spiritually compromised state, the Church forbade members to exercise their vote. Maintaining such distance from civil institutions led to other serious moral and legal dilemmas. 'They were also forbidden from starting legal actions, enlisting in the armed forces, and joining outside organisations - even missionary societies of which the church actually approved.'[25]

Brown makes the comment that the bulk of the members united with the Free Church in 1876 because they found it 'hard to swallow the social isolation and impotence' consequent on such high principles. True as that observation is, it does not do full justice to other principles that drove the search for closer ties with other denominations. The long discussions leading up to the 1876 union, followed on the split of 1863 when the majority of the Reformed Presbyterian congregations accepted the Synod decision to relax church censures on voting and on swearing the oath of allegiance, by declaring them matters for liberty of conscience.[26] A minority Reformed Presbyterian synod held to the older position. From 1863-1876 the majority Reformed Presbyterian Church pursued union

---

[22] See 'Reformed Presbyterian Church', *DSCHT*, 698-9. See also M. Hutchison, *The Reformed Presbyterian Church in Scotland, its Origin and History 1680-1876*, (Paisley, 1893); W. J. Couper, 'The Reformed Presbyterian Church in Scotland', *RSCHS*, ii, 1925, 3-179; J. Robb, *Cameronian Fasti, 1680-1929*, (Edinburgh: Reformed Heritage Press, 1975).

[23] *RPM*, 1863, 231ff.

[24] Callum Brown, *Religion and Society in Scotland since 1707*, (Edinburgh: Edinburgh University Press, 1997), 28.

[25] Ibid., 28-9.

[26] See *Speeches at the Reformed Presbytery of Glasgow, April 7, 1863, on the Synod's Overture anent Discipline for the Exercise of the Elective Franchise, &c.* by the Rev. John M'Dermid and Rev William Symington, (Glasgow, 1863), appended to *RPM*, 1863. Another interesting account of the issues, enriched by several years hindsight, is found in the 'Report of the Committee on Union', *RPM*, 1869, 211.

with the Free Church and the United Presbyterian Church because of a deeply felt ecclesiastical isolation and a genuine desire to be part of a reunited evangelical Presbyterianism.[27]

Dr W. H. Goold, one of the most respected leaders of the (majority) Reformed Presbyterians, chaired the Reformed Presbyterian Union Committee from 1864-1876. As Moderator of the Reformed Presbyterian Synod in 1876 he addressed the Free Church Assembly during the enactment of the union where he described 'the normal condition of Presbyterianism as being that of unity.' The entire address is both irenic and principled. One extract reveals the passion for unity that is often the emotionally obverse side of principled separation, and which surfaced in a number of the previous Committee of Union reports.

> Let me assure you...that we have accomplished this union with you out of no antagonism to other Churches. We cherish a strong feeling of respect and sympathy for our honoured brethren of the United Presbyterian Church.... But I venture to go further, and say, that we are not here in a spirit of antagonism even to the Established Church itself. If anyone has given attention to the negotiations for union, and the speeches and utterances made in connection with them during the past ten years, they will notice a peculiar type and stamp upon all the utterances of my brethren to the effect, that they yearned not merely for the union of the whole of the Churches in negotiation with each other, but for a general reconstruction and reunion of all the Evangelical Presbyterianism in Scotland....[28]

So while there were socially pragmatic reasons for seeking union with the Free Church of Scotland, there was also an underlying theology pushing towards the same goal.[29]

---

[27] *RPM*, 1876, 260. The entire July issue is given over to reporting the proceedings. From 1865 the *RPM* carried a full account of the union discussions. In 1865, it reprinted "Plea for Presbyterian Unity" from *The Princeton Review*, 115-22. The *RPM* printed a number of such pro-Presbyterian union articles throughout the years of the negotiations. As the process came to fulfilment, optimism and anticipation become more evident. See especially 1873, 203-6, and the important Appendix at the end of the volume, additionally numbered 1-60 which gives the full narrative of events including the reasons for the United Presbyterian Church's withdrawal from negotiations, leaving the way clear for the Reformed Presbyterian Church and the Free Church. *RPM*, 1875, 203-12; and 1876, 140-50, include reports and returns from Presbyteries and Sessions.

[28] *RPM*, 1876, 260-1.

[29] See for example 'Plea for Presbyterian Unity', *RPM*, 1865, 115-22; 'Christian Union', *RPM*, 1857, 212-217; 'The Fathers of Our Church on the Subject of Christian Union', *RPM*, 1865, 317-25. *RPM*, 1867, 199-240 is especially valuable as a fully reported account of the discussion of the Report on Union of that year. Several of the contributions show the theological and pastoral care taken in seeking wide and clear understanding of the issues. It is important to be aware also of the minority opposition within the Free Church which had circulated a periodical called *Watchword*. See *RPM*, 1868, 65-70; 153-60; 264-70; 306-12.

Thus James Denney grew up in a congregation that, by the time he was five had split into two separate communions,[30] in a Church which by the time he was seven had split into separate denominations, and by the time he was twenty had united with another denomination. Principled separation and principled union presuppose strong doctrinal convictions, under-girding powerful church affiliations. When circumstances change, and principles are legitimately modified in the light of such changes, to persist in separation is theologically untenable. That is the underlying logic of the reunion process of 1864-1876.[31]

'Particular churches with their specific polities'

It was against this unpredictable denominational background, that the Denney family lived out their local church experience. They were to find life in the local church equally unpredictable. When John Denney moved to Greenock in 1856, the minister was the Rev Andrew Gilmour who, when he died in 1859, had been minister for twenty six years. In the Obituary his achievement is the more effective for the brevity of its summarising statement: 'From having no place of worship, the congregation is possessed of a commodious and comfortable church, free of debt; from a communion roll of nineteen, the numbers have risen to three hundred and sixty nine'.[32]

During such a lengthy ministry Gilmour had become a well known figure in Greenock. He communicated effectively with young people and ran a Wednesday Bible Class, which included young people from several of the town's churches. It was a major source of recruitment for the church's membership. His obituary gives an independent account of the social realities of Greenock's poorer areas. 'The social position of the sufferer caused no difference in the assiduous attentions of this servant of Jesus. In some of the narrow lanes of Greenock, where squalor and vice reign supreme, the gentle tones of his voice might have been heard speaking words of comfort to some weary soul.... Misery and penury never appealed in vain to either heart or purse.'[33]

James Denney was too young to have been directly influenced by Gilmour's combination of evangelism and practical caring, but the

---

[30] See following section in this chapter.

[31] 'In expiscating the real amount of difference [between the negotiating churches], they have but elicited the vast amount of harmony - harmony to a degree that really proves the Churches to be, in a most important sense, already one, and on the footing of which the most close and brotherly communion may be justified.' *RPM*, 1869, 214.

[32] *RPM*, 1859, 254. The West Stewart Street congregation was established in 1824 and the building, with seating for 467 was built in 1838. *New Statistical Account of Scotland*, vol. VII, (Edinburgh and London, 1845), 466.

[33] *RPM*, 1859, 256.

church in which he grew up had come to maturity and stability under a ministry that inevitably shaped its convictions and decisively influenced its ethos. Gilmour was a Reformed Presbyterian who held the convictions of his churchmanship with an adamantine certainty. 'As the author of "Our Political Oaths" and the "Supremacy of the British Crown", he amply vindicated his title to be regarded as one of the ablest expositors of the position which the Reformed Presbyterian Church holds towards the civil institutions of Britain'.[34] Such articulate conviction in a minister has a significant trickle-down effect on the mindset of a congregation. That the church split into two congregations and went their separate ways was perhaps the inevitable result of the power vacuum left by his death, and of the difficulty in a large congregation of maintaining unanimity of opinion on controversial matters.[35]

During the summer of 1860 the Greenock congregation tried on two occasions to call the Rev. A. M. Symington of Dumfries and on both occasions he declined.[36] In July a call was issued to the Rev. Peter Carmichael of Penpont who was duly inducted to West Stewart Street on 17th October.[37] Six days earlier

> those members of the R. P. Congregation in Greenock to whom a disjunction had been granted by the Presbytery of Paisley were organised into a separate congregation by the Rev. Wm. M'Lachlan, Port Glasgow. Four elders and six deacons, who had gone with the disjunctionists, were unanimously elected to take office over them, and the session was regularly constituted. A Committee was appointed to look out for a site for a new church. In the mean time, the new congregation will meet for public worship in the mission house belonging to the Rev. Mr. Morton's (U.P.) Congregation.[38]

No reference is made in the *RPM* about the reasons for the 'disjunctionists' withdrawing from the mother congregation to create Greenock 2nd Congregation. The following year the Magazine reported that the new place of worship in West Shaw Street was almost completed, and that the church had called the Rev. David Taylor from Ayr to the pastoral charge.[39] The New Reformed Presbyterian Church, Greenock, with seating for 536 people, was opened for public worship on 15th December 1861. It was noted that in fourteen months the congregation had raised from their own resources, £630 of the £1500 cost for the building. The editor noted with frankness and admiration, 'We

---

[34] Ibid.
[35] In 1858 the 'Schedule of the State of the Congregations' shows only Glasgow 1st (900) and Penpont (370) as larger than Greenock (340). *RPM* 1858.
[36] *RPM*, 1860, 66, 100, 160, 197.
[37] Ibid., 274, 315, 344, 400.
[38] Ibid., 378.
[39] *RPM*, 1861, 372.

understand there are none of the members who can be called wealthy, but their previous exertions, and above all, the collection of the Sabbath ult., when the highest single sum deposited in the plate was only £5, speaks volumes for their liberality.'[40]

In 1863, as noted earlier, the denomination divided over the relaxation of church censures on voting, resulting in the formation of a (minority) RPC and a (majority) RPC. In Greenock the West Stewart Street congregation attached itself to the minority RPC while the newer West Shaw Street congregation, where the Denneys were members, went with the majority.[41] It was by travelling along this rather convoluted path that James Denney eventually 'passed over to the Free Church, taking with him his stern but warm piety, his appreciation of dogmatic truth, and his hearty interest in the Church of Christ.'[42]

Reference to master James Denny[43] (sic) appears in the denominational magazine in 1867 in a balance sheet showing contributions to "The Children's Boxes", a fund-raising effort to finance the mission ship "Dayspring". Twenty six boxes were returned by children from the West Shaw Street congregation and the amount of their contribution placed alongside their names. Denney gave three shillings and four pence; eighteen of the twenty six gave more.[44] He is next mentioned in connection with his work as a Sunday School teacher in 1869.[45] The same year at the annual church soiree and anniversary 'addresses bearing on

---

[40] *RPM*, 1862, 33.

[41] The Synod records of attendance for 1861, 1862 and 1863 show Greenock as having two congregations. From 1864 onwards it reverts to the simple Greenock and all references are to the West Shaw Street congregation.

[42] *LWRN*, xv. In expressing his admiration for the Rev. J. P. Struthers, minister of the Reformed Presbyterian Church in Greenock from 1882-1915, Fleming paid tribute to the contribution the RPC made to the Scottish church. 'Principal James Denney, a close friend of Struthers, Professor Laidlaw of new College, and Professor J. E. MacFadyen, the Old Testament scholar, ...carried into a wider sphere the impress of their early training in the small Church of the Covenants.' J. R. Fleming, *The Church of Scotland 1875-1929*, (Edinburgh: T & T Clark, 1933), 137.

[43] The spelling of Denney's name was a recurring problem. It is spelt with and without the second 'e' in different issues of the magazine. The census return of 1881 shows the family name as Denny. While lecturing in America Denney was doubly offended by the advertisement 'Dr. Johnston by Dr. Denny.' He commented to his friend J. P. Struthers, 'Only Dr. Johnson's powers of vituperation would have enabled me to say what I thought about such an accumulation of insults.' *LFF*, 83. Denney's own powers of vituperation would have been provoked further by the misspelling of his name on the brass plate of the organ installed in East Free Church in memory of the Reverend Professors Bruce, Denny (sic) and Moffatt.

[44] *RPM*, 1867, 283. The following year he gave three shillings and one and a half pence. His sister Margaret gave eight shillings.

[45] *RPM*, 1869, 426.

the history of the congregation were given by Messrs Milligan, Denney, McKechnie and Scott, members of the congregation.' The Denney referred to would be John Denney. However in 1872, the first year of the West Shaw Street Congregational Bible Class was marked by a special meeting at which Mr James Denney gave the secretary's report.[46]

Such scattered references surfacing in the denominational magazine suggest the family were actively involved in the life of the local church. This is confirmed from an examination of the Congregational and Session minutes. When the new building was opened John Denney was the spokesman for the church Building Committee and initiated the use of tune boards; fourteen years later he reported that 'the church is not so well lighted as he would like'.[47] Between those years, when his family were growing up, John Denney was a significant player in the life of the congregation. He was a ruling elder who on occasion represented the church at the Paisley Presbytery, and at the Synod in 1865.[48] He was the proposer of the call to Andrew Symington in 1869,[49] moderated the Chair during the vacancy, and served as Church Treasurer for a number of years.[50] He was a frequent speaker at the congregational meeting, several years urging support for the work of the Sabbath school,[51] took the chair during the minister's illness,[52] visited members on matters of discipline during the reviewing of the roll,[53] convened the seat letting committee and was appointed to the Committee for the Future Management of Finances following the Union of 1876.[54] All of this argues a commitment and involvement in the life of the local church that inevitably affected home life and the spiritual formation of his family. The active leadership roles he played reflect upward mobility from joiner to small business partner. His practical skills were used in the care of the church's fabric, his financial and business ability applied to the church affairs, and his spiritual leadership clearly respected.[55]

---

[46] *RPM*, 1872, 283.

[47] Congregational Minutes, CH3/669/2, entry for 22 February 1875.

[48] *RPM*, 1872, 207; *RPM*, 1865, 197.

[49] CH3/669/2, entry for June 23, 1869.

[50] In 1870 John Denney warned the congregation that growing numbers would result in the withdrawal of financial help from the Ferguson Trustees, and urged 'increased exertions' in giving. See entry for 7 November 1870

[51] See for example CH3/669/2, entry for 1 November 1869.

[52] CH3/669/2. See entries for February to August 1869.

[53] Minutes of Session, CH3/669/1, 237-8, 75.

[54] CH3/669/2, 5 July 1876.

[55] At the union of 1876 there was much discussion at the congregational meeting about the name of the new church. Of three options John Denney supported renaming the congregation 'Union Free Church'. His motion fell in favour of 'Martyrs Free Church of Scotland', suggesting he was a respected but not dominant presence. Ibid., 26 July 1876.

'I speak of the things...touching the king'

The ethos and concerns of the Reformed Presbyterian Church, and of the majority Reformed Presbyterian Church after 1863, are reflected in considerable detail in the *Reformed Presbyterian Magazine*. It ran from 1855 to 1876 and conveniently covers the life of the denomination in which James Denney spent the first twenty years of his life. This remarkably detailed account provides rich documentation of the ethos and concerns, the history, events and people, the discussions and disagreements, of a denomination coming to terms with a rapidly changing social and ecclesiastical context.

The motto of the *Reformed Presbyterian Magazine* was taken from Psalm 45.1 'I speak of the things...touching the king'. In early years, 1855-63, the editor wrote an annual 'Address to the Readers' in which the aims of the magazine were clearly stated. As the 'only vehicle of intelligence the Church possesses', the magazine was to be a forum in which the denomination's principles were publicly advocated, the church's interests promoted and the events of the denomination's history duly chronicled.[56] A more succinct statement of aims was given in 1860, describing it as 'A Magazine, a Missionary Chronicle and a Journal of Ecclesiastical Intelligence.'[57] The modest but strategic aim was formation by information. So it recorded the day to day history of the churches, informed the denomination about missionary activity, aimed to 'elevate the spirituality of our readers', provided 'some measure of acquaintance with the religious literature of the day', and commented on public issues and affairs from a Christian perspective. For many, therefore, it served as a source of news, creating a network of information between the congregations.

The contributors were mainly drawn from the denomination, though there are regular reprints of articles from elsewhere, frequently *The Princeton Review*. The tone varies with the content from combative polemic and pulpit rhetoric to devotional seriousness and detailed narrative. The editor's motto was 'Truth without compromise, love without dissimulation,' because he believed 'truth can never suffer by discussion, conducted in a spirit of Christian candour and courtesy. The fire only makes the precious metal shine the more brilliantly; whatever is lost in the crucible, it is not the gold.'[58] From an overview of the contents, it is possible to get a more detailed understanding of the church ethos, the particular spiritual interests and the theological outlook that informed the first twenty years of James Denney's spiritual and intellectual formation.

---

[56] *RPM*, 1855 1.
[57] *RPM*, 1860 2.
[58] *RPM*, 1855, 2-3.

'I feel mad at the cheek of the Pope!'[59]

The first volume contained an article "Popery and Bells".[60] It is a scoffing account of a bell being baptised by the Roman Catholic Bishop of Liege, an 'incident at once profoundly serious and ludicrous...the idol, at least, cannot be said to be a dumb one.' The article ends by comparing the bell recently cast and sent to the Reformed Presbyterian mission station at Aneityum with the Liege bell. 'How different the objects for which these bells are used! The one to bolster the superstition of a doomed system, the other to open up, as it were, an highway for our God; the one the badge of slavery and superstition; the other the symbol of liberty, the pioneer of civilisation, and the joyful sound.'[61]

While this is a slight and satirical piece it exemplifies the attitude of suspicious hostility towards all things Roman Catholic that characterises Victorian Reformed Presbyterianism. The spectre of papal power being extended by Catholic nations, Jesuit conspiracies, unprincipled betrayals by liberal Protestant states or unjustified concessions by the British government, loomed large in the consciousness of a small denomination that believed the papacy to be the negation of Christian truth and a credible threat to spiritual and political liberty. Successive volumes warn against and expose the dangers. Jesuit missions to South India,[62] the plight of the papacy during the campaign for Italian Unification,[63] the need for missions to Irish Catholics,[64] the growth of Catholic numbers and influence in England during the nineteenth century,[65] the pronouncements on the Immaculate Conception in 1854[66] and of papal infallibility from the First Vatican Council in 1870,[67] provoked responses ranging from ridicule to outrage. Nearer home a wary statistical eye was being kept on the Roman Catholic presence. Noting that in 1864 there were seventy one more priests in England and an increase of five in Scotland, a sinister trend was highlighted by quoting figures over the previous thirty six years.[68]

The threat behind such statistics was crudely spelt out. 'Irish Papists swarm in our large cities, marry Protestant females whom they prevail on, in many instances, to join their church, and rear Popish families.'[69] A

---

[59] *LFF*, 151.
[60] *RPM*, 1855, 123.
[61] Ibid., 124.
[62] Ibid., 150-2.
[63] *RPM*, 1867, 463-65.
[64] *RPM*, 1865, 134 –35.
[65] Ibid., 197-200.
[66] *RPM*, 1855, 26-8.
[67] *RPM*, 1870, 28-31.
[68] *RPM*, 1865, 108.
[69] Ibid.

different tactic altogether was used in an 1856 article 'Influence of Romanism and Protestantism on Civilization'.[70] Comparisons were made between 'the chief Romanist and the chief Protestant nations'. Tables of exports, absolute wealth, elementary education, proportions of Protestant and Romanist populations educated, and even league tables of murders and illegitimate children,[71] demonstrated that the impact of Protestantism on the culture, morals and economic prosperity of a nation, was overwhelmingly more positive.

The anti Roman Catholic zeal of the Reformed Presbyterians is historic, has been unrelenting, but was not untypical of mid-Victorian anti-Catholicism. The 'Papal Aggression' of 1850 sparked anti-papal riots and conflict with immigrant Irish Catholics.[72] During the Garibaldi Riots of 1862 British working class protesters took to the streets in support of Garibaldi marching on Rome while Irish Catholic workers protested in defence of the Pope.[73] The Oxford Movement fuelled fears of a 'renascent Catholicism' as a serious threat within the Anglican Church. The revival of various ritual practices was seen as part of an increasingly bold Romanising tendency and high profile clerical conversions to Rome, such as John Henry Newman, reinforced such suspicions. It is within the more general context of a Protestantism 'uniformly hostile to papal authority and the main tenets of the Catholic Church'[74] that Reformed Presbyterian anti-Catholicism is best understood.

Living in Greenock in the middle of the nineteenth century, one further deeply significant fact places the young Denney firmly within the anti-Catholic culture of mid-Victorian militant Protestantism, namely the Irish connection. Reformed Presbyterian churchmanship, widespread and fierce anti-Catholicism, several decades of papal encroachments and doctrinal pronouncements anathema to Protestantism, and the attraction of Greenock for large numbers of migrating Irish Catholics, are

---

[70] *RPM*, 1856, 151-4.

[71] Scotland was top of the league with the lowest murder rate of 1 in 270,000, Spain had 1 in 4113. In the three Protestant nations (British Isles, Prussia and Sweden), 1 in 12 children was illegitimate whereas in the three Romanist nations France, Bohemia and Austria) it was 1 in 7. The figures of course don't add up, but they point to the intended conclusion. 'Thus in every particular in this general comparison, the superiority is on the side of Protestantism. A superiority of such a nature cannot be accidental. The superiority relates to the great secular interests of individuals and society. In all these interests Romanism stands at a disadvantage...' Ibid., 154.

[72] Donald M. MacRaild, *Irish Migrants in Modern Britain 1750-1922*, (Basingstoke: MacMillan, 1999), 175. See also D. G. Paz, *Popular Anti-Catholicism in Mid-Victorian England*, (Stanford: Stanford University Press, 1992).

[73] Ibid., 176. See also *RPM*, 1861, 4, for the editor's enthusiastic comments about the Pope's difficulties.

[74] MacRaild, *Irish Migrants*, 169.

cumulatively significant factors during Denney's developing years. Add to them strong interdenominational ties with a sister Synod whose members lived in a country overwhelmingly Catholic, and whose political and spiritual security depended on a British government uncertain how to deal with 'the Irish question', and they present a set of circumstances whose cumulative moulding force on Denney's outlook resulted in long-term antipathy.[75]

Historically the Reformed Presbyterian Church had strong fraternal links with the Irish Reformed Presbyterian Synod.[76] In 1866 the Eastern Reformed Synod of Ireland requested the establishment of 'an organic connection with the Reformed Presbyterian Church of Scotland'.[77] As a result the exchange of deputations between the Scottish and Irish Synods was 'placed on the advanced and more satisfactory footing of an annual appointment'.[78]

Greenock in the 1860s and 1870s was going through a massive industrial expansion. Geographically it was near Ireland and industrially it required an ever-expanding workforce. Official Census figures put the numbers of Irish born people in the Scottish population at around 200,000 throughout the years from 1841-1901,[79] while between 1851 and 1891 around 50% of dockers in Greenock were Irish.[80] The sheer quantity of Irish labourers and their lower wage expectations provided a reservoir of manpower for the growth industries on Clyde side. 'Both inside Glasgow and in nearby towns the Protestant Irish seem to have adapted to the labour and employment characteristics of the area. For example, they were well represented in the high quality skilled textile work and artisan crafts of Paisley, and in the unskilled, casual work which was a predominant feature of Greenock'.[81]

The Irish presence in Scotland was not an undifferentiated mass, but was divided within itself; there were Irish Catholic and Irish Protestant

---

[75] 'The Church-Catholic and Protestant', DEN09-10. See 'The Constructive Task of Protestanitsm', *Constructive Quarterly* 1, June 1913, 213-26, where Denney's appeal for re-thinking the doctrine of the church takes issue with the centrality of ecclesiology in Roman Catholic theology. In the *Thessalonians* commentary Denney fulminates against the system of the Papacy while being careful to acknowledge the saintliness of some Roman Catholics, 317-19.

[76] A contemporary account of the origins and history of Irish Reformed Presbyterians is given in *RPM*, 1857, 48-53.

[77] *RPM*, 1866, 234-5.

[78] *RPM*, 1867, 385-6.

[79] MacRaild, *Irish Migrants*, 43.

[80] Ibid., 54.

[81] Tom Gallagher, 'The Protestant Irish in Scotland', T. M. Devine (ed.), *Irish Immigrants and Scottish Society in the 19th and 20th Centuries*, (Edinburgh: John Donald, 1991), 59.

communities, and for many their religious affiliation was more decisive for their community identity than their nationality. Along the Clyde side, 'Catholic and Protestant workers from Ireland worked in uneasy proximity in the sugar refineries and quays.'[82] By the 1880's Greenock had its own Orange Lodge, and Irish Protestantism had successfully transplanted to congenial soil.

The fears so frequently and pungently expressed in the *Reformed Presbyterian Magazine*, of papist plots, doctrinal error and Romanist expansionism were given daily credence by such a large Irish presence. Denney grew up in a church and in a town where anti Roman Catholicism and anti-Irish sentiment were dominant notes of social and spiritual life. But in the circles of Reformed Presbyterianism, anti-Irish feeling was significantly discriminating; it was Irish Catholicism that was hated. Many Irish Protestants were looked on as ecclesiastical allies.

'The Sabbath – gift to man'[83]

'The nineteenth century was a great age for Scottish sabbatarianism, both for volume of publications and concerted efforts to bring national life into harmony with the fourth commandment.'[84] On the other hand it was also an age of concerted efforts to make the requirements of the fourth commandment more compatible with the demands of a quickly changing culture in which the demands of industry, transport and leisure exerted pressure on strict Sabbath observance. The Scottish historian T. C. Smout describes in his own words the imagined dominance of the church over the majority of the population:

> To native and foreigners alike, the Scottish Victorian Sabbath was the outward and visible sign of the Church's inward and spiritual sway. A universal stillness fell over Glasgow and Edinburgh (except in the unredeemed slums) at the time of the divine service, and pervaded small towns and villages from dawn to dusk...On Sundays the churches held the country in thrall for Christ.[85]

The remorseless clamouring of factory machinery, driven not only by coal, but by the social forces of cultural change and market growth, meant that by the second half of the century the average Scot would be hard pressed to enjoy 'a universal stillness'. In 1865, the *Reformed*

---

[82] Tom Gallagher, '"A Tale of Two Cities": communal strife in Glasgow and Liverpool before 1914', in R. Swift and S. Gilley (eds.), *The Irish in the Victorian City*, (London: Croom Helm, 1985), 110.

[83] Sermon title, DEN01-56.

[84] Needham, N. 'Sabbatarianism', in *DSCHT*, 738.

[85] T. C. Smout, *A Century of the Scottish People, 1830-1950*, (Glasgow: Collins, 1986), 182-3.

Presbyterian Magazine lamented the spoiling of the Sabbath by 'the enemies of godliness'.

> In all quarters the Sabbath is invaded. Railway directors run their passenger and goods trains on that day. The press employs a multitude of hands on the Sabbath in preparing the Monday news. The Post-Office works its officials in assorting, conveying and delivering letters. Shops are open in the large cities for merchandise by the thousand. A new attempt is just about to be made in Parliament to have the Botanical Gardens of Edinburgh thrown open on Sabbath afternoons.[86]

The objections of the Reformed Presbyterians were only a small part of a loud chorus of complaints from outraged sabbatarians in 1865. The North British Railway Company's decision to run passenger trains from Glasgow to Edinburgh sparked so much serious and organised opposition the controversy was nicknamed 'the Sabbath War'.[87] The *Reformed Presbyterian Magazine* sniped at those who had 'invaded the law of God', and were motivated by 'worldly sharpness rather than...spiritual enlightenment.'[88]

Throughout Denney's formative years Sabbath observance was both spiritual discipline and social habit, reinforced by family practice and church expectations. During his early ministry he preached a carefully argued sermon on Sabbath observance at East Hill Street.[89] True to his tradition he weighed the spiritual and social benefits of observance against the spiritual and social dangers of non-observance. Moral benefit flows not only from the physical advantages of regular rest and recreation, but from the promised blessing of God on a society which

---

[86] *RPM*, 1865, 183. See also *RPM*, 1862, 137-8, for the difference in principle between those who equated rest with amusement and recreation, and those who equate the Sabbath with serious religious observance. Quoting Hugh Miller the writer warns, 'But man is not a mere animal: what is best for the ox and the ass is not best for him; and in order to degrade him into a poor unintellectual slave, over whom tyranny, in its caprice, may trample rough-shod, it is but necessary to tie him down, animal like, during his six working days, to hard, engrossing labour, and to convert the seventh into a day of frivolous unthinking relaxation.'

[87] R. D. Brackenridge, 'The "Sabbath War" of 1865-66', *RSCHS* 16, 1966, 23-24; C. J. A. Robertson, 'Early Scottish Railways and the Observance of the Sabbath', *Scottish Historical Review* 57, 1978, 143-67.

[88] *RPM*, 1865, 384. *RPM*, 1866, 80 carries a commendation of a 'Report of Meeting held in Stirling on December 18th [1865], for the purpose of Protesting against Sabbath Trading', first published in the *Stirling Observer*.

[89] DEN03-46 'Sermon on the Sabbath'. In DEN01-67, 'The 4th Commandment', the subject arises in the course of a series of sermons on the decalogue preached during his Broughty Ferry ministry. Two further treatments include an outline address and a full address on Sabbath observance. A more relaxed view is discernible in his article 'Continental Sundays', *Union Magazine*, 1901, 261-2.

honours and obeys the divine law. Denney reflects standard strict Victorian views, making much of Sabbath observance as an identity marker of the Christian community and of a healthy society.

'The good Rhine wine'

Amongst the meagre sampling of Denney's early letters home from Germany there is a playful comment which, had it become common knowledge, would have raised a few hoary Reformed Presbyterian eyebrows.

> I have tasted the good Rhine wine, partly because the water is bad but chiefly because 'there's nothing can cheer the hearts that pine, like a deep, deep draught of the good Rhine wine,' etc., and because you never could drink anybody's health in water! N.B. I will be teetotal again in Scotland, so don't be angry about the drinking. Nobody is teetotal here, and I have only seen one drunk man in Cologne. So that there is no need of my example.

Despite the apparent levity, Denney suspects parental disapproval, and quickly owns his ongoing commitment to teetotalism when he returns to a Scottish context where such an example is an act of witness. In Reformed Presbyterian piety and social concern, temperance was an issue of almost equal importance to sabbatarianism.[90] Year after year, the magazine faithfully reported facts and figures about drunkenness and the liquor trade, passed on comments and news about legislative changes, and generally kept the constituency well educated in the rationale of teetotalism. The 1875 report welcomed increasing support for the temperance position. The British Association and the Congress of Social Sciences had both heard papers on legislative control and on total abstinence. Statistics had been published establishing the links between alcohol consumption and 'a lamentable amount of poverty, disease, immorality, crime and mortality.'[91] The Convenor noted £140 million pounds had been spent in the three kingdoms in the past year and blamed some of that on rising wages for the working classes. Commenting on the recent Moody and Sankey revival meetings the American evangelists were complimented for their strict and public stance on teetotalism.

---

[90] The standard histories often deal with them together, or as issues of similar social significance. J. L. Macleod, *The Second Disruption*, (East Linton: Tuckwell Press, 2000), ch. 1; Brown, *Religion and Society*, 145-50; Drummond and Bulloch, *Church in Late Victorian Scotland*, 21-8. For the broader social significance of drink and temperance see Smout, *Century*, 133-48; D. C. Paton, 'Temperance and the Churches in Scotland 1829-1927', *Scottish Records Association Conference Report*, 7, 1987, 22-9.

[91] *RPM*, 1875, 187.

All of which was balanced by an approach to total abstinence which allowed for freedom of individual conscience but made a persuasive appeal to that conscience.

> While not recommending the temperance pledge as a term of communion in Churches, your Committee would recommend it as not only unobjectionable on Scriptural grounds, but also as having proved abundantly helpful in the experience of individuals. They would, at the same time, welcome the co-operation of all their fellow-members in the Church, though not personally abstainers, in every legitimate effort for the lessening of the evils of intemperance, by the restriction of licences, and by preaching against the evils and causes of intemperance not only once or so, immediately before the close, but also frequently, during the course of the year.[92]

Denney, as a young man on the continent, clearly felt free to enjoy the local wines in a way he never would in Scotland. His later position hardened and he became a leading temperance spokesman within the Free Church and United Free Church General Assemblies.[93] During the war he supported prohibition. In his last letter to William Robertson Nicoll he complained, 'the things I *am* sore at being unable to help at are the Temperance Cause and the Central Fund.[94]

In Victorian Evangelicalism in general, and in Scottish Reformed Presbyterianism in particular, anti-Catholicism, sabbatarianism and temperance were the three high-profile causes which focused on ethical negatives and provoked powerful moral resistance. Total abstinence from drink, from unnecessary work on the Sabbath and from any truck with Romanism, was seen as a necessary spiritual safeguard and as the ethical norm within Reformed Presbyterian circles when Denney was growing up.[95]

---

[92] Ibid., 188. See also DEN04-83, 'Total Abstinence', sermon on Mark 9.42.

[93] Denney addressed the Free Church Assembly in 1898, and the United Free Church Assembly, in 1901, 1906, on Temperance; during the Great War, 1914, 1915 and 1916, he promoted temperance then prohibition.

[94] *LWRN*, 263.

[95] Total abstinence from Romanism, far from being an overstatement, was a seriously proposed argument introducing the 1875 Temperance Report. 'We profess to be, ecclesiastically, the successors of those who totally abstained, unitedly, and in a solemnly pledged manner, from even the most moderate errors of Popery, Prelacy and Erastianism. An evil, which in this land, at the present day at least, is practically as hurtful to soul, body and property, as any, or all of these evils combined, is claiming our attention, and its annihilation our most earnest efforts.' *RPM*, 1875, 187.

Missionary Investment

However, the *Reformed Presbyterian Magazine* also gives evidence of a broader and more open attitude to the modern world. The magazine carried regular news from the Irish and American Synods, important links for the morale of a small 'witnessing remnant'. There are major series of articles on India, China, Israel, and travelogues on such countries as Japan, France, Turkey, South Africa, Polynesia, Italy, Hungary and Switzerland.[96] While much of the writing was about the spiritual and missionary situation in these lands, they gave many people their first insights into life in other cultures and suggest an appetite for information unlikely in a readership content with intellectual insularity. The Reformed Presbyterians, like other Scottish churches in the Victorian age were strongly committed to overseas mission.[97] Often these travel articles were a *preparatio evangelium*, encouraging financial support, advertising the need for missionaries and thereby undergirding the rationale for missionary work.

During Denney's growth from childhood to adulthood the dominant figures in the Scottish Reformed Presbyterian mission story were John G. Paton[98] and John Inglis.[99] Paton's story, from his ordination in 1858 until 1876, is told in his own words in a long series of letters, published regularly in the magazine, remarkable both for their detail and for what they reveal of the motives and attitudes of a mid-nineteenth century Scottish Presbyterian missionary. More impressive still, the letters of John Inglis run in a continuous narrative throughout the entire publishing life of the magazine. It is hard to imagine the first readers of these letters would not be influenced and drawn into the dramas of these detailed accounts of life in another culture.[100] The scale of Inglis' achievement

---

[96] As examples, the 1863 volume of the *RPM* has a series of six articles on China, 15, 86, 121, 157, 281, 360; five articles on 'Travels in Italy' appeared in 1867. They are good humoured, appreciative, gossipy and marked by an enjoyable Victorian loquaciousness. See *RPM*, 1867, 54, 117, 165, 361, 437.

[97] A. Walls, 'Missions', *DSCHT*, 567-74, gives a summary overview of the development of missionary thinking in the Scottish churches during the period. Also Drummond and Bulloch, *Church in Victorian Scotland*, chapter 6, 'The Missionary Scene.'

[98] Paton worked in Vanuatu in the New Hebrides. See John Paton, *DSCHT*, 648. The monthly letters over many years in the *RPM* have an immediacy and detail hard to reproduce in secondary literature.

[99] Inglis arrived in Vanuatu in 1852. Again his series of published letters give first hand primary accounts of over twenty years of missionary service. See John Inglis, *DSCHT*, 430.

[100] It was the Editor's hope that regular, personal and detailed missionary intelligence would 'rivet attention and educe prayers', and he was satisfied that the magazine had 'done

over twenty four years was demonstrated in what amounted to an advertisement for his successor in 1876. 'Aneityum[101] is a cultivated field. Its people have embraced Christianity for years past. Church and manse and schools have all been erected. The climate, with ordinary precautions, Mr Inglis has often pointed out, is not unhealthy. A letter, in which he details in striking terms the advantages of Aneityum, will be found in the Reformed Presbyterian Magazine for 1871'.[102] The unfolding story of a missionary's experience of God, articulated in their own words, and contextualised in the reality of the life they have chosen to lead in an adopted culture, provides an effective and historically specific example of narrative theology.[103]

Not only did James Denney know about the work of Inglis and Paton; he supported it financially. As noted earlier, as a Sunday School scholar his annual few shillings helped buy the ship that serviced the missionary stations. When he finished his theological training he tried unsuccessfully to be appointed to a vacant position in the Free Church College, Calcutta. There is no indication he considered missionary field work outside a college framework. Later he would argue the case for giving to missions as one in a series of lectures on the Free Church, while on other occasions he spoke at missionary meetings on both the missionary vocation and on missionary work in particular places.[104]

Commitment to foreign mission was balanced by an interest in international events, especially as they impinged on the progress of the gospel or on major ethical and political questions. The American Civil War, and its connection to the slave emancipation movement received significant coverage and comment. In 1859 the news was welcomed that the American Reformed Presbyterian Church passed a resolution against slavery and cited the practice as sufficient grounds for not swearing the

---

much to enkindle and keep alive, no less than to increase, the missionary zeal of the church.' *RPM*, 1861, 3.

[101] Aneityum is an area of the South Sea Islands in the New Hebrides. Inglis compiled an Aneityumese dictionary, and prepared an Aneityumese translation of the Bible. He gives a moving and spirited defence of the labour involved in providing a translation for the community of 1500 Aneityumese people amongst whom the missionaries worked. See *RPM*, 1876, 378-83.

[102] *RPM*, 1874, 37.

[103] In 1872 the *RPM* carried two sermons which Inglis preached at the induction of new missionaries. They are examples of Victorian practical missiology, in which common-sense and strategic awareness mix with cultural blind-spots and theological non-negotiables.

[104] DEN08-77, 'Foreign Missions'. See also DEN11-16, 'Free Church Missions'; DEN11-17, 'Missionaries'; DEN11-18, 'Missions in East Africa'; DEN11-19, 'Congo'; DEN11-20, 'West Africa and Missions'; 'The Missionary Motive', in *Missionary Sermons*, (London: Carey Press, 1924), 229-40. In 1910 Denney addressed the Edinburgh World Missionary Conference at an evening session.

oath of allegiance because it required its citizens to 'obey [the Constitution's] unholy practices'.[105] An anonymous article on 'The War in America' offered incisive comment on the alleged causes of the war. The claim that it was Northern protectionist demands colliding with Southern desires for free trade was dismissed. More likely slaveholders attempting to load Congress with representatives from States opposed to emancipation lay behind the conflict. There follows a well-informed account of recent political machinations to back up the main thesis, 'that Slavery, one way or another has been the chief disturbing element in the United States ever since it was a nation'.[106] The article shows considerable political realism about Lincoln's motives; it excoriates the various American church denominations because they 'have a sum total of 665,000 human beings held as chattels by ministers and members of professedly Christian churches.'[107] A series of resolutions was passed at the American Synod in September 1865, the first of which leaves no doubt where Reformed Presbyterian sympathies lay as they thanked God for the 'utter overthrow of the slaveholders rebellion'.[108]

Nearer home, other social concerns found their way into the magazine's pages. Bothies, and the plight of agricultural labourers in tied accommodation and excessively low wages,[109] the need to provide decent housing for working people,[110] a generally supportive and full comment on the Education Act of 1872,[111] advice on how best to fulfil the duty of voting during an election,[112] and firm approval of the Government's suspension of the Habeas Corpus Act in Ireland[113] are a selection of the kinds of issues and public questions that were brought to the attention of the readership.

---

[105] '...the holding of men as property, to be bought and sold as "chattels personal" - is a "malum per se" [an evil in itself], wholly at variance with every precept of the Divine word, and a gross outrage upon every attribute of our common humanity'. *RPM*, 1859, 268.

[106] *RPM*, 1862, 15.

[107] Ibid., 17.

[108] *RPM*, 1865, 343.

[109] *RPM*, 1859, 79-83.

[110] *RPM*, 1855, 159 .

[111] *RPM*, 1871, 139. Passed in 1871, the Act came into effect in 1872 and is generally known as the Education Act of 1872.

[112] *RPM*, 1868, 339-45. This shows how far the (majority) Reformed Presbyterians had moved since enfranchisement and the removal of the Church's censure on voting. Now the duty of electors is linked to the strategic interests of the Kingdom of God.

[113] *RPM*, 1866, 106.

'A widespread relish for the free handling of sacred things'

The period 1855-79 was marked by major changes in approach to the Bible. During these years biblical criticism developed in new directions, largely dictated by the influence of German scholarship, and by the response, positive or negative, of those who interacted with it. The twenty three year old graduate who wrote to his parents from Germany in 1879, worried about his application to be considered as a ministerial candidate, was clearly aware that his own developing views might not be orthodox enough for 'the very reverend the Presbytery of Greenock.'[114] Denney's early interaction with biblical criticism, especially during the years of his theological formation in the Free College, Glasgow, will be considered later. His denomination's magazine sheds light on the attitude of Reformed Presbyterians to the wider developments in biblical study and theological restatement which would present the Scottish Church with one of its most fertile but painful challenges during the last quarter of the nineteenth century.

The magazine rarely presented to its readership the more radical intellectual developments arising from new thinking on the natural and social sciences.[115] The publication of Darwin's *Origin of Species* in 1859, *The Descent of Man* in 1871 and the resultant intellectual and theological controversies over evolution, failed to register in the list of contents. There were however more general and occasional interactions with higher criticism. A helpful glimpse into Reformed Presbyterian attitudes is given in the 'Introductory Address at the Opening of the Reformed Presbyterian Hall, Aug. 5. 1862'.[116] The overarching concern was to maintain the 'old truths', eschewing 'the glitter of theological novelties...the fire-mist of a troubled atmosphere distorting the real and deluding with a thousand phantoms....' Metaphysical speculations and 'the canker of rationalism' were generally held responsible for 'denying inspiration, multiplying paltry and peddling doubts, claiming liberty of thought by a ridiculous misnomer for licentious speculation [and] challenging in various ways the supreme authority of Scripture'.[117] The practical result of 'the rationalism of Germany and the Socinianism of

---

[114] *LFF*, 4.

[115] However Bishop Colenso is subjected to severe and sarcastic verbal abuse for his book questioning the Mosaic authorship and historical accuracy of parts of the Pentateuch, RPM, 1863, 42-6. The authors of the volume *Essays and Reviews* were similarly savaged: 'There is something beyond expression pitiable in the thought that after neology has, in Germany, been cast aside as a covering too narrow for a man to wrap himself in withal, men in England should put on the Teutonic old-clothes under the gowns of professors and the surplices of clergymen'. This is one of the more moderate, and less personal, statements in the article. *RPM*, 1861, 219-23.

[116] *RPM*, 1862, 331-40.

[117] Ibid., 335.

our own country' is the paralysis of mission 'to the lapsed at home or the heathen abroad'.

The defence of tradition against novelty by appealing to old truth vindicated by contemporary thought rightly and reverently used, was the main response of Denney's church in his years from Sunday School scholar to university student. Welhausen's *History of Israel* would not be published in English until 1878. It marked a watershed in relations between the academy and church courts, and exposed the growing gulf between professional critical learning applied to the Bible, and popular perceptions of the nature and status of biblical authority. The serious consequences for the Free Church, for William Robertson Smith and for the future of biblical studies in the colleges and pulpits of the Scottish churches were largely unforeseen in the decade or so previous.

The 'Reviews and Notices' sections of the magazine carried warm commendations of works by the more moderate German biblical critics. During this period the massive series of commentaries by C F Keil and F Delitzsch were being published.[118] Keil's *Minor Prophets* was 'evangelical in tone, learned without ostentatious display, and free from the wordiness and wire-drawn distinctions so often characteristic of German theological writers'.[119] The passage quoted in the review as a sample of the soundness of the scholarship is taken from Keil's treatment of the swallowing of Jonah. 'The great fish...was not a whale, because this is extremely rare in the Mediterranean, and has too small a throat to swallow a man, but a large shark or sea-dog, canis carcharias or squalus carcharius....' Scientific and factual information was used to substantiate biblical history; the more troublesome tension between historicity and miracle was not addressed.

The use of new discoveries to vindicate biblical truth was an important strategy for those who held to a literal view of the Bible. In 1872 an article on Assyrian cuneiform inscriptions by W. H. Green of Princeton was reprinted because it argued 'the new witness in the Assyrian cuneiform inscriptions to the truth of the Old Testament history'. The discovery of these 'sculptured slabs' from 1845 onwards, and the translation of the data they contain, seemed to throw biblical chronology into doubt. For that reason Green took a long, hard learned look at cuneiform as a written language, and raised enough questions to throw enough doubt on the integrity of the translations, to reassure those for whom the historical accuracy of the biblical record was foundational for biblical authority.[120]

---

[118] Denney later translated the third edition of Delitzsch on Isaiah into English.

[119] *RPM*, 1868, 324.

[120] *RPM*, 1872, 13-36. Green was concerned to show that an adequate approach to translating cuneiform required a fixity of meaning and a consistency in the referential value of each symbol. This, he argued, is precisely what Assyriologists lacked. They were

New developments in textual criticism were cautiously welcomed. An article on the importance of the Alexandrian and Vatican Codices, as witnesses in establishing the most reliable text of the New Testament, elicits a rare expression of gratitude to the Vatican for making the Codex Vaticanus available to the wider world.[121] This is not to say there was enthusiasm for the science of textual criticism as such; the value of such minute and painstaking establishing of the biblical text would depend on whether the end result enhanced or diminished the authority of Scripture itself.

New Testament commentaries were noted with various degrees of enthusiasm in the magazine. From 1873 to 1885, T. & T. Clark of Edinburgh issued translations of the entire series of the *Critical and Exegetical Commentary on the New Testament* edited by H. A. W. Meyer, 'perhaps the ablest commentator on the New Testament of modern times', according to Charles Hodge of Princeton.[122] The *Reformed Presbyterian Magazine* agreed: 'Sociniansim and broad Churchism will find no support in his expositions. He holds most distinctly the expiatory character of the death of Christ as a sacrifice for sin.'[123] Meyer in fact stood in a mediating position between a resurgent German Pietism and an emerging liberalism in Tubingen. His work was a combination of philological rigour and theological reflection, and while C. H. Spurgeon warned that his rationalism was a serious drawback, the Reformed Presbyterian reviewers had no such complaint.[124] In the 1860's it is significant that the Magazine reviewed Princeton's Charles Hodge on Romans but not J. B. Lightfoot's landmark commentaries on Galatians or Philippians. The massive J. P. Lange *Bibelwerk* was translated and edited by a team of scholars under the editorship of Philip Schaff and the first volumes greeted with unqualified enthusiasm. 'Those good people who, forgetful that it is the land of Bible-loving Luther and Melanchthon,

---

interpreting a symbolic language without having access to the social and cultural codebooks that a translator requires in order to communicate across the linguistic chasm. Green was a brilliant scholar of the Princeton School, whose energies were focused on defending the authority of the Bible. See Marion Ann Taylor, 'William Henry Green.', in W. A. Elwell and J. D. Weaver (eds.), *Bible Interpreters of the 20th Century. A Selection of Evangelical Voices'*, (Grand Rapids: Baker, 1999), 22-36.

[121] *RPM*, 1873, 341.

[122] On Meyer, see D. L. Bock, 'Meyer, Heinrich August Wilhelm (1800-1873)', in D. McKim (ed.), *Historical Handbook of Major Biblical Interpreters*, (Leicester: IVP, 1998), 340-2.

[123] *RPM*, 1873, 458 and 1874, 434.

[124] C. H. Spurgeon, *Commenting and Commentaries*, (Edinburgh: Banner of Truth, 1969), 145. Compared with Spurgeon's further comment 'apart from his scholarship we do not commend him', the *Reformed Presbyterian* reviews convey an air of intellectual generosity.

associate Germany with everything that is heterodox, will be delightfully surprised to find, ...that it is just as celebrated for admirable commentary on Scripture...'.[125]

'A Bible centred, ethically stringent Presbyterian evangelicalism'

From birth to his matriculation at the University of Glasgow, James Denney lived in Greenock in a working-class home. Unlike many of his contemporaries in the town, the evidence suggests he did not suffer significant deprivation. He had a reasonable education in a school where foundations of learning were laid with care. Life largely revolved around the social and religious programme of the local Reformed Presbyterian Church where the religious atmosphere of tempered spiritual intensity had been forged out of a passionate sense of denominational identity. These are some of the broad contextual outlines of James Denney's early life.

But the details are also important. He remained unashamedly conscious of his father's working background and of his own roots in unfashionable Greenock. He grew up in a large town expanding too quickly for its own good, the labour market acting like a magnet drawing people from Scotland and Ireland. The resultant over-crowding, inadequate sanitation, lack of decent housing and insufficient water supply, created major health and social problems during the 1860's and 1870's. The family church was strict in theology and jealously proud of its historic roots in the Covenanting ecclesiology of the seventeenth century. His experience was of a church which had divided over a local difference, and denominationally had split over matters of strongly held principle. He had known three ministers, his father had been an elder for many years, he had taught and been taught in Sunday school, and had been a leader among the young people.

The ethos in which his early spiritual life was formed was a Bible centred and ethically stringent Presbyterian evangelicalism. The social, intellectual, and moral attitudes of his church dictated the spiritual and ethical guidelines for his behaviour, and equally importantly, defined the intellectual and theological context in which he grew towards maturity. The mental and moral environment of nineteenth-century Scottish Reformed Presbyterianism was informed by several identity-conferring emphases: a deep suspicion of the British government as a secular organism usurping the legitimate kingship of Christ; an implacable opposition to Roman Catholicism as a political and theological system; a protective devotion to public Sabbath observance, and, by the middle of the century, a vocal and highly moral supporter of Temperance

---

[125] *RPM*, 1869, 463. Reprinted in the USA as recently as the 1970's.

principles; a willingness to walk along the path to union with like-minded Christians, and the capacity to make the decision to unite despite having to sacrifice the denomination's own unity; a strong interest in foreign missions and a willing investment in missionary activity; an awareness of the social problems of the nation, and a readiness to comment on them, though at times in terms that gave spiritual and oversimplified solutions to problems structurally endemic to the political realities; a biblical literacy which was so conservative that at times it came near to biblical literalism, and which tended only to approve those fruits of criticism which upheld 'old truth'.

The cumulative pressure of such emphases, exerted on a boy growing into a young man, were such that they were likely to become defining attitudes for the recipient. The formation process can be a positive and personal owning of the received values, a negative reaction against them, or more usually, a mixture of both. Willingness to pick and choose what matters from inherited social values and learned patterns of behaviour is an important part of the individuation process, whereby a person discovers who they are, and what in life will matter most. In other words, values are chosen as well as inherited.

In later life Denney repeatedly stated the moral basis of human life. Each human being is, he said, 'in nature akin to God, capable of fellowship with Him and designed for it, conscious of moral freedom and responsibility, and therefore morally responsible and free'.[126] Such moral maturity is a process of learning and experience, and learning from experience. At the University of Glasgow, and the Free Church College in Glasgow, James Denney would be exposed to ways of thinking that would force a revaluation. Many absorbed assumptions would require reconsideration; much that he had taken for granted for eighteen years would have to stand scrutiny as intelligence was trained in criticism.

---

[126] Denney, *Studies*, 75.

CHAPTER 3

The University Years, 1874-1879

Referring to Denney's time at Glasgow University, A. S. Peake remarked, 'he had a brilliant career in classics under (Sir) Richard C. Jebb [and] in philosophy under Edward Caird'.[1] Peake is one of several contemporaries who commented on the early evidence of Denney's outstanding intellectual ability.[2] Robertson Nicoll also mentioned the influence of Jebb and Caird, but importantly paid tribute to John Veitch, Professor of Logic and Rhetoric at Glasgow. Denney excelled in all three subjects, winning several prestigious prizes and inevitably coming to the attention of his teachers.[3] He later marked papers for Jebb whom he admired, was sufficiently proficient for Veitch to invite him to teach the Logic class[4] and won the Gold Medal in Caird's philosophy class.[5]

While the influence of particular teachers on a high performance student is difficult to gauge, cross-fertilisation of ideas was all but unavoidable in the prolonged interactive relationship between student and professors. It is difficult to trace with precision and certainty, where one person has followed another's intellectual footsteps and where they have travelled independently.

Of his three university teachers Denney expressed explicit indebtedness only to Jebb. In a brief note of appreciation included in Jebb's biography, Denney recalled his classics professor as a role model for those 'who had no idea of what translation could be...He not only did the thing, but created an ideal for us by doing it.'[6] On the other hand, while excelling in philosophy, he remained permanently ambivalent, even

---

[1] *DNB, 1912-1921*, 153-4. Peake was an interesting choice. In 1903 and 1904 he and Denney had conducted a published argument on aspects of Denney's atonement theology in his volumes *The Death of Christ* and *The Atonement and the Modern Mind*. Peake's assessment of Denney's character is coloured, not unfairly, by the exchange.

[2] Walker, *Denney*, is a characteristically overstated account giving Denney's abilities legendary status. Taylor gathers the few fragments of information into a more credible picture in *Principal James Denney*, 19-21.

[3] Denney's name has 15 entries in the Record of University Prizes.

[4] *LFF*, 31.

[5] *LWRN*, xiv and xv.

[6] Caroline Jebb, *Life and Letters of Sir Richard Claverhouse Jebb O.M., Litt.D.*, (Cambridge: Cambridge University Press, 1907), 186-8.

suspicious, of the discipline that helped equip him with the tools of argument. In 1893, while still minister in Broughty Ferry, he described reading Edward Caird's Gifford Lectures as 'unprofitable labour', hardly complimentary to the efforts of his old teacher.[7] However it would be unwise to assume on such evidence that Denney's mind was more influenced by Jebb, the teacher he admired who taught a subject he enjoyed for the rest of his life, than by Caird, a teacher who taught a subject he never fully trusted and whose speculative tendencies left him cold.

Moulding of scholarly attitudes, training in intellectual discipline, instilling reverence for truth and meaning, developing a capacity for organising and internalising ideas so that they become personalised knowledge affecting mental and moral development, these are constituent parts of what is not always a self-conscious educative process. The fact that Denney is later dismissive of philosophical theology, and pays scant tribute to Caird, need not mean Caird's influence was either negligible or short-term. The impact of Caird's teaching on Denney's mind may have lain not so much in the simple absorption of ideas, as in the intellectual stimulus and challenge of being exposed to a first-class mind which questioned received foundational assumptions, and compelled either reconstruction or restatement.

One further reason for caution in evaluating influences on the development of mind and thought lies in the provisional nature of opinion, insight and judgement. Intellectual integrity and mature self-knowledge require that a mind alive to truth holds its judgements and conclusions open to revision. Moffatt records just such a turning point in Denney's mind. At an after dinner speech in the Glasgow Free Church College, Denney told 'how he had been preoccupied as a student with Dr. Bruce's teaching about Jesus and indifferent to Professor Drummond's lectures on science; now he said, he recognised that acquaintance with the scientific outlook on the world was far more vital to religion and religious teaching than he had realised'.[8] Past indifference had given way to discovered relevance.

University Education in Nineteenth Century Scotland

Denney arrived in Glasgow at a time of radical educational change. The traditional Scottish Arts degree was under considerable pressure to adapt to changing social needs. John Coutts describes the Scottish ideal:

> In Arts the old but evergreen subjects of Latin and Greek formed the department of Classics; Logic, Moral Philosophy and English Literature, that of Mental

---

[7] *LFF*, 49.
[8] *LFF*, xii.

Philosophy; while Mathematics and Natural Philosophy formed the third department. Candidates were left free to take the departmental examinations in any order they pleased.[9]

The aim of such an educational approach was the formation of the student's mind, equipping them with essential intellectual tools. The general Arts curriculum was rooted in Scottish philosophical traditions, and aimed to produce thinkers who were in the broad sense learned, well read, and able to hold their own in the give and take of wide-ranging cultural and intellectual discussion.[10] But pressures were building from several directions. One influential interpretation, that of the intellectual historian George Davie,[11] describing what was happening in nineteenth century university education, portrays a struggle between a patriotic core bent on retaining the Scottish general curriculum, and progressive anglicising enthusiasts pushing for the introduction of 'narrower specialisation typified by the single subject honours degree'.[12]

Davie's view has been criticised for being over-influenced by nationalistic concerns, because it was anachronistically modern in its portrayal of English 'specialisation', and for presenting the student experience of the Scottish general curriculum as more standardised and secure than it actually was.[13] By the 1860's Scottish universities were developing science degrees independent of the arts framework. Faculties of medicine did not make an Arts degree an entry prerequisite, and medical science in particular was a major beneficiary of the rapid growth in scientific research. 'The contribution of many distinguished Scots - Kelvin, Simpson, Lyell, Clerk-Maxwell...to the long list of important scientific and medical advances in the nineteenth century was a considerable one'.[14] Humes argues that science was 'perhaps *the* leading concept' and the basis of 'intellectual security and material advancement' in the nineteenth century. A German physiologist summed up the status of science in the nineteenth century marketplace of ideas:

---

[9] J. Coutts, *History of the University of Glasgow, 1451-1909*, (Glasgow: ...., 1909), 436.

[10] 'The chief objective was the production of well-rounded gentlemen, imbued with Christian humanist values and familiar with all branches of polite learning.' R. D. Anderson, *Scottish Education Since the Reformation*, (Dundee: Economic and Social History Society of Scotland, 1997), 15.

[11] G. Davie, *The Democratic Intellect*, (Edinburgh: Edinburgh University Press, 1961).

[12] Anderson, *Scottish Education*, 30.

[13] W. M. Humes, 'Science, Religion and Education: A Study in Cultural Interaction', in W. M. Humes and Hamish M. Paterson (eds.), *Scottish Culture and Scottish Education, 1800-1980*, (Edinburgh: John Donald, 1983), 16-17; Anderson, *Scottish Education*, 32-3.

[14] Anderson, *Scottish Education*, 119.

'If there is one criterion which for us indicates the progress of humanity, it is the level attained of power over nature...Only in scientific research and power over nature is there no stagnation; knowledge grows steadily, the shaping strength develops unceasingly.'[15] Science offered a way of controlling the world, its 'shaping strength' residing in the application of ideas to the physical world. New technology, ideas put to work, gave scientific advances an industrial and social application with obvious commercial, but more questionably, human benefits.[16]

The growing status of science encouraged a more critical mind-set, which sought to understand and construe the world and human nature in a quite specific way. The attachment of science to the methods of inductive rationality, and the resulting epistemology heavily dependent on empirical evidence, inevitably modified worldviews, developing an approach to reality which 'valued rationalism above intuition and materialism above spirituality.'[17] The work of Henry Drummond is an example of how one mind sought to reconstrue science and theology into a worldview in which the truths of both could be reconciled without major loss of credibility. Drummond's inaugural lecture as Professor of Natural Science in the Free Church College, Glasgow, was 'The Contribution of Science to Christianity.' His *Natural Law in the Spiritual World*, published in 1883, was severely criticised in 1885 by Denney.[18] The relations between Drummond and Denney will be examined later in the context of Denney's theological education. Denney's most trenchant criticisms of Drummond's best-seller concern the worldview Drummond implied in his use of an evolutionary framework and the absence of adequate doctrines of sin and atonement.

The ongoing debate on educational reform was therefore conducted throughout a period when competing worldviews suggested differing priorities, and was at its most intense in the 1870s when Denney studied

---

[15] Michael Biddiss, quoted in Humes, 'Science, Religion and Education', 118.

[16] John Veitch reveals the ambivalence felt by many in the face of industrialisation and technological advance driven by the commercial benefits of science. He wrote his observations on the train journey from Peebles to Glasgow: 'The autumn was glorious and pathetic...up to the coal pits of Lanarkshire, when only the naked arms of trees - waeful trees - were horrid against the sky.... Manufacturing industry has much to answer for. It has cursed this country, and deprived thousands of their natural sustenance- the light of heaven and the greenery of earth.' Mary R. L. Bryce, *Memoir of John Veitch, LL.D.*, (Edinburgh, 1896), 171-2.

[17] Humes, 'Science, Religion and Education', 119.

[18] *'On "Natural Law in the Spiritual World"'*, by a Brother of the Natural Man, (Paisley, 1885), was written anonymously by Denney. Drummond's volume was 'the most widely read religious book in the world in its day' according to one Drummond enthusiast. Humes, 'Science, Religion and Education', 121. See D. W. Bebbington, 'Henry Drummond, Evangelicalism and Science', 19-38, in Thomas Corts (ed.), *Henry Drummond. A Perpetual Benediction*, (Edinburgh: T & T Clark, 1999).

Arts and Divinity. The progressive faction, one of whose champions was Edward Caird, believed the production of scientifically trained minds would be facilitated by specialisation, a selection process of the most able students by entrance requirements, and a gradation of degrees awarded on the basis of examination. The more conservative group, which included John Veitch, sought to retain the broad general curriculum, though with the reluctant compromise that specialisation could constitute the second part of a degree after a general foundation had been laid.[19] In educational policy as in philosophical preference, Caird and Veitch were on opposite sides, and Denney was under the tutelage of both.

Later, examining the role of Veitch and Caird as teachers who influenced Denney's intellectual development, it will be important to consider in more detail the decline of the Scottish philosophical tradition, and the shift of interest in Scottish universities to the philosophy of Idealism associated particularly with Germany. Though German thought usually came into Scotland via Oxford,[20] many Scots in the second half of the nineteenth century spent time in Germany, doing further study or simply soaking in the intellectual atmosphere.[21] In German universities divinity faculties enjoyed much greater intellectual freedom and were much more numerous. More generally they were institutions where new tools of historical criticism and laboratory based study of natural science were being rapidly developed. In such ways they modelled a new kind of university, in which teaching coalesced with research and scholarship, providing a much more socially useful *raison d'être* for a major educational institution.[22]

Davie's account of 'the democratic intellect' is acknowledged to be at its strongest in its analysis of what was at stake in the struggle between competing educational ideologies linked to shifts in scientific and philosophical thought. At Glasgow University Edward Caird seemed more in tune with the times than Veitch. Henry Jones, Denney's student friend, recalled, '[Caird] spoke of Kant, and often quoted Goethe and referred to Hegel, substituting as was supposed, for the wholesome home made doctrines, theories which were somehow "unintelligible jargon" and also unsettling and dangerous'.[23] By the end of the century 'most Scottish philosophy chairs were filled by neo-Hegelian idealists trained at

---

[19] Davie, *Democratic Intellect*, 84-8.

[20] A. C. Cheyne, *Studies in Scottish Church History*, (Edinburgh: T & T Clark, 1999), 27-9.

[21] As noted earlier, Denney spent the summer of 1879, the year he graduated, reading philosophy and studying with Henry Jones and Hugh Walker in Germany.

[22] J. W. Rogerson, *The Bible and Criticism in Victorian Britain*, (Sheffield: Sheffield Academic Press, 1995), ch. 5, 'The German Connection'.

[23] Sir H. Jones and J. H. Muirhead, *The Life and Philosophy of Edward Caird*, (Glasgow: Maclehose & Jackson, 1921), 67.

Oxford...'[24] Of these, Edward Caird was a highly influential figure, not least in his impact on generations of students, his Hegelian teaching contributing to the decline of Scottish philosophy and 'moving his students away from Evangelicalism'.[25]

But the changes in educational approach and content were not simply the working out of differing philosophies and educational policies. Social developments, such as the professionalisation of many areas of life, made qualifications and good degrees an integral part of middle-class ambitions.[26] At the same time new technology and the demands of industrial expansion created a corresponding demand for precisely the specialised knowledge a broad-based general curriculum weighted in favour of mental philosophy and classics could not supply. The dominance of the general curriculum crumbled under the vocational demands of professional ambition. Training in skill and professional competence in a chosen career, gradually supplanted a process of equipping the mind with the multi-purpose tools of judgement and reflection, as the primary educational goal.

Denney matriculated at Glasgow in 1874, two years after the 1872 Education Act permanently and comprehensively changed the approach to education in Scotland. For half a century a series of Royal Commissions had highlighted several problems with the traditional general degree, including age of entry and entry-level qualifications, the range of subjects studied and the need for more specialisation. These were not only educational limitations; such problems affected the quality and marketability of the universities' intellectual product.[27] Behind this general account lie powerful changes in intellectual climate, with science and an increasing confidence in the scientific worldview on the ascendant, philosophy becoming much more cosmopolitan and eclectic, strong social under-currents powering the professional aspirations of the growing middle classes, and on the part of the State, an increasing determination to improve educational provision and adapt educational policy to the changing world. In the personalities of Jebb, Veitch and Edward Caird, Denney encountered this changing world by being exposed during his university years to strong cross-currents of educational ideology, philosophical rivalry and personal attraction, all of which played their part in shaping his response to what he learned and in forming long-term disciplines and habits of mind and thought.

---

[24] Anderson, *Scottish Education*, 33.
[25] 'Caird, Edward', *DSCHT*, 116.
[26] Anderson, *Scottish Education*, 31.
[27] Humes, 'Science, Religion and Education', 117.

'Entering into the mind of men eminent in thought and in power of expression'

Richard Jebb was a deeply cultured classics scholar whose translation of Sophocles was deemed 'the most completely satisfactory commentary on a classical author that has been written in the English language'.[28] John Veitch was a Professor of Logic deeply influenced by the metaphysics of Sir William Hamilton. Edward Caird, was an influential populariser of Hegel and a devoted scholar of Kant who twice became Gifford Lecturer. These were the men whose teaching and personalities laid intellectual foundations in the minds of the Arts students who matriculated in 1874. Amongst them was eighteen year-old James Denney,[29] whose mental horizons had so far been fixed by his experience in working class Greenock, in the Highlander's Academy, and in the Reformed Presbyterian Church.

Denney's admiration for Jebb is uncharacteristically fulsome for someone who seldom flattered. 'I have no hesitation in saying that [Jebb] was by far the best teacher I ever knew, and that he made his subject real and inspiring as few are able to do.'[30] Jebb's classics teacher at Cambridge was J. B. Lightfoot who had high expectations for Jebb's future, who became his friend and whose company and conversation enabled Jebb to live 'in a region above the frost-line of perpetual shams and misunderstandings'.[31] For Jebb, above the frost-line was the place of study, whether the classroom or his own desk. His theory of education was memorably explained in his inaugural address, and it sheds considerable light on what motivated him both as scholar and teacher. He asked what it meant to claim that a modern education should bear '*directly* on the things of modern life'. His reply is illuminating:

> It will be useful to remember the distinction between these terms: information - knowledge - science - education. Information is the process of shaping what was shapeless; it may be used, therefore, of anything which defines a notion previously vague... Knowledge is information digested and made a complete, intelligible whole. Science is knowledge extended, not merely to the systematic arrangement of

---

[28] *DNB, 1912-1921*, 368. His edition remains in print over a century later.

[29] Denney's signature is number 627 in the matriculation *Register of the University of Glasgow*.

[30] Jebb, *Life and Letters*, 187. Sir Henry Jones, Denney's friend from university days, paid similar tribute to Jebb's influence. H. J. W. Hetherington, *The Life and Letters of Sir Henry Jones*, (London: Hodder & Stoughton, 1924), 19. Denney's admiration did not extend to Jebb's political acumen or his Christian credentials: 'If there is the faintest whiff of Christianity about the creature, he neutralises it somehow or other with absolute success...he could no more rouse a crowd than John Bright could edit Sophocles'. *LFF*, 52.

[31] Jebb, *Life and Letters*, 25, 119.

particulars, but to the comprehension or illustration of laws. Education literally means not bringing out, but bringing up. Mental education is a training of the mind, whatever the instrument may be by which it is trained.[32]

Quoting Sir William Hamilton's dictum, 'The study of language if conducted upon rational principles is one of the best exercises of an applied logic', Jebb goes on to argue for a thorough grounding in classical literature as a prerequisite for a truly wise and human life. 'The study of literature, to which that of language is the key, is the entering into the mind of men eminent in thought and in power of expression. That is why it is called humanising. It makes you a more representative human being, because it gives you a share in the best things that have been thought and said by the best ones of our race....'[33] This is the gospel according to Jebb, the Classics professor pleading the continuing relevance of studying the classics, with the forceful persuasion of an evangelist, and indicating just how such learning bears '*directly* on modern life'. Used rightly, the classics become instruments of mental education, training the mind by the study of literature, using language as the key, instilling disciplines that humanise and make people more representative human beings.

In the Romanes Lecture for 1899 Jebb further expounded the theme of 'Humanism in Education'. Beginning with a reference to the Renaissance he quickly focused on his theme:

> The Renaissance had its central inspiration in the belief that the classical literatures, which were being gradually recovered, were the supreme products of the human mind; that they were the best means of self-culture; that there alone one could see the human reason moving freely, the moral nature clearly expressed, in a word, the dignity of man, as a rational being, fully displayed.[34]

There follows a long and erudite history of Renaissance humanism as an ideal, essential to human flourishing, nourished by intellectual freedom and endangered by obscurantism. The aim of a humanist education is balance, wholeness, a harmonious coincidence of a person's intellectual powers, so that it may be said the student 'goes through a little Renaissance of his own...'. In the following extract Jebb describes the student's experience of the complex relationship between teacher and student:

> He feels the stimulus of discovery; he perceives in some measure, a beauty of form unlike anything that he has found elsewhere; there is much in the thoughts of those great writers, much of their charm, much of their music, that fixes itself in his

---

[32] Ibid., 184-5.
[33] Ibid., 186.
[34] R. C. Jebb, *Humanism in Education*. The Romanes Lecture, (London, 1899), 5.

memory and becomes part of his consciousness. However dimly and imperfectly, there lives before him a world very distinct from that in which he moves, and yet as he can already feel, by no means wholly alien from it...it is an experience which is not forgotten afterwards. Whatever the man's work may be in after years, if ever he looks back and tries to date epochs in his mental history, he will recur to that early time as a season which made the buds unfold and the leaves grow, which gave him new elements of intellectual life and interest.[35]

Such was the philosophy of education that Denney encountered as a young man, personified in a professor whose humanism was a life passion which left its mark on Denney's mental apparatus for the rest of his life. Denney's own reputation as a teacher rested on an educational philosophy and a teaching style not dissimilar to Jebb's. His passion for precision, both in thinking and expression, mirrors Jebb's approach to education, in which learning was understood as a moral as well as a mental discipline, a humanising influence to be nurtured and sustained in the pursuit of truth and maturity. Denney remained a deeply cultured lover of the classics. He read Euripides on holiday, recommended Epictetus as a book 'to read in, anywhere, now and again', and found deep pleasure in reading the sixth book of Homer's *Iliad* during his last illness.[36]

Words written about Jebb's expository gifts in relation to the classics are equally apt applied to Denney's later work, particularly on Paul. 'Jebb had an exquisite apprehension of every shade of meaning in the most delicate and precise of languages; and there was a natural harmony between the poet and his expositor, by virtue of which Jebb seems to wind his way into the very mind of Sophocles.'[37] Replace Paul as poet and Denney as expositor, and the words suggest the profounder levels at which a gifted teacher passes on an entire tradition of scholarship. The interpretation of the mind of Paul was one way in which his Classics grounding bore fruit, his Romans commentary in particular, a demonstration of mature skills and reliable interpretative instincts first awakened in Jebb's classics class.[38] Denney's work on the New Testament text was characterised by a critical but sympathetic interaction between the authorial and the interpreting mind, a conversation aided by the best tools, and unafraid of conclusions so long as they were supported by

---

[35] Ibid., 25.
[36] *LFF*, 173, 197, 211.
[37] *DNB, 1912-21*, 369.
[38] Denney was delighted that his commentary on Second Corinthians was reviewed in the *British Weekly* by Marcus Dods, who interestingly wrote that Denney 'brings the reader into direct contact with the mind of Paul.' *BW*, 10 May 1894, 22.

available evidence.[39] As Denney himself acknowledged, Jebb not only translated; he created an ideal for his students by doing it.

'He who will not reason is a bigot; he who cannot is a fool; he who dare not is a slave!'[40]

John Veitch, Professor of Logic, had seriously considered entering the Free Church ministry but ran into intellectual difficulties with Calvinistic orthodoxy.

> I cannot but think it is a stain on our Churches, and men in them, to have acquiesced so long and so unthinkingly in the doctrine of Necessitation, or rather of a necessitated volition. I know that this arises from their holding 'Election' views. These I hold too; but we ought not on that account to annihilate the notions of merit and demerit, or at least render them ridiculous.... However I think there is a great deal of rubbish which requires clearance connected with what is termed Calvinism.[41]

The independence of mind and impatience with dogma these words expose were eventually to make it impossible for him to be ordained. His refusal to subscribe to standards of faith and to submit to doctrinal examination demonstrates the mental temper of the scholar who taught James Denney in the logic class. 'I for one am resolved that, though I am stranded on the shore of heresy, I shall never attempt to maintain any theological doctrine which I have not for myself thoroughly sifted and found to be true. "He who will not reason is a bigot; he who cannot is a fool; he who dare not is a slave!"'[42]

Veitch turned to the study of philosophy in Edinburgh where he first became assistant to Sir William Hamilton then to Professor Alexander Fraser. Hamilton was one of the last exponents of Scottish Realism, Fraser a Professor of Logic who was a convinced theist and later Gifford

---

[39] Denney's writing on the mind of Paul began with two contributions to the *Expositior's Bible*, on Thessalonians in 1892 and Second Corinthians in 1894. The chapters were originally preached as sermons in Broughty Ferry, as were several other expository series including 25 sermons on First Corinthians. See DEN06-18 to DEN06-43 and the 85 pages of exegetical notes DEN06-44A. The 1900 Romans commentary was followed by a series of articles on the 'Theology of the Epistle to the Romans' published in *The Expositor* in 1901 and 1902. Six unpublished lectures on 'The Gospel According to Paul', DEN08-13-01 to DEN08-13-06, and a 48 page paper on 'The Christology of Paul', DEN08 14, together represent a full length study on Paul's theology.

[40] Bryce, *Memoir*, 99.

[41] Ibid., 53-4.

[42] Ibid., 96-9, contains a moving account of a young mind refusing to be coerced into an orthodoxy he cannot intellectually own. The quotation is on page 99.

Lecturer on 'The Philosophy of Theism'.[43] The impact of Hamilton was decisive and Veitch became both disciple and biographer, one of the last to advocate Scottish Common Sense philosophy in a Scottish University during the later nineteenth century.

William Robertson Nicoll wrote an affectionate but qualified tribute on Veitch's death. By 1894 Veitch had become an authority on the poetry of the Scottish Borders and as a result, 'on the whole [had] done very little for philosophy'.[44] His philosophical work had been mainly an echo of Hamilton, and even then Nicoll thought his exposition inferior to the essay of Spencer Baynes in that author's *Edinburgh Essays*. But that is the judgement of a widely read and independent mind; Denney had encountered Veitch twenty years earlier, as an undergraduate newly discovering the intellectual gymnastics of mental philosophy, and while Veitch was still an intellectual force to be reckoned with.

In 1877, the year Denney won the class-prize, the Logic examination papers show the importance of Scottish Philosophy in the logic curriculum, and Veitch's own commitment to a Scottish form of Realism as the most viable foundation for intellectual enquiry. By contrast the Moral Philosophy papers reveal the importance of Hegel, Kant and German philosophical concerns in Edward Caird's classes.[45] The presence in the same university and faculty, of two teachers from opposing schools of philosophy created for students who took both classes an intellectual climate of dialectic opposites of almost Hegelian proportions. Students such as James Orr, James Denney and Henry Jones learned Mental Philosophy by excelling in two classes in which, while the syllabuses showed considerable overlap, the professors were poles apart on fundamental questions of epistemology and metaphysics.

Scottish Philosophy: 'To make experience intelligible'

A superficial definition of 'common sense philosophy' might suggest that problems of philosophy such as the relation between mind and matter, or the nature and significance of moral experience, can be settled by a straightforward appeal to the commonly accepted opinions of ordinary people, a sophisticated form of philosophy by opinion poll. To avoid such fundamental misunderstanding, Professor Gordon Graham carefully defines the Scottish philosophy of common sense as expounded by Thomas Reid. The leading exponents of Scottish philosophy, he argues, share 'an almost unspoken assumption that the question of mind

---

[43] For Fraser see *DSCHT*, 333-4. Veitch and Fraser remained lifelong friends. Bryce, *Memoir*, 39.

[44] *BW*, 6 September 1894, 307.

[45] See *Glasgow University Calendar*, 1877, 44-6 for the examination papers on 'Logic and Rhetoric' and 'Moral Philosophy'.

and world lies at the heart of philosophy'.[46] If the mind is accurately to capture or reflect reality there must be some process that includes reason and inference. The assumption of the Scottish philosophy is that 'there is no better ground than common sense. That is to say, at the root of our everyday beliefs are certain principles of judgement and inference which we naturally (in the sense of unreflectively) employ, and which, importantly, we cannot fail to employ without falling into confusion and sceptical error.'[47] This basic point is further refined in a lecture explicating the Scottish philosophy:

> While Reid does indeed invoke in criticism of the 'theory of ideas' certain fundamental principles of thought and reasoning, he does not present them as widely held *beliefs*....The point, in fact, is not to make philosophical theories accommodate themselves to common belief, but to make them accord with the intelligibility of common *experience*. Common belief is often prejudiced, silly or ignorant. Consequently there is no occasion to require philosophy to bring its conclusions into conformity with it. But common experience, which is what I think the phrase Common Sense in Reid refers to (in contrast to its modern meaning), is a datum which philosophy must take account of. Philosophy's task, in short, is to make experience intelligible.[48]

John Veitch shared a similar view; philosophy 'is an attempt...to state the meaning and guarantee we have of reality as applied to man, the world, and God. Metaphysics is a reflection, an awakening to the hidden inner truth of things.'[49]

Veitch's version of the Scottish philosophy as mediated through Hamilton could be stated simply: 'In plain words, it is primarily and essentially the method which Bacon inculcated...an appeal to experience, to our actual knowledge.' In all ordinary experience certain principles are not argued, they are assumed:

> There are laws which guarantee themselves by the impossibility of subverting them even in thought. This impossibility or necessity being fully realised in consciousness, gives them universality. For what *must* be thought, *always must* be

---

[46] Gordon Graham, 'The Nineteenth Century Aftermath', in Alexander Broadie (ed.), *The Cambridge Companion to the Scottish Enlightenment*, (Cambridge: Cambridge University Press, 2003), 344.

[47] Gordon Graham, 'Morality and Feeling in the Scottish Enlightenment', *Philosophy* 76, 2001, 274.

[48] Gordon Graham, 'The Scottish Tradition in Philosophy', *The Aberdeen University Review* LVIII, 201, Spring, 1999, 6.

[49] John Veitch, *Sir William Hamilton. The Man and His Philosophy*, (Edinburgh, 1883), 26.

thought – in a word, is universal in consciousness...no one can assail those principles without assuming them or their equivalents.[50]

The reference to Bacon indicates the importance of inductive reasoning in the quest to understand reality. Graham contends that the Scottish philosophy is best defined in terms of its methodological principles rather than its doctrines. James McCosh, President of Princeton, and one of the most powerful proponents of Scottish philosophy, presented a threefold summary of its characteristics.[51] First, *'it proceeds throughout by observation. It begins with facts and ends with facts'*. McCosh was keen to point out that though the Scottish school uses deduction, it does so 'rather sparingly, and only after it has got its premises by a previous induction'.[52] Second, *'it observes the operations of the mind by the inner sense, - that is consciousness'*. McCosh was referring to a process of introspection, but in his previous book he carefully guarded against any suggestion that a true perception of reality was at the mercy of individual subjectivity.

> He who would obtain an adequate and comprehensive view of our complex mental nature must not be satisfied with occasional glances at the working of his own soul: he must take a survey of the thoughts and feelings of others...from the acts of mankind generally...from universal language as the expression of human cogitation and sentiment; and from the commerce we hold with our fellow men.[53]

Veitch makes the same point and reveals the importance in his own philosophy, of introspection as a habit of the mind, disciplined by constant and conscientious reference to common human experience.

> I am conscious of feeling, perceiving, knowing, willing. This is the first fact for me and beyond its teachings I cannot go. This guarantees itself; this is the ground of knowledge for me...Reality for you and me is in what we think and feel, rather than in what we do. Out of the heart are the issues of life. But do not understand consciousness narrowly. It is not...the arbitrary or passing mood of the individual. It is the consciousness, the mind of humanity which is studied, consciousness in its full content, and its universal laws...Wherever and wheresover man has expressed himself, this method follows him, seeking the origin and genesis of the facts,

---

[50] Ibid., 32-3, emphasis mine.

[51] McCosh wrote a comprehensive history, *The Scottish Philosophy*, in 1874, the introductory chapter of which expounds its methodology. A later article in *The British and Foreign Evangelical Review* rehearsed and expanded the material. The following references are to this later article.

[52] James McCosh, 'The Scottish Philosophy as Contrasted with the German', *BFER*, 32, 1883, 98. See also his earlier article, 'The Scottish Philosophy', *BFER*, 12, 1863, 663-81.

[53] Quoted in Graham, 'Nineteenth Century Aftermath', 342.

without preconceived theory, face to face with the realities. It thus imposes no formula on the facts....[54]

It imposes no formula on facts, but the experience of consciousness is only possible if certain epistemological principles are given the ontological status of facts. This is McCosh's third characteristic. *'By observation principles are discovered which are above observation, universal and eternal.'*[55] Reid called these principles of common sense, explained above as common human experience. Hamilton called them 'reason in the first degree, which discerns truth at once, as distinguished from reason in the second degree which discovers truth by arguing'.[56] Rather than define them McCosh specified the characteristics of these primary principles of the mind. 'I discover that two straight lines cannot enclose a space, that benevolence is good, that cruelty is evil, by simply contemplating the things'; they are thus *self evident* intuitions of things, needing no argument. 'We must hold them, and cannot be made to think or believe otherwise'; they are thus *necessary*. 'Being entertained by all men.' They are, therefore, *universal*.[57]

These main characteristics of Scottish Common Sense philosophy can be further clarified by noting three particular areas of application. First, Common Sense epistemology is based on the conviction that our perceptions reveal the world as it is; they are not merely ideas impressed on the mind. There is a knower and a known, a subject and an object. The world is not constituted by consciousness, rather human beings are so constituted that 'by no reasoning, or voluntary effort, can a man cease to believe that he exists, that he perceives, that he feels pleasure and pain...Many things are so obvious, and so necessarily engage the attention of all rational beings, that we cannot conceive any period of their active existence in which they do not assent to them.'[58] In other words the mind is so structured, that reason compels realist assumptions about the relationship between the perceiving mind, the external physical world and the internal moral world.

This leads to a second area of application, ethical common sense philosophy. There are inherent moral senses corresponding to the physical senses so that ethical knowledge is as surely based in general human experience as empirical knowledge. Reid rooted such powers of moral perception and discrimination in God-given human nature, stating that God 'has given to men the faculty of perceiving the right and the

---

[54] Veitch, *Sir William Hamilton. The Man*, 33-4.
[55] McCosh, *BFER*, 99.
[56] Ibid., 100.
[57] Ibid., 101. Emphases mine.
[58] Reid, quoted in Mark Noll, 'Common Sense Traditions and American Evangelical Thought', *American Quarterly* 37, 1985, 216-38. Quotation at 221.

wrong in conduct, as far as is necessary to our present state, and of perceiving the dignity of the one, and the demerit of the other'.[59]

Methodological Common Sense, a third application, proceeds by the Baconian method, that is, by asserting that 'truths about consciousness, the world, or religion must be built by a strict induction from irreducible facts of experience'.[60] Applied to moral philosophy such a methodology would aim at a science of moral knowledge, gradually providing a secure consensus of agreed 'moral facts', building up into a body of knowledge for further research. Newton himself was quoted in support of such a possibility: 'If natural philosophy, in all its parts, by pursuing this [empirical] method, shall, at length, be perfected, the bounds of moral philosophy will also be enlarged'.[61]

As noted earlier, John Veitch was the last exponent of the Scottish philosophy to hold a university chair in nineteenth century Scotland. The intellectual world he inhabited included much of the above conceptual landscape. However Veitch's appropriation of the Scottish Common Sense tradition was neither wholesale nor original. He was self consciously indebted to Sir William Hamilton who along with Dugald Stewart dominated the intellectual life of Edinburgh in the first half of the nineteenth century, representing the high water mark of Scottish philosophy. Not that Hamilton or Stewart were its most original exponents; but in their day they influenced the cultural and intellectual life of Scotland and beyond. Today's judgement is altogether more realistic, Hamilton's reputation and influence in his own times being considered 'vastly overestimated'. As proof of exaggerated esteem Graham notes that Veitch's study of Hamilton was included in the series *Philosophical Classics* published by Blackwood, 'and thus bizarrely ranked alongside Descartes, Berkeley, Locke, Kant and Hegel'.[62] In the eyes of his contemporaries Hamilton so dominated the foreground of Scottish intellectual life that for a generation it was hard for many to see past him.

That included John Veitch. 'To those of his students…inspired by him, who gave themselves up for a time to his power, and followed from day to day the clear, firm paced, vigorous, and consecutive steps of his

---

[59] Reid, quoted in Noll, 'Common Sense Traditions', 221. See also E. Madden, 'Common-Sense Ethics', in E. Craig (ed.), *The Routledge Encyclopaedia of Philosophy*, vol. 2, (London: Routledge, 1998), 448-51. 'Thomas Reid…and his followers argued that moral knowledge and the motives to abide by it are within the reach of everyone. They believed that a plurality of basic self-evident moral principles is revealed by conscience to all mature moral agents', 448.

[60] Noll, 'Common Sense Traditions', 223.

[61] Ibid., 222.

[62] Graham, 'Nineteenth Century Aftermath', 343.

prelections, he became the moulder of their intellectual life.'[63] Veitch publicly stated a qualified admiration of Hamilton in 1883:

> My own conviction is that Hamilton reached certain results which are thoroughly stable and valid. I do not in this commit myself by any means to all his philosophy, or even to certain fundamental points in that philosophy. I am and always have been a disciple of Hamilton, not in the sense of following his opinions, or teaching these...but in the way of the spirit of the man, and the guiding principles of his method – a method, at the same time, common to him with the whole line of thinkers who, since Descartes, have recognised *the authority of experience, as the only vindicable sphere of human knowledge.*[64]

When Veitch uses the term 'the authority of experience' as 'the only vindicable sphere of human knowledge', he is using an epistemological approach that will recur repeatedly in Denney's later argumentations. This is not surprising. In the more theologically conservative Christian circles of the mid to late nineteenth century, the Scottish philosophy was seen as the philosophical ally of Christian orthodoxy, particularly in America.[65] For example, in Princeton, Charles Hodge built his theology on an epistemological realism rooted in the Scottish tradition. Against the encroachments of Darwinian science, the inroads of biblical criticism into biblical authority and the unsettling speculative philosophies emanating from Europe, Hodge combined commitment to biblical inerrancy and the realist assurance that ordinary sense experience apprehends the real. Denney shared a commitment to the validity and evidential value of experience, but made no such commitment to biblical inerrancy.[66]

That the Scottish philosophy was intimately connected with evangelical theology is of considerable significance in trying to trace the development of Denney's mind, and in evaluating the influence of someone like Veitch. Similarly, Denney's exposure to a quite different

---

[63] Veitch, *Sir William Hamilton. The Man*, 25. The point is emphasised further: 'The electric force of intellect is not to be measured merely by the degree of illumination which it casts over the field of knowledge; it is to be gathered as well from the amount of vitality which it imparts to the minds through which it passes, and which it quickens to the life of thought and feeling and lofty speculative effort', 27.

[64] Ibid., 26-7, (emphasis mine).

[65] See Noll, 'Common Sense Traditions'. The influence on American theology is examined in Sydney E. Ahlstrom, 'The Scottish Philosophy and American Theology', *Church History*, xxiv, 1955, 257-72. Gary Dorrien, *The Remaking of Evangelical Theology*, (Louisville: Westminster John Knox, 1998), 24-7, gives an account of Princeton realism; he places Orr and Denney in the 'non-inerrancy evangelicalism' bracket, see 119. See also, Samuel Fleischacker, 'The impact on America: Scottish Philosophy and the American founding,' in Broadie, (ed.), *Scottish Enlightenment*, 316-37.

[66] See especially chapters 3 and 5 of this study.

and competing philosophy powerfully presented by Edward Caird created an academic context of serious intellectual tension for an intelligent mind at its most malleable stage. Though the Scottish philosophy was all but displaced by German idealism by the 1870s when Denney was a student, the fact that he was taught by a Logic professor who was a convinced philosopher of the Common Sense school, and by a future Balliol philosopher steeped in Kant and Hegel, compelled him, as it did James Orr before him and Henry Jones who was a contemporary, to make his own intellectual choices only after studying and considering two incompatible options.

The experience and later opinions of Orr and Jones help indicate that such a choice was not a foregone conclusion. Jones, who shared Denney's admiration for Jebb, was less enthusiastic about Veitch: 'The food he deals to us is rich in bones and poor in meat. Scraggy and lean is his philosophy, my friend; and I must have another mind before I can enjoy it.'[67] By contrast Caird became his intellectual mentor, his 'perfect sincerity of soul and simplicity of manner' together with 'the pure eloquence of [his] reflective thought' commanding both respect and affection. 'I was born in Llangernyw in 1852, and born again in 1876 in Edward Caird's classroom.'[68] By contrast, a decade earlier James Orr faced with much the same dilemma opted for the traditional philosophy of Veitch. As well as taking Veitch's class, he studied Dugald Stewart's *Elements of the Human Mind* in preparation for the class, and subsequently William Thomson's *Outlines of the Laws of Thought* under Veitch's supervision. In his final year he opted for Veitch's Advanced Logic class as his M.A. Honours choice, and was awarded a Ferguson Scholarship, which tended to be awarded to scholars sympathetic to the Scottish philosophy.[69]

Like Orr, Denney formed a closer attachment to Veitch than to Caird. Similarly, some of Denney's later theological emphases and

---

[67] Hetherington, *Jones*, 19.

[68] Ibid., pp. 20-21.

[69] G. G. Scorgie, *A Call for Continuity: The Theological Contribution of James Orr*, (Macon: Mercer University Press, 1988), 31-5, gives an informative account of life in Glasgow University for students in the 1860's. The influence of the two Cairds was on the ascendant, both of them being instrumental in promoting German and particularly Hegelian Idealism. This at a time when the Scottish philosophy seemed to be running low on credibility as an intellectual option for progressive thinkers. Edward Caird's negative attitude to the Scottish school of philosophy was apparent from the beginning. 'He most rarely referred to the philosophical views which were then current in Scotland in his time, whether as conscious doctrines or as unconscious assumptions, implicit in the traditional morality and religion. Session after session passed and no allusion, near or remote, was made to the Scottish school of Common Sense. No Scottish name later than David Hume passed his lips.' Quoted in Davie, *Democratic Intellect*, 330.

methodology would be built on and supported by argumentation appealing to the authority of experience, assuming moral discernment and accountability as a universal given, and basing theological truth on the historic facts of Christian Scripture attested by apostolic experience and testimony.

'The world is a rational and intelligible system'

The moulding influence of Jebb on Denney's approach to interpreting ancient texts is the more easily established by Denney's own testimony and by observing his respectful criticism of the text itself. This was to become so characteristic of Denney's approach to Scripture, that it underlay his view of the relations between criticism and the Bible. Denney's willingness to be Veitch's assistant suggests a comfortable level of congruence between Veitch's philosophical position and Denney's own developing mind, a suggestion made more secure by the evidence of Scottish philosophical categories shaping Denney's own approach to argumentation.

However, in the case of Caird, Denney nowhere states a sense of direct indebtedness, and it is significant that throughout his life his attitude to German philosophical thought remained ambivalent. But the developing of intellectual muscle, as with physical training, is progressed as much by resistance to what is uncongenial as by relaxed approval of what sits easily with existing presuppositions. The ideas Denney encountered at Glasgow in Caird's classroom were all but contradictory of the Reformed evangelicalism that permeated his upbringing, and were at metaphysical logger-heads with the traditional Scottish philosophy of Veitch, in whose classroom Denney at his most impressionable had his first serious encounter with academic philosophy.[70] The influence of Edward Caird on

---

[70] Attendance at lectures was compulsory, and Caird's course consisted of 120 lectures, delivered at 8 a.m. during the winter session. Students inevitably experienced prolonged exposure to the thought and personality of the lecturer. Jones and Muirhead, *Edward Caird*, 51, 112. Caird was involved in a legal battle for the right of lecturers to retain copyright to the content of their lectures as preserved in student notes. In his own evidence he explains the purpose of his lectures and in so doing reveals the pedagogic significance he attached to the lecture as a formative influence on student intellectual development: 'The effect of lectures as distinct from books, to a great extent depends on the way they are spoken and heard. The students hear my lectures, then they make attempts to reproduce them. They take down notes, which I consider to be a valuable exercise for their minds. If they can save themselves that trouble by taking up some convenient crib... they would really be destroying the work of the class. It would be taking away the freshness of personal address, and would at the same time be furnishing the students with something that they ought to be doing for themselves.' Ibid., 111.

the intellectual life of Scotland was complex and pervasive,[71] and seeking to explain why Denney never fell under Caird's spell may provide important clues to Denney's intellectual and theological development.

Caird's philosophy was so disturbing to the minds of evangelical students that the Free Church considered sending students to an alternative and theologically safer teacher.[72] Caird's educational aim was to commend a restated Christian faith to the 'large and increasing class who have become, partially at least, alienated from the ordinary dogmatic system of belief, but who, at the same time, are conscious that they have owed a great part of their spiritual life to the teachings of the Bible and the Christian church.'[73] In a lecture on 'The Problem of Philosophy at the Present Time',[74] Caird identified the need to reconcile the apparently opposing currents of contemporary thought.

> The need for philosophy arises out of the broken harmony of a spiritual life, in which the different elements or factors seem to be set in irreconcilable opposition to each other; in which...the religious consciousness, the consciousness of the infinite, is at war with the secular consciousness, the consciousness of the finite; or again, the consciousness of the self, with the consciousness of the external world.... The nature of the controversies which most trouble us at present...all, directly or indirectly, turn upon the difficulty of reconciling the three great terms of thought, - the world, self and God.[75]

Following a critique of various intellectual options, Caird identified the religious consciousness as the only principle of universal synthesis adequate to the task of reconciling 'the world, self and God'. The following extract demonstrates Caird at his apologetic best, seeking for Christianity a respected position in the marketplace of ideas:

> Philosophy may therefore begin its work by a vindication of the religious consciousness - the consciousness of the infinite - as presupposed in that very consciousness of the finite, which at present often claims to exclude it altogether,

---

[71] Ibid., 67. For biographical details see *DNB Second Supplement I*, 291-95. The standard biography remains Jones and Muirhead. Drummond and Bulloch, *The Church in Late Victorian Scotland*, ch. 5, 'The Mind of the Church', places both Cairds in their Scottish context. Two introductory articles by Colin Tyler in *The Collected Works of Edward Caird* are available online, full details in Bibliography. See (www.thoemmes.com/idealism/caird_intro). They provide an up to date evaluation of Caird's intellectual emphases; a comprehensive primary and secondary bibliography is also included.

[72] Drummond and Bulloch, *Church in Late Victorian Scotland*, 248.

[73] Ibid., 251. Caird's personal piety is often alluded to by Jones and Muirhead. See 82, *Edward Caird*, where the text of Caird's morning prayer before lectures is printed.

[74] Introductory Address, delivered to the Philosophical Society of the University of Edinburgh, 1881, reprinted in Caird's *Lectures on Literature and Philosophy*, ii, (Glasgow, 1892), 190 -229.

[75] Ibid., 191-2.

or to reduce it to an empty apotheosis of the unknown and unknowable. And having thus taught us to regard the consciousness of the infinite as no mere illusion, but as the consciousness of a real object, an Absolute, a God, who has been revealing himself in and to man in all ages, philosophy must go on to consider the history of religion, and indeed the whole history of man as founded on religion, as the progressive development of this consciousness. Nor can it fail to discover that the idea on which the higher life of man is founded – the idea of the unity of man as spiritual with an Absolute spirit - has in Christianity been brought to light and made, in a manner, apprehensible to all.[76]

Caird's philosophical theology was a fusion of 'Hegel-inspired Idealism'[77] and Christian theism, set in an evolutionary framework. The resultant theology significantly qualified the adjective Christian in order to accommodate an even more qualified form of theism. Christianity's privileged status in this account of spiritual evolution is purchased at the expense of much that makes Christianity distinctive.[78]

When refracted through Idealist metaphysics, Caird's form of Christianity was inescapably monistic. When reality is conceived as one, the dualisms that exist between such categories as transcendence and immanence, divinity and humanity, good and evil, time and eternity, natural and supernatural, are dissolved. The doctrinal core of Caird's thought has been described as 'the dynamic conception of the Absolute'.[79] 'The Absolute (which both Hegel and Caird equate with God) is a self-manifesting impulse of the rational consciousness. In consequence, "the world we live in is a spiritual world - a divine order, the source of which is akin to the principle of intelligence in our own souls. ... I think it can be shown that our whole nature, and the conditions of our existence, and indeed every rational thought we think and every rational act we do, implies that it is so"'.[80] In presenting this view of the world and human life as caught up in a universal process of self-manifesting purposive consciousness, Caird is seeking to provide a

---

[76] Ibid., 224-5.

[77] The phrase is borrowed from Alan Sell who coined it 'to caution myself and others that no British philosopher of note adopted Hegelianism uncritically'. Alan P. F. Sell, *The Philosophy of Religion, 1875-1980*, (London: Routledge, 1988), 12. Sell gives a nuanced assessment of Caird's indebtedness to Hegel in chapter 2 of this work. Sell's volume, *Philosophical Idealism and Christian Belief*, (University of Wales: Cardiff, 1995), is a major and valuable study.

[78] See B. M. G. Reardon, *Religion in the Victorian Age*, (London: Longman, 1980), 308-9.

[79] Tyler, 'Introduction', see footnote 71.

[80] Ibid.; Edward Caird, *Lay Sermons and Addresses*, (Glasgow: Maclehose and Jackson, 1907), 304-5.

philosophical and theological articulation of evolutionary thought, rooted in the self-evident conclusions of the rational mind.[81]

The linking of Idealist metaphysics with evolutionary thought provides an elaborate scaffolding for Caird's intellectual project, and perhaps offers a clue to his widespread popularity and influence in a period of intellectual and cultural flux. Tyler suggests that for Caird

> there could be no true understanding of the Absolute which did not bring to the fore the notion of universal and ceaseless evolution. This belief in "a continuous and all-pervasive evolution" leads Caird to discern "wherever he looks ... progressive development; in the natural world, in culture and civilisation, in nationhood, in human knowledge, in art". Affirmations of such development can be found throughout his work.[82]

The view of God as immanent in the universal historical process, carries serious theological implications for any resultant theism. A conception of the Absolute as an emergent universal consciousness manifested in a universal history reduces the significance of particular historical events to the role they play as part of an evolving whole. As such they become symbols of timeless truths, local relative parables pointing to universal reality: they are realities in the lower case preceded by the indefinite article, which point to Reality in the higher case requiring no article because it needs no such differentiation. It simply is; and It is all that is.

John Macquarrie is alert to the religious consequences of Caird's thought at this point; 'belief in a particular incarnation is of interest not as the assertion of a once-for-all happening but as a parable of the timeless truth of the union of God and man'.[83] This is a direct implicate of monistic thought in which the distinct otherness between God and humanity is dissolved, and the transcendent is internalised within natural and historical processes.

Caird assumed each human being was by nature self-consciously rational and religious, and that all are participants in a universal history evolving upwards towards a realised perfection. Religion shares in this universal upward movement. According to Caird, the objective religion of Greece in which experience of God is perceived in the natural and physical world, along with its reaction in the subjective religion of Israel, in which experience of God is perceived in the moral consciousness, have

---

[81] Caird's view of human history is placed in broader philosophical and theological context in Peter Hinchliff, *God and History. Aspects of British Theology 1875-1914*, (Oxford University Press, 1992), 128-49.

[82] See footnote 73 above.

[83] John Macquarrie, *Twentieth Century Religious Thought*, (London: SCM, 1973), 43. See also his *Jesus Christ and Modern Thought,* (London: SCM, 2000), chapter 10, 'Idealist Christology', which puts Caird in the wider context of Hegelian thought.

found their reconciliation and fulfilment in the universal religion of Christianity. It is this view of Christianity as the manifestation of universal religion that undercuts the very particularity of the Christian faith, a particularity rooted in such unrepeatable historical and doctrinal facts as incarnation, atonement and resurrection. The claim of Christianity that it is founded on a unique set of historical circumstances and events, in which the transcendent God intervened in human history, is clearly incompatible with a view of history resting on a monistic view of reality. In Caird's thought incarnation, atonement and resurrection are evacuated of their once-for-allness and unique, reality-changing significance. The divorcing of essential religious truth from its particular historical matrix in order to isolate what is universally and eternally true, reduces the historical element to a provisional and dispensable status.[84] Applied to such doctrines as the resurrection of Jesus, such drastic ahistoricism undercuts the objectivity and historicity of the Christian Gospel, abandoning historical facts for metaphysical ideas.

'The absolute significance of Christ'

Two quotations illustrate the different doctrinal consequences of Caird's evolutionary idealism and Denney's historical realism. In his 1893 Gifford Lectures, *The Evolution of Religion*, Caird considers immortality, and comments on the optional rather than the essential significance of the resurrection of Christ: 'Even for St Paul himself who...more than any other penetrated to the spiritual meaning of Christianity, the evidence of the Christian law of life through death...rested on the believed fact of the resurrection of Christ.... But I do not think it need rest on that basis'.[85] In Denney's *Atonement and the Modern Mind*, there is a passage of philosophical reflection, in which Denney passes critical comment on Idealism, giving a rare glimpse into his later philosophical opinions. Though, he argued, proponents of idealist philosophy 'make copious use of Christian phraseology, it seems to me obvious that it is not in an adequate Christian sense.... Their philosophy is to them a surrogate for religion, but they should not be allowed to suppose...that it is the equivalent of Christianity...this philosophy only lives by ignoring the greatest reality of the spiritual world.'[86]

Christ's consciousness of himself as the revelation of God and as Redeemer of a fallen creation became for Denney a core conviction that challenged the optimistic anthropology implied in Idealism's view of divine human relations. His most serious criticisms therefore concern the

---

[84] Sell, *Philosophy of Religion*, 20-1; James Iverach, 'Edward Caird', *ExpT*, V, 1893-4, 205.
[85] Quoted in Drummond and Bulloch, *Church in Late Victorian Scotland*, 252.
[86] Denney, *Modern Mind*, 28-30.

inability of Idealist thought to accommodate the greatness of Christ, the reality of sin and the necessity of atonement. With these and similar strictures on idealist philosophy, Denney exhibited such a strong resistance to its central concepts that it is unlikely he ever entertained the admiration for Caird's teaching that people like Henry Jones and Cosmo Gordon Lang[87] expressed. Indeed the mature Denney's most powerful theological writing is an attempt to restate the precise, objective, historical particularity of events he deemed central to Christian history and indispensable to an adequate Christian theology.

'Philosophy and the New Testament', is a substantial and at times lyrical paper delivered to a philosophical society with a passion approaching evangelistic fervour.[88] In it, Denney argued for a Christian philosophy which arises out of the Christian experience of Christ, is rooted in apostolic testimony and is embodied in the New Testament text. The Christocentrism of Denney's paper is uncompromising, relativising all other reality. The apostles' experience of Christ required both a new metaphysic and a revaluation of key concepts, in fact, a Copernican revolution of their thought processes. 'He is a Being of another order than they; it is not that He offers us another account of reality from theirs, but in virtue of His presence in the world we feel that the reality for which we have to account is itself different.'[89] It is worth quoting Denney at length on this point, because here Denney indicates the distance between his and Caird's position, and makes it highly unlikely Denney ever seriously considered adopting Caird's philosophical world view. The apostles' experience of Christ was:

> One in which men became conscious of seeing more deeply into the life of things, of getting a firmer grasp on the <u>ens realissimum</u>,[90] the supreme category by relation to which all things are to be defined, the organising principle by which all things are to be reduced to a unity.... Men are conscious in the presence of Jesus Christ, and in the experience of what He has done for them, that they are in contact with the last reality in the universe, the final and absolute truth which can never be resolved into anything higher, and in which they can build their life (including their intellectual life), as on a sure foundation. And what is this <u>ens realissimum</u>, this last reality of Christian experience, to which everything else has to be subordinated, on which the very foundations of the world must rest? What is the reality apart from

---

[87] 'As a student at [Glasgow] University he was intoxicated by the metaphysics of Edward Caird.... Walking in the park one day he shouted: "The Universe is one and its Unity and Ultimate Reality is God!"' Quoted in D. L. Edwards, *Leaders of the Church of England*, (Oxford: Oxford University Press, 1971), 307.

[88] DEN08-10. See earlier, p.7, for a tentative suggested provenance, for the difficulties in establishing date and context.

[89] DEN08-10, 8.

[90] 'A real thing, especially as opposed to an attribute.' *Collins English Dictionary*, third ed., 1991.

which the world must remain blank, mysterious, chaotic, unintelligible? It is divine redeeming love, the love revealed in Christ and taking on itself the burden of sin, sinner and death of the world.... The impression Christ made on them was so profound, their sense of the absolute significance of the truth given to them in Him was so deep, that they felt bound to reconstruct the universe in their minds with Him as its beginning and its end, its principle, its unity, its goal.[91]

Throughout the paper Denney uses familiar philosophical terms, most of them commonplace to students of Caird. For example the category of absolute is repeatedly Christologised. Given 'the absolute significance of Christ',[92] 'Christianity is not something which has happened to emerge at a particular point in time and space, and is limited accordingly; it is the revelation of the final and absolute truth.'[93] Christ is therefore to be understood as the unifying principle of the entire creation, the one in whom the eternal truth of God as reconciler and redeemer is embodied, revealed and fulfilled. In contrast to the more impersonal and inevitable process at work in Caird's evolutionary Idealism, Denney portrays a personal, purposive process rooted in the eternal nature of God and realised in Christ. 'The Christian world is not a segment of reality which has its place in the whole; the whole world is a Christian world; it has been created in Christ and for Him; in Him all its discords are to be overcome; it is God's eternal purpose to gather together in one all things in Christ.'[94]

The theme of all things being united in Christ, is perceived as being a central emphasis of the New Testament, and in this paper Denney traces its significance to the role of Christ as reconciler. With more than a sideglance at speculative philosophies of an idealist brand he laments the lack of depth in contemporary philosophy, by which Denney means the absence of moral and spiritual profundity in the face of a fractured cosmos where humans exist in the disharmony and dislocation of sin.

> The world is full of contrasts, and of means of transcending them - full of differences, and of reconciliations of them - full of antitheses and of higher unities in which they are merged, and there is no philosophy but deals with these at some level or other; but not till a man realizes what is present in the world in Christ does he recognize how deep and dreadful differences may be, how logical antitheses and contrasts can darken and harden into the most tragic moral antagonisms; nor again,

---

[91] Ibid., 2-3.
[92] Ibid., 2.
[93] Ibid., 3.
[94] Ibid., 3. The Christ-hymn of Colossians and the prologue of John's gospel provide many of the key thoughts in Denney's arguments in this paper.

how there is in God a reconciling love, so real, so passionate and wonderful that it can subdue antagonisms at their worst and make sinful men Sons of God.[95]

Denney's vision of a reconciled creation, and his conviction about how that will be achieved, is presented as nothing less than a Christian philosophy of history which is centred on Christ as both the focal goal and the enabling power of God's redemptive purpose. It is hard to resist the conclusion that Denney's argument in this paper is a repudiation of any theology, including that of Edward Caird, which relaxes the tension between immanence and transcendence, raises universal consciousness to the status of the Absolute, portrays history as the spiritual evolution of the race, or downplays the tragic elements of existence and in the end relativises Christ. At one point Denney made the contrast explicit: 'God is not the category of the ideal; God the Redeemer, the God in whom we must believe if we are to philosophize in a world disintegrated by evil, is the reality of which we are finally assured in Christ'.[96]

It seems obvious then, given such unambiguously orthodox statements of Christian theism, christology and soteriology, supported in his view, by the clear testimony of the New Testament, that Denney had little permanent interest in philosophical theology of the type expounded by Caird. This is confirmed in an unpublished letter sent to Nicoll in 1901. 'All the neo-Hegelian men - Edward Caird and his pupils - are Christian as they understand it; but as far as Christ is concerned, their whole business is to keep him in his own place. He belongs to history but He does not belong to life, in any other sense than that in which every historical person does. This it seems to me, is to annihilate Christianity at a stroke.'[97]

The intriguing question remains though, why Caird failed to make a disciple of Denney, and why, at least in the long term, Denney was so unresponsive to a high profile teacher widely regarded as one of Scotland's most influential thinkers. A number of considerations, taken together, may help explain Denney's refusal to follow Caird's intellectual lead, and at the same time provide a clearer picture of the influences and circumstances which formed the nexus of his development in and beyond his university years.

The first factor was Denney's own theological background. His years of spiritual formation in the Reformed Presbyterian and then the Free

---

[95] Ibid., 7.
[96] Ibid., 10.
[97] MS/3518/27/10. Letter dated 2 April 1901. Yet, when expounding Paul's thought in Romans 8, 'the whole creation is sighing for redemption', Denney recommended Caird's *Evolution of Religion*, vol. ii, 124f, 'for a fine speculative interpretation'. James Denney, *Romans*, in *Expositor's Greek Testament*, (London: Hodder & Stoughton, 1900), 649.

Church, as Sabbath School and Bible Class teacher, provided a thorough grounding in Reformed dogmatic orthodoxy. While such a background was no immunisation to more speculative and liberal thought, it created a conservative mind-set with a critical awareness of theological novelty. The fact that the Free Church was suspicious of Caird, and that some of his students moved away from evangelical convictions, makes it clear that a Reformed background was not of itself a sufficient bulwark against a charismatic, original and forceful teacher. It is possible, perhaps likely, that Denney as a student was initially interested in, even attracted to the brilliant Caird and his thought. Available evidence of Denney's antipathy to Idealism is drawn from the mature Denney, and shows only that Caird's philosophy held no lasting attraction.

'Idealism has always been something of a philosopher's philosophy.'[98] The abstract nature of Neo-Hegelian thought and its remoteness from the daily lives of ordinary people despite its fashionable status in the universities, made it an elitist philosophy not self-evidently practical.[99] Denney was the son of a joiner, and of a home where education and knowledge were valued as much for their usefulness as their novelty. On the other hand Caird was himself the son of a Greenock foundry owner, yet he had clearly found in Idealism a fascinating and convincing intellectual framework for his own attempts to restate Christian thought.

But in Denney's case, the suggestion, arising from his church and family background, that he would have found Caird's thought uncongenial, is perhaps strengthened by evidence from Denney's own letters and writings of a temperament ill at ease with speculative and imaginative thought. While Denney often explains his resistance to speculative and abstract ideas on the grounds that constructive Christian thinking should arise from an engagement with the text of the New

---

[98] S. Wilkens and A. Padgett, *Christianity and Western Thought*, vol. 2, (Leicester: IVP, 2000), 65.

[99] This point has to be balanced by the social activism of Caird, much of which found effective practical outlets. He fought long and hard for the rights of women to be admitted to lectures and degree courses at Glasgow University, he was involved in social work in Cathedral Street, Glasgow, he was active in promoting the work of the Women's Protective and Provident League to improve working conditions for women and children, especially in laundries, he supported Trades Unions for women and was Convener of the Scottish Council for Women's Trades. In addition his abilities as an ethicist were called on to arbitrate in disputes. He characteristically insisted that employers, legislators and socially responsible persons had a 'duty to know' the facts and conditions of existence in order to 'humanise the economy' for the poorer members of society. It may be that his Idealist philosophy can be considered abstract as an intellectual structure, but not as a way of evading moral and social responsibilities. See Jones and Muirhead, *Edward Caird*, 115-25.

Testament, that simply pushes the question back; why did he find speculative thought uncongenial and lacking intellectual authority, while his own mind flourished when encountering a text to which, when it was a biblical text, he gave a normative authority over all other forms of thought? Intellectual taste is both acquired and individual, and given the choice of philosophical or biblical theology, Denney declined the former and relished the latter.[100]

To what extent is a student's intellectual preference determined by the order in which they tackle required courses? It is an intriguing question, because Denney was exposed to Jebb on the classics, and Veitch's logic class from the beginning of his course, a significant time before he encountered the full blown teaching of Caird. By that time he had acquired a fascination and facility with the classics and had absorbed something of the Scottish philosophical tradition mediated through Veitch. The sense of indebtedness, even admiration, felt by a young student to the first teachers who enabled him to develop mental muscle and make new intellectual discoveries would not naturally predispose him to a philosophy seriously at odds with a previous teacher. Combined with the earlier points about his background and temperament, there would certainly be nothing inevitable about Caird's teaching finding ready acceptance in Denney's mind. Yet his performance in Caird's class demonstrates the quality and seriousness of his engagement with the set class syllabus and the mind of the teacher who taught it. Indeed Caird's biographers mention an intriguing connection between Caird and Denney. In 1879 'The Witenagamote', a student's philosophical society, was formed. Denney is noted amongst its earliest members. It was made up mostly of philosophy students, it met in the evening, and was occasionally visited by Caird.[101]

Following his university years, Denney was taught in the Free Church College, Glasgow, by A. B. Bruce.[102] Bruce was an informed and resolute opponent of neo-Hegelian thought,[103] deeply critical, as was the later Denney, of any version of the Christian faith not anchored in historical facts. Whatever Denney imbibed of Caird's philosophy was subjected to penetrating criticism from a teacher who took the historical rootedeness of the New Testament witness with utmost seriousness. Whereas Denney's

---

[100] Denney worried about his friend Jones's health, and the waste of a life devoted to philosophy. It is an interesting opinion given the later fruitfulness of Jones's life, and perhaps an indication of Denney's failure to understand minds different from his own. *LFF*, 8.

[101] Jones and Muirhead, *Edward Caird*, 90.

[102] *LFF*, 182-3. Denney's debt to Bruce will be considered more fully in the account of Denney's college years.

[103] Alan P. F. Sell, *Defending and Declaring the Faith*, (Exeter: Paternoster, 1987), 89. Drummond and Bulloch, *Church in Late Victorian Scotland*, 262.

mature writing betrays almost no discernible traces of Idealist thought, the very subject matter of his later theological concerns, the dialectic of free intellectual criticism and responsible textual interpretation in relation to the New Testament, the passionate exposition of a moral universe redeemed by the once-for-all intervention of God in human history, the centrality of the historical Jesus in any adequate exposition of the Gospel, are all, one way or another, issues addressed by Bruce during and after Denney's college years.

In relation to his own spiritual and theological development, perhaps Denney's greatest debt to Bruce was in the combination of intellectual freedom and spiritual integrity Bruce modelled, and from within a more familiar and congenial theological framework than that expounded by Caird. Following Bruce's death Denney paid generous tribute in words that, if not autobiographical, are freighted with personal significance.

> He never tried to impose his personality or his convictions on others, or to fashion them in his mould. He awakened their minds, liberated them, and left them free. Hence though he was a great teacher, he cannot be said to have founded a school. He taught many but enslaved none. The work he left behind him remains as a ferment in the mind of the church....[104]

New and Disturbing Ideas

By the time Denney finished his degree, he was aged twenty three. The narrow confines of his upbringing had been expanded by a broad based education in the humanities in the traditional Scottish academic mould, but a mould in process of being reshaped to the changing needs of society and the cultural and commercial requirements of a rapidly modernising world. His intellectual powers had been tested and had performed to standards of academic excellence. Study of the classics and philosophy had equipped his mind with mental disciplines and a respect for reason that would shape his theology, both in content and methodology.

The intellectual stimulus of university had forced him to think beyond the industrialised world of Greenock shipbuilding to consider such subtleties as the moral psychology of Sir William Hamilton. The dogmatic world of Westminster Confessional theology and the safe world of received theological opinion in a local Free Church congregation, had collided in the mind of Denney with new speculative ideas about spiritual evolution and Absolute Spirit. His earliest encounters with an ancient text which had centred on the Bible, straightforwardly read and with an assumed perspicacity, were now challenged by a way of interpreting,

---

[104] DEN10-02, 'The Work of Dr Bruce', 13.

criticising and translating ancient classical texts which revealed hidden depths, and raised fascinating questions about the same methods applied to the Bible. In the classes of such teachers as Jebb, Veitch and Caird, the young Denney had encountered new and disturbing ideas. But what to do with them?[105]

At some point in the years leading up to and during his time at university he had begun to think of a future in the Free Church ministry. The only known reference Denney made to this decision was in the letter to his family from Germany, already noted.[106] In the light of the inevitable changes in his own thinking brought about by a broad humanities education, it is not greatly surprising that Denney worried about how his application would be received by the Presbytery of Greenock.

The 1876 union of the Reformed Presbyterian and the Free Church had taken place while Denney was a Glasgow Arts student. The euphoria and spiritual impetus that accompanied such an achievement awakened members to the larger possibilities for an enlarged denomination. Denney's later committed and vocal involvement in the process of reunion amongst the Scottish Presbyterian churches had long roots, reaching back to his experiences of local church and denominational division, and his experience while a student, of denominational reunion. The local impact of such discussions and decisions, their implications for theological and ecclesial principles, the sense of significance which involvement in such changes conferred on members and congregations, together created an atmosphere in which it is likely a high performance student, whose spirituality was moulded within a minority evangelical denomination, would be attracted to the new spiritual and vocational opportunities of an enlarged church context.

In addition, Denney had been an assistant teacher in the Highlanders Academy, he had taught in Sunday School and Bible class, and had been assistant to John Veitch at university level. Teaching was an obvious vocational option, the real choice being whether in university or church. His concern about Henry Jones' projected career in philosophy suggests he had no interest in such a possibility for himself. In the 1870s ministers were still regarded as a major part of the educational resources of a community, trusted providers of both edification and education. The Free Church had an impressive tradition of learned ministers, many of whom moved into theological education. In the absence of personal information about Denney's sense of call, it is not unlikely he would be attracted to a

---

[105] Thirty years later, Denney would defend the process of intellectual questioning that an Arts followed by Divinity syllabus was intended to stimulate in ministerial students. Several of his comments then, seem to carry a personal reference to his own intellectual history. See 169 and 174 of the present study.

[106] *LFF*, 4.

situation which would enable him to combine Christian work, with teaching and scholarship.

CHAPTER 4

College Years, 1879-1883

On 26 November 1879 the Free Church Presbytery of Greenock approved Denney's application for admission to the Theological Hall in Glasgow.[1] Despite Denney's initial anxiety about his acceptability, at each subsequent annual review he continued to satisfy the Examining Committee's enquiries about academic progress and continuing doctrinal soundness.[2]

The 1870s and 1880s were pivotal years in the history of Scottish religious thought. The relationship of new scientific thinking to religious faith had become an acutely disturbing issue which could not simply be wished away, denied, or ignored by more conservative thinkers. German scholarship, particularly the application of historical criticism to the biblical texts, produced conclusions seriously threatening to the traditional doctrine of inspiration, and was perceived by traditionalists as a frontal assault on scriptural authority.

In the Free Church of Scotland, between 1875 and 1881, the progressive energies of these intellectual changes collided with the reactionary forces of religious intellectual conservatism. The removal of William Robertson Smith from his professorship would have far reaching consequences for Denney, since several of his teachers were vocal supporters of Smith, and one, A. B. Bruce, was a pioneering exponent of German inspired higher critical methods in Free Church circles. In the decade 1873-83 Moody and Sankey had conducted campaigns in Scotland, the 1873-74 visit coinciding with Denney's early university years and that of 1881-82 taking place while Denney was a senior college student. Moody's advent significantly affected the religious climate in which Denney would preach and teach.[3]

The impact of such changing fashions of thought contributed to the steady erosion of Westminster Confessional Reformed Orthodoxy as the

---

[1] *Minutes of the Free Presbytery of Greenock*, CH3/166/4, 396.

[2] Ibid., 421, 450, 470.

[3] For an assessment and explanation of Moody's impact see John Coffey, 'Democracy and popular religion: Moody and Sankey mission to Britain, 1873-1875', in E. F. Biagini (ed.), *Citizenship and Community. Liberals, Radicals and Cultural Identity in the British Isles, 1865-1931*, (Cambridge: Cambridhe University Press, 1991), 93-119.

most authoritative expression of Reformed faith. Consequently, many were beginning to look for a broader, more accommodating framework within which thoughtful Christians could continue to 'work out their own salvation' whether or not 'with fear and trembling'. The continuing growth of Glasgow in the last quarter of the nineteenth century provided a context dominated by social and economic changes, giving rise to human problems with which Denney would have to engage, when at the end of his training, he was called as a mission-worker in the Gallowgate.

Tracing the influence of these intellectual and cultural changes in church and society as they impinged on Denney's mind; measuring the role played by his teachers and his College education in equipping Denney towards independent thought; weighing the effects of events such as the Robertson Smith case and the Moody revivals on the formation of mental and moral attitudes; these are necessary explorations of the context within which Denney matured.

The Free Church College, Glasgow

Following the Disruption, the Free Church established ministerial training colleges in Edinburgh (1843), Aberdeen (1843) and Glasgow (1856).[4] During the earlier years of the Glasgow College, from 1857-1874, Patrick Fairbairn was Principal. Self-taught in Hebrew, conversant in German, a facility he developed while minister in an isolated church in Orkney, Fairbairn had 'a thorough acquaintance with contemporary biblical and theological literature in [German]'.[5] His own views remained conservative, but were expressed by a learned mind, well organised and relatively open, evidenced by his editorship of *The Imperial Bible Dictionary* on the one hand, and his support for Moody's evangelistic campaigns on the other. The other Professors, James Gibson, W. M. Hetherington and George Douglas[6] held similar conservative views.

In 1875, following Fairbairn's death, Douglas became Principal and Alexander Bain Bruce, Fairbairn's replacement, was appointed Professor of Apologetics and New Testament Exegesis. Three years earlier James S. Candlish and T. M. Lindsay had been appointed to the chairs in Systematic Theology and Church History respectively. Candlish was the son of R. S. Candlish, the most prominent and respected Free Church leader in the quarter century following Chalmers' death. Lindsay had

---

[4] 'Education, Theological', *DSCHT,* 278-85.

[5] 'Fairbairn, Patrick', *DSCHT,* 313. Fairbairn's reputation in Reformed circles was based on several massive studies in conservative hermeneutics. *The Typology of Scripture,* (Edinburgh, 1845-7); *The Interpretation of Prophecy,* (Edinburgh 1856); *The Hermeneutical Manual,* (Edinburgh, 1858).

[6] Biographical details of the Glasgow College staff are given in *DSCHT* under their respective names.

previously been R. S. Candlish's assistant at Free St George's, Edinburgh. In September 1877, Henry Drummond was appointed for an initial year, then for subsequent years, as Lecturer in Natural Science, becoming Professor in the newly established chair in 1884. These were the men with whom Denney would interact over four years. Lindsay would become a close friend and colleague.

Ministerial training is a complex educative process involving the assimilation of various kinds of knowledge, stimulus to constructive and exploratory thinking, nurturing mental disciplines that facilitate the search for truth and instil moral disciplines which respect and interpret facts, the building blocks of truth. But importantly for Denney, all of this took place within a collegiate and religious context where what was taught, learned and established as true, had implications for personal faith and spiritual liberty. In a Divinity Hall such as Denney attended, funded by the Free Church, and founded on the same strong confessional basis as that Church, the criterion of orthodoxy imposed an assumed regulatory limit on how far and how fast new thinking could go.

By 1879 Denney had passed through four years of academic formation, and was in possession of a mind now less likely to be fazed by having to think new thoughts in relation to his faith. On holiday in Germany in June 1879, he had already expressed alarm at the way events were unfolding in the Free Church as the Robertson Smith affair simmered on. By November the Presbytery of Greenock had found nothing unsound in his interviews, despite Denney's unease about those in his church who adopted an aggressive and hostile stance against teachers propagating higher critical views.

The Robertson Smith Affair

Considering the influence of Denney's college years on his overall development, involves studying the thought and opinions of his teachers, weighing their stature and role within the Free Church and examining Denney's own long-term relationships with them. While in this chapter particular attention will be paid to Denney's teachers, and the part they each played in the evolution of Denney's own theology, this must also include more generally College ethos and the role of staff-student relationships in forging intellectual tastes and loyalties. The stamp the Glasgow College impressed on the minds of its students, was more complex than can be accounted for by the individual contributions of its professors. Directly or indirectly, key members of the Glasgow faculty were involved in the protracted proceedings against Robertson Smith. It is impossible now to appreciate the excitement, the common-room discussions, the side-taking and head-shaking that accompanied each stage of the unfolding drama.⁷ No student living through such events could be unaffected. After 1882, the place of moderate biblical criticism was secured, albeit at the cost of one of the Free Church's most gifted scholars, and not without several after-tremors triggered by Dods, Bruce and George Adam Smith.⁸

Denney's theological education took place during the climax and immediate aftermath of the affair and at the hands of some of Robertson Smith's most vocal and loyal supporters. It is this ethos of supportive, even combative sympathy with Smith, which was highly significant in the formation of Denney's views on the nature and authority of Scripture, and its relation to criticism.

Of all the Professors, Principal Douglas remained conservative and most resistant to Smith's views. Significantly though, he was Smith's colleague on the Old Testament Revision Committee working on the Revised Version, and Smith believed he could rely on Douglas 'to defend the rights of criticism'.⁹ However, in 1878, when Smith's position was becoming more difficult, Douglas published a pamphlet, *Why I still believe that Moses wrote Deuteronomy: some reflections after reading Professor Smith's Additional Answer to the Libel*. This was reviewed in 1879, in the *British and Foreign Evangelical Review*, by A. B. Davidson, previously Robertson Smith's teacher.¹⁰ Davidson was careful to point out Douglas had never doubted that '"critical opinions" regarding Deuteronomy might be embraced and advocated by one who was as sincerely attached to evangelical truth as he was himself'.¹¹

---

⁷ In 1877 'Professor Lindsay of Glasgow stood on the back of one of the forms and frantically waved his hat to express his joy and triumph....' Macleod, *Second Disruption*, 62, n. 106.

⁸ See Cheyne, *Studies*, 'The Bible and Change in the Nineteenth Century', 123-38, for the longer historical and broader theological context of the Robertson Smith affair and its aftermath.

⁹ J. S. Black and G. W. Chrystal, *William Robertson Smith*, (London: A & C Black, 1912), 191.

¹⁰ Candlish had requested the article as 'from the Smith side'; Davidson's compliance broke his silence during the Smith case. The article attracted serious criticism to Davidson himself in 1880. R. E. Riesen, *Criticism and Faith in Late Victorian Scotland*, (Lanham: University Press of America 1985), 346-7.

¹¹ A. B. Davidson, 'Review of Works on Old Testament Exegesis', *BFER*, 1879, 338. Davidson subjected the book to a fifteen page critique, closing with the following comment. '[Douglas] has no difficulty in pronouncing a verdict of irrelevancy upon the whole critical direction of the Protestant mind of Europe during a century past.... This whole direction of mind with its premises and its results is without meaning, so far as truth and progress is concerned, in the history of the church and of mankind. A great intellectual movement can hardly be conceived so completely abandoned by the spirit of truth, and carrying on its operations so entirely outside the region where God himself is

It is evidence of the complexity of the issues surrounding the Robertson Smith case that many shared Douglas's position, personally disagreeing with the practice and conclusions of higher criticism, yet uneasy about judgmental condemnation of those who promulgated critical views, and about the use of church courts to settle matters of scholarship.[12] In a tendentious article on 'The Critical Movement in the Scotch Free Church', T. M. Lindsay, Professor of Church History in Glasgow, explained the ambivalence many felt. Referring to the decision of the Aberdeen Presbytery and Synod in 1877, that there was no heresy case to answer, he remarked:

> They had declared that the opinions which [Smith] held might be held in the Church. His critical views were not adopted – they were rather repudiated – but it was held that it was no business of the Church to deal with private critical opinions if they did not trench upon the great doctrines of Scripture. The Presbytery, in short....maintained the possibility of critical freedom combined with dogmatic orthodoxy.[13]

It seems Douglas's position was not dissimilar, strongly disapproving of Smith's conclusions but not questioning Smith's dogmatic orthodoxy. Indeed, Douglas was involved with Candlish, Lindsay and Smith's other supporters in trying to advise him as the crisis later came to a climax.[14] If this is a fair representation of Douglas's stance, then students such as Denney trained in a College where none of the senior staff, not even the Principal, 'a scholarly conservative, sceptical of higher critical views',[15] supported a formal ecclesial attack on critical freedom.

'Men full of the new learning of the times, and not afraid of it'

Throughout the crisis Lindsay was a major player.[16] His 1878 article already cited was premature in its celebrations and its conclusions. But

---

present as the source of all true advancement, as this view implies.' Ibid., 361. Davidson could hardly have been more pointed about where his own critical sympathies lay.

[12] Nevertheless, the theme of Douglas's introductory lecture for the new session in 1891 was 'The Old Testament and its Critics'. It is a defiant rebuttal of the critical method and its conclusions, which, in its printed form, is prefaced by his letter of resignation on health grounds, from his Principalship. The refusal of the College Committee to provide an assistant may indicate they considered Douglas yesterday's man. His successor was George Adam Smith, a figure more congenial to the other Glasgow Professors.

[13] T. M. Lindsay, 'The Critical Movement in the Scotch Free Church', *The Contemporary Review* 33, 1878, 30.

[14] Black and Chrystal, *Smith*, 341.

[15] *DSCHT*, 253.

[16] For an account of Lindsay's career see McKim, D., 'Thomas Martin Lindsay', 351-375, in M. Bauman and M. Klauber, *Historians of the Christian Tradition. Their*

what is significant for understanding the theological development of Denney is the way Lindsay based his defence of Smith on an appeal to the Reformation doctrine of the witness of the Spirit.

> Historical criticism, in fact, if only the doctrine of the witness of the Spirit be kept clearly in the foreground, resolves the Bible into scene after scene of fellowship and communion with God. It multiplies, deepens, and broadens the sight and experience of that fellowship which the Scripture brings us.[17]

Lindsay's positive appraisal of the role and value of higher criticism was supported by an appeal to Calvin and Melanchthon as Humanists, 'men full of the new learning of the times, and...not afraid of it.'[18] The historian in Lindsay discerned in his own times, two opposing cultural movements in the response to new knowledge. On the one hand where new knowledge is perceived as threatening to religious truth, such knowledge will be seen, not as God's gift but as a wile of the Devil to be resisted. In such circumstances the timid religious mind seeks the security of an external authority, as in mediaeval times. Lindsay's polemical edge, at times razor sharp,[19] woundingly compared the present appeal to authority 'in not a few of the Churches of the Reformation' (including his own), with recent Roman Catholic moves to consolidate and centralise spiritual authority.[20] The fearful mind forges its own spiritual and intellectual shackles when it surrenders the obligation to pursue truth wherever it leads, and relies instead on an external arbiter other than the Spirit of God.

On the other hand, Lindsay discerned in the spirit of the age an unbridled Humanism 'accompanied by all the intellectual extravagance and moral heedlessness...which distinguished the Renascence period', and which 'neither fears God nor regards man'. If the appeal to external authority is the surrender of a God-given freedom, then the appeal to intellectual *laissez faire* is a denial of God-given authority. Both responses to new knowledge pose a threat to the moral and spiritual welfare of

---

Methodology and Influence on Western Thought, (Nashville: Broadman and Holman, 1995).

[17] Lindsay, 'Critical Movement', 25.

[18] Ibid., 24.

[19] Lindsay refers to those prosecuting Robertson Smith as 'pamphleteers' who used letters to newspapers and pamphlets as 'heavenly weapons' with which they as 'self-constituted defenders fight the battles of orthodoxy'. Smith's opponents are 'alarmists' who use 'garbled extracts', and 'theological doctrinaires' who have 'commonly the modest assurance to consider [themselves] the standard of human intelligence, and to be angry with all who do not accept [their] pet notions.' Ibid., 26-8, 32. This is good rhetoric, but reckless diplomacy.

[20] Almost certainly a reference to the First Vatican Council 1870, and the declaration of papal infallibility.

church and society. 'All churches have confronting them now what the Church of the Reformation had; the revolt of a revived paganism, accompanied by its unfailing attendant, a revival of Church authority and priestly pretension.'[21] The response to the present crisis, in Lindsay's view, should therefore be the same as the response of the Reformers facing the same cultural realities:

> ...if this doctrine of the witness of the Spirit which had helped Calvin to steer clear of so many difficulties in his day, and which had been put down in the very forefront of the doctrine of Scripture in the Westminster Confession of Faith, were used now as it had been used then, it would not only be as serviceable now, but those who used it would be the real heirs of Reformation theologians and the true upholders of their Church's confessional theology.[22]

In 1878 when Lindsay wrote this, he clearly believed the matter was all but closed. With premature optimism he concluded, 'The Free Church of Scotland has not denied her old confession; but she has declared practically, if not formally, that criticism and dogma are not antagonistic things; that critical freedom may co-exist with dogmatic orthodoxy'.[23] These sentiments about criticism, backed as they were by appeals to the Reformers' doctrine of the inner witness of the Spirit, would be absorbed by Denney as he attended Lindsay's classes on historical theology, and later be reproduced in the articulation of his own theology of Scripture.

The likelihood of Lindsay's opinions being publicly aired, and permeating his College teaching, is strengthened by the prominent place occupied by Lindsay amongst those dissenting from the final report that led to Smith's removal. Note 10 of Lindsay's Dissent is worth quoting, along with the part of the Report to which he took great exception. 'I dissent from the statements made about Professor Smith's historical criticism and also from the paragraph on page 8 of the printed Report beginning "Moreover the general method..."'.[24] The paragraph in question, with the preceding sentence, reads:

> The whole tendency of the writings examined by the Committee is fitted to throw the Old Testament history into confusion and at least to weaken, if not destroy the very foundation on which New Testament Doctrine is built. Moreover the general method on which he proceeds conveys the impression that the Bible may be

---

[21] Lindsay, 'Critical Movement', 24.

[22] Ibid., 25.

[23] Ibid., 34.

[24] 'Dissents taken from the Report of Committee appointed by the Commission anent the Writings of Professor Robertson Smith', 9.

accounted for by the same laws which have determined the growth of any other literature, inasmuch as there is no recognition of the divine element in the Book.[25]

Several other details support the view that Lindsay's defence of Smith was a *cause celebre* amongst the student body, and that Denney's sympathies lay with his teacher. The Colleges were facing mounting criticism, evidenced by a pamphlet published in 1880, *The Uncertain Theology in the Colleges of the Free Church*. Denney's College Notebook for Church History, dated 1881, has survived, and has considerable interest as a record of Lindsay's lectures. But of at least equal interest are the notes and doodles on the back pages.[26] Several entries bear the marks of notes written for the amusement of a neighbouring student in the lecture hall. 'I have heard him tell this story three times before'; 'I have got a fine motto in Melanchthon for my controversial'; and of more significance for the present discussion, 'We should ask Lindsay who slandered us and bring an action against him before the Sheriff.' It is an intriguing question who, in 1881, said what about the College, to provoke a pencilled note of threatened (tongue-in-cheek?), legal action.

'He helped to win intelligent acceptance of this truth'

Thirty three years later, Denney preached at Lindsay's funeral. The text was 'I know whom I have believed, and am persuaded, that He is able to keep that which I have committed unto Him against that day' (2 Tim. 1.12). In the first section Denney summarised the Christian religion in words that encapsulated a key element in his mature theology, 'The Christian religion can be put as simply as this: it is knowing and trusting the Person who speaks to us in the gospel. The whole value of the gospels is that they put us in communication with this person, and enable us to say, I know whom I have believed.'[27]

But speaking of Lindsay's personal faith, Denney found it impossible to avoid reference to Lindsay's role in the Robertson Smith controversy. The sermon manuscript has several significant deletions, all of them still legible.[28] Several times Denney excised references to his student days, probably to give what he did say the authority, not of personal reminiscence, but of now accepted fact. One sentence, frustratingly scored out before it was completed, comes immediately after Denney referred to the Robertson Smith crisis, 'I was a student in Dr Lindsay's class at the

---

[25] The section Lindsay quotes is on pages 7 and 8 of the 'Report of Committee on Professor W. R. Smith's Writings'. See *PDGAFCS*, 1880.

[26] DEN12-01. There are no page numbers. The assorted doodlings are on the last eight pages.

[27] DEN07-77, 2.

[28] All references in this paragraph to DEN07-77, 2-4.

time and I remember well the....' Previous to this comment, an entire paragraph is crossed out. In it Denney commented, 'One of the great services Dr Lindsay did to the Church, a service for which I, for one, will always be grateful to him, was that he helped to win intelligent acceptance for this truth.' It is important to put that sentence in context by quoting Denney at length, and showing just what 'truth' it was that earned Lindsay Denney's lifelong gratitude. The rewritten paragraph is not substantially different from the crossed out passage, apart from omitting personal references, diplomatic softening of a few phrases and tidying up the syntax. It can therefore be taken as Denney's view of the affair and of its lasting intellectual implications for Denney himself. It is seldom that Denney's intellectual indebtedness is so explicitly stated and precisely documented in his own words.

> Fully thirty years ago our church was in the throes of the great controversy about the Bible associated with the name of Robertson Smith...and the great scholar and teacher whose loss we mourn today, took a leading part in it. [I was a student in Dr Lindsay's class at the time and remember well the...][29] It is easier today than it was then to see what was really at issue in those confused and passionate debates. It was the simplicity of the true religion, the title of the humble man, to whom God had spoken through the Scriptures, to say without being troubled by any questions of Biblical criticism, I know whom I have believed. There were those then who argued that a man could not be a minister of the Free Church- nay that he could not be a true Christian, unless he held such and such views about the date and authorship of certain books in the Bible. But views about the date and authorship of books in the Bible are no part of the sum of saving knowledge. They are not given to us in spiritual experience. It is a fact worth remembering that in the Bible itself the expression 'the Word of God' is never applied to anything written. No document is ever so described. 'The Word of God' is never anything less than God speaking to me, convincing and persuading me that it is He who speaks, and enabling me to say, I know whom I have believed. One of the great services which Dr Lindsay did to the church, a service which we gratefully recal [sic] today, was that he helped to win intelligent acceptance for this truth, and to bring men's minds back to the simplicity which is in Christ. It is better to have right than wrong opinions about the date of Deuteronomy, or the authorship of certain Psalms, or the composition of the gospels. But after all, it is not vital. Dr Lindsay loved his Bible because through it he had communion with God, a communion which is independent of all such questions. This was its value to him, and in the last resort its only value. Its unity and inspiration lie in this, that the living and true God speaks to us through it as a whole, and bears testimony to it in our hearts through His Spirit.[30]

During the Assembly of 1881, on the Sunday before the decisive vote which removed Smith, Lindsay was preaching at the Free High Church in Edinburgh. His text was 'He shall turn the heart of the fathers'. It was a

---

[29] This is where the deleted sentence comes in the rewritten paragraph.
[30] ibid., 3-4.

plea for understanding and acceptance between the generations. The ironic and combatant mood of Lindsay's previous publications and speeches gave way to a persuasive appeal in which old and young, who represent the Church's past and future, have to live together in the present. The fathers are a thinly veiled reference to the fathers of the Free Church, the young are the new generation of leaders and scholars, and Robertson Smith, though unmentioned, stands in the emotional foreground. The first extract shows the direction of Lindsay's argument, and reveals the intellectual stance underlying Lindsay's approach to history and criticism; the second reveals the resentful psychology of a generation gap which, unless hearts are turned, results in cultural collision with dire spiritual consequences.[31]

> Spiritual life in the church and among men is possible when the past and future meet in harmony in the present, when the past and future are not arrayed against each other as two opposing forces fighting for the possession of the present but as two mutually complementary elements. The law of spiritual life is that the old look forward to the future and that the young look back to the past, that the fathers turn to the children and that the children turn to the fathers: when each know that they are not the whole of the present, when the past knows that there is a future, and when the future knows that there is a past.[32]

> The prophet does not ask the fathers to think exactly as the children, nor the children to think exactly as the fathers. They are to feel with each other. It is a meeting of heart, not of heads, that brings deliverance from coming evil or impending doom.... Each age must think for itself in its own special fashion, and commonly that special fashion is somewhat different from that of the age that went before and from that of the age that will come after. I do not mean that God's truth changes, or that the great fundamental doctrines of God's revelation change. They do not. They are there, eternal verities. But who has ever got at the whole of each of these truths? New knowledge is coming before us and we must attend to that... The fathers had their own way of looking at things and thinking about them, and the children have theirs. And the one can never become the other.... The fathers cannot change to see and think exactly as the children, and the children cannot see and think exactly as the fathers. And yet both are seeing and thinking about the same

---

[31] See J. W. Rogerson, *The Bible and Criticism in Victorian Britain*, (Sheffield: Sheffield Academic Press, 1995), ch. 4, 'A Tale of two Cultures'. Rogerson's account of the trials and of what he calls 'the German connection' balances others which tend to caricature Smith's opponents as ignorant obscurantists. J. C. O'Neill, *The Bible's Authority. A Portrait Gallery of Thinkers from Lessing to Bultmann,* (Edinburgh: T & T Clark, 1991), illustrates the ferment created by German intellectual engagement with the Bible in the eighteenth and nineteenth centuries.

[32] T. M. Lindsay, *College Addresses and Sermons*, (Glasgow: Maclehose and Jackson, 1915), 111.

things.... Each generation must act up to and think up to the light that God has given it. [The prophet] asks for sympathy, not exact similarity of thought.[33]

The hoped for rapprochement between fathers and children did not materialise. The removal of Robertson Smith was a seismic shock which acted only to confirm in men like Lindsay, Bruce and Candlish a profound sense of moral responsibility with respect to new knowledge. They practised before their students, an ethic of criticism, displaying a moral commitment to truth which must satisfy the conscience as to its intellectual integrity. The discipleship of the mind imposes obligations to follow truth where it leads, in the confidence that the Spirit of Truth cannot deceive.

Truth's capacity to defend itself became theologically axiomatic for Denney. As events unfolded, and Denney's senior Professors took prominent positions on Robertson Smith's side, Denney's own mind was being made up about the relation of Scripture to criticism and of both to truth. In 1894, lecturing at Chicago Theological Seminary, Denney spoke on the doctrine of Holy Scripture. The published version of the lecture echoes much of Lindsay's arguments and terminology and refers approvingly to Lindsay's article printed in *The Expositor*, 1894, as a 'full and lucid account of Professor Robertson Smith's doctrine of Scripture'.[34] Denney's *Studies in Theology* will be considered later, but one quotation suggests the lasting influence of a teacher like Lindsay, and why it was that Denney later counted on Lindsay's friendship as a kindred spirit, and made him the obvious choice to speak at Lindsay's funeral.

> A Christian who knows that God does speak to the soul through the Scriptures ought not to speak of criticism as an alien or hostile power, with which he may be compelled, against his will, to go so far, but which he must ever regard with suspicion....true criticism is a science, and will go its own length, and we will all go along with it. Even to speak of moderate and extreme opinions in criticism is out of place. The answers to the critics questions are not moderate or extreme, but true or false; and of all men a Christian ought to be willing to go any length with truth.[35]

'The authority of Scripture independent of criticism'

Denney was confronted with issues of Scriptural authority from the outset of his course. The College opening lecture was delivered by Candlish in 1879, Denney's first year. It was one of the first lectures Denney heard in

---

[33] Ibid., 113-5.
[34] Denney, *Studies*, 271.
[35] Ibid., 213.

College and was delivered just as the Smith case was again referred by Aberdeen Presbytery to the Assembly. Smith himself was in Egypt, and Candlish was anxious about the turn events were taking. Significantly the title was 'The Testimony of the Spirit to the Word of God'. This lecture, along with several of Candlish's recent publications became the focus of hostile attention.[36] He had become editor of the *British and Foreign Evangelical Review* in 1875 and within the year had made his editorial article 'Soundness and Freedom of Theology' a statement of editorial intent. *The Authority of Scripture Independent of Criticism*, followed in 1877, and his article on 'Dogma' was published in the Ninth Edition of the *Encyclopaedia Britannica*. Each of these publications contributed to the theological pre-history of Candlish's lecture.

But for Candlish there was an additional personal element in the Robertson Smith case. Robertson Smith attended Candlish's church while Candlish was still a minister in Aberdeen. By Smith's own severe standards Candlish was, on the whole, worth listening to. He reported. '[I] find him an instructive and in a measure stimulating preacher. He has a "sense" for scientific theology, but I don't think that he is quite free from the faults of our present Scotch theology.'[37] Over the years they had become friends and as the crisis deepened, 'Candlish became day by day a more firm and affectionate ally.'[38] In 1877 Smith wrote to his brother, 'Candlish and Bruce are members of Assembly expressly, as I understand, in order to give me fair play.'[39] As editor of the *British and Foreign Evangelical Review* he had personally seen some of Smith's articles into print and was again in trouble on Smith's account, when he commissioned A. B. Davidson to submit the review mentioned above, which was critical of Douglas.

In the light of Candlish's friendship with Smith, and his publication track record as Smith's defender, it is not surprising that *The Scotsman* report on Candlish's 1879 start of session lecture alarmed Smith's opponents. When the offending part of the press report is read it becomes clear Candlish was virtually making a policy statement about the continuing role of biblical criticism in the College curriculum.

---

[36] See *Professor Smith and His Apologists: A Few Words Concerning a pamphlet entitled 'The Authority of Scripture independent of Criticism, By James S. Candlish. D.D.,' and a pamphlet entitled ' A Plain View of the case of Professor W. Robertson Smith, by the Rev W. Miller, MA*, By a Minister of the Free Church of Scotland, (Edinburgh, 1878); Edward A. Thomson, *The Uncertain Theology in the Colleges of the Free Church*, (Edinburgh, 1880).

[37] Black and Chrystal, *Smith*, 135.

[38] Ibid., 239.

[39] Ibid., 228.

They would not shut their eyes to the fact that the researches of historical enquiry were continually bringing new materials to light bearing on the outward form of the Bible, and they could not stand upon any foregone conclusion in regard to these. They might require to alter many preconceived opinions about the sacred books, to regard them or their contents in a light different from that they had been accustomed to. But if they heard the voice of God speaking to their spirit in these books, they should be sure that no results of criticism could shake that great truth that God had been speaking at sundry times and in divers manners to the fathers by the prophets and in the last days by His Son. And they should best show their confidence in the Divine authority and infallible truth of Scripture as the rule of faith and life by being willing that it should be cast unreservedly into the crucible of free enquiry, assured that whatever that might destroy in their preconceived opinion, the words of God would come out as pure words, as silver tried in the furnace of earth purified seven times. Such was the faith in which they desired to carry on the work of theological study in that College.[40]

For the ancient texts of the Bible to be 'cast unreservedly into the crucible of free enquiry' was a provocative assertion for those fearful of higher criticism, and already prosecuting a case against Robertson Smith. For a student of Denney's recent academic background in Philosophy, Classics and a recent six-month immersion in German culture, the lecture was more likely reassuring. It is possible Denney had read Candlish's *Authority of Scripture Independent of Criticism* before he came to College, perhaps in Germany. When Denney wrote home in June 1879, arguing that the orthodoxy of students could not be secured by silencing their teachers, his words are very close to Candlish's concluding argument.

> For it is vain to think that [new opinions] can be kept from the knowledge of our ministers, students and thinking people in general. They must be studied and discussed, and the discussion of them is surely far safer in the hands of men who are thoroughly evangelical in spirit, and who think they can reconcile them with the doctrines of the evangelical churches....[41]

Like Lindsay, Candlish was not defending the validity of Robertson Smith's conclusions, but the neutrality of critical methods applied to Scripture. The proper authority of Scripture is secured if the scholar in question accepted the status of the Bible as God's word, and understood authority to lie not in the text *per se*, but in the dynamic activity of the

---

[40] *The Scotsman*, 4 November 1879. Quoted in *Uncertain Theology*, 34.

[41] Candlish, *Authority of Scripture*, 28. Compare *LFF*, 4. The point is conceded by one of Candlish's critics. 'It would not be right of them to keep the young men in ignorance of prevailing errors; but like the man at the railway switches, if they open the up-line for the down-train, or the down-line for the up-train; if they open and leave open the inlets of error and unbelief without displaying the danger signal, they are responsible for whatever collision or disaster may ensue.' *The Uncertain Theology*, 19.

Holy Spirit communicating Christ and creating communion with God through the written words of Scripture.

It is important to consider in some more detail Candlish's publications on the relations between criticism and the Bible, in order to be clear about his doctrine of Scripture. Like Lindsay, he was a prominent voice both in the public forum and the College classroom, his views as cogently and pungently expressed in the one as the other. When Denney came to work out his own views of Scripture, as minister and later as College lecturer, clear lines of dependence can be traced back to these pivotal years in the history of biblical interpretation in Scotland

'We also adopt the rationalistic principle'

In David Bebbington's study of British Evangelicalism, the scholarly aims and methods of Robertson Smith are placed within the broader philosophical category of German Romanticism. Citing Alfred Cave, one of Smith's most hostile critics, he comments that Cave 'did no justice to [Smith's] views. The explanation is to be found in the title of one of Cave's later books: *The Inspiration of the Old Testament Inductively Considered* (1888). Cave was tied to Enlightenment categories such as induction that made constructive engagement with Smith impossible.'[42] Rogerson's tale of two cultures personified in Begg and Robertson Smith, was in reality the tale of a doomed conversation because the participants did not share a common language or conceptual framework. Perhaps this explains the inability of Smith's opponents to take at face value his repeated and clear statements concerning his doctrine of Scripture, or to understand how he reconciled orthodox sentiments with an approach to Scripture free of dogmatic constraint and yielding such unorthodox results. In his *Answer to the Form of Libel* he gave what he believed was an adequate defence and sufficient reassurance:

> If I am asked why I receive Scripture as the Word of God and the only perfect rule of faith and life, I answer with all the Fathers of the Protestant Church, because the Bible is the only record of the redeeming love of God, because in the Bible alone I find God drawing near to men in Christ Jesus and declaring to us in Him His will for our salvation. And this record I know to be true by the witness of His Spirit in my heart, whereby I am assured that none other than God Himself is able to speak such words to my soul.[43]

---

[42] D. W. Bebbington, *Evangelicalism in Modern Britain*, (London: Unwin Hyman, 1989), 185.

[43] W. R. Smith, *Answer to the Form of Libel now before the Free Church Presbytery of Aberdeen* (Edinburgh, 1878), 21. This defensive statement of Smith's is embedded in

Candlish made no bones about where the communication breakdown had occurred, and who was to blame. Criticism is an exercise in reason while Scripture is a spiritual exercise. What gives the results of criticism authority are rational criteria; what gives Scripture authority are spiritual criteria. Thus in *The Authority of Scripture Independent of Criticism*, Candlish began by contrasting rationalistic theories with a spiritual understanding of the nature of the Bible.

> The purity, heavenliness, and spiritual power of Scripture are qualities with which no criticism, lower or higher, has to do; and therefore a faith that rests on them is secure, whatever criticism may say. But if we lay down such propositions as these:- Scripture, being divine, must have an absolutely pure text, or must be written in perfect grammatical style, without solecisms or irregularities, or must be always literally interpreted, or cannot contain an exhibition of mere earthly love, or a work of imagination: we endanger our faith by making it depend on the replies to questions that can only be answered by criticism...by any such proceeding we also adopt the rationalistic principle. For that principle is just this: that we are able to judge antecedently what a revelation from God must be.[44]

In its purest and strictest form, rationalism denies that anything in Scripture is beyond the grasp of reason. In its naturalistic form it denies the supernatural *a priori*. Those who accused Smith and other higher critics of rationalism, Candlish warned, were guilty of a more dangerous rationalism by linking the authority of the Scripture to an *a priori* concept of what a revelation must be.

> Now it is very undesirable that we should fall into a similar error in regard to criticism; and by a dogmatic rationalism which maintains that the Bible, because divine, must be written in some particular form, should open the door for that sceptical rationalism which argues that because it is not written in that way, it cannot be divine. Rather let us occupy the humbler, but far safer position of true faith, that we are sure that the Bible is divine because of its self-evidencing light and power....[45]

In support of the contention that critical opinions can co-exist with evangelical soundness, Candlish peppered his article with the names of 'many of the most cautious and conservative expositors' who held more relaxed views of critical matters. Amongst those cited as witnesses were Keil, Delitzsch, Hengstenberg and Kleinert 'cautious and orthodox critics' from the Continent; James Bannerman, Thomas Chalmers, Dr Fairbairn, a triumvirate of revered Free Church Fathers; Charles Hodge, J.

Denney's Chicago lecture on Holy Scripture as published in *Studies in Theology*, Denney's first major articulation of his own theology. 204-5.

[44] Candlish, *The Authority of Scripture*, 4.

[45] Ibid., 5.

A. Alexander and Moses Stuart representing American evangelical orthodoxy; and almost as a footnote, Calvin.

The term rationalism is almost always pejorative in conservative theological circles. In the Robertson Smith case the description can, with appropriate qualification, be applied to both sides. Candlish however, was seeking to claim the high ground by insisting decisive weight be placed on the inner witness of the Spirit communicating Scriptural authority as textually mediated truth spiritually experienced, rather than on any antecedent dogma determining what a revelation from God must be. His claim that his approach placed biblical authority on a more secure basis was strongly disputed.[46] But judging from Denney's mature position on matters of biblical authority and its relations to criticism, he found the Lindsay / Candlish view an attractive and persuasive basis for his own thought.

'Christianity is essentially a historical religion'

In 1900, following the death of A. B. Bruce, Denney was appointed to the chair of New Testament Language and Literature. There is an appropriateness in Bruce's mantle falling on Denney, because Bruce's influence on Denney, as on generations of students, was decisive. Mention has already been made of Bruce's role in counter-balancing the neo-Hegelian thought of Edward Caird.

> The pantheizing tendencies of speculative theism are resolutely to be opposed. Pantheisms of all kinds, whether Spinozistic or Hegelian, founder on the historical Jesus...History is not to be escaped from, either by the idealistic way, or by the experience-centred way of which Schleiermacher was the prophet.[47]

But Denney's debt to Bruce was less in apologetics and refutation of inadequate philosophical theology, than in the positive impetus Bruce gave to Denney's mind in the direction of New Testament studies. For Bruce, Jesus as revealed in the gospels, when subjected to honest intellectual and historical enquiry, is the central reality of the Christian gospel. No dogmatic construct must be used as a grid to harmonise the gospels into theological consistency, for this obscures rather than clarifies the revelation of God given in Jesus.

Bruce's role in the Robertson Smith case was as prominent and public as Candlish and Lindsay, and his position in relation to criticism and Scripture, if anything even less influenced by *a priori* dogmatic considerations. His closing appeal on Robertson Smith's behalf, followed by his historic statement of dissent, placed Bruce firmly amongst those

---

[46] See especially *The Uncertain Theology* and *Professor Smith and his Apologists*.
[47] Sell, *Defending and Declaring*, 115.

publicly committed, whatever the consequences, to believing criticism. He looked forward to a future in which the Free Church 'shall appear orthodox yet not illiberal, evangelical yet not Pharisaical, believing yet not afraid of enquiry.'[48] Bruce's reasons of dissent, stated in the Assembly, were adopted verbatim into the signed protest and stated the future agenda unambiguously: 'We also declare that the decision of the Assembly leaves all Free Church ministers and office-bearers free to pursue the critical questions raised by Professor W. R. Smith, and we pledge ourselves to do our best to protect any man who pursues these studies legitimately'.[49]

Not only did Bruce awaken in Denney a fascination with Jesus, the gospels, and the Gospel, he also demonstrated that historical investigation provides the most fruitful way of understanding the relations between these three realities. In several significant areas of thought, Bruce left his mark on Denney's mind. Bruce believed that the critical questions for the modern mind were historical not metaphysical, and that Christianity 'is essentially a historical religion'; Denney came to believe likewise. Bruce regarded the New Testament documents as witnesses to be heard and their evidence weighed, not as authorities to be uncritically accepted on *a priori* grounds; Denney also defended the self-authenticating character of the historic documentation of Christian faith. Bruce was impatient with creeds as controlling mechanisms, and urged a restatement of doctrine more suited to contemporary thought; Denney shared the antipathy to credal formulations and later urged a simplifying of doctrine in *Jesus and the Gospel*. Bruce found in Jesus Christ, the controlling centre of theology and devotion, the supreme authority in matters of faith, the decisive hermeneutic principle in relation to Scripture; much of Denney's most characteristic writing built on that same Christological hermeneutic. Bruce insisted on the moral impact of such doctrines as incarnation, atonement and Christology on the human conscience; Denney's preaching and theologising powerfully echo similar notes of ethical passion. All of this is not to suggest Denney absorbed Bruce uncritically. He came to see serious limitations in Bruce's methodology, gaps in his work, and flaws of temperament, which at times prejudiced his scholarship.

'To look on Him with open face'

Following Bruce's death in 1899, Denney expressed some of his judgements about the lasting value of Bruce's work.[50] Though not

---

[48] Black and Chrystal, *Smith*, 439.
[49] Ibid., 450.
[50] 'The Theological Work of Dr. Bruce', DEN10-02. There are several close similarities in words and content to W. M. Clow's article for *The Expository Times*,

uncritical, he is unmistakably respectful, even affectionate. Bruce combined in one mind an interest in apologetics and in the New Testament, and managed to bring the two into relation with each other. His lifelong commitment to 'deal with anti-Christian prejudices in such a way that Christianity may get a fair hearing' originated in his own experience of being spiritually unsettled by reading Strauss's *Das Leben Jesu*. Yet, Bruce was no philosopher, 'he had no philosophy of religion and never wanted one. His mind was scientific rather than speculative, and he distrusted everything which promised too much...he had a profound sense of the limitations of the mind.' Personal experience of 'the solid earth on which he had believed himself to stand crumbling under his feet', gave Bruce's apologetic work an evangelistic and pastoral edge.[51] His own faith recovered through a commitment to investigating and confirming the historic facticity of the gospels.

Throughout his work in both apologetics and New Testament 'the impulse of all his work was to get into immediate contact with Jesus, and to look on him with open face.' Denney went on, 'No man could more legitimately have taken as his life's motto - Jesus only; Jesus as opposed to the churches and their traditions, Jesus as opposed even to those who at the best were but witness to Jesus. Jesus as he lives before our eyes in the pages of the evangelists, speaking to us with his own lips, appealing to us by his own grace and truth'.[52] Personal reminiscence informs the comment:

> He made it his business to open the eyes of his students as his own had been opened, and hundreds of men who are now preaching the gospel owe him this immeasurable debt. He took the veil from the gospels for them; instead of being a mere picture book or source of illustrations to the gospel, Matthew, Mark and Luke were raised into a place of pre-eminence, and the gospel was sought in the first instance from them alone.[53]

In describing Bruce's lifelong fascination with the gospels Denney commented on the Pauline bias of Protestant theology and traditional Scottish preaching as a 'presentation of the truth in forms determined in the main by Paul's thought.... Even when the gospels are used, and made the text of a discourse, this intellectual construction of their import

---

September 1899. Denney's manuscript is headed by his home address and 'From James Denney'. Bruce would have enjoyed the questions of literary dependence, authorial style, verbal agreements, external and internal evidence the two documents raise. Denney's is the fuller version and contains personal comments not in Clow's article. Clow having been one of Bruce's students perhaps asked several others to provide information for his piece.

[51] Ibid., 2.
[52] Ibid., 3.
[53] Ibid., 3-4.

prevails. It is as though we read them through the epistles; the mind we bring to the task is a mind that has been Christianised already in another medium.'[54] Denney wrote as one who was himself soaked in the gospel according to Paul from his early years. Being taught the gospels by Bruce was to experience a radical rearrangement of mental furniture.

> He had heard Jesus himself, and could not listen to anybody else in precisely the same way. He never focussed the realities of revelation exactly as Paul did. His Christ was Jesus of Nazareth; Paul's Christ was the Lord of Glory.... The life and teaching of Jesus were for Dr. Bruce the inmost shrine of revelation.... Dr Bruce did not go to Paul for the gospel, he went to Paul with the gospel. He had learned to know Jesus elsewhere.[55]

While much of Denney's thought expounds Pauline concepts rooted in Pauline texts,[56] his published work, sermons and unpublished lectures, give considerable attention to the gospel texts and to the figure of Jesus. Early in his Broughty Ferry ministry he decided to preach on the gospels at least once a week.[57] A simple text analysis of the surviving sermons that span his lifetime, show a clear weighting towards gospel texts. Denney's interleaved copy of Huck's Synopsis reveals an accumulation over time of careful textual and lexical notes.[58] Unpublished papers and class lectures demonstrate that his engagement with contemporary gospel criticism was given at least as much attention as Pauline studies. The significance of these details is that they draw attention to a balance in Denney's thought easily overlooked.

His contribution to the theology of the atonement tends to dominate in any inventory of his most significant work, and that in turn might suggest his own mind was more Christianised in the Pauline medium than was the case. It will be important when considering his major writings to examine the weight Denney gives to the entire sweep of New Testament evidence, and in particular the role played by the gospels, and the figure of Jesus discovered through the gospel texts, in his overall theology. It is likely then that Bruce was largely responsible for setting Denney's mind in the conviction that Jesus Christ as revealed in the gospels and as witnessed to in apostolic testimony, is the sum and centre of Christian theology. If, as Denney later claimed, eternal love bearing sin is the last reality of the universe, then, as Bruce never tired of claiming, the Word made flesh in

---

[54] Ibid., 3,9.

[55] Ibid., 2, 9.

[56] His three commentaries are on 2 Corinthians, 1 and 2 Thesalonians and Romans. See also the eight articles on 'The Theology of Romans' published in *The Expositor* in 1901-2; and six unpublished lectures, 'The Gospel according to Paul', dated post 1909, DEN08-13-01 to DEN08-13-06.

[57] *LFF*, 33.

[58] DEN10-11.

Jesus of Nazareth is the starting point for understanding that and every other reality.

However much Denney later differed from Bruce on points of New Testament interpretation, and however dismissive he was of Bruce's apologetic efforts, he owed much to Bruce for his understanding of the person of Jesus as the content of the gospel, as the fundamental datum from which any treatment of the work of Christ must begin. That Scripture bears witness to Christ and that Jesus Christ is therefore Scripture's definitive hermeneutical principle; that the testimony of the Evangelists as to who Jesus is, is embedded in historic documents on which critical scholarship must work to excavate the real Person to whom they bear witness, these may be part of that same 'Bruceian' mindset which left its mark on Denney. The following words are so similar in theological sympathy with some of the writings of both men that, without knowing their source beforehand, they would be hard to attribute with confidence to either of them:

> The Gospel writers have no independent historical interest, and what they give us is not the representation of Christ as He really was, but Christ as to them He must have been, Christ transfigured in the luminous haze of faith. The task of the historian is to dissipate the haze, to see Jesus as He really was, to reduce Him to the historic proportions in which alone He can have lived and moved among men. To faith it may seem an ungrateful task, in performing which it is impossible to avoid wounding the tenderest feelings; yet faith in God can have no interest superior to that of truth, and ought to be confident that whatever it may lose in the process the end can be nothing but gain.[59]

It would be hard to find in Denney's writing a better example of the interpretative consequences of the Lindsay/Candlish/Bruce view that the authority of Scripture is, and must be, independent of criticism. On the other hand, in 1894, Denney's challenge to the Chicago Theological Seminary students reveals a certainty verging on naiveté reminiscent of Bruce, that an open mind reading the gospels will assent to their essential truthfulness:

> Read these books with your eye on Christ, and it will be as certain to you as anything is certain to the mind, heart and conscience of men, that the character of Christ there exhibited is a real character. It is not a fancy character; it is not a work of imagination; the evangelists did not make it up out of their own heads.[60]

One other aspect of Bruce's theology, mentioned by Denney, was important in setting the tone in much of Denney's theology. 'Next to the grace of the gospel, Dr Bruce was impressed by its severity; in its moral

---

[59] James Denney, *Jesus and the Gospel*, (London: Hodder & Stoughton, 1908), 56-7.
[60] Denney, *Studies*, 207.

demand there is something original and inexorable.'[61] For Bruce true religion carried profoundly moral implications. Faith, he believed, 'was a kind of moral inspiration; it gave intellectual and moral originality to people'. Far from being an alternative to ethical demand, faith in the gospel 'is the thing which alone gives moral value to all we are and do.' Denney's exposition of Bruce's doctrine of election demonstrates how Bruce translated the most perplexing of dogmas into moral terms:

> [Men] were elect not to the exclusion of others from God's good will, but to be by their suffering and service the ministers of God's good will to the world. Election, in short is a divine method of using some men to bless all; the elect are privileged in that they are made ministers of blessing; it is theirs to drink of Christ's cup and to be baptized with his baptism. A Calvinist may say that however true this is, it is irrelevant to what he means by election. Perhaps it is, so much the worse for what he means. When Jesus said to his disciples, you have not chosen me, but I have chosen you, he said all that is true in Calvinism.[62]

In this extensive account of Bruce's theological legacy, criticism is couched in an appreciative tone. Evaluating Bruce's *Synoptic Gospels*, Denney balanced endorsement with hesitation, and in doing so showed where he was in sympathy, and where he must part company, with his teacher:

> What may seem a more extraordinary thing, and in a man desirous of coming to close quarters with the facts an almost incredible thing, is that he had almost no historical interest. He did not feel much the need of background in reading the gospels. He did not look for the points of attachment, in the common mind and common life of the first century, for the words and deeds that meant so much to him. He fastened on them as they stood in the record, with no mediation of any kind, as if they were directly addressed to the nineteenth century intelligence...he read what the evangelists wrote not as history but as eternal truth.... Hence in spite of what is not to be found in it, his commentary on the Synoptic Gospels is for the man who reads with a religious interest the most illuminating and inspiring of guides.... Here and there it may strike the reader as whimsical, for Dr Bruce had not that oppressive sense of responsibility by which some vain people are burdened, and was capable of saying even in print just what rose in his thoughts to say - without feeling solemnly bound to answer to all time for it. Those who knew the man and loved him know and love him in these idiosyncrasies, and are not blinded by them to the immense contribution he made to the better understanding of the gospels.[63]

In his pupil several of Bruce's convictions and emphases exerted lasting influence. Not that they were merely borrowed; Denney was too independent of mind to borrow even Bruce's armour. But certain

---

[61] DEN10-02, 'Dr. Bruce', 7.
[62] Ibid., 8-9.
[63] Ibid., 4-5.

important emphases in his work at least echo the convictions of his teacher, even though Denney refined and developed them to better fit the shape and ethos of his own mind. Amongst these were Bruce's conviction that the gospels were their own best apologists, his tireless pre-occupation with the historical facts of Jesus' person, words and work, the meaning of these facts for the modern mind, his strong sense of doctrine as truth that must command the conscience with moral rather than legal or credal authority. In the theological formation of Denney, it may be the faith and character of the teacher, and the manner of the teaching rather than its content, that had long-term effects, not primarily on what, but on how, his student thought.

Before leaving Bruce, one other important comment by Denney should be noted. In 1901, responding to Nicoll's question about whether Bruce's posthumously published article on Jesus, in the *Encyclopaedia Biblica*, indicated he had lost his faith, Denney loyally defended his teacher:

> I don't know under what restrictions Bruce wrote his article - I mean restrictions imposed by the editors. There are evidently to be articles in the Encyclopaedia Biblica on the resurrection, the nativity narratives etc by other writers and Bruce may have been warned off all these, and restricted to write on the life and teaching and death of Jesus: I don't know. It is open to any one to say that a believer in the deity and resurrection of the Son of God should not have consented to write under restrictions which virtually involved a suppression of his faith: but however much I regret the absence from the article of much that might have been expected, I dare not answer your question in a way which would imply [such] a judgement upon Dr Bruce so severe as it suggests. I would rather say that he wrote this article in a bad week - in one of the times at which he suffered from the temporary eclipse of faith - than that he had ceased to be a believer. There certainly were ups and downs in the fight of faith in him, and he may have done this in one of the downs. But whatever the explanation may be, nothing short of an express statement from his own lips would ever justify me in saying that he did not believe in the deity and resurrection of Christ.[64]

'A light, a challenge, an enigma, a reflection of his Master'[65]

The affection discernible in Denney's relationship to Bruce is in considerable contrast to his relationship with Henry Drummond. Part of Drummond's significance for Denney lies in the fact that his book *Natural Law in the Spiritual World* so annoyed him it provoked Denney

---

[64] Unpublished letter. MS 3518/27/10/James Denney/April 2, 1901.
[65] R. F. Horton, *An Autobiography*, (London: Longman, 1917), 134.

into writing his first published work.[66] A trawl through the reviews of Drummond's runaway best-seller shows Denney was more severe than the substantial majority of reviewers. There is a personal edge to his treatment of the book and its author that suggests more than the usual tones of Victorian literary rhetoric, praise and critique laced with mild sarcasm and courteous restraint. Denney's treatment is neither mild nor restrained, and barely courteous.

Born in 1851,[67] Drummond was described as 'a radiant boy who lived in the sunshine and reflected it in his life'.[68] He was educated at Morison's Academy in Crieff, then Edinburgh University and New College, though it was 1876 before he passed the second part of the exit examination. He was invited to be geology tutor under Professor Geikie at the age of 21, and volunteer speaker and follow-up worker at the Moody revival meetings in 1873-74 and 1883. Assistant at Barclay Church Edinburgh in 1876-7, he was appointed lecturer in Natural Science at the Free Church College, Glasgow, in 1877.

As colleague with Marcus Dods he was pioneer missionary in Possilpark mission station, visited the Rockies and Africa on geology field trips, and developed his evangelistic work at well attended meetings of working men, students and upper class socialites in Glasgow, Edinburgh, Aberdeen and London. He was offered a diplomatic post in Dublin and Gladstone invited him to stand for Parliament. When the Boys' Brigade was formed in 1883 he was an early supporter and Honorary Vice President. In the 1890's he travelled world-wide promoting student ministries, destinations including Australia, Fiji Islands, Hong Kong and Japan. He was invited to be speaker at Moody's Northfield Convention in 1893. It was in the context of such a hyper-active and bewilderingly varied Christian lifestyle that Drummond wrote his two most significant books, *Natural Law in the Spiritual World* and *The Ascent of Man*.

Denney's pamphlet is a perceptive theological critique of a work, which popularised ideas he believed deeply inimical to orthodox Christian faith.[69] Written in an attractive style, *Natural Law* is crammed with interesting and novel illustrations from natural history. Composed largely of papers first presented to the working men of Possilpark, purporting to combine science with religion in a way that removed the fundamental conflict between the two, interacting with some of the

---

[66] *On 'Natural Law in the Spiritual World'*, by a Brother of the Natural Man, (Paisley: Alex Gardiner, 1885).

[67] For biographical details see George Adam Smith, *Henry Drummond*, (London: Hodder & Stoughton, 1908); J. Y. Simpson, *Henry Drummond*, (Edinburgh: Oliphant, 1901); Cuthbert Lennox, *Henry Drummond*, (London: Melrose, 1901); Thomas E. Corts, *Henry Drummond. A Perpetual Benediction*, (Edinburgh: T & T Clark, 1999).

[68] Simpson, *Drummond*, 13.

[69] Bruce may have encouraged Denney to write it. Walker, *Denney*, 37.

leading secular thinkers of the day,[70] it was a publishing phenomenon. The theological shortcomings of the work were widely recognised and many major reviews expressed serious hesitations.[71]

Like other reviewers, Denney seized on the Preface and Introduction and easily exposed the philosophical and logical flaws, doing so with references to Euclid, Plato, and untranslated quips in Greek, Latin and German. The book's popularity as an answer to those 'haunted now by a sense of instability in the foundations of their faith' made it for Denney a dangerous book because based on a highly speculative, selective and ultimately heterodox version of Christianity. Against Drummond's speculative, analogical and *a posteriori* arguments, Denney insisted 'it is on a fact basis science rests.'[72] Key concepts such as 'Biogenesis', 'Continuity' and 'Life', were left undefined by Drummond, in Denney's view, 'the most irritating characteristic of the book'.[73] Denney, who gained a distinction in Natural Philosophy at Glasgow, confidently corrected Drummond's science:

> The true meaning of the principle of continuity is apparent if it is called the principle of the conservation of force in all its transformations. A real example of its application is seen in... the transformation of the kinetic energy of a cannon ball shot upwards into potential energy, which as the ball descends again is re-transformed into kinetic energy equivalent to that with which it started.[74]

The point is important because Denney took issue with Drummond's claim that his book was scientific when it was based on only one branch of science, biology.[75] 'The very difference between the life of a serpent, for instance, and the life of a saint, *qua* saint - for in their purely animal aspects they are equally subjects for the biologist - should make us hesitate to find in the mere use of the words "spiritual life" a justification of the use of biological formulae to interpret sanctity.'[76]

The most substantial criticisms, however, went to the very core of Christian doctrine and experience, because Denney was, and was to remain, fiercely protective of 'the spiritual God of Christianity revealed in

---

[70] Herbert Spencer, John Ruskin, Thomas Carlyle, R. W. Emerson, and F. W. Robertson were amongst Drummond's intellectual mentors.

[71] See the list of twenty one reviews in Lennox, *Drummond*, 233-5.

[72] Denney, *'On Natural Law'*, 18.

[73] Ibid., 25.

[74] Ibid., 19-20.

[75] Drummond was the son of a seeds man and well informed biologist.

[76] Ibid., 22-3. The point was made with some feeling again: 'We cannot afford to disinherit ourselves of the unsearchable riches of Christ, to pass by all the other helps He gives to understanding, because the Christian "life" is a topic on which a Christian biologist finds it easy to preach'. 64.

the Man Christ Jesus.'[77] According to Drummond the natural man is dead to God, excluded from the spiritual world. Not so, replied Denney: 'The very heart of the Gospel's attraction is this, that the Son of Man is the revealer of God the Father; and the revelation of the divine Father in the human Son means that man, not natural nor spiritual, but man *simpliciter*, has an indefectible kinship with God, in the recognition of which he is born again.'[78] Regeneration according to Drummond is something over which the natural man has no control, but is a process governed by laws outside human determination. This, said Denney,

> is election and reprobation with a vengeance.... The truth about regeneration is, on the one hand, that it is divine, because it is dependent on the love of God; on the other that it is human, because it depends on the free moral appropriation of that love.... The relation of all souls to God is not casual, but essential; God is the Father of the most natural of natural men, however unworthy he may be to be called His son; and the work of redemption is the work of winning men to recognise their true nature.[79]

The determinism Denney detected in Drummond's application of natural law to the spiritual world had more far-reaching consequences still. 'Faith in the Atonement - that is faith in a divine goodness which is wounded by human sin, yet outlives the offence, and precisely on the cross reconciles the world to itself - this faith it is that regenerates. And the new life, to call it so, is a stream flowing from the spring of conscious pardon. But is there any analogy to this in the physical world?'[80] The nature of atonement and the experience of forgiveness arise from spiritual principles that have no mirror image in the physical world, they are moral realities that presuppose a moral relationship between God and humanity. Several times Denney inveighs against the moral passivity implied in Drummond's view of human life where 'growth can only be synonymous with a living *automatic* process...for life *must* develop out

---

[77] Ibid., 53. Drummond's work has been called the '"Spencerization" of evangelicalism.... It amounted to an attempt to find a law of continuity connecting the material and spiritual worlds, and was widely interpreted as an underwriting of faith by the latest science. In the long run its opiating strategy contributed significantly to...the naturalization of the supernatural.' This was precisely what Denney feared. David N. Livingstone, 'Situating Evangelical Responses to Evolution', in David Livingstone, D. G. Hart and Mark A. Noll, *Evangelicals and Science in Historical Perspective*, (Oxford: Oxford University Press, 1999), 204. The full impact of Spencer's thought on Drummond is examined in James R., Moore, 'Evangelicals and Evolution. Henry Drummond, Herbert Spencer and the Naturalisation of the Spiritual World', *Scottish Journal of Theology*, 38, 1985, 383-417.

[78] Denney, *On Natural Law*, 32.

[79] Ibid., 47, 42-3.

[80] Ibid., 43.

according to its type; and being a germ of the Christ-life it *must* unfold into *a Christ*.'[81] Even the Incarnation, which Drummond affirmed as 'God making himself accessible to human thought - God opening to man the possibility of correspondence through Jesus Christ'[82], was not safe when natural law was applied to the spiritual world. In response Denney remarked, 'That has something like a Christian sound at last; but it cuts the ground from under Mr Drummond's argument.'[83]

In the light of such serious doctrinal errors Denney drew a drastic conclusion: 'This doctrine destroys the Christian character of God'.[84] Doctrinal deficiencies and the mass appeal of what to Denney were erroneous views, drove his argument throughout. The last sentence is a clever summation of its failings as Denney saw them, 'A book no lover of men will call religious, and no student of theology scientific.'[85]

'Not anything that he said so much as what he did not say'

Denney excelled at one line reviews of other people's work. But this last sentence of his pamphlet is only one of many sharp-edged comments. Why was Denney's treatment of his former teacher's work couched in impolite, if not insulting, tones? Repeatedly Denney gave valid criticism an extra twist: 'this off-hand refutation', 'the argument is refuted, as is usual with Mr Drummond, by an illustration', 'he is surely frightened by a word', 'it is not easy to be patient with such confusions as these', 'the author, I say it without the slightest disrespect, is a biologist', 'as vague as a fourth dimension in space'. This is good knock-about literary sparring, unremarkable in itself except that Drummond was Denney's teacher, recently elevated to Professor. It is hard to imagine Denney savaging the work of Candlish, Lindsay or Bruce in quite the outspoken manner of this anonymous pamphlet.

Is there residual resentment at wasted lecture-time on fanciful scientific theories and geological field-trips to Arran,[86] underlying Denney's deceptively mild observation, 'Beautiful words seem to come so naturally to the writer, that he is sometimes unable to break the charm of them, and see that they are only words, and that the picture they paint is painted in

---

[81] Ibid., 38-9.
[82] Ibid., 54.
[83] Ibid.
[84] Ibid., 46. On pp. 61 and 63 Denney appeals (echoing Bruce?) to the Synoptic Gospels as 'the primary and authentic documents of our Lords teaching...may we not protest with some energy when he tells us that there is no Christianity at all except a mysterious possession by something which Matthew, Mark, and Luke never heard of?'
[85] Denney, *On Natural Law*, 67.
[86] Smith, *Drummond*, 273.

the air'?[87] The suggestion that Bruce encouraged Denney to write, and the similarity between some of Denney's criticisms and Bruce's emphases, may have encouraged a more cavalier approach.[88]

Perhaps Drummond personified a number of issues facing Denney at this time. By the time *Natural Law in the Spiritual World* was published, Denney was finished college, coping with the disappointment of not getting the job he wanted in Calcutta, and working as missioner in East Hill Street. At the same time Drummond, only five years Denney's senior, was in Possilpark, in great demand as an evangelist and celebrated author, and, with far inferior qualifications,[89] holding a lectureship about to be upgraded to a full professorial chair.

The second wave of Moody-Sankey revival meetings took place in 1882 and Drummond commented to his friend Robert Barbour, 'I have got a few students to come to the inquiry room, but the attitude of the College as a whole is largely one of simple tolerance.'[90] What was Denney's attitude? An early sermon entitled 'He was a good man', preached at the Hill Street mission, indicates Denney looked on Moody-style evangelism with a mixture of intellectual disdain and grudging admiration. The sermon refers to mass evangelistic campaigns of the kind in which Drummond took a leading part.

> Evangelistic meetings, and other unlicensed church agencies, are repugnant to many for reasons of various sorts. They sometimes keep rather questionable hours; they often adopt very questionable methods of working people up into an excited and impressionable condition; sometimes their catchwords embody very questionable doctrine. But the characteristic of the good man is, that while he is not insensible to these drawbacks, he can see the grace of God thro' them if it is really there. He has faith in the power of goodness to work off these crudities, to correct all distempered extravagance and to shape for itself a glorious body after its own kind. And instead of indulging in cynical criticism of an evangelist who makes light of grammar, and is guileless of moral philosophy, or it may be even of common sense, he rejoices at the sight of God's working and joins in it himself, heart and hand.[91]

So while Drummond's evangelistic activities might have raised the students' eyebrows, Denney adopted a more Gamaliel-like attitude, giving

---

[87] Denney, *On Natural Law*, 6.

[88] Walker, *Denney*, 37. Bruce offered his own criticisms in 1886 in *The Miraculous Element in the Gospels*, (London, 1886), 44, 70-8.

[89] Drummond never completed his Edinburgh Arts degree. Smith, *Drummond*, 30, 43.

[90] Ibid., 134.

[91] DEN05-49, 5. The impact of Moody's campaigns on religious thought and practice in Scotland will be considered further in the next chapter in relation to Denney's own mission work.

the benefit of the doubt lest unwittingly, however improbably, he obstruct the working of God.

Denney's own explanation for his treatment of Drummond is full of interest. Denney was impatient with bad science and suspicious of mysticism.[92] In Henry Drummond's personality love of science and mystical experience fused into a winning evangelistic combination. The two men stood at opposite ends of the temperamental spectrum, a fact recognised by Denney later in life. On Drummond's death in March 1897 he wrote to Robertson Nicoll concerning the fascination Drummond had over others:

> One felt as if an advantage were being taken of his mind by a power not of the nature of reason and [I] was irritated by it. At least I felt so, and I daresay when I criticised 'Natural Law in the Spiritual World' a good while afterwards I allowed this kind of irritation too free expression. I am sorry now when I think of it, for Drummond was the most gentle and generous of men, and it must have been to him inexplicably and gratuitously rude.[93]

But it is Denney's next sentence that makes most sense of his irritation and of the inability of the two men to think in the same way about Christianity. 'Probably what riled me...was not anything that he said so much as what he did not say - the airy way in which he seemed to do without all that to common Christianity was indispensable. He approached the subject so disinterestedly, with such an entire disregard of its one presupposition - sin - that it was impossible to get upon common ground with him.'[94] On receipt of Simpson's biography four years later he wrote:

> [I am] more interested in Drummond at the moment than ever I was before. You make one who somehow never appreciated him feel how much he lost – I don't know how it was, but he and I seemed always to look at things through opposite ends of the telescope, but I always did admire *The Ascent of Man*...not for the science of it, which I could not appreciate at all, but for the intuition and inspiration of it. He had divined at last what we need if we are to hold anything else than a materialistic philosophy, namely, that the highest thing must be at the very foundation of the world. They called his first book Calvinistic, and so in a way it was, bad Calvinism with its double decree of election and reprobation. But this last one was the genuine Calvinism which makes the redeeming love of God the alpha and the omega, the ultimate reality on which the universe rests, and which in ways we cannot divine must be working through it all. That there is one ray of this celestial light all

---

[92] W. M. Macgregor, recalls Denney saying 'a Mystic is simply a daft man.', in *Persons and Ideals*, (Edinburgh : T & T Clark, 1939) 17. In Denney's class note-book the list of Lindsay's lectures on pre-Reformation mystics is decorated by the word 'Wearisome' in large elaborate script. Den12-01.

[93] Darlow, *Nicoll*, 155.

[94] Ibid.

through the Ascent of Man is the glory of it, and of the writer as a Christian thinker.[95]

The mind of Denney only later appreciated what Drummond was trying to do. *Natural Law* may have been a flawed attempt at bringing modern science and Christian doctrine into a creative, mutually informing dialogue. But that the attempt had to be made, and that Drummond succeeded in putting the issue on the agenda of the thinking elite,[96] is to Drummond's lasting credit. Denney concedes as much. In his teaching years Denney would wrestle with the issue, it would appear in book reviews,[97] inform his thinking about ministerial training,[98] and be a subject of discussion with colleagues such as Orr.

In 1883 Denney graduated from the Free Church College in Glasgow. Judging from the confidence and competence of his first publication he had integrated and brought under control considerable reserves of knowledge. Whether consciously or not, he had been exposed to influences which broadened and opened his understanding of what Christian truth is and requires. His future handling of Scripture, as minister and professor, was decisively shaped by the events and influences of these four years. When later he succeeded Bruce to the New Testament chair, he would do so with a mind thinking different thoughts from Bruce on many core issues, but thinking them with a level of intellectual integrity and with a freedom of thought in relation to Scripture which owed much to his teachers.

---

[95] *LFF*, 109-110.

[96] Bebbington, 'Henry Drummond, Evangelicalism and Science', in Corts, *Perpetual Benediction*, 29. Bebbington places Drummond in the intellectual context of Romanticism, 'the currents of thought reacting against the Enlightenment of the previous century.' See pp. 33-6. His comment that for Drummond the Romantic, the leading human faculty is not 'as had been supposed in the past, the faculty of reason; instead it is imagination' provides a further example of why Drummond and Denney failed in the meeting of minds. See also Cheyne, *Studies*, 'The Religious World of Henry Drummond', 185-198.

[97] *LWRN*, 83, 205, 235. There is an intriguing pencil note in DEN-07-157, a Communion Address on love in 1 John; 'contrast Darwin and Drummond'. Almost certainly a reference to Drummond's *Ascent of Man* with its theme of altruism as self-giving for the survival for others.

[98] *LFF*, 160.

CHAPTER 5

Hill Street and Broughty Ferry, 1883-1897

On 16 May 1883, Denney was licensed 'to preach the Gospel of Christ, and exercise his gifts as a Probationer for the Holy Ministry'.[1] Having been unsuccessful in gaining appointment to a teaching position in the Mission College at Calcutta,[2] Denney was looking for work. When Free St John's, Galsgow, were seeking a new missioner for Hill Street, Gallowgate, the Eastern Young Men's Religious Society wrote to the Deacons, suggesting 'from experience of his abilities that Mr Denney would be particularly suitable for Missionary and would do much to promote the general interests and usefulness of their society'.[3]

When Denney began work in July 1883,[4] responsibilities included assisting the minister with preaching in St John's, regular preaching to the mission congregation, visitation evangelism in the mission district, overseeing the Sabbath School and supervising other work within the mission premises, for which he received £130 p.a.[5] Hill Street was one of a number of Free Church congregational missions in Glasgow, part of an evolving but failing strategy intended to 'assert church influence in an industrialising economy against a predominantly urbanised population'.[6] The phrase accurately described Glasgow in the 1880s.

---

[1] Minutes of Free Presbytery of Greenock, CH3/166/4, 470, 475-6.

[2] There was an urgent need for a missionary professor at the Duff College Calcutta. Rev. W. McCulloch, 'a brilliant student', was appointed in March 1883. *Free Church Monthly and Missionary Record*, 1883, 75.

[3] *Session and Deacons' Minutes of St John's Free Church of Scotland*, Glasgow, CH3/1162/3, 163.

[4] *LFF*, 31.

[5] *Minutes St John's Free Church*, CH3/1162/8, 149. Abstract accounts for 1883-4 show Denney's pay was made up of £17/3/4d from Mission income, £19/3/4d from Home Mission funds and £15 from the Ferguson Bequest; the balance made up by St John's. He also received most of the £23/15/- paid in Pulpit Supply that year.

[6] Keith Campbell, 'The Free Church of Scotland and the Territorial Ideal', (PhD, Edinburgh, 1999), 1. Campbell covers the theological rationale, social impact and historic significance of territorial missions. See *Memorials of St. John's Congregation, Glasgow*, (Glasgow, 1871), 45-9, for the origins and educational role of 'St. John's Local Mission'.

In 1867, the year after the City Improvement Act was passed, Dougall MaColl commented in the narrative account of his mission work in socially deprived areas of Glasgow,

> I look upon [city improvement] as one of the larger results of the Christian work carried on in this city during the last 50 years....In healthier streets, better dwellings for the poor, in the abundant supply of fine water from Loch Katrine, in open parks and free libraries, in a wider application of our advancing sanitary science, in a deepening sympathy of one class of the community for the other, in enlarged efforts for universal and superior education, in the larger co-operation of earnest men and women not merely for their own things, but also for the things of others, I see the elements on which the Gospel can seize to work out another and a better life for our great cities.[7]

These aspirations summarise the social needs and civic goals of mid-Victorian Glasgow.[8]

'Some good must come from these meetings'

During Denney's time in Hill Street Mission he lived in lodgings in Grafton Place, developing friendships with the minister, John Carroll, and his elder John Salmon, an architect who believed improving the city infrastructure might prevent social problems fuelling social unrest.[9] The weekly programme in Hill Street was fairly typical. Activities in congregational missions included district visiting using a band of co-ordinated lay visitors, Sunday school, day, evening and industrial training classes, savings banks, libraries, lectures in popular science and clothing societies.[10] Evangelism and church extension fuelled busy programmes of contact with, and facility provision for, the local population, but as congregational missions gradually took on the aspect of extension churches they reflected the gathered church model rather than the territorial.

The problem of retaining existing members and adherents dominated Free Church thinking throughout the 1870s and 1880s.[11] The search for

---

[7] Dougall MaColl, *Among the Masses. Work in the Wynds*, (London, 1867), 350-1.

[8] See the encyclopaedic study by W. Hamish Fraser and Irene Maver, *Glasgow. Volume II:1830-1912*, (Manchester: Manchester University Press, 1996).

[9] Walker, *Denney*, 37. Fraser and Maver, *Glasgow*, 491.

[10] Stewart J. Brown, 'Thomas Chalmers and the Communal Ideal in Victorian Scotland', in *Victorian Values*, Proceedings of the British Academy, 78, (Oxford: Oxford University Press, 1992), 61-80; Charles D. Cashdollar, *A Spiritual Home. Life in British and American Reformed Congregations, 1830-1915*, (Pennsylvania: Pennsylvania State University Press, 2000), 124-50.

[11] *PDGAFCS* (1878), Appendix XX, Report of Committee on the State of Religion and Morals. *PDGAFCS*, (1880), Appendix III.; *PDGAFCS*, (1882), Appendix, XX.

a strategy to stem the slow haemorrhage of existing members diverted energy and resources from more overtly evangelistic efforts to win new converts. Repeated calls for new programmes of church extension co-existed with the difficult reality that the church was struggling to hold on to those already reached. The centenary celebrations of the birth of Chalmers in 1880 evoked calls for renewed commitment to territorial missions, despite the financial problems congregational mission initiatives created for the denomination.[12] By 1879 the Home Mission Committee was subsidising 100 congregational missions at a cost of £2,507. In 1868, when congregational missions were introduced, it had been stated that not more than £500 of the Home Mission budget should be allocated to subsidise them.[13]

At a time of increased social mobility existing social networks dissolved and re-formed, but many migrants did not join the church in the area to which they moved. In particular, rural migrants commonly lapsed in the more anonymous city environment. Other factors blamed for lapsing included poverty, intemperance, poor housing and under provision of churches.[14] In expanding cities like Glasgow more pressure was put on congregational missions by the rise of new suburban communities linked to the city centre by a rapidly improving public transport system. Since this enabled the middle classes to live outside the city centre, the Free Church opted to build new churches in new areas rather than risk members not travelling to the older churches nearer the more densely populated city centre. This effectively transferred crucial resources of leadership personnel and finance to new housing developments, weakening city centre congregations, many of which supported congregational missions. A further result was the loss of contact between those who lived in poorer working class districts and the upwardly and geographically mobile middle classes. Residential segregation would eventually create a damaging social ignorance, the one half not knowing how the other half lived.[15]

Coinciding with significant social changes, economic factors played a part in shaping and limiting church mission policy. The recessions of the 1880s forced the Glasgow Council to initiate special relief operations from 1884-1887.[16] In response to the social and human problems the Council became more interventionist. A programme of building affordable, habitable housing was put into operation, public baths and wash-houses were built, and in 1881 it was decreed all hospital patients

---

[12] *Free Church of Scotland Monthly Record*, 1 July 1880, 173.
[13] Campbell, *Territorial Ideal*, 244.
[14] Ibid., 182ff.
[15] Fraser and Maver, *Glasgow*, 419.
[16] R. A. Cage, *The Working Class in Glasgow c.1750-c.1914*, (London: Croom Helm, 1987).

should be treated free of charge.[17] Such measures gradually shifted responsibility for social improvement, and the resources to achieve them, from voluntary groups to local government.[18]

The 1872 Education Act reduced the educational role of the churches in mission charges. Increased leisure and the provision of facilities for recreation pushed the churches further down the list of options for those looking for interesting ways of spending time off work. The regulation of working hours, an increased margin of disposable income, less physically exhausting work, the growth of spectator sports, provision of municipal parks and gardens, and improving public transport, all conspired to provide those who could afford it, with new life possibilities.

At a less tangible level the impact of Moody revivalism with large well-organised, widely publicised and packed meetings, modelling successful ecumenical co-operation and boasting a strong link with temperance, provided a glamorous and apparently more successful model for evangelising the masses. Such techniques as the free breakfasts at the Tent on Glasgow Green, which peaked at 2,000, gave public evidence of people being 'reached'. Crowded meetings, with big personalities and high entertainment value though successful, by that same success eroded confidence in territorial, grass-roots, locally specific and small-scale day to day mission work. Inevitably a more emotionally warm and theologically inclusive gospel, combined with a spirit of ecumenical co-operation, impressed many students and ministers, visible success converting them to a more pragmatic theology of mission. A broader Gospel message provided a more democratic and egalitarian form of personal spiritual experience and public religious affiliation. 'The use of revival experience in formulating atonement theology was a general feature of Scottish theology in the period [1845-1920].'[19]

It is against the background of a growing city with a strong but unpredictable economy, and of a denomination struggling to find an effective mission strategy during times of theological and cultural shift, that Denney began work at Hill Street. The Session minutes record regular increases in membership. At each communion during his two years of work in the Gallowgate, Denney presented the names of those applying for membership on their profession of faith, or by certificate of transfer. On every occasion the numbers were in double figures; these were people 'he had met with...several times, as well as at the meetings,

---

[17] Fraser and Maver, *Glasgow*, 321-5, 367.

[18] See Ibid, the chapters on 'The social problems of the city' and 'Tackling the problems', 352-441. These detail the transition from voluntary to interventionist policies.

[19] Malcolm Kinnear, 'Scottish New Testament Scholarship and the Atonement, 1845-1920', (Edinburgh PhD, 1996). 349; Coffey, 'Democracy and Popular Religion', 104-5.

and found all to have an intelligent understanding of the solemn step they contemplated'.[20]

A report in 1883 from the Hill Street management committee to the Session describes weekly life at the mission:

> The Committee consists of 28 members drawn from those attending the meetings of whom 8 are office-bearers who also form the Finance Committee to attend to the church door collection. The Mission district is divided into sections and each member has his own section to visit and report on. The meetings are well attended, the average number present being 202. Each Thursday we have a Musical Entertainment before the Lecture. There is also a Reading Room with Draught Boards, which is largely taken advantage of. We have also two special Sunday lectures in the evening, one by Rev Mr Carroll and the other by Rev Mr Denney and we feel sure that some good must result from the meetings.[21]

Denney experienced the characteristic tensions of congregational life in a late-Victorian Reformed context;[22] the diplomatic tip-toeing required to introduce an organ and professional singers,[23] money for new church hymnals,[24] collisions with another church about a suggestion the Mission should move further down the Gallowgate to a more needy area,[25] and bookings and security for the let of the hall to the Mizpah Band. While there was widespread uncertainty about the future of church mission extension, apparently Hill Street was still an active and well supported cause in the early 1880s.

Around thirty of Denney's sermons can be dated to 1883-85. Read in chronological order, noting theme and audience, there are discernible traces of a mind in transition from academy to mission hall congregation. In these years Denney embarked on a process of theological ownership, the construction of a theology fitted to his own mind and conscience, meeting the requirements of intellect, temperament, and the implicates of his own spiritual, moral and pastoral experience.

Robertson Nicoll suggested Denney passed through a brief period of 'Broad Churchism' and was 'led into a more pronounced evangelical creed' by his wife.[26] A study of the early sermons proves inconclusive.[27] There are sermons in which his interpretation of the Kingdom of God, his

---

[20] St John's Free Session Minutes, CH3/1162/3, 198-9.

[21] Ibid., 174.

[22] See Cashdollar, *Spiritual Home*, a richly textured account of life in British and American Reformed congregations from 1830-1915.

[23] CH3/1162/3, 216.

[24] St John's Free Deacons' Court Minutes, CH3/1162/8, 161.

[25] CH3/1162/3, 217.

[26] *LWRN*, xv-xvi.

[27] Denney's review of Drummond's *Natural Law*, from this period, is equally difficult to place on the sliding scale of theological opinion.

view of grace, and even his view of the cross, can be construed as moralistic and liberal. But equally there are sermons in which the moral psychology of sin, the meaning of God's love and the necessity and finality of an objective atonement, are expounded with an evangelical power equal to some of his best mature writing. The following review of his Hill Street preaching considers theological content, contextual references and homiletic technique.

Theological Content

A preacher's theological stance cannot be fairly determined on the basis of one sermon, or extrapolated paragraphs. Over two years Denney preached and lectured in Hill Street, his theological style developing through regular public articulation. One obvious theme to consider in the light of his later theology is his early treatment of the atonement. A sermon on Romans 6.14, dated January 1885, follows the traditional line of the Law as a remorseless but necessary accuser which reveals sin but cannot redeem, 'it has great power to stimulate sin, but none to generate righteousness'.[28] By contrast grace is 'unmerited love', 'the deep and primary relation between God and man'. Two homiletic applications surprise those familiar with the later Denney. The first describes an organic view of spiritual life. '[Men's] strength as moral creatures is to lay their nature open to all divine influences, as the plant spreads its leaves to air and sun and rain. But is this what men do?... Instead of recognising the truth, that they are dependent by nature, or if you like naturally under grace, they set up a false kind of independence of their own.'[29] Nowhere in this sermon is pardon linked to the cross. Instead, in a closing passage, Denney expounded a subjective exemplary view of forgiveness:

> Grace...gives life only because it supplies a new motive in the knowledge of God's love as revealed in the death of Jesus Christ. And if there is a man to whom that awful and tender revelation does not appeal, it gives no life to him, and he has added this to all his other sins. God does not save men by main force, plucking them out of the fire whether they will or no; but he shows us his infinite goodness, he comes to meet us with his mercy even in our sin; he proclaims anew the truth of man's creation that all his life is of God...and when all that is done the solemn responsibility is laid on man of believing the witness God has given of himself...in preaching to sinful men we preach grace,...the mercy that pardons is not something they have to work for, but something that comes to meet them and gives them strength to work; assuring them that Love is God's First and Last name....[30]

---

[28] DEN06-07C, 'Not under law but under grace', 3.
[29] Ibid., 5.
[30] Ibid., 7.

The cross is here reduced to being an illustration of God's love. Near the end of his life, in a comment on Moberley's *Atonement and Personality*, Denney stated what he thought the theological weakness of a subjective view of the atonement: 'No matter how potent the Passion of Christ may be as a motive to reproduce in us its own characteristic moral qualities, the Christian attitude to it is not that of repeating it; it is that of depending on it, believing in it, trusting it to the uttermost'.[31] In 1893, in a more outspoken comment to Nicoll on Rashdall's 'Abelardism', Denney expressed vividly the theological rationale for sin, penalty and substitution as the apostolic substructure of the doctrine of atonement: 'A martyrdom in plain English, no matter how holy and loving the martyr, is an irrelevance. There is a fascinating way of preaching Abelardism, but as a fisher-evangelist once said to me, to preach it is like fishing with a barbless hook; your bait is taken but you don't catch men'.[32]

Several other sermons deal substantially with Denney's view of salvation and atonement,[33] but his last sermon at Hill Street, in June 1885, was on Colossians 2.10 and is of particular interest. Speaking of the fullness of God in Christ he focused on holiness as God's primary attribute. In Jesus Christ, God's holiness is revealed as 'an all searching, all-penetrating light', 'an infinite holiness to which all sin is an infinite affront.'[34] But it is a merciful holiness, revealed in Christ's life and death, the source of 'a love which forbids the guiltiest to despair...higher than heaven and deeper than hell'. Therefore 'a Christian can never go outside Christ for his religion':

> There are many who try to think of reconciliation to God, of acceptance with God, of life in God's favour, as a thing which comes to them without ado; they say we have sinned, no doubt, but God is gracious...that is true, but not all the truth...it hides from those who speak so the unspeakable sacrifice, at the cost of which God's pardoning and reconciling love comes to mankind...there is a great mystery in the atonement, there is abundant room for raising hard questions even about the morality of it; but if we are to hear Christ and the apostles and let the NT be the rule of our religion, there is no doubt about the fact of it...it is a fact accomplished. Christ came to do this very thing for us.[35]

For the remainder of the sermon Denney expounded the holiness of the reconciled heart, moving towards the climax by way of a rare

---

[31] James Denney, *The Christian Doctrine of Reconciliation*, (London: Hodder & Stoughton, 1917), 284.
[32] *LWRN*, 2.
[33] DEN06-76, 'This do in Remembrance'; DEN04-251, 'It is expedient for you'; DEN03-55, 'They that make them are like unto them'; DEN07-138, 'Be clothed with humility'.
[34] DEN07-27, 'In Him dwelleth'.
[35] Ibid., 4.

autobiographical passage which, as a rhetorical device, carries a powerful emotional payload:

> I felt constrained on this last occasion on which I could [speak to you] rather to present in one view the fullness of that Gospel which I came here to preach.... Everyone will make mistakes at times, even with the honestest intentions, and no doubt I have sometimes missed the truth, sometimes disguised it in foolish words, sometimes confused it with explanations, sometimes corrupted its simplicity by reasoning about it...but I would not address you for the last time on anything but what is fundamental in the gospel, and in the plainest words.[36]

In the plainest words, 'it is the death of Christ which is the life of the Church. There is no gift of the Spirit until He is glorified, and He is glorified on the cross.... Atonement must precede regeneration.'[37]

Whatever development can be traced in these early sermons, there is no evident chronological pattern. Rather than theological ambiguity, what these sermons reveal is a theology in the making, as Denney's preaching compelled an integration of his spiritual experience, formal education and pastoral responsibilities. For example one wonders if Bruce is in the background when he lectured on miracles and concluded 'faith in the incarnation is rather the cause, than the effect, of faith in miracles'; or that miracles are 'signs of a present redeeming power whose real mode of operation was to regenerate the spirit within by bringing it into sympathy with the Redeemer himself, and then working from the centre to renew the whole round of life.'[38]

Again, while such sentiments suggest a softer theology, several other passages describe the tragedy of sin, and the moral psychology of human accountability in terms that would not significantly change in Denney's later thought. 'Forgiveness is not impunity.... You think your sin once done is dead and buried, and that you are clear of it forever. But it is not a lifeless corpse: it is a living seed which will spring up and bear fruit on which you must feed...no repentance enables a man to shirk the consequences of wrongdoing...or stop God's mouth when he comes to judgement.'[39] In one sense this sermon never gets out of Romans 1, with its litany of reasons for human guilt. The role of conscience as the inner

---

[36] Ibid., 6.

[37] DEN04-251, ' It is expedient for you', 2-4.Yet in DEN04-223, a sermon on John the Baptist two years earlier in 1883, the view of the Kingdom of God echoes the Ritschlian liberal view, 'a spiritual kingdom in human hearts.' 2.

[38] DEN04-175, 'The Gospel Miracles'.

[39] DEN03-31, '*Haec fecisti et tacui*', 6. On moral accountability see especially DEN04-132, 'The Strong man'. This sermon on the devil, temptation and the experience of moral captivity is reminiscent of C. S. Lewis in its spiritual subtlety. This is thought-provoking, complacency-smashing, morally interrogative preaching, remarkable in such an inexperienced minister.

monitor of all moral experience, and as the conduit for God's voice convicting human sin and convincing of divine righteousness, is already being established as a fundamental principle informing all Denney's later dogmatic and pastoral theology.

Contextual References

In several passages Denney describes pastoral care with the vividness of one newly engaged in it. Whether care took the form of poor relief, moral guidance or spiritual concern, resistance and resentment was easily provoked by the wrong attitude: 'the smallest suspicion of patronage, of condescension or self complacency in his would-be benefactor shuts the door against him, and it is right that it should...[the carer's] despondency is disappointed vanity, and the only good they have done is...the awakened spirit of honest independence that refused to cater to their humour.'[40] Much of Denney's time would be spent in the homes of people whose poverty, housing conditions, or state of health raised concern. Gallowgate in the 1880s was overcrowded, populated by workers in the nearby heavy engineering works, and lacking many basic amenities taken for granted in the newer parts of an expanding city.[41] In his preaching he outspokenly criticised bad housing and its effect on childhood development. 'Who are the chief sufferers by the neglect in ordinary life of the means of keeping life vigorous? Are they not the children...It is pitiable to see the children of the poor who have lived with the conditions of life against them for generations, and who, if they grow up, will transmit their weakness weakened further still to a new race of miserables.' Perhaps recalling cholera and typhus outbreaks during his childhood in Greenock, he continued, 'people who have lived in bad air, eaten unwholesome food, drunk impure water and been careless about cleanliness are swept away in their tens of thousands as when cholera first came to our country...'.[42]

Within a month of his appointment he lamented the 'relaxation of the bonds of family life',[43] and impressed the need for the amelioration of social problems, but in ways that supported rather than supplanted attitudes of self-help and independence. A sermon on 'The patient continuance of well doing' urged Christians to love their needy neighbours, 'to spend and be spent in the teeth of all discouragement'

---

[40] DEN06-02, 'Patient continuing in well-doing', 6.
[41] The collapse of the Glasgow bank in 1878 halted redevelopment of slum housing in areas like Gallowgate, where poverty was endemic. See Fraser and Maver, *Glasgow*, 21, 33, 122, 164.
[42] DEN03-03, 2-3, 'Meaning of Suffering'.
[43] DEN01-44, 'God's revelation of Himself', 7.

and to shrink from 'the impiety which seeks in successful work the ground of self-glorification'.[44]

Addressing social problems such as bad housing, unemployment, crime and drunkenness, Denney was no sentimentalist. Rejecting the growing fashion to take mitigating circumstances such as environment and upbringing into account, he scorned the tendency to more lenient sentencing of criminals. 'I do not doubt that much of the odious tenderness for criminals, which the just severity of the law so regularly excites, is due to neglecting this truth (that by God kings reign and princes decree), and to the foolish fancy that the world is to be ruled as a weak father misrules a weak family.'[45] Denney's lifelong opposition to the drinks trade drew significantly on his experiences of misery in the working-class homes off the Gallowgate.[46]

Religious issues were also subjected to Denney's uncompromising approach. An oblique reference to Moody-style evangelistic meetings has already been noted in connection with Drummond. Another comment from October 1883 conveys the same disdain of the objective spectator. 'We have had opportunity enough to see in the religious experience of our own country in recent years that there is a natural human excitement in spiritual work on a large scale, an excitement in which a man may share without feeling anything repulsive, even although he is far from gaining a permanent spiritual benefit.'[47]

He alternately praised and scorned Roman Catholic faith and practice. A history lesson laced with strictures on monasticism as an unbalanced view of life nowhere commended in the Bible passed for an entire sermon.[48] On the other hand, while strongly rejecting the Roman Catholic doctrine of the Church and the Sacraments, he commended the stability and spiritual authority that a strong doctrine of the Church and faithful regular partaking of the Sacraments instils.[49] This whole sermon against the sectarian spirit makes remarkable reading and must have been provocative to hear in a Free Church Mission in East-End Glasgow. Not only did he quote Roman hymns, and use Catholic sacramental seriousness to rebuke his own Communion's occasional observances, but

---

[44] DEN06-02, 'Patient continuance', 5. On Denney's opinions about other problems see DEN03-03, 'Meaning of suffering' (housing); DEN03-31, 'Haec fecisti et tacui' (black slavery). DEN 06-102, 'Bear one another's burdens', is an important example of late Victorian ambivalence about government intervention on health care, unemployment benefit and housing improvements.

[45] DEN03-55, 'They that make them are like unto them', 6.

[46] The links between unemployment, poverty, bad housing and drunkenness are described in Fraser and Maver, *Glasgow*, 394ff.

[47] DEN04-223, 'He was a burning and a shining light', 2.

[48] DEN04-150, 'He that is faithful'.

[49] DEN06-67, Let no man glory in men'.

he gave early evidence of resistance to credal subscription and imposed standards in the interests of a Christocentric spirituality. He warned:

> You must not let [men] limit the infinite truth of God into propositions numbered in a catechism, nor cut off your Christian liberty by any rail fence of use and wont. You must not subscribe any creed or attach yourself to any party, as though one or the other had the exclusive and perfect apprehension of the faith and Christian morality...openness of mind and willingness to recognise and assimilate new truth is a duty and one that is often disowned and still oftener neglected. A deep-seated slothfulness of intellect which makes us disinclined to examine our thoughts or enter into communication with others is a sin...'[50]

The remainder is a courageous apologia for Christian liberty based on the gospel principle 'all things are yours and you are Christ's'. Here, as often in the coming years, Denney explicitly championed spiritual and intellectual freedom exercised within the parameters of the apostolic gospel, centred on Christ-crucified and risen. Indeed the last few sentences are so rhetorically forceful, one wonders what created such a powerful homiletic head of steam.

> Qualify, qualify is the cry of the cautious moraliser.... But it is characteristic of all deeply religious men, and pre-eminently of Paul, not to qualify.... Remember the Christ of God is no fiction. His life was a true and perfect human life. It appropriated all human experience; it turned it all to account; it consecrated it all to God. Remember that you are His; and that all that He conquered is yours. Do not disinherit yourself in timidity or sloth; do not be afraid to go in and possess the land. Walk through it in the length thereof and in the breadth thereof...do not say to yourself all this should be mine; say rather all this is mine. All this God has given me to inherit; and no sectarian blindness, no mental sloth, no moral cowardice shall keep me from enjoying his unspeakable gift.[51]

Four years after Robertson Smith's removal, and almost a decade before the Free Church passed the Declaratory Act, Denney had arrived at a position from which he would not significantly move. Intellectual freedom to explore the Gospel was for Denney a constituent part of spiritual integrity and a *sine qua non* of New Testament Christianity.

Homiletic Technique

> The Greek word which is translated 'good' in this verse and which occurs just more than a hundred times (103 in Hudson's concordance)...had a long and interesting history. It really means 'good of its kind', and the precise shade of meaning to be attached to it has to be determined from the content in which it stands, the

---

[50] Ibid., 6-7.
[51] Ibid., 8-9.

substantive which it is used to qualify and the social environment in which it is applied.[52]

So begins one of Denney's sermons, in East Hill Street, off the Gallowgate, Sunday, 6 January 1884, about 7.30.p.m, in mid winter, in a gas-lit hall, filled with mainly working people. The last person to talk down to a congregation, Denney aimed at lucidity of language, not commonplaces of thought. In any case, many of those attending mission churches lacked educational opportunity rather than intellectual ability.[53] The sermons are laboriously written. After his first Sunday Denney explained why to his lifelong friend, J. P. Struthers of Greenock: 'I had to speak three times, which is rather too much and will not be repeated, but was surprised with a half agreeable and half ominous feeling to find that my tongue hung so loosely...unless I make a science of writing all or almost all that I mean to say, I will degenerate into a pure haverel'.[54]

Lexical information, semantic statistics, references to Latin and Greek poets, Plato, Aristotle and even untranslated Greek script, found their way into his sermon manuscript. Quotations are used sparingly but in one sermon, entitled 'Be clothed with humility', Schleiermacher, Nietzsche and Calvin are quoted,[55] while in others Spurgeon, Bunyan, Liddon and Faber are used to underpin points. In his lecture on miracles he quoted the Gospel of Thomas to illustrate the differences between spurious and authentic accounts,[56] while on the sensitive question of Davidic authorship he was straightforward: Psalm 115 'has all the marks of the period after the exile'.[57] Critical opinions were considered valid sermonic material.

Illustrations, Denney admitted, were his downfall. In Hill Street he used a variety of material. His love of Burns was well known in later life; in one of his first sermons he used the annual Burns Supper as an example of the hero remembered, to illustrate the commemorative basis of the Lord's

---

[52] DEN05-49, 'He was a good man', 1.

[53] Explaining the origins of *Natural Law* as lectures originally given to working men in Possilpark, Drummond wrote: 'I am asked: Were these papers...not above the people?... My conviction grows stronger every day that the masses require and deserve the very best work we have. The crime of evangelism is laziness; and the failure of the average mission church to reach intelligent working men rises from the indolent reiteration of threadbare formulae by teachers often competent enough, who have not first learned to respect their hearers.' Smith, *Drummond*, 147. Denney's work shows he was equally respectful in his assumptions about the intelligence of his audience. It is an important insight into nineteenth century pedagogic practice in urban church mission situations.

[54] *LFF*, 31.

[55] DEN07-138.

[56] DEN04-175, 'The Gospel Miracles, 3.

[57] DEN03-55, 'They that make them', 1.

Supper, a connection which must have caused some consternation.[58] In the same sermon his retelling of the crucifixion is almost Moravian in its graphic intensity, establishing as central, the sacrificial nature of the atonement. The rise and fall of Rome and the brutality of the French Revolution illustrated the judgement of God on paganism,[59] the heartlessness of a Christless God is argued with reference to the history of Unitarianism,[60] and in a style reminiscent of Drummond he used contemporary scientific theory concerning 'perpetual flux' to illustrate spiritual truth.[61]

Biblical narrative and allusion was the material used most comfortably, suggesting his congregation were mostly Christians who would recognise metaphors about rotten fruit, brackish water, fruitless trees and make the connections between stories of prophets and kings and contemporary spiritual experience. The truth is, Denney's mind worked best with ideas. 'I never have an illustration', he confessed to Struthers, '- the analogical faculty seems to be totally lacking. Not totally either, for I can see the force of them, when another man produces them; but overweighted, for I see as promptly when they break down - which is discouraging.'[62]

The importance of this comment for understanding Denney's approach to preaching, and the essential relationship he assumed between persuasive preaching and sound theological exposition, he argued in the same letter to Struthers: 'The prime requisite, I think, in writing is not illustration but lucidity. If your idea is luminous, from within, you don't need to depend for its being visible or intelligible on casual rays of coloured light turned on to it from unexpected quarters.'[63] The significant word is *writing*; whatever notes Denney used in the pulpit, many of his surviving sermons exist in full manuscript and were written with care before preaching.[64] Accounts of Denney's preaching refer to such qualities as 'moral force', 'precision', 'feeling for truth', phrases which describe an effective presentation of ideas rather than a persuasive appeal to emotion. Thus the rhetorical force is often built up through argument, information, the provoking of mind and conscience to assent

---

[58] DEN06-76, 'This do in remembrance', 3.
[59] DEN04-132, 'The Strong man'.
[60] DEN03-55, 'They that make them', 7.
[61] DEN06-71, (untitled), 4.
[62] *LFF*, 36.
[63] *LFF*, 36.
[64] Some sermons, and most Bible studies are written on two or three A5 sheets. A large number of sermons are A4 and vary from five to eight pages. Expository series such as Samuel, Ezra, John, Acts, 1 Corinthians and James are all full manuscript A4. Undated series probably date from Broughty Ferry since they presuppose consecutive Sundays and frequently refer to previous passages. In the cases of Deuteronomy, Ezra and James, this is confirmed in correspondence between Denney and Struthers.

to truth and so bring the will into line in obedient response. Denney's hesitation about revivalist preaching which appealed to emotion, was not only the prejudice of a more restrained personality embarrassed by religious fervour. His preference, temperamentally and technically, was for presenting the Gospel as an appeal to the whole person, mind, conscience, will, and, yes, emotion, but emotion reached and converted through the more durable process of intellectual persuasion, moral conviction and spiritual surrender. For Denney, lucidity in writing precedes luminosity in preaching, and careful thought beforehand is the consecration of words in the service of the Word.

At East Hill Street, his preaching was thoughtful, thin on theological clichés and substantial in content and argument. In the process, his theology took on more definite shape, and he began to make connections between pastoral involvement in people's lives, and the preaching responsibilities that go with an effective cure of souls.

Dundee's Country House

Denney left East Hill St in June 1885. He preached in a number of churches including Troon and Westbourne Kelvinside.[65] When he received the call from Broughty Ferry East Free Church, in February 1886, the Presbytery 'resolved to take the necessary steps for Mr Denney's ordination' and prescribed the ordination trials to be heard at the next ordinary meeting.[66] On 10 March 1886, 'Mr Denney having been examined orally on the prescribed subjects, the Presbytery having taken a conjunct view of the trials, expressed their high satisfaction with the manner in which Mr Denney had acquitted himself'.[67]

Denney was ordained and inducted on 22 March, at the age of 30,[68] the fourth minister of a church formed by a secession 'carried out with great good feeling and success'.[69] Broughty Ferry in 1886 was a suburban retreat known as fashionable Dundee's 'country house', and an increasingly popular holiday town. John Lyon had been minister in the town during its transition from small strategic ferry port to commuter suburb, attractive for its 'pleasant site, fine air and good sea bathing'[70]. Writing in 1884 he recalled,

---

[65] Several sermons contain dates and place of preaching.

[66] *Minutes of the Dundee Presbytery of the Free Church of Scotland*, CH3/91/5, 159.

[67] Ibid., 162.

[68] *Minutes of Dundee Presbytery*, CH3/91/5, 165-66.

[69] John Lyon, *Sketch of the History of the Free Church of Broughty Ferry*, (Broughty Ferry, 1884), 38-41.

[70] 'Broughty Ferry', in *Ordnance Gazetteer,* (Edinburgh: Thomas Jack, 1882), vol. 1, 194.

> The town itself is a contrast to what it was in 1843...There were no pavements or footpaths. But now our streets are all macadamised, and our footpaths covered with clean and beautiful concrete. Forty years ago there were but few good houses in Broughty Ferry, and the inhabitants generally were of the working class – now our good houses are multiplied to an extraordinary extent, and are quite palatial in appearance. During the times of good trade in Dundee, the merchants made liberal fortunes, and part of the wealth of these times found its way to Broughty Ferry....I am happy to be able to say that our churches shared in the abundance that flowed around us, and that our merchant princes are still among the best supporters of our religious schemes.[71]

The population had risen from three and a half thousand in 1861, to five and a half thousand in 1871. During Denney's time the number was around eight thousand and rising.[72] The town itself had a diverse economy of fishermen, labourers, gardeners, weavers, female servants, shopkeepers, slaters, cooks, washerwomen, surgeons, upholsterers, vintners and carters. But it was also a town in transition. For example by 1882 trawlers started fishing in the traditional line-fishing grounds. From 1885 to 1890 the herring bounty fell from £60 per boat to £6, and many traditional fishermen moved to work with the Dundee trawlers.[73] Tourism was becoming an important element in the local economy, stimulating civic amenity improvements such as a band-stand for Sunday concerts, despite Sabbatarian objections, and plans to extend the concrete esplanade as far as the castle.[74] This particular issue provoked invidious comparisons:

> If Broughty Ferry were down the Clyde, there would be a pavilion on the castle green which would be laid out with walks and flowers, and a band would give nightly concerts. The town ought to have its aquarium and public gardens for open air concerts, flirtations and gossip and Broughty Street could be laid out with trees to form a boulevard and pleasant lounge on a hot afternoon.[75]

Many of these changes occurred just before or during the decade Denney lived in Broughty Ferry. East Free had its share of professional and wealthy businessmen. 'I had rich merchants, secretaries of financial companies, schoolmasters, shopkeepers, tradesmen and coachmen in my session, and we were as true a brotherhood in Christ as a minister could wish to have part in.'[76] While Broughty Ferry's growth was due largely to

---

[71] Lyon, *Sketch*, 43-4.
[72] Nancy Davey, *Broughty Ferry. Village to Suburb*, (Dundee: City of Dundee District Council, 1976), 3-5.
[73] Ibid., 12-14.
[74] Ibid., 35-6.
[75] Ibid.
[76] *LWRN*, 107-8.

an influx of the well-off who wanted to escape the noise and smell of the factories, textile prosperity made Dundee a powerful centre of gravity for those seeking work, encouraging a strong migration flow from Angus, Perth, Kinross and Fife.[77]

Details of those who joined the East Free Church in Broughty Ferry during Denney's ministry reflect something of these migration flows. One example from May 1895, shows that the session approved membership applications of people moving from Hawick, Bothwell, Monifeith, Newport, Cupar, Chicago, four from other Free churches in Dundee, three from other churches in Broughty Ferry, and twelve young persons including two recently married couples.[78] Those transferring from Dundee may reflect a continuing trend of upwardly mobile migration, which had been on the increase from mid-century. In 1850 only one of the leading thirty Dundee manufacturers had a residential address in Broughty Ferry; by 1870 eleven of the original thirty had either died or gone out of business, but of the remaining nineteen, seven now lived in Broughty.[79] It was to this kind of economically diverse town, suburban haven of the well-off, popular tourist and day-trippers attraction, a town with three Free churches, two Established Churches, two United Presbyterian, and one each of Baptist and Episcopal, that James Denney came in 1886.

'They had for one another a mutual passion'

On 1 July 1886 Denney married Mary Carmichael Brown. Mary Denney has been subjected to considerable hagiographic treatment in her own right, making it difficult to assess the impact her personality exerted on her husband. Walker wins the prize for the least helpful of a number of non-descriptions of what Mary Denney was actually like. 'Mary Carmichael Brown's memory - a very precious one and too sacred a topic to be written of here - is indeed blessed.'[80]

Robertson Nicoll's suggestion that Mrs Denney encouraged her husband to read Spurgeon and so was instrumental in leading him into a more 'pronounced evangelical creed', is more convincing given the psychological fit of Nicoll's further comment that Denney had been inclined to despise Spurgeon. His condescending comment about

---

[77] S. J. Jones, *Dundee and District*, (Dundee: Dundee Local Executive of the British Association for the Advancement of Science, 1968), gives details of population movements.

[78] *Session and Deacons' Minutes of Broughty Ferry East Free Church of Scotland*, CH3/1156/2, 21-2.

[79] Louise Miskell, Christopher Whatley and Bob Harris, *Victorian Dundee. Image and Realities*, (East Linton: Tuckwell Press, 2000), 65.

[80] Walker, *Denney*, 52.

Moody-style evangelists who 'make light of grammar and are guileless of moral philosophy', makes it credible that Denney may have been less than impressed by a populist preacher whose sermons sold by the thousand every week, and who was a Baptist. Following his visit to America in 1894 he wrote to Struthers, 'There are many things strong which I dislike...Baptist principles, belief in the millennium...and in general the fads of the uneducated and half educated man'.[81]

The intensity of the married relationship evoked comment from a former student; 'she was the possessor of a vigorous native intelligence that made her a worthy partner even in the loftiest reaches of his endeavour; and they had for one another a mutual passion which was beautifully, but not distressingly obvious....'[82] Experience of marriage, coupled with the emotional and relational demands of long-term pastoral care in one congregation, served to humanise the new minister who already had a reputation for shyness verging on aloofness.[83]

During their time at Broughty Ferry, the Denneys holidayed in places like Grantown and Auchterarder, and their capacity for fun is evident in letters to Struthers. 'Grantown is a delightful place for a holiday. It is high enough to dispense you from climbing altogether, if you don't wish to climb, and to give you a decent start if you do...in a fortnight's idleness I fell into the mania for golf, which is pretty bad up there....'[84] A year or two later in Auchterarder, 'a long drawn out and dreary town', he reported. 'Mrs Denney and I have been gaining health and losing our tempers, balls etc. over [the golf course] every morning.'[85] Whether golf, hill-walking on the west coast, frequenting agricultural shows, or foreign travel to Italy, Germany or Switzerland, such activities suggest an appetite for life and enjoyment beyond the intellectual and theological.

Golf, however, did not displace literary and scholarly pursuits. In a lecture to the Broughty Ferry Literary Society, 'Reading, Writing and Speaking', Denney revealed a number of personal likes and dislikes.[86] He told the young men money was better spent on books than 'the soothing tobacco'. He commends Browning as 'perhaps the richest of our poets since Shakespeare', while Scott and Burns he rated as highly as any other English language poet except Shakespeare. Jane Austen he had read only

---

[81] *LFF*, 56. Nevertheless Denney did preach in the Baptist Church at Broughty Ferry during his time in the town.

[82] This comment, almost comic in its fine-drawn sentiment, was made by J. W. Coutts, quoted in Taylor, *Denney*, 28.

[83] CH3/1156/2, 239. Memorial Minute reproduced in this volume as Appendix 4, 239.

[84] *LFF*, 42.

[85] Ibid., 62.

[86] See DEN10-09 for all quotations in this paragraph. See also Denney's article 'The Best Hundred Religious Books', which begins with the discouraging assertion that there aren't a hundred *good* religious books. *BW*, August 30, 1894, 290.

since coming to Dundee. In his younger years he had read through Pope's translation of *The Iliad*, Macaulay's *Historical and Biographical Essays*, and Carlyle's *Sartor Resartus*. Arnold's first series of *Essays on Criticism* he valued greatly but most of his other writings contain 'nothing that is new, and not much more that is true.'[87]

His favourite authors were of the eighteenth century, the neo-classicism of the Augustan age appealing to someone striving for lucidity, precision and a persuasive simplicity in language. He strongly encouraged the reading of Pope, 'if we want to see wit and sense and precision in the use of language, he is the incomparable teacher'. He appreciated the crisp prose of Walpole,[88] Gibbon, and Burke. By far his favourite literary work was Boswell's *Life of Johnson*, a book he read through a number of times. The moral perceptiveness, casually acquired erudition and larger than life humanity of Dr Johnson fascinated a mind like Denney's, classically trained and with highly tuned moral antennae.[89]

Theological reading during the period can be gleaned from various letters, footnotes in his two commentaries,[90] and books he reviewed for *The British Weekly*. In judging the intellectual significance of what Denney read, what is important is less what he read as what he thought of each volume. Mozley's *Essays Historical and Theological*, Jowett's *Life*, Caird's *Gifford Lectures* and Newman's sermons, were all critically dissected. He reviewed Beyschlag's *New Testament Theology* favourably; Andrew Murray's devotional exposition of Hebrews from a Keswick holiness slant, he treated with surprising warmth; the Duke of Argyll's *Philosophy of Belief,* predictably failed to enthuse him; A. B. Bruce's *Synoptic Gospels* he praised with the understandable prejudice of a former student.

One of Mrs Denney's *obiter dicta* shows the strategic importance of the minister's wife acting as honorary shop steward, voicing the grievances of the congregation. 'A man never knows how dull he can be', she warned, 'until he tries to lecture right through one of Paul's Epistles.'[91] The week before their marriage, Denney had begun a course

---

[87] In 1913, the *Glasgow Herald* reported a lecture on 'Johnson in His Own Works', in which Denney spoke incidentally of his enjoyment of Gaskell, the Brontes, Scott, Macaulay and Carlyle, *Glasgow Herlad*, 29 February 1913, 10d. Denney remained most at home with the literature of an earlier age.

[88] His set of Walpole was bought for him as a Christmas present from his wife. It was while purchasing this that the first intimations of her illness were felt.

[89] Unfortunately Denney's lectures on Johnson are not extant. One is reported in the *Glasgow Herald*, 29 February 1908, 10d. The lecture on Johnson was amongst those whose ownership was contested after his death at the Court of Session.

[90] The Notes in *Studies*, reveal familiarity with up to date technical academic theology, much of it German.

[91] Macgregor, *Persons*, 19.

of twenty lectures on First Corinthians lasting till the following summer. Forty lectures on Acts, twenty four on Thessalonians[92] and twenty eight on Second Corinthians followed, creating a substantial corpus of expository material. With numerous other occasional sermons from Paul over the years, even Denney was beginning to wilt, confessing to Struthers, 'I think I have done my duty by Pauline exegesis, and want a little leisure to devote to other aspects of this interesting universe'.[93]

Denney's preaching is a study in itself, made more difficult by a self-confessed act of intellectual barbarism; 'when I left Broughty Ferry I burned nearly all my sermons and was horrified as I did so to see the amount of repetition there was in them.'[94] Fortunately a considerable number survived and it is interesting, if precarious, to speculate why those which did were spared the flames.[95] Of 951 sermons, 26 are from 1883-5, and 65 individual sermons can with confidence be dated to Broughty Ferry. In addition around 200 expository sermons or lectures can be dated within the period. The distinction between the sermon and the lecture was mainly a matter of style; the lecture, or expository discourse, was more didactic but no less Bible-based, less personally applied to the congregation, and usually delivered in the evening.[96] The entire Bible is represented in the corpus, except Ruth, Esther, Ecclesiastes, Song of Solomon, Lamentations, Proverbs and Philemon. There are several series of character studies, an increasingly popular didactic approach in Victorian devotional writing.[97]

'A confession the utterance of which touches the conscience'

Three very different extracts from the early series on First Corinthians reveal the concerns Denney chose to address as a new minister embarking on his first major expository work in a pastoral setting.[98] On 1 Corinthians 11.2-16 he tackled the issue of hats in church:

---

[92] Bible study outlines on A5 sheets survive, the same format as a series of thirty one studies on the Pastorals delivered at the Broughty weekly prayer meeting.

[93] *LFF*, 70-1.

[94] *LWRN*, 190; *LFF*, 53, 96.

[95] Struthers, *Life and Letters*, 171, refers to a series of lectures Denney prepared on Joshua in 1888. None survive. See Appendix 1.

[96] Cashdollar, *Spiritual Home*, 35-40.

[97] See Alexander Whyte's six volume *Bible Characters*, (Edinburgh: Oliphant, 1896-1902). Others such as W. M. Taylor and Alexander MacLaren fuelled the trend.

[98] Since the work in this volume was completed several previously unknown manuscripts have become available and are now deposited in New College Special Collections awaiting incorporation into the catalogue of the Denney Papers. One item is a lecture on First Corinthians 1.26-2.5, dated B.F. 24/10/86, listed in the catalogue as 'Missing', and whose recovery now completes the set. The others are mostly written on

It is easy to make merry over such a discussion and to deride the solemn folly of a man who tried to control the fashionable by arguments that few can understand.... Why should an inspired apostle deliberately sit down, and write a page hard of comprehension on such an absurd question as whether men should keep on their hats in church, or whether women should put theirs off? The answer to such a question must be, that what is apparently frivolous, may be of very real importance, and require a thorough discussion in the light of right principles. For instance, the attitude in which one worships may seem a very little thing, not worth speaking about in a religion purely spiritual; but if a man stands up to pray, or to sing praise to God, with his hands in his trouser pockets it is not a little thing; the posture of ease and negligence says plainly that he who assumes it does not see God and it would not be unworthy of an apostle to animadvert upon it.[99]

For one otherwise open to critical methods, the interpretation makes no concessions to the culturally specific nature of Paul's directions. Twenty years later in a paper on 'The Current Aversion to St Paul', he still maintained the apostle's strictures on cultural accommodation.[100]

On 1 Corinthians 12.1-11, Denney gives further early evidence of a position for which he was to become an outspoken champion. He valued Creeds and Confessions as useful didactic resources, but not as an imposition on the conscience. In any case, credal subscription was an ineffective safeguard of doctrinal orthodoxy. Paul's claim that 'No one can say Jesus is Lord except by the Holy Spirit', drew Denney into a discussion that became central to his later thought.[101]

This passage is a strong plea for a short and simple creed. A creed miscarries completely, and fails to serve any good purpose, when it has no moral impressiveness. Most of the Reformed Churches, our own among the number, have confessions and testimonies of excessive length. They work out a scheme of Christian truth with the minutest details; and even if the result were a body of infallible doctrine, which those who most admire it would never claim, it could not be asserted that no man could say this or that in it without the Holy Ghost. There are plenty of things in an elaborate confession, like that which ministers and elders of our church subscribe, which have no such critical character. A man might say them

---

A5 notepaper, Denney's preferred paper for Bible study notes. These are notes of twelve studies on Hebrews which Denney delivered at Broughty Ferry, probably at the midweek meeting. The manuscripts were previously owned by the Rev. W. P. Gilmour who had been a close friend of the Rev. J. P. Struthers, Denney's good friend. While minister in Greenock, Struthers was in the habit of borrowing Denney's sermons and studies for his own use, and these were probably borrowed during his Greenock ministry, and not returned.

[99] DEN-06-34, 1.

[100] DEN08-84, 5. Denney's conservative temperament is well illustrated by his attitude to women. *LFF*, 191-3; 'St Paul and Women', *BW*, August 24, 1911. See further *LWRN*, 183 and 187, and chapter 6 of this study.

[101] See Denney, *Jesus*, 373-412.

though he had not the Spirit of God; and a man with the Spirit might deny them. They do not appeal to the spiritual nature in any way at all; and they are quite unsuited according to the tenor of the passage before us, to be tests of any kind within the Christian body. What we want in the church is a confession, the utterance of which touches the conscience, and brings he who makes it to a practical recognition in word and deed, of the Supreme Authority of Christ. In a long confession the conscience gets lost among details which never touch it....[102]

The placing of Christ at the centre of Christian faith and devotion, at the centre of the church's life and worship, and at the centre of a redeemed universe, was for Denney the only secure confessional basis. The worshipping heart guides the enquiring mind to such truth as can be understood. Going back to his post-university anxiety about his church's attempts to secure orthodoxy, and the college years when his views on the nature of biblical authority were inextricably linked with his professors' defence of Robertson Smith, and building on convictions about spiritual liberty in Christ contrasted with man-made traditions first articulated publicly in Hill Street, Denney had reached settled convictions about the limits of detailed confessions and creeds.

There was nothing radically novel in what he was saying. Throughout the decade from the close of the Robertson Smith case to the passing of the Declaratory Act, discontent with credal subscription and the imposition of the older doctrinal standards had been building towards crisis. It was to be expected that people of Denney's intellectual calibre would seek to give biblical warrant for a less constrictive approach to faith. The conviction that Christological confession arising out of Christocentric experience, is the only way to preserve the spiritual liberty of the individual, and secure the orthodoxy the church rightly requires, was a position Denney held consistently throughout his mature years.[103] Not that, in Denney's opinion, credal subscription to any standard could ever guarantee orthodoxy. Only a confession morally rooted in the conscience, and evoked by the experience of reconciliation in Christ, can govern the will and give Christian doctrine the only hold that ultimately matters in the believing mind. Nevertheless, Denney sufficiently valued the didactic function of creeds to deliver a major series of lectures on the Apostle's Creed to the Broughty Ferry Congregation.[104]

Denney was passionately protective of the Lord's Supper.[105] A third extract based on Paul's instruction, 'let a man examine himself', explains

---

[102] DEN06-36, 4-5.
[103] The issue was to exercise Denney and the other participants in the talks on Union between the Church of Scotland and the United Free Church from 1908 onwards.
[104] DEN08-16 to DEN08-24.
[105] Examples of Communion sermons, DEN07-177, 'These are they'; DEN04-21, 'A Ransom for Many'; DEN07-157, 'We love because he first loved us'. DEN06-75 to

why he expected communion to be a central experience in Christian devotion.

> Let a man examine himself. Examine himself of what? The context leaves us in no doubt...the intending communicant should say to himself, Do I know what is meant by the bread and wine which I am about to partake? Is it in my mind, is it in my heart, that these are the symbols chosen by Christ himself to keep his dying love in remembrance? Do I feel the infinite importance of that death as he did who ordained the Supper before he died, and ordained it anew from his throne in glory? Do I feel that apart from that death, the revelation of God gives me no assurance of the forgiveness of sins? Do I confess that upon it is founded the New Covenant of grace, in which I draw near to God as a child reconciled to his father? If I do so, if I approach the holy table, penitent, truly adoring, affectionately dwelling upon the love with which Christ has loved me who gave himself for me, then, though I am unworthy to communicate; I do not communicate unworthily.[106]

Amongst the pastoral problems regularly discussed by the Session was a concern, voiced early on by Denney himself, that the Supper was not as well attended as it ought to be, and an assumption that non-attendance implied an undervaluing of the ordinance which was interpreted as spiritual indifference. One year after his induction, Denney complained that only three out of four members regularly communicate, lamenting 'the comparably small number who availed themselves of the privilege of being present at the Sacrament'.[107] The Session noted the concern, and by 1889 prayer meetings were organised for every week-day evening before the Communion preparatory service on Friday, 'in an endeavour to awaken more interest in this solemn service'. At the next communion two hundred of the three hundred and three members attended, only 66% compared to the 75% of the previous year![108] Communion sermons from the Broughty years provide significant examples of Denney's theology taking a pastoral and cruciform shape. However, in his lecture on 'The Passion of the Son', part of the series on the Apostle's Creed, Denney pinned down, with precision and passion, what he considered the crux of the apostolic gospel, in the process demonstrating why a high view of the Lord's Supper was integral to his pastoral theology.

> I feel the vital importance of this truth for Christian faith and life...Christ died for our sins according to the Scriptures... The Cross is in the foreground of the

---

DEN06-79, expound Paul's *locus classicus* in 1 Corinthians 11. See further Denney, *Jesus*, 356-66; Denney, *Death*, 134ff; DEN09-23-10, 'Practical Theology Lectures: Sacraments'; DEN11-13, 'Duties of Church Members'. Cashdollar, *Spiritual Home*, 45-55, gives an overview of Reformed practice in the period.

[106] DEN06-35, 7. It seems the Session's efforts to stimulate spiritual interest failed.
[107] Broughty Ferry East Free Church Minutes, CH3/1156/1, 292.
[108] Ibid., 302-3.

Apostolic Gospel and it occupies that place, not as a symbol of devotion, but as a refuge of despair. Christ for us- bearing our sin in his own body on the tree, dying that we might not taste death, bearing the hiding of his Father's face that the light might never be withdrawn from us, made sin for us that we might be made the righteousness of God in him. Here is what comes first in the gospel that subdued the world. Once grasp this, and every other truth and duty connected with the passion finds its appropriate place. Though Christ is not crucified with us, but in us, we are crucified with him. His love, (the love which bore our sins), constrains us to identify ourselves with him, to share in his sorrow for sin, his love to men, his faithful obedience to God. The cross that covers sin inspires with sympathy and devotion: but if there be no blotting out of the hand-writing that is against us, where can the new life begin?... What Christian is not ashamed to love Christ so little? And who that is not yet a Christian can refuse his allegiance any longer?[109]

It was that view of the Passion which pushed the communion table centre-stage in Denney's church. Significantly, for years after he left Broughty Ferry, it was Denney who was invited regularly to conduct the Spring Communion.[110]

'Laboriousness as love's characteristic'

The tedium and trials of church life and pastoral issues are all too evident in the Session minutes. Denney was only months settled when the first rumble of thunder was heard in the distance. In November 1886, Alexander Tocher presented a petition in favour of instrumental music. The generic term was preferred to the more provocative 'organ' or 'harmonium'.[111] The resignation of the Precentor cannot be unconnected with the consequent discussion about the theological, diplomatic, liturgical and pastoral fallout that might result from such a controversial innovation.[112] May 1887 found the Session playing for time, announcing financial considerations dictated a delay though the Session agreed in principle. Six months was set as a period of further consideration.[113] On March 7, 1888 'some remarks having been made as to the present condition of the Psalmody and the necessity of taking immediate steps for its improvement, the matter was remitted to the Psalmody Committee to consider and report'.[114]

Six weeks later the Committee brought a unanimous recommendation 'for the introduction of [an] instrument to assist in the Service of Praise.' Voting papers were issued 'to test the feeling of the congregation

---

[109] DEN08-18, 7-8.
[110] CH3/1156/2, 114.
[111] CH3/1156/1, 279.
[112] Ibid., 275.
[113] Ibid., 289.
[114] Ibid., 293.

regarding the introduction of instrumental music at public worship in the church'. The result was 130 for, 15 neutral and 14 against. The Session decided 'Members of Session should call on those members who had voted against the introduction of an instrument in the Service of Praise, ascertain the nature of their objections, and report back as soon as possible'. Following the elders' reports it was minuted, 'only one man...still holds out'. The decision was taken to proceed in consultation with the deacons and 'by this means it was hoped that without causing any ill-feeling, the Psalmody might be placed on a more satisfactory basis'.[115]

Five years later, in 1893, permission was sought for the organist to play over the tune before singing each hymn, a reasonable request at a time when new hymns and hymnbooks were being more widely introduced.[116] The Session could not agree and the matter was dropped. Three years later the deacons asked that the organist play tunes before singing, but the Session did not consider it advisable to take action in the meantime. Six months later the Session gave in and tunes or parts of tunes could thereafter be played over when the organ was in use. In 1897 the organist and choirmaster resigned. In the ensuing discussion notice of motion was presented that 'the new organist be allowed to play voluntaries at least before the service begins.' At the March meeting it was agreed 'voluntaries may only be played while the congregation is assembling', as background music, not as a valid element in worship.[117] The music by stealth approach may indicate Denney's shrewdness, ensuring that proposed changes were swallowed by being introduced in manageable mouthfuls, and at suitable intervals. He had already witnessed in Free St John's in Glasgow, a Kirk Session in serious disagreement over the introduction of professional musicians to train the choir and lead the praise on Sunday evenings.[118]

If a high view of the Lord's Supper, centred on the Cross, and a lengthy process of cautious diplomacy about the theological ambiguities of an organ, represents the sublime and the arguably ridiculous, then adultery in the church brings a salutary reminder that human beings are a complicated mixture of moral ambiguity and spiritual aspiration. In 1894

---

[115] Ibid., 295-7.

[116] CH3/1156/ 2, 11. On hymnal developments generally see Cashdollar, *Spiritual Home*, 82-84. Denney lectured on some of the better known hymn-writers, including Bonar, Cowper, Havergal, Keble, Newman, Watts and Wesley. See DEN08-47 to DEN08-54. He also included 'Praise' in his Practical Theology lectures, DEN09-23-08.

[117] Ibid., 28-31.

[118] CH3/1162/3, 216 and 220. Cashdollar aptly comments, 'The organ question took more than a century to play itself out'. *Spiritual Home*, 85-92. The convoluted negotiations at Broughty Ferry were typical rather than unusual. The saga had lasted throughout Denney's ministry.

the same Alexander Tocher who had petitioned for instrumental music, confessed to adultery and the case was referred to Presbytery who remitted it back to the Session.[119] Mr Tocher 'compeared and after making confession of his sin, and expressing penitence, was suitably addressed by the Moderator [Denney] and suspended from church privileges'. A year later the Session regretfully recorded, 'Mr Tocher had again committed that sin with the same woman'. One of Denney's last acts before leaving Broughty Ferry was to receive Mr Tocher back into full church privileges.[120] Other concerns included discipline over matters of drunkenness and sexual scandals, changing from communion tokens to cards, summer evangelism, complicated changes in election procedures for the eldership, membership roll purges, personality problems in the choir - in short the usual human agenda created by fallible people pursuing the sometimes conflicting goals of personal interests and community integrity.

'Lots of good people, and an extraordinary mass of indifference'

Balancing these matters of church politics and spiritual discipline, there is evidence of Denney's growing happiness and fulfilment in pastoral ministry. He made friends over these years with whom he corresponded for the rest of his life. During his time the church roll grew from 236 in 1886 to 366 in 1897. The Sunday School numbers peaked at 149 during Denney's ministry, and there is a regular place on the Session Agenda, year in and year out, for young communicants seeking membership on profession of faith. In 1893 he had 65 in his Bible class,[121] and the Presbytery return for 1893 showed young people under 5, fifty two; 5-14 years, one hundred and nineteen; and 14-20 years, fifty four.[122] The Denney's had no children, yet those who knew Denney best remarked on his ability to relate to young people. An unpublished letter written to Miss Edith Currie is a playful example of a quite different Denney treating children with humorous affection.[123]

Denney wasn't over-impressed by figures or by appearances. He saw clearly enough the slow but sure drift away from the faith and from the church as an essential component in personal and community life. 'I don't know if this place is more wicked or worldly than others, but though there are lots of good people in it, there is an extraordinary mass

---

[119] CH3/1156/2, 15.
[120] Ibid., 22, 34.
[121] *LFF*, 48.
[122] CH3/1156/1, entry for 7 June.
[123] The letter, dated 1915, is in the possession of the writer. One example of Denney's more serious views on children and church is in DEN08-84, a talk at a children's service.

of indifference.'[124] 'My congregation has been everywhere but in Broughty Ferry',[125] he complained, with the resignation of every minister not yet on holiday, looking at a poor turn-out on a glorious summer day. 'There are people here in my church who would let me say what I liked, because they did not care what I said';[126] a rueful comment by a minister singularly lacking in naiveté.

A request from a member of the Free Church, to all the ministers in the town, that they alter the dates of communion to avoid a clash of dates with the Choral Union Concert, he dubbed a piece of 'thoroughbred unconscious impertinence'.[127] And while many in the town wanted bandstands and boulevards, Denney saw Sabbath day tourism in a less positive light:

> the church [was] full of strange faces in the morning, and the Monifeith Road in the evening. Strangers in church have a weakness for attending to everything but the service. They have to accommodate themselves to a new situation, before they have eyes or ears to spare for the direction of the pulpit....That at least is the most charitable explanation of their behaviour – the only alternatives I can see are the ungrateful one that I am an uninteresting preacher, or the insolent one that they are not accustomed to listen at home. An honest sleep is not so provoking as wide awake listlessness.[128]

But Denney's written sermons make it unlikely he was uninteresting. Eschewing pulpit histrionics, devoid of anecdotal highlights, often lacking formal structure, the sermons display instead careful argument, informed believing criticism of the text, and a sharp psychological instinct for the moral point of Christian doctrine. They reflect the pastoral variety of congregational life including election and charges to elders, deacons and congregation, festive season remarks to the Youth Fellowship, prayers with the children, and sermons for Christmas Day and Boxing Day.[129]

The sermon preached on the Queen's Diamond Jubilee is a restrained panegyric on Victoria's qualities, 'conscious of capacity and not afraid of responsibility...loyal to the constitution of a free people'.[130] It reveals a social conscience alert both to the blessings and shortcomings of the nation these past sixty years. The extension of the franchise to almost universal (male) suffrage, the role of universal education 'because an uneducated democracy might do anything', the changes in the conditions of labour, the need for provision of good housing and pension security,

---

[124] *LFF*, 35.
[125] Ibid., 38.
[126] Ibid., 49.
[127] Ibid., 38.
[128] *LFF*, 49-52.
[129] See respectively, DEN07-17; DEN06-74; DEN04-152; DEN04-101; DEN01-128.
[130] DEN03-39, 2.

not only for public officials, but for 'the ploughman, the day-labourer and the tradesman...who are as much entitled to consideration in age as any official'; these and other social concerns were aired and argued.[131]

He recited a litany of recent wars which brought no credit to the British Empire; the Afghan, Chinese, Kaffir, Burmese, Soudan and Crimean wars and the Indian mutiny, each provoked atrocities and inhumanities he found offensive and unchristian. 'One could think with more pride of the gallantry of our soldiers if the nation had employed them oftener in disinterested services - if their victories had sometimes been won for ideal ends - if the wars had been of emancipation rather than conquest - and their issue something other than the extension of the British Sphere of influence.'[132] These were politically charged words, courageous in criticism and reflecting a mind which consulted ethical criteria in reaching political judgements and which presupposed objective moral standards as foundational to a Christian worldview.[133] In closing he refers to biblical criticism and Darwinism as two intellectual movements of the highest importance. 'The mind of the church has not yet digested or accommodated itself to either; and the process of making the necessary adjustments will be difficult and tedious.'[134] By 1894 Denney would discover just how difficult and tedious.

'One coherent intellectual whole'

In August 1893 Denney informed the Session of an invitation to lecture at Chicago Theological Seminary the following year.[135] He had trouble deciding on the subject matter and finally opted to 'review the chief *loci communes theologica* with reference to current ideas, especially those of Ritschl...'.[136] Ritschlian thought dominated Continental theology in the last quarter of the nineteenth century, and though severely critical of it, Denney owed more to aspects of Ritschlian theology than his severe criticisms suggest.

Ever since his holiday in student days Denney had remained open to the positive gains of German biblical and theological scholarship. His 1894 commentary, *The Second Epistle to the Corinthians*, contains many more references to Continental NT scholars, is more rigorously

---

[131] Ibid., 3.

[132] Ibid., 3-4.

[133] There is no record in the surviving correspondence of Denney's views about the Boer War 1899-1902, nor is there any treatment of the issues it raised in Denney's signed contributions to the *BW*.

[134] DEN03-39, 7-8.

[135] CH3/1156/2, 13. They warmly supported the invitation and instructed him to take Mrs Denney and have three month's holiday!

[136] *LWRN*, 3-4.

exegetical, and reads less obviously as recycled sermons, compared with his Thessalonians volume published two years earlier.[137] As translator of Delitzsch's *Commentary on Isaiah*[138] he had come to the attention of the Chicago Seminary's Professor of Hebrew, an acquaintance of Delitzsch's.[139] Throughout his sermons and other written material he was at ease with his adopted position on criticism and the Bible. For example in the Thessalonians commentary he took Lapide and Calvin to task for twisting Paul's words into a 'pious fraud' to explain how Paul's expectation of remaining alive till Christ's return, was unfulfilled. 'Is it not better to recognise the obvious fact that Paul was mistaken as to the nearness of the Second Advent, than to torture his words to secure infallibility?... I hope, if we had the choice, we would all choose rather to tell the truth, and be mistaken, than to be infallible, and tell lies.'[140]

Such daring dismissal of exegetical casuistry in the service of inerrancy was quite consistent with Denney's view of biblical authority as independent of criticism. But when worked out into a stated theology of Holy Scripture in his ninth Chicago lecture, audience reaction was robust and critical. He later commented ruefully in the Preface to the published volume, *Studies in Theology*, that the lecture on Holy Scripture 'excited considerable discussion in the circles to which it was first addressed. It has been re-written', he explained, 'not with the view of retracting or qualifying anything, but in order, as far as possible, to obviate misconception, and secure a readier acceptance for what the writer thinks true ideas on the authority of Scripture'.[141]

These lectures examine key elements in theology at a pivotal point in Denney's life. They represent an interim report on his theological development, with the important qualification that several core ideas nascent here, would not essentially change, but remain recognisably related to these early attempts at a constructive dogmatic. The footprints

---

[137] Hoffman, Holtzmann, Meyer, and Schmiedel are some of his conversation partners. Not that Denney uncritically assimilated German exegetical efforts. On the subject of God's wrath, he defended Paul against German critics. 'I cannot understand how any one should feel entitled either to flout the Apostle on this matter, or to take him under his patronage. If any one ever had the sense to distinguish between what is real and unreal in regard to God, between what is true and what is false spiritually, it was he; even with Ritschl on one side and Schmiedel on the other, he is not dwarfed, and may be permitted to speak for himself'. Denney, *2 Corinthians*, 213.

[138] Franz Delitzsch, *Biblical Commentary on the Prophecies of Isaiah*, translation from the third edition by James Denney (London: Clark's Foreign Theological Library, 1890-91). An important exercise in cross-cultural hermeneutics; in the translation process, rendering verbal equivalence was no more significant than the translator's continuing exposure to moderately critical German exegetical methods.

[139] *LWRN*, 5.

[140] Denney, *Thessalonians*, 177.

[141] Denney, *Studies*, Preface. This lecture will be examined in the next chapter.

of Denney's mature thought on the relation of Scripture to criticism and to the Spirit, the problem of sin, the death of Christ, the person of Jesus and the authority of the Gospel, and the Christocentric nature of Christian existence, can be traced back to these lectures.

The necessity of bringing biblical Christianity into meaningful relation with 'the modern mind'[142] was, to Denney, a key theological task and a moral and intellectual imperative. Throughout his life, from the cultured dogmatic ethos of Reformed Presbyterianism, through the educational enlightenment and acquisition of scholarly disciplines attained by studying Classics and Philosophy, followed by exposure to theological reflection in the orbit of a Glasgow College staffed by intellectually adventurous professors, supplemented by more than a decade of pastoral experience in which theology and mental engagement necessarily had to relate to the life of the world, Denney had come to presuppose the intellectual coherence of New Testament faith as an *a priori* principle.

The first lecture was an apologia for his own way of thinking. He rejected the division of faith and reason, God and nature, religion and science, into separate compartments each with their peculiar epistemological criteria. The influence of Enlightenment assumptions is woven throughout the entire lecture. The supremacy of reason in judging matters of fact and truth, whether scientific or religious, was coloured in Denney's case by an inner affinity with and exposure to Scottish Common-sense philosophy. The lecture bristles with verbal clues.

> *All* that man knows - of God and of the world - must be capable of being constructed into one coherent intellectual whole...the attempt to distinguish between the religious and the theoretic, to assign separate spheres to reason and faith...amounts to a betrayal of the truth; it is really an attempt to build religious certainty on indifference to reason, or scepticism of it; and reason always avenges itself by keeping in its own power something which is essential to faith.[143]

Denney strongly affirmed the prior claims of reason in exploring and analysing human experience of God in nature and history. 'The division between the religious and the scientific interpretation of events is one to which the very nature of intelligence must refuse its consent...the mind will inevitably revolt against this schism in its life...the mind cannot have two *unrelated* explanations of the same thing.'[144] There can be no bifurcation in the Christian's mind, but rather a commitment implying 'moral effort' a 'certain condition of the heart, the conscience and even the will,' aiming at 'combining and harmonising in his theology all his

---

[142] The phrase has programmatic significance in Denney's theology.

[143] Denney, *Studies*, 4, 8. Emphasis Denney's.

[144] Ibid., 10, 12. Denney believed Ritschl's rejection of natural theology and metaphysics created such epistemological problems.

knowledge and experience, physical, metaphysical, historical and religious'.[145] The lecture closes with a plea that each age must endeavour to come to convictions, insights, and a system of its own:

> Recognising the importance of great historical decisions and formulations of the faith, we shall feel that the ground on which these were made must be as accessible to us as to those who have gone before; and that the mind's mastery of itself and of the world around it may have given us instruments of precision which in earlier times were wanting. Our intellectual environment..., whatever may be said of our intellectual equipment, is not that of the Nicene Age, or the Augustinian or even the Reformation. Our religious experience with all that it presupposes and involves has to be read in new light, and set in relation to a new world...It will be the utmost I can aim at if I can help you to be true to all you know, and at the same time to keep a complete and joyful faith as Christian men.[146]

'Not to stultify reason'; the 'mind's mastery'; 'moral effort' of 'heart, conscience and will'; 'the instinctive motion of the mind to seek an explanation'; '*all* that man knows...constructed into one coherent intellectual whole'. These are the phrases of one who was unashamedly, perhaps because unconsciously, a child of the Enlightenment, with complete confidence in reason as arbiter of truth; but reason applied to the revelation of Scripture, and that revelation illumined by the Spirit working in the mind and conscience of human beings, endowed with the capacity to grasp truths self evident to any 'sensible' person.[147]

'One who gladly acknowledges a great debt to the person from whom he dissents'

'By far the most influential, most interesting, and in some ways most inspiring of modern theologians.... I refer to the late Professor Ritschl.'[148] Throughout his theological career, Denney was ambivalent about the thought of Ritschl. In the 1894 Chicago lectures Ritschl was the target of outspoken and unsympathetic criticism, the language so unguarded it was described as 'uncompromisingly hostile', indulging in 'sweeping allegations' and 'hasty misinterpretations'.[149] When published, this harsh treatment of Ritschl was rebuked by A. E. Garvie, in his much more positive account of Ritschl's theology. Garvie did not spare Denney's blushes, pointing out unjustified overstatement, shaking his head at Denney's excesses, and wondering how 'any theologian who weighs and measures words with care' could so misrepresent another. He particularly

---

[145] Ibid., 15-17.
[146] Ibid., 23.
[147] The appeal to common sense is a favourite rhetorical tool.
[148] Denney, *Studies*, 2.
[149] James Richmond, *Ritschl. A Reappraisal*, (Glasgow: Collins, 1978), 29, 170.

deplored 'the insinuation of insincerity, which...in all courteous, not to say Christian controversy...is quite out of place'.[150] The shortcomings of Denney's interpretation were spelt out:

> He misunderstands the value judgements; he charges on very slight grounds, and in spite of strong evidence on the other side, the Ritschlians with the denial of miracles generally, and the resurrection especially; he does not justly represent their attitude to the virgin-birth, the pre-existence, and the incarnation of the Logos, while his own position that these alone give "objective character" to "Christ's Godhead" is one which, in the interests of a theology that seeks to cast its roots deep into the soil of Christian experience, must be seriously questioned.[151]

That Denney was not attempting a systematic construction, but presenting a critique of an increasingly influential school of thought of which he was highly suspicious, does little to lessen the force and fairness of Garvie's criticisms. Denney, like many others, found Ritschl difficult to understand, inconsistent, and capable of changing his mind mid-volume or between editions. He said as much, and more, in his review of volume three of Ritschl's *Justification and Reconciliation,* complaining, 'Reading Ritschl is like learning to see in the dark. It is provoking, because you strike against things where you did not expect them; you fancy you see things looming through the haze, but they recede as you approach; and you want to find things, but cannot lay hands on them.'[152] However, Denney also spoke generously about Ritschl's theology:

> Its thinking is at all events live thinking, and its representative men are animated by a real enthusiasm for the man Christ Jesus...their devotion to the ethico-historical line of interpretation has restored...a great deal that the traditional orthodoxy was in danger of losing. But it is possible for us to appropriate all that it has won without letting go our hold of these still deeper and greater things which it either ignores or denies...in proceeding to make some critical points.... I do it as one who gladly acknowledges a great debt to the person from whom he dissents.[153]

In 1900 he openly endorsed two of Ritschl's most important contributions to constructive theology. 'The supreme merit of Ritschl's work', he affirmed, 'is that it never loses sight of the fact that the centre of gravity in the New Testament is the idea of reconciliation, and that it never ceases to bring theological propositions to the test of Christian

---

[150] A. E. Garvie, *The Ritschlian Theology*, (Edinburgh, 1899), 363, 286, 287. Both were young theologians making their voices heard.

[151] Ibid., 295. Orr in turn criticised Garvie's 'uncalled for severity', *The Ritschlian Theology and Evangelical Faith*, (London, 1899), 78.

[152] 'Ritschl in English', *ExpT*, xii, 1900, 137.

[153] Denney, *Studies*, 146, 141,

experience.'[154] From 1900 onwards reconciliation became the centre of gravity of Denney's own theology,[155] and the testing of theological propositions on the touchstone of Christian experience a key hermeneutical principle. Denney's debt to Ritschl, however was more extensive than even these primary colours of his own theology.

Direct influence on intellectual development is difficult to establish, as influence can take numerous forms, from borrowing, to dependence on the one hand, to positive critique or negative reaction on the other. Influence can be direct, indirect, or mediated through a third party. A. B. Bruce was an early and discerning critic of Ritschl, and some of what Denney owed Bruce was payable to Ritschl.[156] 'All we really know of God in spirit and in very truth we know through Jesus; but only on condition that we truly know Jesus Himself as revealed to us in the pages of the evangelic history. Knowledge of the historical Jesus is the foundation at once of a sound Christian theology and of a thoroughly healthy Christian life.'[157] The words could be a programmatic summary of Denney's mature work, from *Jesus and the Gospel* to the *Christian Doctrine of Reconciliation*. Equally they could be understood as an outline of key principles in Ritschl's theological approach.

In fact they are Bruce, in his 1892 book on *Apologetics,* pursuing truth without dogma, impatient of metaphysical presuppositions, and regarding revelation as 'consisting not in the impartation of truths which the human mind cannot conceive, but in the conversion of conceivable possibilities into indubitable realities'.[158] Just as in Bruce, so in Ritschl, there was much to which Denney did not assent. But by negative reaction, or by direct learning and incorporation of insights into his own intellectual armoury, or yet again by a process of osmosis, conscious or unconscious, some of Ritschl's more assimilable theological and methodological insights became permanent characteristics of Denney's own thought.

The historical positivism of Ritschl had its counterpart in Denney's passionate insistence, that the historical rooted-ness of Jesus represents and reveals the presence of the eternal in time. In one of his many sideswipes at Idealism, Denney showed the importance of holding the Jesus of history and the Christ of faith in a historical and ontological unity:

---

[154] Denney, 'Ritschl in English', 139.

[155] Reconciliation terminology was prominent in the treatment of the atonement even in the 1894 *Studies*.

[156] Moon Sang Kwon, 'A Study of Scottish Kenoticism: The Interpretation of the Self-Emptying of Christ in Ethical Categories with particular reference to A. B. Bruce and H. R. Mackintosh', (Aberdeen PhD, 1999). Ritschl's influence on Bruce is examined on pages 87-99.

[157] J. K. Mozley, *Tendencies in British Theology*, (London: SPCK, 1951), 110-11.

[158] Ibid.

> Faith attaches itself to something historical and clings to it....what is absolute idealism, what are eternal truths of reason, to a man shut out from God by a bad conscience, and lost if he is left to himself? But to such a man the Son of God in flesh and blood, receiving sinners like *him* in salvation; his conscience gives him an eye for the history and its meaning, and the inward and outward witness unite in an assurance which has history at its heart yet can never be impaired.[159]

The historical record of Jesus as revealer of God, embedded in the canonical gospels through the testimony and experience of the Evangelists, and given coherent articulation by apostolic theological reflection, appropriated anew in the continuing experience of the Christian community, provided an integrated epistemological foundation. That foundation, dependent on historical fact critically established, upon verifiable experience given the ontological status of fact,[160] and upon the evidential value of experience communicated through reliable testimony, compels a recognition that the truth of God is not, therefore, reached by speculative reason unaided by historic revelation, or by ahistorical mysticism. It is reached by historical enquiry into the definitive and originating apostolic experience of Jesus, and the confirmation and corrective of a community rooted in common testimony as it perpetuates and appropriates for its own time, the apostolic experience.[161]

Denney's resistance to Hegelian idealism, the metaphysical speculations which underlay much traditional dogmatic formulation, and suspicion bordering on outright hostility to mysticism, are attitudes in which the echoing voice of Ritschl is clear, and not always distant. As late as 1917, Denney acknowledged the originality and importance of Ritschl's work, placing it alongside Schleiermacher and McLeod Campbell.[162] Even in this, his last book, Denney praised and criticised, learned from and contradicted Ritschl; but in the end the influence of Ritschl on the exposition of *The Christian Doctrine of Reconciliation* is not in this or that idea, but in the overall methodology of a book that privileged the evidence of experience, restated doctrine with no sense of binding obligation to traditional dogmatic constructions, took with absolute seriousness the veracity of the historical revelation of God in the person and work of Jesus as given in the New Testament, focused on

---

[159] 'Christianity and the Historical Christ', *Exp*, Series VIII, vol. V, January 1913, 26.

[160] 'The life of trust in God is a fact, not so much to be explained as to explain everything else.' For Ritschl and Denney, experience was the 'positive religious datum' of theology. *Encyclopaedia Britannica,* (New York: Encyclopedia Brittanica 11th ed., 1910-11), vol. 23, 367.

[161] G. W. See McCulloch, 'A Historical Bible, A Reasonable Faith, A Conscious Action. The Theological Legacy of Albrecht Ritschl', in D. Jodock, (ed.), *Ritschl in Retrospect*, (Minneapolis: Fortress, 1995), 31-50.

[162] Denney, *Reconciliation*, 115.

reconciliation as the 'centre of gravity' in Christian theology, and eschewing mystical and philosophical categories, focused on the moral import of reconciliation for human life.

On central and crucial issues such as the nature of sin, the death of Jesus interpreted as unprecedented, vicarious and substitutionary, as essentially and eternally related to sin, and the precise relations of divine love and righteousness, each fulfilling and expressing the other in the appalling tragedy of Calvary, Denney remained at serious odds with Ritschl.[163] Such convictions, evident in his earliest work, and reaffirmed late in life in the context of the Great War, underlay the Pauline doctrine of reconciliation, 'that makes Christ's death a solitary phenomenon in the universe....This solitariness of Christ, this uniqueness of His work, is to be maintained over all analogies.'[164] The Word God spoke in Christ, is, for Denney, *hapax legomenon*.

'What I have learned among you'

In 1895 Denney was awarded a Glasgow D.D. to add to the one he received from Chicago.[165] It was only a matter of time till he was called to serve in one of his church's Divinity Halls. The Free Church has a long tradition of seeking its professors amongst working ministers. When J. S. Candlish died in 1897, Denney was appointed to the chair of Practical and Systematic Theology. His farewell sermon to the Broughty Ferry congregation was on the text 'We have known and believed the love which God has for us'.[166] He spoke of the 'sacred privilege' of sharing people's ups and downs, their high hopes and high spirits, their disappointments, defeats, struggles, sorrows and pain. He confessed, 'It is one of the things for which I can never be sufficiently thankful that so many of the members and of the families of the church allowed me to be intimate with them, both in joy and in sorrow'.[167]

Predictably, all roads of human experience led to the cross, and evoked an exposition anticipating themes which later inspired some of his most powerful writing:

---

[163] Denney, *Studies*, 141-51, shows Denney in a better light as constructive critic. MacQuarrie, *Jesus Christ*, 252-258, indicates the strengths and weaknesses of Ritschl's theology viewed from a sympathetic modern perspective.

[164] Denney, *Studies*, 147,151.

[165] *LFF*, 57-9. 'It is with peculiar pleasure that I accept such a distinction from my own University, and I hope I shall always have a proper sense of its worth, and of the obligations it imposes.' Letter of acceptance, 23 March 1895, GUA 4066. Aberdeen and Princeton later added to Denney's honours.

[166] DEN07-156. All further references are to this text.

[167] Ibid., 7.

> The tragedy of guilt is answered by the tragedy of redemption...blood is the strongest word that can be used to reach our hearts; it is the word which means life and death, agony and passion, Gethsemane and Calvary. Leave out that propitiation in blood and you leave us without the love of God at the very place where our need of it is most desperate...God is love. Great words must have great things behind them to fill them with meaning, and what fills these particular words with meaning is the cross...God is love, the most intelligible as well as the most unfathomable of truths.[168]

He went on to say 'I have tried in these eleven years I have been with you...in preaching the gospel and in administering the sacraments to give [the gospel] that fundamental place, that awful character, that all-determining power.... I feel today how little I have been able to speak of it as it should be spoken of, and that I have not felt nor preached enough its patience, its tenderness, its unvaried faithfulness.'[169] The corrections and insertions in the manuscript evidence carefully chosen words, conveying his belief that his years in Broughty Ferry decisively opened his personality, refined his theology and shaped his understanding of what ministry should be.

> We have been part of each other's life in Christ Jesus- you of mine and I of yours - and no changes can undo that. I have tried to be of service to you as I could, and I cannot tell you of what service you have been to me.... We have not been wilful in seeking to go away... I shall still be a minister of the word of God, a servant of Christ in the gospel; if it were not so, I should certainly not go.... If I can be of any service to the future ministers of the church, it will be through what I have learned among you; it will not be possible for me to think or speak of anything connected with the church or the ministry except through the medium of my experience here.[170]

The connection with the church was never broken. Year after year he returned to conduct the Spring communion. He preached the funeral service of his successor, the Rev. McGillvray in 1907. He took charge of the pastorate on occasion during the summer recess from College. He corresponded with church members for years afterwards, and complained that leaving Broughty Ferry, 'I lost all my open doors'.[171] When he died in 1917 the Session inserted in the Minute Book a beautifully written tribute, which summed up the lasting impact of his ministry in Broughty Ferry.[172]

---

[168] Ibid., 4.
[169] Ibid., 6.
[170] Ibid., 8.
[171] *LFF*, 163.
[172] CH3/1156/2, 239. See Appendix 2. Denney's farewell was reported in *BW*, 16 September 1897, 356.

'I shall still be a minister of the Word of God', he had said. What he understood that Word to be, and which the intellectual and spiritual principles that govern its interpretation, were questions that would exercise, and at times, vex him, for the twenty years of life that remained.

CHAPTER 6

The Glasgow Years, 1897-1907

> In Dr Denney they had a man of singularly massive, penetrating, and luminous intellect, a man of rare independence of judgement, a man who was in bondage neither to the past nor to the present, a man whose supreme reverence was for the truth and the truth alone, a man who had the rarest intellectual and moral courage, and who would therefore, without hesitation, make plain to his students and to the world, the results at which he arrived.[1]

The speaker, Dr Patrick, addressed the 1897 Free Church Assembly, presenting Denney for the Glasgow College Chair of Systematic and Practical Theology. 'He hoped the house would not require of him a certificate of Dr Denney's orthodoxy.... If orthodoxy consisted in truth...they had in Dr Denney the most orthodox of men, for he desired to know truth, and to obey truth, and that alone.'[2] Patrick had hoped to avoid a vote, and to forestall questions of Denney's theological acceptability, but he was disappointed. Moving the name of the Rev John MacPherson, the opposing speaker argued the church should only appoint

> Professors whose orthodoxy was above suspicion... He admired Dr Denney's brilliant talents and abilities, he admired some of his writings, and perhaps had derived some benefit from them; but at the same time there were certain things in Dr Denney's writings which he disapproved of and would not like that they should be taught in their Halls. He had given utterance to certain thoughts on the canon of Scripture and on the inspiration of the Bible which it would be most disastrous for their students to imbibe.[3]

In view of Denney's subsequent career and reputation for orthodoxy as forceful proponent of substitutionary atonement, and his diagnostic skill in tracing the invasive malignancy of sin, the words of Mr Macaskill, who

---

[1] *PDGAFCS*, 1897, 71.
[2] Ibid.
[3] Ibid., 72. This was not the only time the word disastrous was used by the more orthodox against Denney's views. See J. Kerr, *The Higher Criticism: Disastrous Results. Professors Smith, Dods and Denney*, (Glasgow: privately published, 1903).

had known Denney since childhood but rose to second the opposing motion, now ring with unintended irony.

> In respect of [Dr Denney's] statement on the doctrine of sin and man's original condition, he was under the necessity of saying he could not vote for him. Dr Denney was to teach systematic theology; he was to teach the doctrine of redemption; but how could he begin it without having any true conception of the doctrine of sin? It was impossible for a man who was wrong on the doctrine of sin to continue long right on the doctrine of the atonement.[4]

The appointment was carried 456 for Denney, 76 for MacPherson. But the push for a vote was significant. The election of Professors in 1897 shows that opinion was divided on Denney's orthodoxy, particularly over perceived deficiencies in his doctrine of Scripture.

During the Glasgow years Denney would grow in stature, becoming a trusted scholar and senior churchman within the United Free Church and beyond. He increasingly became an established authoritative source of theological reflection on central themes of Christian faith in which the interests of criticism and modern thought, and the interests of apostolic Christianity, were brought together. Yet unresolved tension remained between Denney's passionate evangelical faith, and his 'desire to know the truth, obey the truth, and that alone.' Criticism and the Bible, intellectual freedom and dogmatic authority, the relations of criticism to faith and church, these persisted as polar tensions in Denney's constructive thought.

The discomfort dated back, at least in its public expression, to 1891. In an Assembly debate on the Confession of Faith, Denney spoke with 'the utmost frankness' on the matter of inerrancy. His intervention in the debate goes far to explain the hesitations felt by those who later opposed his election.

> The infallibility of the Scriptures was not a mere verbal inerrancy, a historical accuracy, but an infallibility of power to save. The Word of God infallibly carried God's power to save men's souls. If a man submitted his heart and mind to the Spirit of God speaking in it, he would infallibly become a new creature in Christ Jesus. That was the only infallibility he believed in. For mere verbal inerrancy he cared not one straw. It was worth nothing to him; it would be worth nothing if it were there, and it was not...he did not think anybody has a right to accuse them or to

---

[4]*PDGAFCS*, 72. But see DEN09-14–DEN09-16, 'The Doctrine of Sin'; Denney, *Reconciliation*, ch. 4, 'The Need of Reconciliation'. The objector was probably alluding to Denney's ahistorical view of the Fall. But Denney upheld the *religious* and *experimental* truth of original sin.

suspect them in the very faintest degree of falling away into rationalism, or denying the Divine authority of the Word of God. Authority was not authorship.[5]

The level of unguarded frankness in a young minister betrays strong feeling and Denney's temperamental inability to discount truth in the interests of tact. He believed that an untenable view of the Bible[6] was being presented as the agreed mind of the Confession of Faith Committee, and took the unusual step of opposing the unanimous motion of a Committee on which he served. In his reply Denney stated his view of infallibility noted above, but went on to call the motion 'two faced' and 'equivocal'. He understood the motive was to allay fear and alarm, an intellectual timidity with which he obviously had no patience. 'The only real way of allaying anxiety and alarm was to deal truly with the truth. There were other anxieties to be considered, much more respectable than this timidity which really insulted the truth - the anxieties of those who had at heart the interest of Biblical science, the interest of Christian liberty, and the interest of the honesty and good name of the Free Church.'[7] In such debates Denney took no prisoners, but neither did he turn enemies into friends. The reverberations of this speech could still be felt on the assembly floor in 1897 at the election of professors.[8]

'He was nothing if not a biblical theologian'

The first decade of the twentieth century represents Denney's most theologically productive years. His commentary on *Romans*, a major series of articles in the *Expositor* on 'The Theology of Romans', *The Death of Christ, The Atonement and the Modern Mind, Jesus and the Gospel, The Church and the Kingdom* and *The Way Everlasting*, a volume of collected sermons, were the published evidence of a fertile mind. But it was a mind which treated the Bible in apparently paradoxical fashion, as both normative guide in its spiritual application, and fallible text in its literary form.

It was Denney's refusal to tie the normative authority of Holy Scripture to the notion of an infallible text which had created the conservative backlash in Chicago in 1894, and which caused Lecture IX, 'Holy Scripture', to be rewritten for the published volume, *Studies in Theology*. The tension between Denney's sensitivity to those criticisms,

---

[5] *PDGAFCS*, 1891, 111-12. Denney preached before the Assembly that year, on 31 May, five days after this exchange.

[6] Ibid., 111: 'the absolute inerrancy of Scripture as originally given.'.

[7] Ibid., 112.

[8] Macaskill, who seconded the opposing motion, was a focus of conservative resistance to biblical criticism. See Kenneth Ross, *Church and Creed in Scotland*, (Edinburgh: Rutherford House, 1988), 186-8.

and his reluctance to make concessions to a view of Scripture reminiscent of that which fuelled the case against Robertson Smith, is obvious in the published Preface:

> The ninth lecture has been rewritten...not with the view of retracting or qualifying anything, but in order, as far as possible, to obviate misconception, and secure a readier acceptance for what the writer thinks true ideas of the authority of Scripture.[9]

This is a key statement, not only of Denney's mind in 1894 in the considered aftermath of his personal experience of theological controversy, but of the purpose that would inform most of Denney's subsequent published work. In books, articles and public lectures, his teaching aimed to 'secure a readier acceptance of what the writer thinks true ideas on the authority of Scripture', and that not only in Chicago, but in the ecclesiastical and theological flux of the Scottish Church at the beginning of the new century.

In tracing the forty years of his life so far, a number of influences and circumstances, some decisive and some suggestive, whether through the conscious decision of a reasoning mind grasping perceived truth, or the unconscious absorption into the mind of congenial attitudes and insights, and whether reacting against or responding to those teachers who made up the rich pedagogic networks within which he moved at University and College, these influences and circumstances represented a slow process of maturation towards settled conviction. By 1894 when he lectured at Chicago, he had had a first taste of public controversy. More than a decade of pastoral experience had provided ample opportunity for his use of Scripture to be tested in the one place and context where 'true ideas on the authority of Scripture' mattered most to him, in the pulpit, preaching to a worshipping community.

Any account of Denney's subsequent life in Glasgow as theological educator and writer; any attempt to understand how his mind habitually addressed theological questions; any adequate evaluation of his overall significance as a church leader of increasing stature as the years passed, must reckon with Denney's use of Scripture, and the paradox of an evangelical theology constructed upon a view of Scripture of which many evangelicals were suspicious. Along with Lindsay, Candlish, Bruce[10] and Orr, Denney expounded 'non-inerrancy evangelicalism', a phrase some would call oxymoronic.[11]

---

[9] Denney, *Studies*, Preface.

[10] Denney would not have hesitated to include Bruce within a generous definition of evangelicalism.

[11] The phrase is from G. Dorrien, *Remaking of Evangelical Theology*, (Nashville: Westminster John Knox, 1998), 119. Undoubtedly opponents within his own communion would find the phrase 'two faced'!

> It was in Scripture that his thought reached its full height and found its most creative and constructive dimensions. He was nothing if not a Biblical theologian.... He actually wrote very little about its place or its nature or its use; he simply used it...and in that use asserted its own nature and assumed its own place.[12]

With the Bible as normative source and primary resource, for the remaining twenty years of his life Denney tackled fundamental theological themes such as atonement and Christology. In his writing and churchmanship he helped the Church adjust to intellectual and cultural changes, encouraged the churches towards a recovered unity, and later reflected with a chastened confidence, on God, the Great War and the Christian doctrine of reconciliation.

All of this can be documented in his published work. Taylor's reconstruction of Denney's theology of Scripture gives a thorough and plausible account which acknowledges the ambiguities and unresolved tensions of a doctrine of Scripture less evangelical than the theology it was used to construct.[13] But the account inevitably flattens out the contours of historical context, imposes a system on textually dislocated fragments, and lacks the additional dimension of unpublished material which contributes significantly to an understanding of Denney's thought, and the circumstances which compelled its articulation.

The overall purpose of this chapter then, is to place in context the more general developments in Denney's life and thought during the first decade in Glasgow when his writing, lecturing and involvement in Church issues were the expression of a mind reaching the peak of its power. But so much that is characteristic of Denney's mature thought depended on a doctrine of Scripture which transcended dogmatic quarrelling over inerrancy, and appealed instead to the dynamic quality of biblical inspiration as evidenced by the impact of God on those who read the Bible for themselves.

His writing was shaped in content and governed in tone by the biblical and theological methodology he invariably followed. Honest scholarship handling the ancient text with reverent attention to details of text and context, he first learned from Jebb. The application of reason and logic in the work of interpreting the relationships between text, history, doctrine and experience, was an approach influenced by Veitch the Common Sense apologist; but it was reason in pursuit of spiritual truth as finally revealed in Christ, and this he learned from A. B. Bruce. The fate of Robertson Smith, and the examples of Lindsay and Candlish as champions of spiritual liberty, left on Denney an indelible sense both of the risks and consequences of critical scholarship, and of the inner imperative to stand fast in the liberty of mind and conscience, constrained

---

[12] J. R. Taylor, *God Loves Like That!*, (London : SCM, 1962), 133.
[13] Ibid., Chapter VIII. 'Listening for a Voice'.

by neither creed nor dogma of inerrancy, but only by loyalty to Christ and Gospel. A decade of pastoral ministry had provided ample opportunity to test his theology of Scripture in the demanding arena of a Christian community.

'The ninth lecture excited considerable discussion'

Denney never explained what 'caused the fluttering in the ecclesiastical dovecots'[14] in Chicago. What exactly did he say that compelled a diplomatic rewrite before publication? Amongst the papers in New College is a manuscript, which is almost certainly the original lecture. The title 'Holy Scripture',[15] is preceded by the roman numeral IX, which corresponds to the revised chapter in *Studies*. No other papers from the series are extant, which is true of the original manuscripts of all Denney's major publications, suggesting that the other chapters, plus the rewritten one, were sent on the usual non-returnable basis to the publishers, leaving the offending original manuscript in Denney's hands.[16]

All such surmising tilts the balance further towards a certainty all but established, when the written manuscript is read alongside the published version. Large portions of text are exact verbal parallels, many of them in the same structural order, serving as part of the same cumulative argument. At the same time, and more significantly in historical terms, excisions and re-phrasings indicate areas where, in the original lecture, Denney was less than tactful and had failed to appreciate the recent theological arguments and anxieties distressing North American Evangelicals in the 1890s. It is this 'fit' of the theological climate in Chicago, the combative tone of the original lecture, and the evidence of a more domesticated text in the published version, which provides persuasive evidence that this is the lecture manuscript which 'excited considerable discussion' in Chicago.

While space does not permit a comprehensive account of the theological controversies concerning the Bible, which erupted in America in the 1880s and 1890s, it is important to place the Chicago lecture within the theological atmosphere of late nineteenth century American Presbyterianism. Princeton was the dominant conservative evangelical

---

[14] A brief but unenlightening account is given in Walker, *Denney*, 85-6.

[15] DEN09-17. The full text is reproduced in Appendix 2.

[16] None of the sermons reproduced in his commentaries on Thessalonians and 2 Corinthians are extant, nor any manuscripts of his major works. On one occasion Denney requested material back from Robertson Nicoll, despite such requests being against the publisher's policy, suggesting Hodder and Stoughton kept the original manuscripts. See *LWRN*, 28. Much of this remains speculation as the Hodder and Stoughton archives were destroyed during the Second World War. See David Wells, 'Introduction' in the reissue of *Studies in Theology*, (Grand Rapids: Baker, 1976), xvi.

school, its most erudite and prolific apologist being B. B. Warfield, successor to A. A. Hodge. In an 1881 article on 'Inspiration', Warfield and Hodge penned what has become a *locus classicus* in evangelical theology.

> The historical faith of the church has always been, that all the affirmations of Scripture of all kinds, whether of spiritual doctrine or duty, or of physical or historical fact, or of psychological or philosophical principle, are without any error when the *ipsissima verba* of the original autographs are ascertained and interpreted in their natural and intended sense.[17]

By 1891 there was an open controversy over inerrancy between Princeton and Union Seminary, New York, personalised by B. B. Warfield, Professor of Didactic and Polemical Theology at Princeton,[18] and Charles Briggs, Professor of Hebrew at Union Theological Seminary till 1891 and of Biblical Theology thereafter. Eventually, in a lecture on 'The Authority of the Bible', Briggs overstepped the mark in the eyes of the church courts and in 1893 the General Assembly suspended him. Amongst the conservative 'barriers' Briggs attacked were verbal inspiration and inerrancy. In his views of inspiration, the critical enterprise and the spiritual stakes involved in holding true ideas on the authority of the Bible, Briggs was a kindred spirit to Denney.

In 1883 he had defended the view of inspiration favoured by theologians like Lindsay, arguing that it represented the true Reformation faith.[19] In contrast to the 'inerrancy-literalism' of continental scholasticism, he affirmed 'the dynamic interaction of biblical word and the Holy Spirit', appealing to Luther and Calvin in the process. Two quotations illustrate how close Briggs came to the sentiments of Denney and Lindsay.[20]

> Inspiration lies back of the external letter - it is that which gives the word its efficacy, it is the divine afflatus which enlightened and guided holy men to

---

[17] Quoted in Mark A. Noll, *Between Faith and Criticism. Evangelicals, Scholarship and the Bible*, (Leicester: Apollos, 1991), 19.

[18] See B. J. Gundlach, 'Warfield, Benjamin', in T. Larsen (ed.), *Biographical Dictionary of Evangelicals*, (Leicester: IVP, 2003), 698-701.

[19] Charles, Briggs, *Biblical Study: Its Principles, Methods and History*, (New York, 1883). He taught that the Bible and reason were 'each a fountain of divine authority which savingly enlighten men'. See further, Briggs' *The Bible, the Church and Reason*, (New York, 1892). *Encyclopaedia Britannica*, 11th ed., vol. 4, 566.

[20] In 1895 Lindsay published, 'The Doctrine of Scripture. The Reformers and the Princeton School.', *The Expositor*, 1895, 278-93. The year earlier Denney's *Studies in Theology* was published. While written independently, the coincidence of content and viewpoint in the three treatments suggests Denney's views as expressed at Chicago in 1894 were not idiosyncratic but part of a live debate.

apprehend the truth of God in its appropriate forms; assured them of their possession of it; and called and enabled them to make it known to the church by voice and pen.

True criticism never disregards the letter, but reverently and tenderly handles every letter and syllable of the Word of God, striving to purify it from all dross, brushing away the dust of tradition and guarding it from the ignorant and the profane.[21]

The first places inspiration in the dynamic relationship of letter and Spirit whereby the living inner witness of the Spirit enables possession and proclamation. The second mirrors the attitude to criticism Denney adopted and defended in preaching, teaching and controversy.[22]

In 1894, the year following Briggs' suspension, Henry Preserved Smith was suspended by the Presbytery of Cincinatti for disbelief 'in the perfect inerrancy of the biblical autographs'.[23] Warfield, who had already published on the inerrancy of the original autographs, wrote a lengthy critical article the same year, 'Professor Henry Preserved Smith and Inspiration'.[24] By the time Denney arrived in Chicago, the Presbyterian church was divided over the issues of biblical inerrancy and inspiration. With the trial and removal of Briggs and Smith, the precise definition of these terms had ceased to be an academic exchange of opinion and had become a required rubric of evangelical orthodoxy.

While in 1894, Denney was lecturing in the Chicago Congregational Theological Seminary, in the same city and at exactly the same time, the University of Chicago was busy developing its Department of Biblical Studies under W. R. Harper, Ernest Burton and Shailer Matthews.[25] The Chicago school of biblical interpretation 'emphasised empirical experience, history and social backgrounds,'[26] believed critical study of the biblical text could be pursued without prejudice to its spiritual authority, and therefore distinguished between *textual* interpretation which is concerned with *meaning*, from resultant theological formulation which is concerned with dogmatic *truth*.[27] The comment that the Chicago school became 'impressed with the weight of experience as equal with

---

[21] Gary Dorrien, *The Making of American Liberal Theology. Imagining Progressive Religion*, (Louisville: Westminster John Knox, 2001), 351, for both quotations.

[22] In several important unpublished papers shortly to be placed in context, Denney was a frontline apologist for believing criticism in the newly formed UF Church.

[23] Dorrien, *Making*, 366.

[24] *Presbyterian and Reformed Review*, 5, 1894, 600-52

[25] Funk, Robert W, 'The Watershed of the American Biblical Tradition: The Chicago School, First Phase, 1892-1920', *Journal of Biblical Literature*, 95, 1976, 4-22.

[26] J. Hayes (ed.), *Dictionary of Biblical Interpretation*, (Nashville: Abingdon, 1999), vol. 1, 483.

[27] Funk, 'Watershed', 11.

and later, as more important than the witness of Scripture',[28] identifies the direction Denney took in working out his doctrine of Scripture. However Denney did not concede that experience was more important than the witness of Scripture, but that experience and Scripture, Spirit and Word, stood in a relation of mutually informing exegetical dialogue.[29] But the developments in the approach to Biblical Studies in Chicago from 1892 onwards, were not irrelevant in trying to estimate the theological climate into which Denney sailed in 1894.

In the background to the heated inerrancy debates was the deeper alarm of conservative Presbyterians at the gathering momentum for a revision of the Westminster Confession. Ironically Briggs was resistant to revision and would have preferred a relaxation of the terms of subscription. Those like Briggs who supported a believing criticism of the Bible were caught up in a powerful conservative reaction in which those who battled to uphold a strict inerrancy identified their cause with a defence of the Standards of Faith. Victory in the inerrancy debate ensured the defeat of the revision movement.[30] Where controversy over biblical criticism, doctrinal standards and credal subscription coalesced, there was no safe middle ground to support those who wanted the best of both worlds.

The visit to Chicago Congregational Theological Seminary took Denney into unfamiliar cultural territory. It was also unknown academic territory. He had no idea how many he would teach or what level of theological acumen to presuppose.[31] The Seminary, while not Presbyterian, would have been fully aware of the heresy trials, not least through the involvement of their own Professor Curtiss, the one who had extended the invitation to Denney in the first place. It is hard to believe Denney did not appreciate the need for tact and moderation at least in the style and tone of his lectures.

'The most stupendous example on record of lying for God'

Given the context outlined above, and even allowing for the fact it was a non-Presbyterian institution, the original lecture is at times electrifyingly direct in its anti-Princetonian rhetoric. The best evidence of this is to hear Denney at his most devastating, deconstructing concepts such as 'inerrant original autographs', dismissing any notion of an 'infallible text', rejecting out of hand the dogma that the canon of Scripture is to be

---

[28] Hayes, *Dictionary*, 2, 135.
[29] In *The Christian Doctrine of Reconciliation*, published over twenty years later, Denney demonstrated both the strengths and limitations of spiritual experience and biblical exegesis mutually informing each other in the task of constructive theology.
[30] Dorrien, *Making*, 366.
[31] *LWRN*, 5.

identified as the Word of God without remainder, and all this before an audience highly sensitised by recent controversy and heresy trials which focused on precisely these issues.

> ...a more melancholy contrast can hardly be found in history than that which is presented when the religious liberty of the sixteenth century is put side by side with the scholasticism of the seventeenth.... Protestant theologians betook themselves to the Bible. In spite of the fact that the Bible is a collection of books, is only a piece of the Christian tradition, they set it in opposition to the tradition.... They committed themselves to the principle that the canon of scripture is the word of God, that these very words, no more and no less and all alike, are the one divine and infallible rule of faith and practice.... God, said Quenstedt, is the sole author of Holy Scripture...a more extraordinary perversion than this of the Reformation doctrine of the word of God no ingenuity could imagine. This Protestant doctrine of inspiration is literally the most stupendous example on record of lying for God; of deliberate shutting of the eyes to the most palpable and obtrusive facts [of deliberate distortion of the most simple and easy truth].[32]

Little wonder the lecture excited considerable discussion! The Reformation view of Scripture, particularly Luther's preferred canon within the canon, established by the criterion of whether or not the Gospel of justification by faith is clearly taught, is given extensive treatment. Denney based his appeal to 'the original Protestant attitude to Scripture' on Luther's loose treatment of the canon, and Calvin's more restrained but still relaxed view of the relative status of the biblical books. 'The Church tradition,' Denney argued, 'even in the form of the Bible...was itself human and liable to all the infirmities and errors of humanity.'

> Indeed a divine authority for the canon - an authority fixing its limits beforehand and establishing the right of everything within them to be recognised as infallibly true and perpetually binding - neither does nor can exist. God it is true, speaks to the soul and gives it a sure hold of his grace in Christ, thro' the Scripture; and the assurance of God, and of one's own relation to him, so gained, is one against which no human authority can plead its rights; but this does not justify us in dogmatic assertions about the authority of Scripture as a whole. It does not bar criticism, either historical or spiritual, but rather gives us the standing ground and the liberty for it. Such is Luther's opinion, and it seems to me to be the true one.[33]

---

[32] DEN09-17, 6. The bracketed clause is scored out. It is included in this quotation because it indicates Denney's mood. A similar deletion near the end of the lecture suggests Denney's scorn was generated by pastoral concern that a doctrine of textual inerrancy was an apologetic embarrassment. 'We do a great injury to the gospel, we put an immense stumbling block in the way of faith, when we barricade the approach to Christ with a doctrine of inspiration that no man can defend, not to mention a crude assertion of inerrancy of scripture which is simply not true.' Ibid., 15.

[33] DEN09-17, 4.

In this appeal to the more relaxed view of the canon held by the magisterial Reformers, there are strong echoes of the earlier debate in Scotland, and in particular Lindsay and Candlish's defence of Robertson Smith. The main point also chimes closely with Briggs' appeal to the Reformers published in his volume *Biblical Study. Its Principles, Methods and History*.[34] Much of this argumentation was omitted in Denney's revision.[35]

The appeal to Luther on the status of the canon was accompanied by appeal to the Reformer's doctrine of the inner testimony of the Spirit, again recalling the basis of Robertson Smith's defence. Crucially, Denney's exposition of the role of the Spirit in the interpretation and application of the Bible rested on the Gospel of Christ crucified. The Spirit does not bear inner testimony to the inerrancy of the words in the text, but to the message of the Gospel they contain. 'The Holy Spirit, bearing witness by and with the word in our hearts, gives us a full persuasion and assurance of the infallible truth and divine authority of the revelation of God made in [Christ], but it is in the fullness of grace and truth, and not the innumerable historical details of the gospels, to whom we give our faith.'[36] The unbroken connection that Denney then makes explicit, between 'true ideas on the authority of Scripture' and securing an adequate doctrine of the atonement, is a historical snapshot of a mind made up about what is primary and what secondary in the articles of faith.

> The doctrine of an atonement for sins, made in Christ's death, has never been accepted in the church simply on the ground that it was taught by three carnal men, Peter, Paul and John. The authority it enjoys, ...is due to this, that the Holy Spirit has borne witness by and with that doctrine in man's heart, making sure that in accepting it they were accepting the very soul of God's redeeming love. If there is one truth in the whole Bible which is guaranteed by the *testimonium internum Spiritus Sancti*, and by the consenting witness of Christians in all ages, it is this. It has an authority in it, or along with it, by which it vindicates itself to faith as divinely and infallibly true....[37]

The exposition of atonement as the heart of the Christian revelation, and the apostolic testimony to it, preserved in words, but bearing witness to the

---

[34] Dorrien, *Making*, 337-70, has a full account of Briggs' trial and the underlying tensions over confessional revision which drove the controversy to its conclusion in Briggs' dismissal.

[35] The revised lecture intriguingly quotes Warfield and Hodge to support his view of Scripture as primarily a means of grace. Their names are not in the original manuscript, though they are present as primary targets of Denney's anti-inerrancy polemic. One wonders if their inclusion was irenic or ironic.

[36] Ibid., 13.

[37] Ibid., 18,19.

death of Christ as objectively atoning in history and subjectively appropriated in experience, became the central pursuit of Denney's theological career. *The Death of Christ, The Atonement and the Modern Mind, Jesus and the Gospel,* the 'Theology of Romans' and the commentary on *Romans,* and the later *Christian Doctrine of Reconciliation,* are not only titles of the books he wrote, but represent the spiritual *curriculum vitae* of his mature theological career. And all this later work would be shaped in content and theological conviction, by a view of the Bible that, in his view, retained its spiritual authority while preserving in the face of criticism its historical integrity.

Once again, pastoral and apologetic concern injected passion into a mind already well equipped to challenge dogmatic restrictions which prevented thoughtful people from believing the gospel. Denney's antipathy to inerrancy, infallibility and an antecedent dogma of inspiration was the negative mood of one who positively insisted that a critical approach to the Bible, combined with a spiritual commitment to Christ, enhances the Bible as a means of grace and as the vehicle of the Gospel.

> The best thing we can do for the Bible is to keep it open; but very often it is so jealously defended that the truth is made not only impregnable but inaccessible. Nobody can reach it over the ramparts of inspiration, infallibility, inerrancy and so forth. Let Christ have a chance, whatever becomes of the evangelists...the Gospel which is attested in the gospels will put forth victorious and subduing power all the more easily when men are not prejudiced against the books by irrational and untrue claims on their behalf.[38]

Much more than the sanitised revision, this lecture reveals Denney as logic on fire, combining in his most powerful writing, a rationally driven methodology with a passion driven motivation. The hearers of the original manuscript were left in no doubt that Denney was angered by what he took to be untrue ideas about the authority of scripture, and inspired by what is possible in the lives of people, if with true ideas about the Bible, they are able to encounter not an infallible text, but an infallible God.

> If we must assert an *infallibility* for [the Bible], let it not be an infallibility of verbal accuracy, which it does not possess, but an *infallibility* of saving power, which it does. The man who humbly gives up his mind to the teaching of that Spirit which speaks in the Bible will *infallibly* be brought to that faith in God which characterises its writers from first to last; he will *infallibly* be brought by the NT to

---

[38] Ibid., 15.

faith in the God and Father of our Lord Jesus Christ. The Bible has no other *infallibility* than this; but is not this enough? [39]

So the lecture ends with a rhetorical flourish, Denney using the terminology most favoured by those he opposed to demonstrate that *infallibility* far from being intellectually constricting, can carry a meaning spiritually liberating.

The lasting significance of the Chicago experience lies in its impact on Denney's future thought. In the lecture as delivered, there is an overwhelming impression of inner certainty about how the Bible is to be interpreted. His adamantine assurance that Bible and criticism not only could, but ought to inform each other in a dynamic relationship between human mind, biblical text and the Holy Spirit, set the tone for all Denney's subsequent writing and teaching. Here, more than anywhere else in his thought, his intellectual debts are documented, not with footnotes, but with keynotes.

Themes and attitudes had been assimilated, which, when fused with a reserved yet passionate temperament, produced a theology which while lacking overall systematic organisation, was held together by the writer's consistent commitment to lessons learned in younger more impressionable years. Jebb the classicist, Veitch the Common-sense logician, theological mentors such as Lindsay, Candlish and Bruce, memories of the Robertson Smith affair and the price paid for scholarly freedom within the community of faith, pastoral experience of using the Bible not as inerrant text but as dynamic source and resource of the Christian life, these and other voices are unmistakably audible in the lecture, and in what is most characteristic in Denney's subsequent work.

The reasons for expounding Denney's view of Scripture at length at this point in the study are several. First, the Chicago experience provides clear and documented evidence that Denney's views were a clear echo of Candlish and Lindsay's approach, especially the appeal to the 'true Reformation' attitude to Scripture, and the safeguarding of the rights of a moderate criticism. Secondly, comparing the two versions of the lecture raises intriguing questions about the psychology of a minister in whom a reserved personality expressed theological conviction with a combination of popular rhetoric and lucid argument. When truth or tact were the options in public debate, Denney often without intending offence, was positively tactless. Thirdly, by 1897, as a result of the publication of *Studies in Theology*, Denney's views were more widely known and largely explain the reservations of those who opposed his appointment. But then, fourthly, during his first decade in Glasgow, he wrote and spoke on major issues such as biblical criticism and the church, theological restatement and the modern mind and urged radical changes in patterns

---

[39] Ibid., 19. Emphasis mine.

of ministerial education. Each of these as they emerge in his thought is intimately related to the 'non-inerrancy evangelicalism' that informed his views on the nature of Scripture.

In each case he based his argument upon the same core convictions about what he considered 'true ideas on the authority of Scripture'. It can be plausibly argued that the richness of his published corpus, the regular dissemination of his opinions in the *British Weekly*, the influence of his lectures on generations of students, the confidence he inspired in many ministerial colleagues by demonstrating the fruitful co-existence of biblical criticism and theological loyalty, his status as increasingly trusted churchman, helped establish the theological temper of the United Free Church, the fruit of which would be borne in later negotiations and theological adjustments leading to reunion.

'There is an inexhaustible truth in trying to understand Christ'

The first few years in Glasgow were years of major readjustment for Denney. By leaving Broughty Ferry and pastoral ministry, he had lost his primary community, the place where he had an acknowledged status and network of relationships, and where he knew and understood the pressure of expectations. The Denneys moved into Lynedoch Street next to the College, six years later moving to Lilybank Gardens in the fashionable West End.[40] The rest of their lives were spent there, and they joined College Free Church where Denney was an elder.[41]

The close connection between College and Church meant students and lecturers came under the influence of an impressively able congregation. 'If the Chamber of Commerce were summoned to meet within the Session Room of the College Church, a quorum could be formed by its office-bearers.'[42] The minister George Reith was a cultured man, of wide sympathies, mystical temperament, 'jealous of the truth of Scripture', and a preacher for whom Denney had deepest respect. He had lectured on Savonarola, Leonardo da Vinci, Michaelangelo and John Ruskin[43], and he was a staunch defender of Dods, Bruce and Robertson Smith, illustrating

---

[40] *LWRN*, 31. This house was later left in Denney's will for the use of his sister Catherine during her lifetime, after which it was to be sold or rented and the proceeds applied to the Women's Foreign Mission of the UFC. SC36/44/3, 453.

[41] *Free College Church Annual Report*, 1897-8. Unfortunately there is no record of holdings for College Kelvingrove United Free Church, 1900-1919, at NAS or Glasgow Mitchell Library. The building was destroyed by fire in 1925; possibly the church records were destroyed then. W. M. Clow, *George Reith. A Scottish Ministry*, (London: Hodder & Stoughton, 1928), 180.

[42]Ibid., 113.

[43] Ibid., 116.

the kind of scriptural truth of which he was so jealous.[44] He was minister of the church that had established the North Woodside Mission in response to the Moody and Sankey mission and where the Boy's Brigade was founded by William Alexander Smith, Reith being the Brigade's first chaplain.[45] Congregation and minister were deeply congenial to Denney and some compensation for the loss of a pastoral relationship with a congregation of his own.

Within months Denney was writing to Miss Wilson of Broughty Ferry, the start of a correspondence that lasted the rest of his life. Feeling inadequate for the task of expounding the person of Christ he confessed, 'Ignorance and inexperience combined make one fumble and stumble dreadfully, but the sense that there is an inexhaustible truth to deal with in trying to understand Christ, and the light which Christ as the Truth throws on all that is, is very reassuring'.[46] Earlier, writing to his friend Struthers about his struggle to write a lecture on providence he admitted, 'I find at the end of everything - and sometimes a great deal sooner - that there is room for a tremendous lot of agnosticism in theology. Fancy a man having to be inducted to a chair of dogmatics to discover that he cannot by searching find out God.'[47]

A full set of fifteen unpublished Practical Theology Lectures survives from these early years of teaching.[48] They cover only those aspects of ministry specific to a minister's liturgical role. Sacraments, liturgical practice, prayer, scripture reading, praise, preaching and a number of other topics are carefully, at times ponderously expounded, though occasionally enlivened as Denney laid down the law from his own experience.

> Often in a church there is trouble with the choir.... A little diplomacy, a little good temper, a decided appeal to the highest motives, usually settles it. One thing that ought not to be tolerated is seen often enough - a badly behaved choir, in which there is whispering, looking up the next hymn while the Scripture is being read or during the prayer; this is quite gratuitously offensive to the church, as well as irreverent, and the minister should stop it - privately.[49]

The weariness discernible in his comment, 'we have had such questions as instrumental music and its lawfulness discussed <u>ad infinitum</u>', suggests vivid memories of long meetings at Broughty Ferry. 'Prayer' and 'Scripture Reading' demonstrate the same use of anecdote and personal

---

[44] Ibid., 116, 161.
[45] Ibid., 136ff. See 'Boys' Brigade' and 'Reith, George' in *DSCHT*, 92, 782.
[46] *LFF*, 97-8.
[47] Ibid., 74.
[48] DEN09-23-01 to DEN09-23-15.
[49] DEN09-23-08, 'Praise', 6.

experience. 'The Lord's Supper' contains a characteristic discussion of the relation of Sacrament to Word; 'we do not believe the sacrament carries grace of itself; it carries grace as an appendix to the word'.[50] But knowing the profundity of Denney's thought, the reader of these lectures is aware that his mind was made for deeper soundings, 'the plunge of lead into fathomless waters'.[51] With his move to the New Testament Chair in 1900, he found adequate depth in the apostolic testimony.

'Sensitive to all the intellectual influences which breathe around him'

In 1897, Denney delivered his inaugural lecture entitled 'Dogmatic Theology'. It is an important programmatic statement of how he understood the dogmatic task, setting out fundamental assumptions that were to shape his theological approach. He never constructed a systematic theology, but had he done so, this lecture would have formed a suitable basis for the prolegomenon. He began by insisting that truth and reality have an ontological correspondence. 'Dogmatic does nothing effective if it does not present in scientific form the truth of Christianity.... In Christianity the mind of man is put in contact with realities which attest themselves to it as real, and which it is bound to interpret, to the best of its ability, in consistency with each other, and with all that it knows.'[52] These realities were, according to Denney, historically rooted in the apostolic experience of and testimony to Jesus Christ. Indeed in this lecture the historical and experienced reality of Christ is presented as the interpretative criterion and controlling content of dogmatics.

> That power or virtue of the soul which grasps the divine in the historical, and so brings true religion to the birth, is faith... Unless we have renewed the experience of the first Christians - unless in the exercise of faith we have come into contact in Christ Jesus, with divine eternal truth - all that is called Christian doctrine must remain unreal to us...the fullness of eternal truth is only given to faith historically, and we must always revert to what we have in Christ as the measure of rationalized religion.[53]

Religious truth is only apprehensible as truth to 'a mind which is open to religious impression'.[54] An open mind, contact with Christ, an apprehension of the reality and truth that underlies religious experience, these are merely the presuppositions required to understand 'what is

---

[50] DEN09-23-12, 'Liturgical Practice', 4.
[51] Denney, *Death*, 45.
[52] Denney, 'Dogmatic Theology', *Expositor*, Series V, vol. VI, 1896, 422-3.
[53] Ibid., 424-5.
[54] Ibid., 426.

fundamentally and characteristically Christian...the consciousness of reconciliation to God through the atoning death of Jesus and His gift of the Holy Ghost'.[55] That which lies at the heart of the Christian revelation for Denney is not Jesus Christ *simpliciter*, but God in Christ reconciling the world to himself.

The death of Christ as revealing the reconciling love of God, and realising it in human experience, is a reality fundamental not only to dogmatics, but to metaphysics. Denney thought of Christ on a Colossian scale, as the one in whom 'all things consist', the one by whom all things are reconciled, in whom the fullness of the Godhead dwells bodily. Because Christ is to be understood as the central reality of the universe, the reconciling centre of all creation, Denney insists here, as elsewhere, on the wholeness of knowledge, the unity of truth, the final reality of Christ crucified and risen, as the One whose reality is so definitive that consistency with that which he reveals validates or disqualifies all other truth claims.

> The attempt to expel metaphysics from theology is well intentioned but it will not succeed. It is really a plea to decline consideration in the science of theology, of the unity of all truth.... It is an appeal not to think, and such an appeal, addressed to the intelligence, must finally be in vain.... Instead of expelling metaphysics from theology, we must urge the claim of theology to be the only true metaphysics. Metaphysics is the science which deals with the ultimate reality of things, with the truth which is beneath, and through all things, and makes them what they are. To a Christian man, that ultimate reality is the reconciling love of God with which faith has brought him acquainted in Jesus Christ.[56]

Such absolute conviction about the cosmic significance of the death of Christ, and of God's reconciling love as the last and ultimate reality in the universe, co-existed with a conviction, as deeply held, of the provisionality of all dogmatic formulations of that truth. As will become clear, Denney's first decade in Glasgow coincided with a broader move amongst the churches towards doctrinal restatement, and a relaxation of credal subscription as a preferred method of establishing Christian orthodoxy. Within this lecture, Denney left his hearers in no doubt about his sympathy for such a relaxation, and in a passage of spiritual autobiography reveals just why the more conservative ranks of the Free Church resisted his appointment to a position of strategic influence in shaping the minds of future ministers.

> The creeds and confessions are sources, but not laws, for dogmatic theology. Faith comes to us, no doubt, as an inheritance, yet it is a new birth in every man; and he who lives by faith does not live under law. Sympathetic faith will find in the

---

[55] Ibid., 431.
[56] Ibid., 438.

confession under which it has been nurtured a weighty testimony to the essential truths of the Christian religion; yet it may find also, and may with all loyalty to the Church say that it has found, inconsistent or unchristian elements inadvertently bound up with these, or positions laid down as essential to Christianity which wider experience or more matured reflection show to be really indifferent.[57]

Following this confession of a man who valued the tradition which nurtured him, but recognised the need to grow within and beyond it, Denney, perhaps inadvertently, penned his own intellectual portrait.

The dogmatic temper must be the temper of a man who belongs to his own time, but who is at the same time, in virtue of his Christian faith, quickly and keenly sympathetic with all that is Christian in the past, and especially with all endeavours to work out the contents of faith into some kind of Christian science.... No one has more need than the dogmatic theologian to cultivate the spirit which is appreciative equally of what has been and of what is yet to be.[58]

The reconciling love of God in Christ as the focal emphasis of Christian theology, and the dogmatic temper which combine assured conviction and openness to new truth, these became underlying continuities in Denney's most important work.

'Do what you can, or get the chance of doing'

From 1897 onwards Denney gained in stature as scholar and churchman as he became increasingly involved in denominational and public life. On the initiative of Bruce, the Glasgow professors had become accustomed to preaching regularly in the churches. George Adam Smith and Denney became College ambassadors through the quality of their preaching.[59] There are many hints at the busyness of Denney's itinerary in his letters. In one week he preached at the opening of two new Glasgow churches, in Garscube Road and in Cunningham.[60] He complained about travelling to preach at poorly attended evening Synod meetings, he preached often for his friend Struthers in Greenock, at Carluke, Stepps, and elsewhere. Struthers, aware of the strategic effect of sound preaching on a denomination's perception of its professors' theological trustworthiness, encouraged Denney to preach frequently.[61]

As minister, elder and professor, Denney was an active member of Glasgow Presbytery. His minister George Reith recalled him as a conscientious elder, 'faithful in the common work belonging to that

---

[57] Ibid., 427.
[58] Ibid., 428.
[59] *LFF*, 75-6.
[60] Ibid., 75.
[61] Struthers, *Life and Letters*, 237.

office...who thoroughly identified himself with [our] work and worship'.[62] On important occasions Denney spoke on behalf of the College Church. He spoke in 1902 at the afternoon inauguration services for Stevenson Memorial Church, erected at the expense of the College Church to house the Woodside Mission congregation.[63] The year before his death, Denney preached at the fiftieth anniversary of Reith's induction on the text 'I magnify mine office'. The mutual esteem between Denney and Reith is evident in the letter accompanying Denney's gift of his published sermons, *The Way Everlasting*. 'I know how inappropriate it is that I should offer you a volume of sermons: it is a commodity in which you can easily give gold for brass to the rest of us...'I have need to be baptized of thee.'[64]

From 1900 till 1904 Denney and Orr edited the *Union Magazine*, a chore undertaken in the interests of the church, and an example of duty eclipsing discretion. Neither Orr nor Denney could afford the time or creative output to be responsible for a denominational magazine, nor did the task allow them to play to their strengths. But in fairness to Denney, he realised the importance of congregational news, information flow and a public forum reflecting and shaping opinion amongst the churches, in the search for denominational identity, especially in the aftermath of the Union of 1900. The anxieties and pressures of soliciting material, making the magazine attractive, marketable and financially viable, became unsustainable and publication finally ceased in 1906.[65]

Within the College Denney became minute secretary to the Senate, showing ability in the details of administration and organisational management. In 1903, during the Assembly discussion concerning allocation of capital to the Colleges, he intervened to recommend additional funds for the Glasgow College, because its condition of 'squalor and disrepair' was not 'creditable to the Church'.[66] Of more and recurring concern was the shortage of candidates for ministry, and the need to develop new forms of training. Structural changes such as lengthening the session,[67] or increasing the number of lectures,[68] he thought superficial. Denney was a vocal critic of ministerial training dependent on old models no longer relevant or effective in the changing world of knowledge and society. Instead of the disproportionate time

---

[62] Reith, *UFCMR*, 163.
[63] Clow, *Reith*, 144.
[64] Ibid., 124.
[65] *LWRN*, 69-71. The index reveals the frequency with which Denney sought Nicoll's advice on editorial and publishing matters.
[66] *PGAUFC*, 1903, 54.
[67] *LWRN*, 34.
[68] *LWRN*, 46.

spent on Hebrew, Greek, and textual and historical criticism, he advocated thorough grounding in the English biblical text.

> I do think it no better than a superstition to believe that every man who is to preach the Gospel and do pastoral work must affect to be a student of Greek...as for finding the word of God in Holy Scripture, and presenting it for the edifying of the Church, the men who cannot do this with the English Bible - which is all the church itself has to depend upon - cannot do it at all.[69]

Principal Iverach called Denney's paper 'the work of a person who is quite clear, quite sure that he is right, very plausible, but entirely, hopelessly, and, if he cannot be suppressed, fatally wrong'.[70] In this as in other areas, Denney's independence of mind reflected a pastoral concern that the Church be provided with the most effective training for the kinds of ministry needed in the new century.[71] More important than the traditional academic specialisms were a thorough understanding of the Gospel, a mind conversant with intellectual currents and scientific movements and development of the practical skills necessary to communicate the Gospel clearly and effectively to the modern mind.

The impression gained in reading the volumes of letters, is of a man in danger of dissipating his energies trying to do too much. Denney was aware of the temptation to do a multitude of things instead of *the* thing for which he was appointed. Perhaps his sense of duty was the practical expression of that deep moral seriousness which informed all his theologising, and which drew energy from a psychology strongly driven by vocational obligation. Yet, despite the high level of self investment in the work of College and denomination during these years, Denney still produced powerful theological writing.

'I hope we are not in for a time of panic, or of apathy either'

In 1902 he wrote thanking Robertson Nicoll for the gift of *The Church's One Foundation*, a book on Christ and criticism. He was acutely aware of denominational unease about where biblical criticism might lead. His words give a revealing insight into Denney's mind, careful, constructive, measuring the relations between scholarly integrity and pastoral realities.

> I am at the subject all the time.... What troubles me is not how to blow the trumpet, or sound an alarm, but how to teach in detail, and persuade people who are alarmed

---

[69] *LWRN*, 34-6.

[70] *LWRN*, 35.

[71] DEN09-18 'The Theological College Today.' This address at the opening of the College in 1906 will be considered in detail in the next chapter. See also DEN09-22, 'The Training of a Minister'; 'The Education of a Minister', *The London Quarterly Review*, CII, July 1904, 1-16.

not to close their minds in impatience, but to face the kinds of questions criticism raises and to meet them with the composure of intelligence, as well as the assurance of faith. One tries to do it in teaching and with time and pains it can be done, but who will give time and pains? I hope we are not in for a time of panic, or of apathy either, but may be brought through the strait into a larger room.[72]

Facing questions with the composure of intelligence and assurance of faith was more than a personal credo for Denney in 1902. His colleague George Adam Smith's volume, *Modern Criticism and the Preaching of the Old Testament*, had provoked a Memorial from Edinburgh Presbytery to the 1901 General Assembly complaining of the 'deep anxiety and unrest' raised by 'the revolutionary opinions therein set forth'.[73] By January 1902 Smith had appeared before a special College Committee to defend his views, the time between then and the next Assembly raising the spectre of yet another heresy trial, this time threatening to split the newly formed United Free Church. For theological teachers like Smith, Orr and Denney, the priority was to allay anxieties and win the confidence of the majority in the United Free communion

Several unpublished papers deal with the general themes of Bible, criticism and church. 'The Authority of Scripture' contains extensive verbal correspondences with the published version of the Chicago lecture on Holy Scripture, but arranged in a different order. The paper is an apologia for constructive criticism in the service of truth, laced with Denney's characteristic optimism about the spiritual outcome of the critical enterprise when pursued within the household of faith. 'What we have to consider is whether, after resigning what we cannot but resign, we can regain at first hand a conception of the true authority of Scripture which will serve all our purposes as Christians, evangelists and theologians. I believe we can.'[74]

'The Church and the Bible', is another impassioned defence of believing criticism and an important discussion of the relation of Word and Church. 'The Church is begotten by the Word of God, it lives by it, and it bears witness to it.'[75] The paper reiterates Denney's known position on infallibility, that Scripture infallibly leads the sincere soul 'to acceptance of Christ and obedience to him.' Luther's view of Scripture is

---

[72] *LWRN*, 23-4.

[73] Reissen, *Criticism and Faith*, 1. See I. Campbell, 'Sir George Adam Smith, 1856-1942', (PhD, Edinburgh, 2001), for a comprehensive account of Smith's outstanding contribution to ecclesiastical, academic and cultural life in Scotland. Pages 132-9 recount the 1902 episode. On Smith, see also Iain D. Campbell, *Fixing the Indemnity: The Life and Work of Sir George Adam Smith (1856-1942)* (Carlisle: Paternoster, 2004).

[74] DEN09-04, 'The Authority of Scripture', 1. Possibly a further revision of the published chapter in *Studies*, though other than long exact verbal parallels, no other direct internal evidence confirms this.

[75] DEN09-02,1.

rehearsed, 'He extolled everything that he found in harmony with that word of God which had saved his soul, the word which comes straight from God to the sinner, and it brings its own certainty with it.'[76]

What is more surprising is a rare defence of subjective mysticism as a valid but subordinate element in each individual's interpretation of, and appropriation of the Word, though only if that subjective interpretation was controlled by the inner witness of the Spirit and was congruent with the experience of the Christian Body.[77] The passage sheds an important light on how Denney conceived the dynamic relation between Word and Spirit and the responding human heart, and it supports Denney's own contention that he was not so devoid of mystical sympathies as, for example, Robertson Nicoll suggested.[78] 'I can imagine someone with a difficulty in their mind', he conceded,

> A difficulty with the idea that an assurance that God speaks to the soul in the scripture is guaranteed by the Spirit of God alone. It seems quite mystical and unscientific to say so. If one man says he gets this assurance, another may say he does not; and here we are at a stand. It is true there is something mystical here; there must be, whenever God speaks to man, and must do it himself, and no other, whatever the channel thro' which he speaks. But I say this does not open the door to infinite delusion, for in point of fact, men agree as to which God speaks. They are united by what he speaks. His word joins them to each other in the great brotherhood of the Church, and the fact that it does so proves that word to be no vain conceit of one brain, but an independent truth that has quickened countless hearts.[79]

Here Denney affirms the principle of Christian experience tested by ecclesial consensus, and puts his faith in the creative dialectic between church and Bible which takes place in the mind and heart of the believer honestly seeking truth. It was upon this underlying assurance of the sufficiency of Scripture as an infallible means of grace that Denney built his defence of believing criticism. Bible and Church need each other, and the believer needs both.

> The dependence of the Bible and of the Church on each other - their common function as witnesses to the truth - their inseparableness in all Christian experience make abstract questions about their relations somewhat unreal. The Church is the

---

[76] Ibid., 9.
[77] Ibid., 4.
[78] MS3518/27/10/ Envelope 6/19 October 1905. This letter is quoted in edited form in Darlow, *Nicoll*, 400-1.
[79] DEN09-02, 13.

home of the Bible; the Bible is the heart of the Church. The Church is the ark; the Bible is the testimony which it contains.[80]

Since neither of these papers was published it seems likely they were prepared as lectures or occasional papers, delivered in College or elsewhere. A third paper, written with measured care and theological tact, in the light of subsequent events may lay claim to being one of the most important Denney ever delivered. Though undated, several clues suggest that the context of 'Christian Faith and the Criticism of the Bible' was the looming trouble over George Adam Smith's orthodoxy in 1901. Denney began, 'It is as an association of office-bearers in the church that you are here, and it is as a minister of the church that I address you'.[81] We know Denney was largely responsible for the Glasgow United Free Church Office-Bearers Association being formed, and would be a natural choice to address them on such a crisis-laden subject.[82]

In addition, there are several explicit references to the subject 'at this present moment exciting grave interest in the church', the invitation to speak was 'proof of its urgency', and several times Denney referred to the 'present anxiety' and 'the present distress' while expounding the now familiar themes of legitimate criticism and the true nature of biblical authority.[83] Several times in 'Christian Faith and the Criticism of the Bible' Denney affirmed a personal confession of faith and trust in Scripture as God's durable Word, unaffected by believing criticism in its efficacy and infallibility as the medium through which God speaks in the finality of Christ crucified and risen. One passage may offer oblique but eloquent support for his colleague Smith.

> Whoever believes in Christ who made Atonement for sins by his death, and who by his Spirit quickens men into new life - believes in the inspired meaning of Scripture as a whole. There is an expression in use among us sometimes with a shade of Pharisaism, sometimes with a shade of contempt, "believing criticism". What I should take it to mean was criticism as practised by a man to whom the faith I have just described was the element in which he lived and moved and had his being. And that there is such a thing, and that it has a right to be, I do not doubt.[84]

---

[80] Ibid., 12-13.

[81] DEN09-07, 1.

[82] *UFCMR*, 1917, 164.

[83] Denney delivered the start of session College Address in October of 1902 on 'The Gospels and the Gospel'. In seeking wider publicity for it he told Nicoll it had been written 'for the present distress', and asked that it be published. *LWRN*, 28. It was the leading article in *The British Weekly* on 6 and 13 November 1902. It is a robust defence of historical criticism as servant of a historical Gospel bearing witness to the reality of the historic manifestation of God in Christ.

[84] Ibid., 3.

The rest of the paper is a response to 'the present anxiety which many feel about criticism as at present practised within the church',[85] the tone is uncharacteristically reassuring and conciliatory, indicating an assumption to himself of pastoral concern for the future of the church. The paper ends with one of several rueful comments on the dilemma of those expected on the one hand, to articulate the church's concern, and on the other, to defend the church's interests in maintaining spiritual freedom. In the light of the later Assembly decision in 1902 not to proceed against Smith, the closing appeal provides an historically precise example of Denney growing into leadership. It is also a counterbalance to the impression Denney himself often gave, of being impatient, even dismissive of minds less able than his own to overcome anxieties about the impact of biblical criticism on the spiritual life of the church.

> It would be affectation in me to speak as if the subject of faith and criticism were one in which we had only a speculative interest. You would not have asked me to speak about it if this had been the case, and I would not have been doing so. It is because I appreciate and to some extent at least sympathize with the kind of anxiety which is felt by many Christian men in connexion with this subject that I think it worth while to speak of it at all. It needs to be spoken about. It needs to be elucidated, and I could wish that those who understand its bearings or think they do, would take the responsibility of trying to help others to understand them.

> But I hope I shall not be thought presumptuous or obtrusive if I venture to deprecate, in a meeting of office-bearers, any action or movement in the church which while it would be certain to excite strong feeling would not, in all probability contribute anything to the convincing solution of questions about Scripture which the human mind cannot but ask, and therefore would not contribute anything to the relief of the present distress. The problem presented by the relation of faith and criticism is one of the trials of faith for our age, and therefore one of the great forces in its spiritual education. Whatever may be uncertain about it, this is certain, that it cannot be decided by impatience or by zeal, by strong language or even by strong resolve. It can only be worked out by a process in which Christian intelligence and Christian conscience co-operate; not by the renunciation of intelligence, or the renunciation of the gospel in haste or passion, but by the patient adjustment and enlargement of the mind to match reality on the NT scale.... Let us hope and pray that in the United church[86] - a church which owes much to this association - God will guide us through the perplexities which disquiet so many into the path of truth and peace, and enable us always, to preach the gospel, according to the Scriptures, in the power of the Holy Spirit.[87]

---

[85] Ibid., 4.
[86] This is one of the clues suggesting the provenance of the paper was around 1901.
[87] Ibid., 15.

The Death of Christ

The Death of Christ, published in 1902 was preceded by the *Commentary on Romans* (1900) and six lengthy articles in *The Expositor* on 'The Theology of Romans'(1901), and was followed by three published lectures on *The Atonement and the Modern Mind*, (1903). Together they constitute a cluster of theological projects arising naturally from Denney's personal interests, his lecturing responsibilities and from ideas he had been forced to defend and articulate as he constructed a theology of Scripture resistant to theories of textual inerrancy and adequate to the apostolic testimony to Christ's atoning death.

By 1903, when arguing for his view of inspiration and infallibility, Denney habitually located the centre of revelation in the cross. The sympathy of his mind for Paul and for Pauline categories of thought had been obvious in his earlier commentaries on *Thessalonians* and *2 Corinthians*. But in *The Death of Christ* Denney tackled the harder task of understanding the death of Christ by a critical but believing interpretation of the entire New Testament. In doing so, he again arrived at a cruciform understanding of revelation.

> Scripture converges upon the doctrine of the Atonement; it has the unity of a consentient testimony to a love of God which bears the sin of the world. How this is done we do not see clearly till we come to Christ, or till He comes to us; but once we get this revelation from Him we get it for revelation as a whole. To Him bear all the Scriptures witness; and it is as a testimony to Him the Bearer of sin, the Redeemer who gave His life as a ransom for us, that we acknowledge them. This is the burden of the Bible, the one fundamental omnipresent truth to which the Holy Spirit bears witness by and with the word in our hearts. This, at bottom, is what we mean when we say that Scripture is inspired.[88]

The familiar arguments concerning the inner testimony of the Spirit, the Christological focus of revelation, the eschewing of textual inerrancy in favour of the dynamic impact of objective truth evoking subjective response in mind and conscience, are rehearsed at the end of a sustained theological exploration into the heart of the Gospel. In this book Denney demonstrates the gains of believing criticism in the hands of a skilled practitioner. In systematic argument, interacting with all the major texts, unafraid to raise and address critical questions, Denney delved into the core of New Testament faith.

Motive as well as method drove Denney's mind in certain directions. He believed the death of Christ had been pushed down the agenda of preachers as a doctrinal embarrassment, and had been displaced by theologians from the central position it occupied in the writings of the New Testament. His book was intended to reverse these trends and

---

[88] Denney, *Death*, 313-4.

interpret Christ's death taking account of 'the critical investigation of the Scriptures', and to demonstrate how 'an adequate apprehension of New Testament teaching on Christ's death will be found to contain the solution...of many practical and theological problems'[89] then exercising the mind of the Church.

While insisting that the atonement of Christ provided a unifying motif throughout Scripture, Denney's treatment of the various New Testament writers gave proper attention to differences of perspective and theological emphasis. Throughout he conversed with leading German critics such as Holtzmann, Wendt, Weizsacker, and Kahler. The method might be called that of the exegetical theologian, giving due weight to literary and textual analysis, but bringing the conclusions into the most constructive relationship possible, with what he believed was the infallible truth and the saving finality of the Gospel. In each chapter the textual evidence and theological exegesis points to atonement as substitution, to Christ's death as penal, and to sin as the necessitating reality which evokes the divine response of Christ's surrender of His life in the sinner's place. 'A ransom is not wanted at all except where life has been forfeited, and the meaning of the sentence unambiguously is that the forfeited lives of many are liberated by the surrender of Christ's life, and that to surrender His life to do them this incalculable service was the very soul of his calling.'[90] In describing Christ's death as a divine necessity, Denney avoids the note of impersonal fatalism. 'A divine necessity is not a blind but a seeing one...His death is not only inevitable but indispensable, an essential part of the work He has to do. Not blank but intelligible and moral necessity is meant here.'[91]

The central section of the chapter on Paul dealt with key texts which provided seams rich for excavation. The *locus classicus* is 2 Corinthians 5.14-21. Here Denney refused to allow mystical union terminology to displace the regenerating moral exchange of a substitutionary atonement appropriated by faith. 'The love of Christ constrains us. He who has done so tremendous a thing as to take our death to Himself, has established a claim upon our life. We are not in the sphere of mystical union, of dying with Christ and living with Him; but in that of love transcendently shown, and of gratitude profoundly felt.'[92]

---

[89] Ibid., vi.

[90] Ibid., 45. Mark 10.45.

[91] Ibid., 81.

[92] Ibid., 143. Denney's aversion to the idea of a mystical union, and his insistence that the essential union between believer and Christ was moral, provoked an exchange between A. S. Peake and himself. Peake had reviewed Denney's *The Death of Christ* in the *Primitive Methodist Quarterly Review*, differing from Denney's interpretation of union with Christ. Denney took him to task in his lectures on *The Atonement and the Modern Mind*, published in 1903. Peake's 'Reply to Dr Denney' was published in *The Expositor*

Encountering Denney in the full flow of a theological exegesis of such texts, it becomes clear why he insisted throughout his life that theology must be preachable. 'If our gospel does not inspire thought, and if our theology does not inspire preaching, there is no Christianity in either.' [93] Preaching in Denney's view, was itself something constrained by the love of Christ. The final chapter of the book contains a powerful plea for preaching which makes atonement in Christ the central emphasis. Interestingly Denney quotes with approval Wesley's[94] words *'full salvation now'*, as the phrase he thought adequate to describe the effect of the finished work of Christ.

> It is this great gospel which is the gospel to win souls - this message of a sin-bearing, sin-expiating love, which pleads for acceptance, which takes the whole responsibility of the sinner unconditionally, with no preliminaries, if only he abandon himself to it. Only the preaching of full salvation now, as Wesley tells us - and who knew better from experience than he? - has any promise in it of revival.[95]

It is significant for our understanding of Denney that we note his confirmation of a theological fact by exegetical conclusions supported by testimony to experience. While Denney had no intention of subscribing to Wesleyan perfectionism, he borrowed the phrase *'full salvation now'* to describe a perfect atonement as the foundational fact in experience which grants a perfect assurance. In a church tradition where the moral psychology of sin, guilt and forgiveness could become oppressively ambivalent, the pastoral application of doctrine evident in this chapter shows Denney being pastorally effective by being dogmatically persuasive.

> Christ died for sins once for all, and the man who believes in Christ and in His death has his relation to God once for all determined not by sin but by the Atonement. The sin for which a Christian has daily to seek forgiveness is not sin which annuls his acceptance with God, and casts him back into the position of one who has never had the assurance of the pardoning mercy of God in Christ; on the contrary, that assurance ought to be the permanent element in his life. The forgiveness of sins has to be received again and again as sin emerges into act; but when the soul closes with Christ the propitiation, the assurance of God's love is laid at the foundation of its

---

in January 1904, a further reply from Denney appearing in February 1904. Peake had the last word 13 years later when he wrote the entry in the *DNB* on Denney, and recalled with barely restrained pique, the sharpness of Denney's pen. He wasn't the only critic of Denney's anti-mystical stance on the interpretation of union with Christ. Nicoll wrote in November 1903 saying that to interpret the mystical union as merely a moral union was to 'clip and sweat the spiritual coinage'. Darlow, *Nicoll*, 353.

[93] Denney, *Death*, 283.
[94] He had been reading Wesley a year or so earlier. *LWRN*, 14-15.
[95] Denney, *Death*, 289.

being once and for all. It is not to isolated fact that it refers, but to the personality; not to sins but to the sinner; not to the past only, in which wrong has been done, but to time and eternity.[96]

Major themes of Denney's soteriology are woven through this passage; sin, atonement, broken and restored relations, God's love as foundational, propitiation, personality, assurance, each of them key motifs in Denney's theology.

The Atonement and the Modern Mind

Criticism and comment on *The Death of Christ*[97] prompted Denney to pursue the theme in three lectures at an Aberdeen Summer School, later published as *The Atonement and the Modern Mind*. In the Preface to the combined edition Denney insisted that much of the material dealt with real objections and questions communicated to him, and that they were 'not men of straw'.[98] The first lecture sets out Denney's view of how mind, truth, experience and Scripture combine in a Christian epistemology. 'Once the mind has come to know itself, there can be no such thing for it as blank authority...this is not the sin of the mind, but the nature and essence of mind, the being which it owes to God.'[99] Truth is self-confirming in its power to win the mind. In relation to truth and Scripture, Denney acknowledged a tension between them, but the prior authority lies in truth, because Scripture is proven true when that to which it bears witness, is realised in experience.

> Belief in the inspiration of Scripture is neither the beginning of the Christian life nor the foundation of Christian theology; it is the last conclusion...to which experience of the truth of Scripture leads. When we tell, therefore, what the Atonement is, we are telling it not on the authority of any person or persons whatever, but on the authority of the truth in it by which it has won its place in our minds and hearts. We find this truth in the Christian Scriptures undoubtedly, and therefore we prize them; but the truth does not derive its authority from the

---

[96] Ibid, 293.

[97] One intriguing aspect of this volume is the appearance of Kierkegaard as one of Denney's conversation partners. He had read Kierkegaard in German translation and asked Nicoll if there was a market for a small anthology. *LWRN*, 55. More intriguing still, Bruce Metzger in his review of the 1952 edited reprint of *The Death of Christ*, complained 'Tasker has once or twice introduced something from Kierkegaard, as well as from several other authors more recent than Denney', *Princeton Seminary Bulletin*, XLVIII, May, 1955, 56-7. Tasker excised but added no material. Kierkegaard was in the first edition, keeping company with Wesley, Halyburton and Bushnell in the section on preaching and atonement. See Denney, *Death*, 297-300.

[98] Denney, *Death* (rev. ed.), 1911, vii.

[99] Denney, *Atonement*, 7-8.

Scriptures, or from those who penned them. On the contrary, the Scriptures are prized by the Church because through them the soul is brought into contact with this truth.[100]

To the charge that this is uncontrolled subjectivity Denney retorted, that is 'like urging that a man does not see at all, or does not see truly, because he only sees with his own eyes.'[101] Throughout these lectures Denney tried to articulate a theology of experience, or at least a theology in which experience is given a validating authority over dogma. 'We are dealing here with things too great to be simply told. If they are ever to be known in their reality, they must be revealed by God, they must rise upon the mind of man experimentally, in their awful and glorious truth, in ways more wonderful than words.'[102] By which Denney means all words, including the biblical texts. 'There was more in Christ than even His own wonderful words expressed, and all that He was and did and suffered, as well as what He said, entered into the conviction He inspired.'[103]

In a later passage Denney sought to establish the status of religious experience in relation to the truth claims of the Gospel. 'The only apologetic necessities which give rise to fundamental doctrines are those created by religious experience. The apologetic of any religious experience is just the definition of it as real in relation to other acknowledged realities.'[104] Fundamental Christian doctrines such as the atonement do not originate in dogmatic argument, but in convictions rooted in the experience of Christ, the One to whom apostolic testimony bears witness in the light of a historically mediated revelation. Mind interpreting experience, experience as the subject of rational thought and intuitive reflection, the appeal to what is real and to the force of testimony, reliance on reason as the power to establish veracity in experience, these are thought forms which recall the epistemology of the Scottish Philosophy. Experience giving birth to conviction, testimony confirming historical fact, Scripture bearing witness to the Christ of history and experience, here in this combination of subjective experience and objective evidence, Denney located the peculiar authority and inspiration of Scripture.

> There is no proper contrast between Scripture and experience. Scripture so far as it concerns us here, is a record of experience or an interpretation of it. It was the Church's experience that it had its redemption in Christ; it was the interpretation of that experience that Christ died for our sins. Yet in emphasising experience the

---

[100] Ibid., 9.
[101] Ibid., 10.
[102] Ibid., 13.
[103] Ibid.
[104] Ibid., 54.

modern mind is right, and Scripture would lose its authority if the experience it describes were not perpetually verified anew.[105]

In seeking to present the atonement in more persuasive terms to the modern mind, Denney wanted to challenge latent presuppositions which disqualified truth in advance. He detected a world view in which the mind 'has an instinctive consciousness that it cannot accommodate them, and a disposition therefore to reject them *ab initio*'.[106] There follows a passage in which Denney reveals the evangelist's sympathy with the predicament of the modern mind, and the theologians task in addressing it.

> We have to take men as we find them; we have to preach the gospel to the mind which is around us; and if that mind is rooted in a view of the world which leaves no room for Christ and His work as Christian experience has realised them, then that view of the world must be appreciated by the evangelist, it must be undermined at its weak places, its inadequacy to interpret all that is present even in the mind which has accepted it - in other words its inherent inconsistency - must be demonstrated; the attempt must be made to liberate the mind so that it may be open to the impression of realities which under the conditions supposed it could only encounter with instinctive antipathy.[107]

Three powerful and legitimate influences were discernible in the modern mind, each of them partial in their portrayal of reality, 'and because of their very partiality they have, when they absorbed the mind, as new modes of thought are apt to do, prejudiced it against the consideration of other, possibly of deeper and more far-reaching truths'.[108]

The triumph of the physical sciences, particularly biological science, had created a popular mindset instinctively sceptical of religious truth. Yet Denney saw gain for a theology of the atonement in the 'biologist's invincible conviction of the unity of life, and of the certainty and power with which whatever touches it at one point touches it through and through'. An atomic view of personality and of every human being as a closed system had been discredited by biology, 'and so far the evangelist must be grateful. The Atonement presupposes the unity of human life, and its solidarity...a common and universal responsibility...such a conception of the unity of man and nature as biology proceeds upon.'[109] This comment gives a glimpse of how Denney's mind assimilated and reinterpreted knowledge, building it into a theological framework which had foundations independent of historical change, because rooted in an event that was uniquely definitive for all history.

---

[105] Ibid., 38-9.
[106] Ibid., 19.
[107] Ibid., 19-20.
[108] Ibid., 20.
[109] Ibid., 22.

His own fundamental theological presuppositions gave him criteria with which to criticise the methods and conclusions of contemporary thought. He simply refused to capitulate to the inherent tendency to reductionism which characterised science in its imperialist mode. 'Every physical science seems to have a boundless ambition; it wants to reduce everything to its own level, to explain everything in the terms and by the categories with which it itself works.' [110] What follows strongly echoes his critique of Drummond's *Natural law in the Spiritual World* twenty years earlier that the realities of personal experience cannot be explained by sub-personal categories.

> The biologist would like to give...a biological explanation of self-consciousness, of freedom, of religion, morality, sin. Now a biological explanation...is a physical explanation, and a physical explanation of self-consciousness or the moral life is one in which the very essence of the thing to be explained is either ignored or explained away. Man's life is certainly rooted in nature, and therefore a proper subject for biological study; but unless it somehow transcended nature and so demanded other than physical categories for its complete interpretation, there could not be any study or any science at all.[111]

Idealism was the second major influence shaping the mindset of Denney's contemporaries. His opinion of the philosophy of Hegel mediated through Caird has been discussed earlier. The Christological criterion disqualifies Idealism as a vehicle adequate to Christian categories. 'There can be no Christianity without Christ; it is the presence of the mediator which makes Christianity what it is. But a unique Christ, without whom our religion disappears, is frankly disavowed by the more candid and outspoken of our idealist philosophers.'[112]

The third 'modification of mind characteristic of modern times' was the rise of historicism and a mindset equally guilty of 'pronouncing absolute sentences which strike at the life of the Christian religion.' The claim that everything historical is relative, that nothing historical can have absolute significance or condition the eternal he simply rejected as wrong.

> It is no more for historical than for physical science to exalt itself into a theory of the universe or to lay down the law with speculative absoluteness as to the significance and value which shall attach to facts. When we face the fact...of Christ's consciousness of Himself and His vocation...are we not forced to the conclusion that here a new spiritual magnitude has appeared in history, the very

---

[110] Ibid., 23.
[111] Ibid., 23-4.
[112] Ibid., 29. See chapter 2 for a fuller account of Denney's refutation of Idealism.

differentia of which is that it has eternal significance, and that it is eternal life to know it.'[113]

That this is a dogmatic statement, Denney conceded; but as a dogmatic interpretation of historical evidence rather than the dogmatic habit of historicism excluding such interpretations from the outset. 'To set aside an interpretation of Christ's death as dogmatic, on the ground that there is another which is historical, is like setting aside the idea that a watch is made to measure time because you know it was made by a watchmaker.'[114] The eternal significance of the historical was, Denney believed, an absolutely essential theological and philosophical principle. 'If the eternal is not to be seen in Jesus, He can have no place in our religion; if the historical has no dogmatic content it cannot be essential to eternal life.[115]

The first decade of Denney's tenure at the Glasgow College was full, and fulfilling. He confirmed his reputation as a scholar, left the mark of his personality and teaching on successive generations of students, and gave himself to the life of the Free Church, and after 1900, the United Free Church, in College, church, presbytery and Assembly. He built close and important friendships with William Robertson Nicoll who provided an avenue for much of his thought and opinion in the *British Weekly,* with George Adam Smith whose case he advocated during the crisis of 1902, with James Orr as erstwhile co-editor and respected close colleague,[116] and with Lindsay former teacher and Principal. He became involved in more strategic areas of Church life, such as credal revision and developing new approaches to ministerial training. He published major monographs, articles, popular books, and a substantial amount of regular journalism and reviews. They were rich years, and Denney would never experience a time of such happiness and security again.

'In the shadow of his sorrow'

In December 1907 Mary Denney took ill and within days had died of a brain haemorrhage. The impact on Denney was predictable and permanent. The surviving information about her is fragmentary, allusive and second-hand.[117] What is beyond doubt is the role she played as a

---

[113] Ibid., 33.

[114] Ibid., 35-6.

[115] Ibid., 37.

[116] Orr's inscribed copy of Denney's *Romans,* (in the possession of the writer) was given with 'kindest regards' from Denney. See also DEN07-95, 'Death of Dr Orr'.

[117] See *The Temperance Leader and League Journal,* 28 December 1907, 830. Apart from a comment that she was 'a zealous worker in Temperance and religious work', this obituary is more an expression of condolence to Denney for the loss of his 'helpmeet',

dependable emotionally supportive influence whose social abilities compensated for her husband's more reserved personality.

During the Chicago trip in 1894, Denney's emotional dependence on his wife was incidentally observed:

> I don't know if [Americans] consult their wives about what they do; but here is an extract out of a paper which has been very complimentary to me. 'Mr Denney is accompanied by his wife, to whom he evidently instinctively turns for counsel in practical affairs.' Pretty good testimonial to both of us, eh?[118]

That they had no children deprived them of those elements of human experience which while they diffuse the focus of love and commitment as they include others, also broaden the base on which emotional fulfilment depends. Consequently their two-way affection, the responsibility they felt for each other, the mutual meeting of emotional and physical need, the trusted companionship which both challenged and protected, their shared interests and expectations of life, the encouragement of each other towards achievement, and the personal investment that underlies all long-term fidelity in human relations, had, after twenty years of marriage, become primary identity conferring human experiences. The loss of his wife was therefore the loss of the one person whose love, practical support, social instincts and personal friendship, gave everything else he did its primary human meaning, and gave him a securer sense of self.

Bereavement shook and all but disabled Denney. To Nicoll, now one of his closest friends, he spoke of not knowing what had befallen him, of being stunned, of being in a dream. 'We had been married for more than twenty-one years, and in all that time I never had a thought of which my wife was not part, and I hardly know what has befallen me.'[119] But even in grief, Denney's sense of duty and obligation rekindled the resolve to carry on so that for her sake he would 'not be faithless but believing and do what I can.... There is nothing to do but work, and every inducement except the one which once made every other needless'.[120] Resolution, believing, doing, represent the vocabulary of survival for one who knew life had changed irrevocably. Almost as a steeling of self, suggesting defiance if not denial, the same letter eulogises on Horace, comments on Gore's latest book and recalls memories of his father and of his

---

than an account of his wife's life. More helpfully, her contribution to temperance is noted in the *British Weekly*. She was one of the main organisers of the Broomielaw 'Holiday Club' for recovering alcoholics, and regularly engaged in temperance work at the Feeing Market. Practical, formidable, organised, well-informed, the description is of one who could hold her own. See *BW*, 26 December 1907, 341, and 2 January 1908, 373.

[118] *LFF*, 55-6.
[119] *LWRN*, 104-6.
[120] Ibid., 109.

congregation at Broughty Ferry. It is a mixture of uncomprehending and poignant confiding, expressed in the privacy of trusted friendship, and determined resumption of normality as his mind reasserted control over the things he *could* understand.

The psychological tension between inconsolable loss and determined gratitude for what had been given, was occasionally expressed in letters. 'I have had goodness and mercy since, beyond belief, but there are things that never change and that nothing can replace.'[121] Returning home from his first holiday alone, to an empty house,[122] the absence of the one who shared stories and laughter,[123] the loss of George Adam Smith to the Principalship of Aberdeen, and frequent complaints of loneliness, are all symptoms of grief subsiding into sorrow, then becoming a bearable, but never absent sense of incompleteness. Such glimpses into the private emotional life, yielded under the pressure of a sorrow that must occasionally be told, reveal levels of emotional vulnerability, that, when balanced with the impression in his writings of intellectual self-confidence, help explain the complex mixture of hard edged reasoning and existential passion that characterised his greatest writing.

The years following Mary Denney's death produced only two more major works. *Jesus and the Gospel* was well advanced by December 1907, and was published in 1908. Apart from articles, a volume of sermons, and several small books of republished articles, he wrote only one other monograph, published posthumously from the manuscript he had prepared. In *The Christian Doctrine of Reconciliation* Denney returned to the atonement, but this time with a different tone, some would say with a different theology. It is an important question whether any change of tone in Denney's exposition of reconciliation and the Christian hope owes anything to the inner brokenness of a man who had lived in the shadow of his sorrow, through his own personal Calvary.

---

[121] *LFF*, 177.
[122] Ibid., 131.
[123] Ibid., 137.

CHAPTER 7

The Glasgow Years, 1907-1917

In the 1906 College Opening of Session address, Denney promoted a modern, open-minded approach to theological education as an essential part of the church's mission strategy. To those suspicious of the effects of a liberal arts and divinity education on the student's spiritual life, he retorted:

> It is not education which destroys piety or faith. What happens...is that one has had no help in enlarging his thoughts of Christianity at the time when all his other thoughts were being enlarged. If the gospel is to be to a man of five and twenty what it was to a boy of fifteen, it must be a greater thing than he used to think. The function of the theological school is to show that it is greater, and that in the vaster system of nature and history which a scientific education has established in his mind, Christ can still fill all things and subdue them to Himself. The old ardour which had died down will be rekindled when this is done; it is by Christian faithfulness to the mind's requirements, not by unchristian coercion of them, that the soul is made strong to keep its faith and to secure its own generation to the gospel.[1]

The purpose of the theological school, Denney argued, was to train leaders who, by their apprehension of Christ and their application of Christian truth to the ethical concerns of contemporary culture, would be capable of providing the Church with intellectual and spiritual leadership.

> It is by these two processes - the simplification and vivifying of theology by returning to its source in our Lord's consciousness of Himself and His work, and the enrichment of Christian ethics by the ampler application of the ideals involved in Christianity to the world in which we live - that a school like this can render to the church the service it most urgently requires.[2]

In making these points Denney touched on the highly sensitive area of supernatural events in the Bible. Describing the intellectual problems posed by modern scientific and historical thought for ministerial

---

[1] 'The Theological College of today: Its difficulties and its duties', DEN09-18, 5. This is a programmatic address which, because it raises a number of key issues in Denney's later thought, is given full consideration in the first part of this chapter.

[2] Ibid., 17.

candidates encountering theology for the first time, Denney used their attitude to the supernatural as an example. 'It is not necessary to ask the student to bind himself beforehand to this or that miraculous story', he cautioned. 'No given incident, taken by itself, is necessarily vital.'[3] The fundamental question the student must face is the one that the Christian church has always answered in the affirmative:

> Is there among the realities which enter into human experience, a reality which we cannot explain by reference to nature or to human nature, and of which all we can say is, here God has interposed for the salvation of lost men? It is vital...that this question which the Church has always answered in the affirmative should be answered in the affirmative still.... The redemptive action of God is the only miracle which is indispensable to Christianity, but it is indispensable, and everything which conveys it, everything which is integral to redemption as an essential element or force in it – is indispensable too.[4]

Denney was not denying the reality or theological significance of the miraculous events of the biblical story; he was arguing that belief in these miraculous events was not an initial and primary prerequisite for ministerial candidates, nor the focal concern of theological training. Denney's point was that each student's redemptive, life-transforming encounter with Christ would secure the Church's gospel more effectively than an apologetic capacity to uphold the historical veracity or intellectual credibility of this or that miraculous story.

> We do not ask the student who comes to the theological college from the university to accept the supernatural precisely as it is presented in Christian tradition; but neither can we concede a claim to set the supernatural aside which means that the Christian experience of God is to be reduced to a non-Christian scale. On the contrary we must christianise the conceptions of nature and of history to make room for that experience. A Christian view of the world admitting the vital miracle of redemption and all that is constitutive of it is not meaner, or less intellectual, or less scientific than a purely naturalistic one: quite the reverse. It requires a larger and more subtle comprehension of reality; it implies the lifting up of nature into a spiritual system which has its being in personal relations and in moral ends.... When we invite the student of theology to adopt this attitude to the supernatural, we virtually announce that the centre of interest and effort in the work of the College will be Christ Himself.[5]

It is difficult to believe Denney was unaware of the implications that could be drawn from these words. What he went on to say in the address, about the formative impact of Christ-centred study in the spiritual and intellectual training of ministers, and on the application of the Gospel in a

---

[3] DEN09-18, 6.
[4] Ibid., 6-7.
[5] Ibid., 7.

changing world by theologically and ethically equipped ministers, was lost on those who only heard a Church College Professor discounting the evidential value of miracles. Just as significant, in a central section of the address he raised the question of doctrinal restatement, and the need for the church to move beyond the Westminster Confession and other 'accumulated traditions of past generations'.[6] To publicly render belief in even some of the Bible miracles optional, and to consign the Westminster Confession to obsolescence, was to ask for trouble. It came in the following days, as opponents fired off a volley of mostly hostile correspondence to the *Glasgow Herald*.[7]

The Christian Attitude to Christ

Several differently motivated letters indicate the heat generated by Denney's views, demonstrating the anxious awareness of intellectual flux and spiritual insecurity which characterised the ethos of the Scottish Churches in the first decade of the twentieth century.

> Sir, the opening address by Professor Denney to the students of the UF Church College must excite the indignant rage of every true disciple of Our Lord Jesus Christ and the contempt of every person who is determined to know the truth so far as he is able to ascertain it and to have no juggling with his intellect. That Professor Denney and his colleagues should have arrived at the condition in which, while accepting the Bible as the one and only standard, they do not feel any necessity to believe this or that miraculous story – that they should never have seen and never expect to see a miracle themselves – is proof of the spiritual blindness which has fallen upon them, and which God invariably metes out to those who seek to hack and hew out of His Word something conformable to their own imaginations and to supposed scientific facts.[8]

A more theologically liberal correspondent rose to Denney's defence.

> [The Free Church] stands by the literal infallibility of a book which is one of the most fallible in existence, and never even pretend to give any solid reason for their belief. Further, they are continually showing their unchristian spirit by carping at those professors who are devoting their lives to finding out the truth about the Bible, and who cannot help saying so when they find in it what is not true. It must of course be admitted, that thought is at present a little indefinite in the United Free body; but it is quite the same...in every church that can claim to be living. It cannot

---

[6] Ibid., 9.

[7] For the full correspondence see the *Glasgow Herald*, 19 October, 9c; 22 October, 5gh; 23 October, 10b; 24 October, 5c; 25 October, 3c; 26 October, 11d; 27 October, 3h; 29 October, 9g; 30 October, 3c. There is no response from Denney.

[8] *Glasgow Herald*, 22 October, 5,g.

be otherwise...when so many beliefs, previously firmly held, are in the melting pot.[9]

An enthusiastic unbeliever, revelled in the embarrassment Denney's address had caused the church, and looked forward to the day when all could 'bask in the light that shines from a thousand minds, in order to get quit of the mind-dwarfing shackles of antique superstition'.[10]

By late 1906 when this address was delivered, Denney was writing the early chapters of *Jesus and the Gospel*, a lengthy vindication of Christian faith centring on Jesus' self estimate. Writing to Nicoll, he explained his main thesis:

> The Christian religion is what it is, and what it has been all through its history, in virtue of the place which Jesus holds in it; and the one question which really exercises men's minds at the present time is whether the place which the Church has given Him is one which He Himself claimed: in other words whether there is a historical basis adequate to support the spiritual phenomenon of Christianity.[11]

The urgency Denney conveyed in October 1907 when he wrote this letter, had provoked a compelling plea in the 1906 College Address:

> Open the New Testament anywhere and we find ourselves in presence of a complete religious life. We see a whole world of spiritual experiences - convictions, emotions, hopes, energies, a whole life...equal to all the demands which the world makes upon life...Christ has his unique and transcendent place in the faith of the church; He is, in the Christian apprehension of Him, what no other can be; He is what no other can be to God – the only begotten Son; He is what no other can be to humanity – Lord; it is on this that the life of Christianity depends. But what if, when we go back to Christ's own mind about Himself and His work and His relations to God and man, we do not find anything to sustain these conceptions of Him? What if the Jesus of history turns out to be a being unable to sustain the attributes of the Christ of faith?[12]

The rhetorical questions of the preacher thinly veil the urgent enquiries of a scholar alert to the real vulnerabilities of faith encountering the questions of a contemporary culture in search of historical certainty confirmed by the canons of historical criticism. The stakes for Denney were too high to permit either politically correct re-affirmation of the old certainties, or non-committal theologising about abstract Christology, which evade the practical question of faith's ultimate historical foundation and final focus.

---

[9] Ibid., 30 October, 3.c.
[10] Ibid., 27 October, 3,h.
[11] *LWRN*, 95-6.
[12] DEN09-18, 11.

For my part, I frankly admit that it would be fatal to Christianity if when we turned to the historical investigation of the mind of Jesus we found nothing to justify that attitude of the Christian soul to Him which is characteristic of the NT.... I believe it is as easy as it is essential to show from the life of Christ that in His own consciousness He was, alike in relation to God and man, what no other could be; and that He had, in His own consciousness, that absolute significance for all man's relations to God which has always been assigned to Him in the church's faith.[13]

When *Jesus and the Gospel* was eventually published in 1908, he reiterated his conviction that the recognition of the centrality and finality of Christ, renders all other articulations of faith relative.

Amid the vast unsettlement of opinion which has been produced by the emancipation of the mind and its exercise on the general tradition of Christianity, [the present volume] calls attention anew to the certainty of the things which we have been taught. The Church must bind its members to the Christian attitude to Christ, but it has no right to bind them to anything besides. To be a Christian means in one aspect of it, to take Christ at His own estimate....[14]

Faith as taking Christ at his own estimate, Jesus' Christology concerning Himself, convincingly established as the primary hermeneutic principle applicable to all that is meant by Christianity, whether in its biblical revelation, in Christian experience, or in the articulations of dogmatic tradition: that was the ambitious interpretative project Denney attempted in *Jesus and the Gospel*.

'The burden of the accumulated traditions of past generations'

From 1908 onwards, as the two largest Presbyterian Churches began to entertain serious thoughts about reunion, Denney was already wrestling with the problem of formulating a universally acceptable Christian confession.[15] As a known opponent of credal subscription applied as a form of dogmatic control, it is not surprising that in the 1906 address he had tackled the issue of traditional theological formulations, and the need for theological restatement. There he defended the liberal arts followed by divinity pattern of ministerial education.

A man cannot pass through the curriculum of the university, and come out absolutely unaffected by it; or if he can...he is not the man we want as a teacher in

---

[13] Ibid., 11-12.
[14] Denney, *Jesus*, vii, ix.
[15] DEN09-08. 'What a Creed ought to be.' This paper has several verbal parallels with *Jesus and the Gospel*, and possibly dates around 1906, when discussions in the United Free Church culminated in the Act Anent Spiritual Independence of the Church, 'making the Church master of, not subject to, its creed'. *DSCHT*, 838.

the Christian church. The student on whom university training has told as it ought to tell comes to the theological school with ideals of science and truth in his mind which are now the light of all his days. He comes, consequently, with demands to make upon his teacher and upon his faith, which may no doubt be too impetuously urged, but which as the instinctive and irresistible movement of the mind which God has given us, deserve the most serious consideration.[16]

Perhaps a hint of autobiography recalls the impact of University education in the opening up of his own mind. Early in the address he registered serious criticism of those who would restrict the role of theological teachers to mere confirmation of old certainties without confronting contemporary questions.

> Instead of the free and exhilarating search for truth, and the joyful recognition of it, in which the mind really lives, there is the task of finding justification for something which very likely cannot be wholly justified. The attitude it requires us to assume is fundamentally wrong; it is bad for the intellect, bad for the character, repellent to the mind and conscience which have the simplicity and magnanimity of youth.[17]

The argument for intellectual liberty became increasingly important to Denney, not only to allow the church freedom to construct an effective apologetic for the gospel, but to create a climate in which entrenched doctrinal loyalties would not frustrate negotiations towards Presbyterian reunion. The defence of intellectual liberty and spiritual freedom expressed in Glasgow in 1906 was entirely consistent with his known position. But now it was being said in a programmatic address by a Professor of a United Free Church College, to a denominational constituency already nervous about the pace and direction of intellectual change; and it was said with Denney's characteristic flair for outspoken reasonableness.

> It cannot be questioned that the inherited systems of doctrine have largely lost their interest: vital Christianity, men feel, is not dependent on the Westminster Confession...but on Christ's consciousness of Himself, and on the powers which have entered into human life through Him.... What unites us as Christians is not an agreement in all the truths which Christian experience involves - we may have many of these yet to learn; it is our agreement in Christian experience itself - that is, in a common debt to Christ, a common attitude of the soul to Him.... It is perhaps not sufficiently recognised that when Jesus cried Come unto me all ye that labour and are heavy laden, and I will give you rest, the burden under which He saw men crushed was that of a religion which had become identified with the accumulated traditions of past generations. It ought to have been an inspiration, a fountain of

---

[16] DEN09-18, 2.
[17] Ibid., 3.

joy and strength, a well of water springing up unto everlasting life, but these traditions had made it a perplexity and an oppression.[18]

That Denney viewed the Westminster Confession as a 'perplexity and an oppression', when used as a form of control over the Colleges, is a clear sub-text of the address.

> Whether they are intellectual or moral, systems of doctrine or codes of behaviour or methods of Christian work, they are certain sooner or later, to become a burden to the Christian soul of which it must get rid. Not that we would disinherit ourselves, or cast away the intellectual or ethical achievements of Christianity in the past; but true Christianity is nothing if not original; it can be satisfied with nothing but experiences, reflections, inspirations of its own; it is burdened not quickened, till it turns its back upon the traditions, intellectual or moral, and learns for itself what God and man and truth and goodness are at the feet of Jesus.[19]

All of this was becoming a familiar recurrent argument in Denney's writing, revisited and repeated with evangelistic zeal. 'The historical Christ who reveals the Father and through whom we receive the Holy Spirit is the proper subject of the creed; all that is realised in the Spirit, the communion of saints in the catholic church, the forgiveness of sins and the hope of immortality, owes its realisation ultimately to Him.'[20] As early as 1903 in *The Atonement and the Modern Mind*,[21] in a major article 'Preaching Christ',[22] in another paper from the same period, 'The Restatement of Doctrine',[23] and in the final section of *Jesus and the Gospel*, he pleaded for freedom to counter 'disintegrating criticism'[24] by allowing the Christian mind to 'grasp the whole compass of Christian truth, to give an independent, original and consistent statement of it'.[25] That freedom would have its own spiritual constraint by applying the Christological hermeneutic, not a developed Christology complete with metaphysical and dogmatic apparatus, but such an experience of Christ as ensures Him the central place in the life, worship and faith of all Christians.

> It is this truly Christian work of removing the yoke of tradition and putting on the yoke of Jesus which has to be carried on in the divinity school of today.... Loyalty

---

[18] Ibid., 8-9.
[19] Ibid., 10.
[20] 'What a Creed ought to be', DEN09-08, 4.
[21] Denney, *Atonement*, 30.
[22] James Hastings, *A Dictionary of Christ and the Gospels*, (Edinburgh: T & T Clark, 1906-1908), vol. II, 393-403.
[23] DEN09-06.
[24] Ibid., 4.
[25] Ibid., 7.

to the Redeemer, and to the truth as it is in Him, is the supreme duty; and only through such loyalty and through the assurance and emancipation which it brings, can men be inspired to render to the church and the world the service which their own generation requires.[26]

'The symbol of the church's unity'

Denney was certain the Christian experience of Christ was its own guarantor. He conferred final authority on the living Christ, the eternal rooted in historical reality, experienced by apostles and verified by testimony, crucified and risen as the Redeemer. His claims on humanity are absolute, yet gracious, and when yielded to in present experience, evoke self-giving loyalty and grateful obedience. 'It is the combination of the historical fact in the present, in which the whole weight of the evidence lies; and it is the testimony of believers, speaking in the power of the spirit, which is used by God to make the historical eternal - that is, to make it living, present, and divinely strong to save.'[27]

These words are taken from the concluding section of *Jesus and the Gospel*, where Denney declared, in unequivocal terms, his belief that heart loyalty to Christ is the surest safeguard of the historic faith and the unity of the Church. He was nervous about his concluding chapter being taken out of context,[28] because its validity depended upon all that had gone before. Only if Christ is confessed as the object of faith, made the focus of the church's doxology, given the place 'assigned Him in the faith of the historical Church'; and only if that conception of Christ and the soul's spiritual assent to it 'is vindicated when we look to Christ Himself as the oldest records disclose Him',[29] only then can the religious life of the Christian be free to articulate that experience and conception in a summary but universally valid form of words.

In a personal letter to George Adam Smith, thanking him for the gift of his volume *Jerusalem*, Denney linked his own effort in *Jesus and the Gospel* with Smith's volume:

> You touch the difference between the OT and the New to the quick when you say that whereas before there were men who could say I know, now there was somebody who could say I am. The is the <u>differentia</u> of Christianity...The whole end and aim of the thing I am trying to write is to hammer out that one fact so plain that even the blind

---

[26] DEN09-18, 10.
[27] Denney, *Jesus*, 376.
[28] *LWRN*, 129.
[29] Denney, *Jesus*, 381.

may see, or at least that even the wayfaring man however simple may not miss it...[30]

Denney admitted he had not set out to write *Jesus and the Gospel* with the conclusion in mind.[31] But having embarked on a vindication of Christianity by appealing to the place Jesus has held in the historic faith of the Church, he was inevitably compelled to think through the implications for churches seeking a basis of rapprochement. He was concerned that the book should be persuasive to those in his own church, 'especially those under forty', and he refers to 'the present distress', the 'intellectual crisis in the Churches', and 'the most urgent needs of the churches' as his motivation.[32]

> There can be no Christianity to maintain if the evangelical truth is not asserted that Christ must have in the faith of men no less or lower a place than He has had from the beginning, or than He himself...deliberately assumed; but there can be no hope of appealing to the world in which we live to give Christ such a place in its faith if we identify doing so with the acceptance beforehand of the inherited theology or Christology of the Church.... The problem is to find a way of securing two things: unreserved recognition of the place which Christ has always held in evangelical faith, and entire intellectual freedom in thinking out what this implies.[33]

Entire intellectual freedom, pursued within a shared devotion to Christ, was for Denney the spiritual prerequisite for church reunion in Scotland. 'It is certain...that before Christians can combine to face with effect the problems presented by society to the spirit of Christ they must overcome somehow the forces which perpetuate division among themselves. The important question is whether they can find the true principle of union.'[34]

Denney suggested a radically summarised form of words to which all Christians could assent as a 'true principle of union': 'I believe in God through Jesus Christ His only Son, our Lord and Saviour'.[35] He anticipated several of the key objections. Although the ultimate object of faith is God, for Christians the nature of faith and the nature of the God believed in, are determined with reference to Jesus Christ. Given that Jesus is to God what no other can be, this, he believed, is safeguarded by the confession Son of God. Similarly, because Jesus must be to humanity what no other can be, this is secured when He is called Lord and Saviour.

To the criticism that the Holy Spirit is omitted he pointed out that the New Testament nowhere speaks of faith in the Holy Spirit. The proper

---

[30] ACC/9446/ No. 142, letter from Denney to Smith, 20 May 1908.
[31] *LWRN*, 129.
[32] Denney, *Jesus*, 381, 383, 410.
[33] Ibid., 383-4.
[34] Ibid., 390.
[35] Ibid., 398.

place for the Spirit is in the interpretation of Christian experience, since it is through the Spirit that all the work of Christ is appropriated by, and applied to, the lives of believers. The Spirit as the mediator of Christ's work, and the interpreter of Christ's person, was, for Denney, implied in the confession. However it was this approach to the Holy Spirit as implicate, rather than as fully acknowledged divine person, that has led critics then and later, to question the adequacy of Denney's Trinitarian views. It is one of the most jarring theological characteristics of Denney's writing, and an indication of how loosely he hung to metaphysical constructions of the Trinity, that he almost invariably refers to the Spirit in the third person neuter.[36]

The suggestion that the confession is too indefinite and could be repeated by an Arian or an Athanasian, he dismissed as beside the point.

> Arianism and Athanasianism both give answers to a question which multitudes of genuine Christians never ask. Once it is asked, the mind must be allowed to find the answer to it freely. It is not on the answer at all that a man's Christianity depends, but on something antecedent even to the question; and it is this antecedent something - the believing Christian attitude to Christ, and the sense of Christ's unique place as determining all other relations to God...and not the metaphysics of Christ's Person, which alone is entitled to a place in the creed. If we wait for unity in the Church till all Christians accept the same Christology, we may as well give up the thought of unity at once.[37]

The objection that the confession makes no reference to the atonement has no substance because, Denney argued, neither does the Nicene or Apostles' Creed. Nevertheless, 'The Christian consciousness of being indebted to Christ for salvation - of owing Him what we can never repay - must find a place in every confession of faith; and it does so when we call him Saviour.'[38]

---

[36] Sell, *Defending and Declaring*, comments, 'All the more strange therefore that Denney did not begin his symbol of unity with the words, "By the Holy Spirit I believe..."'. 205. This might have muted the criticism of James Cooper, 'Here comes Professor Denney, one of the foremost theologians of the United Free Church, dismissing as the doctrinal basis of reunion not only the Nicene Creed, but even that core of all the creeds, the Threefold Name in which we were baptised.' Augustus Muir, *John White*, (London: Hodder & Stoughton, 1958), 162.

[37] Ibid., 408. Denney's impatience with Athanasian, Nicean and Chalcedonian metaphysics, as inadequate intellectual vehicles for a contemporary Christology or ecumenical consensus was more an apologetic concern than a doctrinal judgement. But it ignored the unarguable fact that the church has always sought an intellectual framework for Christological reflection and has based its canons of orthodoxy on an adequate conceptual and propositional rendering of Christology within a Trinitarian theology.

[38] Ibid., 407.

Denney put forward his suggested confession as a basis for mutual trust and acceptance amongst genuine Christians, by which he meant those who gave to Jesus the place he has ever been given in the historic faith of the Church, and which the entire New Testament confirms he claimed for himself. That was the thesis of the book, and persuading others to accept it was his aim in writing it.

> We can all have, with a clear intellectual conscience, the same religion - the religion preached by the apostles and answering to the self-consciousness of Jesus - the religion in which Jesus holds the place He has held from the beginning, the only place He ever consented to hold - the religion in which we recognise Him as the only Son of God, our Lord and Saviour: we can all have the same religion - provided that the intellectual questions it raises are left to the free consideration of Christian intelligence.[39]

It was this generous, perhaps too optimistic, view of Christian experience informed by apostolic testimony and focused on Jesus, that explains Denney's growing sympathy for and support of the moves towards reunion within the Presbyterian churches in Scotland. His brief confession was, for him if not for others, a sufficient basis on which to build relationships and trust within a reunion process.

'Christian doctrines justified by their moral results'

Alongside doctrinal restatement the theologising of moral experience is a key component in the later Denney's theological profile. He consistently connected doctrine to ethics, relating the intellectual structures of Christian faith to the realities of Christian experience and behaviour. For Denney, practical theology was both an essential component of the divinity curriculum, and the obvious outcome of a faith that is thought through, experienced as transforming power at the core elements of personality and character, and lived at the level of practice and lifestyle with Christ as focus and goal. At the conclusion of his paper 'The Restatement of Doctrine',[40] he pointed to the required outcome of doctrine in ethical behaviour, practical applicability being for him a primary criterion of truth.

> The Christian mind must think; it cannot be smothered from within the church, and must not be intimidated from without. It must think in the world in which it lives, and with the faculties and resources at its disposal. And if it can say of all Christian doctrine (1) that they are the fruits of revelation - truths and convictions generated in the soul by the manifestation of God in Jesus Christ; (2) that they show their vitality by victoriously confronting and adapting themselves to the world of nature

---

[39] Ibid., 408.
[40] DEN09-06.

and history as science discloses it; and (3) *that they are justified by their moral results*, then it does not need to be ashamed.[41]

This was what Denney meant when he had argued in the 1906 address that the task of the divinity school involved, 'unfolding the moral ideals involved in Christianity, and throwing upon the world in which we live the searching and creative light of the law of the gospel'.[42] In the first decade of the twentieth century the Glasgow College had been making repeated overtures to the General Assembly to fill the vacant Chair of Christian Ethics and Practical Theology.[43] The protracted debate was not only over allocation of scarce financial resources, but indicated an implicit undervaluing of practical training, compared with the more overt commitment to academic theology and biblical studies.

In 1906 Denney was concerned enough about the Cinderella status of Christian Ethics and Practical Theology in the Colleges to include comment on it in his address. The passage has 'omit' written beside it, making it uncertain whether his Glasgow audience[44] heard his opinion on the matter.

> The interest of divinity schools has been more in the truth of Christianity than in its ethical requirements: they have proceeded as though the truth admitted or required demonstration and defence, while the ethical import of the gospel was self-evident...the very term truth is hardly found in the NT in the abstract intellectual sense in which it is here employed. What we find in the NT is truth embodied or incarnate in a person: man's relations to it are ethical and have ethical presuppositions and consequences...We want the light of the ethical ideals of Christianity cast upon the moral standards by which we act, and the social order in which we apply them.[45]

In order to do justice to the Gospel, the Church must show a commitment to the ethical principles implied in a Gospel which aimed at the moral transformation of human life. Further, as Denney pointed out, the Church's perceived complacency about the great social and ethical issues arising from a changing national and international social order, when contrasted with the Church's doctrinal defensiveness about issues of little

---

[41] Ibid., 17. Emphasis mine.

[42] DEN09-18, 14.

[43] *Minute Book of Senate, United Free College, Glasgow*, 84/1/1/1, 328. The issue rumbled on for several years. The Professors' persistence suggests those training the students were more aware of the need to modernise ministerial training by increasing the elements of applied theology, than those who controlled the finances.

[44] The same lecture had been delivered at Bristol Baptist College a month earlier. Denney solicited Nicoll's co-operation in not reporting it before the Glasgow College opening. Perhaps 'omit' suggests it was less relevant there. *LWRN*, 71-2.

[45] DEN09-18, 15.

practical import to the majority of people, was a serious stumbling block to 'a large proportion of educated people, perhaps a larger proportion of the labouring classes'.[46] The Church could not afford to overlook the apologetic value of relevance and sympathetic engagement in life. 'There are people in the world with causes at heart which are essentially Christian who do not find in the Church the sympathy and support to which they are entitled. The Church ought to be the most powerful force in society on the side of justice and freedom; it ought to reinforce spontaneously every movement which has the education of humanity in view.'[47]

And, Denney urged, if the Church is to be socially aware and ethically engaged in its given historical context, it must have ministers trained in Christian ethics and aware of the features of a society in which Christian values, if they are to be seriously considered, must be demonstrably and practically worthwhile as an enrichment of human society.

> The ethical contents and requirements of Christianity must be unfolded with constant reference to the world in which we live.... A minister should know something of the laws under which men live, and of their moral operation and tendency. He should know the ethical working of land laws, licensing laws, educational laws, factory laws, poor laws, all laws in short, which are a constant factor in the life of society, and which work to ethical issues.... Whatever else the church is, it ought to be the moral generator of moral ideals and of moral energy, and while it can never commit itself to any party, it ought to lead spontaneously and impel irresistibly every movement which makes for the moral uplifting and liberation of men.[48]

While, to use an anachronism, that is hardly a full-blown liberation theology, Denney's vision does represent a significant call to the Church of his day, to shift its intellectually formative resources away from self-concerned doctrinal conservation, to the provision of other-concerned morally informed leadership. The Church's own interests would be better served by a shift from doctrinal protectionism to social relevance.

'The Spirit of liberty, justice, generosity, and mercy'

In 1884-85, while in Hill Street, Denney encountered complex social problems, but showed himself politically cautious about finding workable solutions. In Chicago, ten years later, he lectured his hearers on the limits of Christian political involvement in such areas as disputes between capital and labour. His views at that time reflected the general failure of the

---

[46] Ibid.
[47] Ibid.
[48] Ibid., 16-17.

church to respond to growing criticism, particularly from the working classes, of its traditional fence-sitting support of the status quo.

> People cry out fiercely that the Church ought to mediate, that the Church ought to be on the side of the poor and oppressed...The Church ought certainly to be on the side of justice and of mercy; but it needs an accurate knowledge of the whole circumstances of the case, and that it is impossible and unnecessary for the church to have... It is no part of the business of the Church...to understand mining, docks, engineering, railways, or any industry, so as to give sentence in cases of dispute...we shall not assume that because we are Christians we are experts in economy or in legislation, or in any branch of politics, any more than in science or in art. We shall believe that the church which cultivates in all its members the spirit of humanity, the spirit of liberty, justice, generosity, and mercy, will do more for the coming of the kingdom than if it plunged into the thick of every conflict, or offered its mediation in every dispute.[49]

There is little evidence here of social criticism, or an alternative vision of more equitable social structures. For much of Denney's life, the intellectual liberty for which he argued, his vision of the Christian mind freed from systems of doctrinal control in order to meet the changing demands of the contemporary world, was not matched by a similar vision for changed political and economic thought, aimed at freedom from systems of social control as they affected, for example, workers and women. Yet the need to change the way society was organised in relation to such fundamental social realities as labour, capital, poverty, social provision, and voting rights, was just as great; and in terms of the church's ability to present itself as an ally to the mass of the population, would be of decisive importance.

His views on Socialism as a political programme were dismissive, confessing in 1908 that he had 'no scientific opinions' on the subject. 'I cannot say I could make out any ground for distinguishing between property which would or would not, or could or could not, be socialised.'[50] At a time when Trade Unions were consolidating their hold on working-class aspirations, strikes were becoming a major social lever, and those resentful about the basis of wealth distribution were being provided with an increasingly popular political alternative, Denney, in common with the majority of Scottish Presbyterian churchmen, was unable to see the consequences for the church of such a change in social expectations.[51] As late as 1914, on the eve of war, he was negative about

---

[49] *Studies*, 200-201. Westcott, Bishop of Durham, successfully mediated in a North East mining dispute in 1892.

[50] *LWRN*, 112.

[51] Brown, *Religion and Society*, 132-142. This general overview conveys the church's uncertainty, at times its divisions, over how to respond to the rise of new

Lloyd George's proposed measures to alleviate the situation of the poorest, demonstrating how an over-developed pragmatism can paralyse political vision.

> Lloyd George's intention to benefit the poor is unquestionable, but though I do not grudge my share on the income tax, I think it is a fair question whether the increase of the income tax and the spending of it as it is spent does nothing to benefit the poor. And there is always the further trouble that when we claim justice for ourselves, we act as judges in our own cause and almost inevitably claim more. Just because democracy is omnipotent, it would need to be composed of unusually good men if it is to produce an unusually good and just Government.[52]

This is political scepticism informed by hamartiology! To Denney's mind, the inherent prejudices and selfishness of human nature pass a cloud over any sunny optimism about democracy. But he was expressing attitudes seriously out of sympathy with the aspirations of those working people he hoped could be attracted back to the churches. By contrast, George Reith, Denney's own minister, not himself a known advocate for wealth redistribution, as Moderator of the United Free Church Assembly in 1914, urged that, 'A reunited Church of Scotland should present itself in the eyes of their fellow countrymen as one concentrated force, bent in Christ's name, on grappling with and ending the social sores from which our beloved land has suffered'.[53]

Denney was not opposed to improving living conditions and economic circumstances, even when it implied significant social change. His negative attitudes were not so much about the end in view, as the means of attaining it.

> The hopeful thing in our present situation is that everybody's conscience is on the same side as to the end to be aimed at: where people differ is as to the means. This is not a question which conscience can settle, though people who are very much in earnest about the end are apt to accuse those who differ from them about the means, of having no conscience.[54]

Underlying Denney's lukewarm attitude to political change, was a deep suspicion that, however desirable social improvement might be, the involvement of the church in the political manoeuvring necessary to achieve such change, was an illegitimate taking to itself of secular means. His study of the gospels had convinced him that the contemporary interpretation of the Kingdom of God as progressive social improvement

---

institutions dedicated to improving the position of working people by challenging the status quo.

[52] *LWRN*, 239.
[53] Brown, *Religion and Society*, 138.
[54] *LWRN*, 238.

of the human situation, was entirely wrong. In 'The Church and the Kingdom of God', published in *The British Weekly* in 1909, he insisted, 'Nothing could be more remote from [Jesus'] temper than the suggestion that if only all men had their rights - political, economical, educational - the Kingdom would have come'. He continued:

> There is a strong tendency to a kind of Christian secularism in much of the labour spent for what is called the Kingdom of God. There is love to men at the heart of it, and in that it comes from Jesus: but in the stress it lays on worldly situations, in the vast consequences it attaches especially to unfavourable or unfair economic conditions, its connection with Jesus is open to question.... We may think it right or wrong or peculiar, but the fact is not open to dispute, that His conception of the Kingdom of God made Jesus conspicuously indifferent to many things which at present are frequently identified with the Kingdom. He never had a vote; He never had economic security; He never had a right to work; and He never spoke of these things to others.[55]

Denney would have been scathing of anyone else invoking special pleading and rhetorical use of anachronism as in this argument. Even had the cultural parallels been valid, the particular and unique vocation of Jesus, as powerfully expounded in Denney's own writings, places Jesus beyond such facile comparisons. Jesus' conception of the Kingdom was tied up with his own passion, making him indifferent to many things which are not thereby invalidated as human aspirations and Christian moral goals.

'To legislate is to take the sword'

In 'The Church and Legislation', another *British Weekly* article, Denney was more persuasive in his rejection of the church's role as agent of political change, and more supportive of its role as embodiment of the kind of life a just, equitable and peaceful society might look like. Whatever people's conception of the Kingdom of God, Denney believed there was unanimous agreement on one point.

> It is that every region of human life is to be Christianised. All the relations of men are to be regulated - which in many cases means revolutionised - by the spirit of Jesus. Not only the life of the soul within, but all the activities of the man without, are to undergo this change. Trade and commerce, property, politics, social life in all its bearings, are to become manifestations of the mind of Christ. In the faith of Christians, Christ fills all things, and He is to fill all things in fact. The question on which men's minds are not clear is what methods are open to the church in

---

[55] James Denney, *The Church and the Kingdom*, (London: Hodder & Stoughton, 1910), 101-102. The book is a selection of six articles published in *The British Weekly* during 1909.

working toward this end. In particular they are not clear how far it is the duty of the Church to work directly for such legislative action as may contribute to its attainment.[56]

This and similar articles help explain his caution about the Church's role in propelling social and political change.[57] He believed strongly that moral change could not be enforced by legislation, and since the church is concerned with a gospel which aims at the spiritual and moral regeneration of the individual, it uses a wrong means when it tries to promote change by Acts of Parliament. In more whimsical mood he commented to Nicoll that Parliament can fix the minimum wage no more than 'it can fix the amount of sunshine there is to be next year'.[58] Comparing his £400 a year at Broughty Ferry with his father's much lower income, he conceded, 'The distribution of the rewards of labour between us was absurd and I long to see it corrected, but I have no conviction that the minimum wage and the right to work and in short any legislation that has yet been conceived, is likely to do much in that direction.'[59]

What would redress the balance was not legislation, but the presence in the market place of ethical principle applied to the benefit of human life. This view of improved wages and working conditions by employers of Christian principle, was earlier stated, in 1895, in his paper 'Preaching and Christian Ethics'.[60] Speaking of industrial relations he said it was unsafe to make money out of people working seven days a week, or to exhaust the strength of workers then throw them aside, or to make money out of any business, like the liquor trade, that results in misery, vice or crime.[61] Then he asked a question touching more fundamental principles.

---

[56] Ibid., 110.

[57] Nicoll thought it 'an omission that you do not sufficiently insist on Christians taking part in politics'. Darlow, *Nicoll,* 207. However in his funeral sermon for James Orr Denney expressed admiration and approval for Orr's dual emphasis on the advocacy and application of gospel principles in the life of the wider community. DEN07-95, 'Death of Professor Orr'.

[58] *LWRN,* 197.

[59] Ibid., 239. This suggest he was fully aware of economic inequities, but had found no solutions that seemed politically workable.

[60] DEN09-21. This paper can be dated to around 1895. The audience was ministers. It refers to the recent miners' strike, (probably 1894) and refers to the working conditions of women in Dundee. Its contents include the role of women, the use of brothels by the military, strikes, unacceptable working conditions in Calcutta and Dundee, business and wealth creation, the liquor trade, international relations, democracy and the relations of church and state. It demonstrates in the wide variety of topics, an equally wide range of opinion. Progressive thought, Christian compassion, undisguised prejudice, common sense, moral frankness and theological reflection, are all in evidence.

[61] Ibid., 7-9.

Is it safe for a Christian to make profit out of a business which does not yield to those by whose labour it is carried on the means of living a decent human life? Perhaps 'a living wage' is not an expression that economists can define: it has no necessary relation to the production of wealth, considered as an end in itself. It had its birth in consideration of humanity, not of economy. But it has a real enough meaning, nevertheless; and what is more it has a Christian meaning. The labourer is worthy of his hire...of what will enable him, in the circumstances of the case, to live with self respect, and with faith in God.[62]

By 1909 he still held to the principle that ethical business practice could not be legislated into existence as a way of improving the conditions of labour, or tackling 'the vested interests of iniquity which trample on human souls'. To 'those at the forefront of social revolution who call loudly on the Church to join them in appeals to the legislature', he replied,

Sometimes they impeach the Church of insensibility, and of contemptuous disregard for the spirit of its Master, if it is slow to respond to their call. Perhaps it does not occur to them that legislation is force. To legislate is to take the sword, and while there is no doubt a power which has this as its divinely appointed function, it may well cross the mind of the Church whether the function is hers...the Church's direct interest is not in framing Acts of Parliament, no matter how Christian their motive; it is in regenerating men, who will give expression, indeed, to their new life, in their laws as in all their activities.[63]

It would take the emergency situation of the Great War to bring Denney to the forefront as a vocal and effective lobbyist for prohibition by Act of Parliament. In this, as in a number of areas of social concern and policy,

---

[62] Ibid. Denney here provides a remarkable comment on the social and spiritual significance of strikes. 'A great strike, like the recent one among the miners, is not simply an economical phenomenon; it is a spiritual phenomenon of the first magnitude. There is a display in it of all those qualities which dignify and degrade human nature; of selfishness and of sacrifice, of cowardice and of courage, of forethought and precipitancy, of discipline and disorder. There is an awakening of sympathy and of antipathy through the whole mass of the population such as few political issues could evoke, and such as we have not seen produced by the gospel for at least a generation. The whole process in humanity which Christ claims as his own, which it is His to inspire, direct, and control, are in powerful operation here; would it not be strange if here, precisely, the minister of Christ had nothing to say.' Ibid., 6. He had an altogether more hostile view of strikes in 1912, supporting the use of soldiers to curb intimidation. *LWRN*, 196.

[63] Denney, *Church*, 113-15, 122-3. The issue was important to Denney. Two of the sermons in his published volume, *The Way Everlasting*, show the same reticence about the Church using direct intervention in the political arena, and the same moral urgency about Christians being examples of an ethical and compassionate social responsibility. See 'The Rich Man's Need of the Poor', 164-76; 'Wrong Roads to the Kingdom', 189-203.

Denney oscillated between pragmatism and principle in his quest for the ethical transformation of society by Gospel means. Underlying his resistance to Church involvement in politics, was a particular view of the Church as a spiritual community whose primary means and ends are therefore, spiritual, ethical and beyond the compulsion of law.

'Thae Unfidel Suffragettes'[64]

On one contentious issue Denney was prepared to be outspoken and provocative, on grounds of self-confessed prejudice rather than argument. He was a staunch opponent of extending the vote to women. He strongly supported a woman's right to equal opportunity in work, a legacy of his days in Dundee where in a population of 150,000, available women exceeded men by 17,000.[65] Single women who had 'to make their way on their own', he believed should have the same employment and remuneration opportunities as men. He makes no mention of the many married women in Dundee who had to work to help support their family.

But the political emancipation of women he simply saw as misguided, unreasonable and socially disruptive. For those already predisposed to resist the enfranchisement of women, there was sufficient evidence in the tactics of the more militant activists, to fuel fears of social destabilisation. The movement was largely made up of middle-class women. It did not agitate for universal suffrage, but for 'votes for women on the basis of the existing property franchise'.[66] A number of women's organisations sympathetic and active in the cause, had connections with churches where middle class women were both numerous and experienced in networking and promoting causes.[67] When Denney said that his late wife and her sister (now his house-keeper) disagreed with him, and that they were 'altogether on the wrong side',[68] he was saying so on the eve of the formation of the Scottish Churches League for Women's Suffrage.[69]

In August 1911 Denney published an article on 'St Paul and Women' which coincided with the visit of Mrs Pankhurst to Largs.[70] Despite a

---

[64] *LWRN*, 183.

[65] DEN09-21, 4.

[66] Tom Devine, *The Scottish Nation, 1700-2000*, (London: Penguin, 2000), 540. Devine sets the historical context of the movement in Scotland, describing several of the more spectacular stunts likely to have outraged an Edwardian academic clergyman with a preference for social stability.

[67] Leah Leneman, 'The Scottish Churches and "Votes for Women"', *RSCHS*, xxiv, 237-52.

[68] *LWRN*, 187.

[69] *DSCHT*, 'Women's Suffrage and the Churches', 891.

[70] *BW*, 24 August 1911, 505-6.

disclaimer that his 'innocent article' had nothing to do with 'thae unfidel suffragettes',[71] he followed a line of reasoning from Scripture that argued divinely intended difference in the role, function and authority of male and female, and by implication, that government is intended to be male. Another paper, 'The Current Aversion to St Paul', argued that Paul's teaching on women had contributed to the Apostle's current unpopularity.[72] As the Liberal Government faced an uncertain future he wished them good luck - 'except in their Women's Votes business'.[73]

Like many who hold an opinion based more on prejudice than argument, Denney admitted the prejudice and sought arguments to rationalise it. On the more general question of the role of women in the Church, he again revealed caution as his default setting on this matter. About the forthcoming discussion of the role of women at the Glasgow Presbytery, he wrote to his sister, 'I am going to vote in favour of letting well alone. I never did know a woman who wanted to be an elder, or who wanted another woman to be an elder, or who would have rejoiced in getting a woman as her minister; but we live in interesting times.'[74]

His more considered opinion was appended as a note to the 1916 Assembly *Report of the Committee on the Recognition of the Place of Women in the Church's Life and Work*. He distinguished between the Roman Catholic view of ordination by which once ordained a man can never be anything else, and is permanently differentiated from the laity, contrasting it with the view of his own tradition. Ordination, he argued, is simply the setting apart by prayer 'to special and regular service, such persons as the Church calls and appoints to the service in question'.[75] There is no reason why the person should not be a woman, and every reason why they should be if the service is one to which women are peculiarly fitted. Denney had in mind Church Sisters ordained as visitors and ordained Sunday school teachers, the standard roles in which women could serve 'appropriately'. 'To say this, however, does not answer any question as to what the kinds of service in the Church are to which men or women may appropriately be called.'[76]

It is anachronistic to judge Denney by the standards of today. His views represented a significant section of opinion within his own denomination and in the wider public. When questions on the role of women in society or church were raised, he freely acknowledged 'I have a prejudice stronger than all reason, but quite convinced of its own

---

[71] *LWRN*, 183.
[72] DEN08-84, 1, 5.
[73] *LWRN*, 195.
[74] *LFF*, 191. See also 'Women's Work in the Church', *CWP*, 71, 1907, 53-6.
[75] *LFF*, 192.
[76] *LFF*, 193. See further 'Christ and the World's Women', *CWP*, 74, 1908, 361-4.

rationality'.[77] This was one area where a mind that demanded spiritual and intellectual freedom to explore new insights in a changing world, and to think generously with Christ as its horizon, in the social context of his time was unable to apply such principles in ways that seem to later generations obvious. [78]

'They freely recognised each other's Christianity'

> The primary function of the Church is to assert its origin; it is to bear witness to Christ as the author of all the blessings it enjoys. Its first duty, as its primal impulse, is worship; and worship is the adoring confession of the God revealed in Christ and possessed in the Spirit as the Redeemer of sinful men. There is nothing so characteristic of the Church's life as doxology.[79]

A high view of the church's role and function was a constant throughout Denney's ministry. At Broughty Ferry, in the 1890s, in his lectures on the Apostles' Creed, he had insisted the words holy and catholic should have their full force.[80] The church is holy because it is what it is by the indwelling of the Spirit and by obedience to the Word of God; it is catholic because open to all who have faith in Christ.[81] In his Chicago lectures of 1894, Denney more explicitly stated an ecclesiology that assumed spiritual unity as theologically distinct from corporate unity achieved by the re-organisation of institutions. The New Testament paradigm was found not in any one trans-local church, but in the relationship of mutual recognition between churches.

> These local [New Testament] churches, reciprocally independent as they were, were nevertheless one; they were a church; they were the church of the living God. The bond that united them to each other as churches was...their common reception of the love of God in Christ Jesus [and] their common acceptance of the obligations which receiving that love imposed. They freely recognised each other's Christianity - each other's membership in the church.[82]

---

[77] *LWRN*, 160-1.

[78] In 1907 Denney became Clerk to the Senate of the College. One of his first entries reads, 'It was decided to admit women to the College at the same fees as men.' *Minute Books of Senate of the Free Church/UF/Trinity College, Glasgow 1857-1977*, held at Glasgow University Archives, 84/1/2/2, 16 October 1907.

[79] Denney, *Church*, 7.

[80] 'The Apostle's Creed and the Church', DEN08-22. See DEN09-10, 'The Church Catholic and Protestant'.

[81] DEN08-22, 7.

[82] Denney, *Studies*, 187-8.

A communion sermon on 'Church Unity' is a masterpiece of homiletic diplomacy and pastorally applied theology. The usual themes are there; church unity as spiritual not institutional;[83] Christian fellowship based on loyalty to Jesus not subscription to creeds;[84] the sinfulness of schism perpetuated for historic reasons no longer valid. It would be exaggeration to call this sermon an eirenicon, it is too outspoken for that. But it represents a powerful plea for that form of unity which must always be prior to any positive rapprochement between differing factions. Instead of acting like duellists, each claiming God's truth and intent only on 'killing their man', existing oneness in Christ demands that Christians bear and forbear. The presence of God's Spirit in the heart 'brings to their consciousness again the truth - always so apt to be forgotten,'

> that the reality with which we deal in framing a creed,...the love of God as it comes to us through Jesus, is so vast that it passes knowledge - a breadth and depth and length and height that we can only comprehend at all if we comprehend it, with all the saints. To recognise this will not make differences in creed seem insignificant: the intellectual statement of Christianity in a form to which all can assent who live in the unity of the Spirit will not lose its fascination or its obligation; to read all things, to interpret the world and the life of man in the highest truth as the truth is in Jesus, will still be a duty as inspiring as it is arduous and endless; but we will not break the bond of spiritual fellowship in Christ with others because they do not spell out the infinite truth precisely as we do ourselves.[85]

In 1909 the UF and Established Church agreed 'to enter into unrestricted conference on the existing ecclesiastical situation...in the earnest hope that, by God's blessing, misunderstandings and hindrances may be removed, and the great object of Presbyterian reunion in Scotland be thereby advanced'.[86] Denney represented the United Free Church, working within the sub-committee considering 'the liberty of the Church in relation to creed'.[87] Here Denney championed precisely the kind of spiritual liberty he had long upheld within his own communion. He was

---

[83] DEN08-75. Referring to 'much talk amongst us of Presbyterian reunion', Denney was dismissive of the use made of John 17 to justify denominational reunion. 'Surely the unity of an ecclesiastical corporation is the last thing in the world to be likened to the unity of the Father and the Son', 8.

[84] Ibid. On pp. 4 and 5 Denney is so pointed in his criticism of those who are insisting on a common system of doctrine as the basis of fellowship, that the sermon could plausibly be dated either around 1904, in the aftermath of the Free Church case, when hard thoughts and recriminations tended to colour discourse, or around 1909-10 when precisely this matter was exercising the joint committee of the two churches.

[85] Ibid., 5-6.

[86] Quoted in Douglas Murray, *The Rebuilding of the Kirk. Presbyterian Reunion in Scotland, 1909-1929*, (Edinburgh: Scottish Academic Press), 34.

[87] Ibid., 36.

resistant to the views of those like James Cooper and Arthur Wotherspoon, representing the Scoto-Catholic position, and who believed the Church should 'keep whole and undefiled the Faith once delivered to the saints and to bear explicit witness to the same'.[88] Denney's quarrel was certainly not with the Faith once delivered to the saints', but rather with its encapsulation in a fixed form of words imposed on others.[89]

During the period of negotiation, and up to their suspension at the outbreak of war, Denney's antipathy to denominational reunion gradually gave way to an acknowledgement of the moral obligation of visible union, unless to do so compromised essential principle. Initially he was deeply suspicious of the motives of the Established Church. Expressing his strong resistance to theological halls being absorbed into University Divinity faculties, he complained to Alexander Martin, 'The Machiavellian tactics of the Establishment - for that is what the continued negotiations amounts to - should be made clear and frustrated'.[90] Yet when the Conference meetings clashed with his College lectures he was 'loth to lose contact with it'.[91] By 1912 he was using the language of hope, responsibility, and optimism complaining in 1913, 'I am astonished to find how unenthusiastic and even suspicious great numbers of our best people are'.[92]

'Spiritual freedom is an important principle'

From the outset Denney saw clearly that, for the United Free Church, two fundamental questions, both heavy with historical grievance, lay across the path to reunion. In 1912, by which time negotiations were well under way, he confided to Nicoll, 'The first is that the Church of Scotland does not possess something which we think indispensable - spiritual liberty; and the second is that the Church of Scotland does possess something which we regard as impossible - political privilege.'[93] As the negotiations progressed and concessions were forthcoming from the Established Church, Denney's views had gradually tilted towards a more generous interpretation of intentions. His support for Lord Sand's Memorandum at the UF Assembly in 1913 is now seen as a decisive intervention which reassured the United Free Church. They would not be compromising their spiritual liberty, nor conceding political privilege, if they were part

---

[88] Ibid., 49.

[89] Denney, *Way*, 270-3. This strong passage on spiritual freedom from credal subscription was published in 1911, when negotiations were delicately balanced.

[90] M/17/7/27. June 12, 1911.

[91] *LWRN*, 165.

[92] Ibid., 219. See also, 204, 'I will certainly be on the side of peace...'; *LFF*, 198 'I dread civil war in our camp'.

[93] *LWRN*, 199.

of a church which *represented*[94] the Scottish Christian churches at those times when the State required such ecclesial presence and participation.[95] If this form of words satisfied both sides, Denney argued, then there was hope of real progress. A unanimous Assembly decision in 1913, made it possible for the two communions to begin work on a joint constitution.

In undertaking the framing of Article I, which expressed the doctrinal references of the proposed Constitution, the problem was how to secure the fundamental doctrines of the Christian Faith, while also securing to the Church the spiritual liberty to alter its subordinate standards. On the Established side, John White's statement reveals the tensions within which the Church of Scotland had to work. 'Spiritual Freedom is an important principle which must have an important place in the Articles and be clearly and unambiguously stated, but Spiritual Freedom cannot alone be the basis of a Christian Church.'[96]

Not even Denney, representing the theological left wing of his Church, wanted unqualified spiritual freedom. His earlier attempt at a doctrinal basis of union was characteristically Christocentric, apostolic and experiential. But it did lack doctrinal precision exactly where precision was desired by people like Cooper, namely the Trinitarian and incarnational fundaments of historic Christian Faith.[97] However, against the call for doctrinal exegesis in orthodox terms, Denney argued that the terms of the doctrinal references 'were in religious rather than theological language',[98] and as such their claim on the conscience of the believer was relational, and based on obedience to the authority of Christ. To Denney's mind, no ecclesiastical authority, imposing doctrinal propositions, could rival such a sovereign hold on the believing mind. In a letter to Alexander Martin,[99] dated 15 July 1914, he drew a highly significant distinction:

> The truth is that they still intellectualise religion more than we, but if you put a religious confession of faith in Article I it will inevitably in the coming

---

[94] A recognised representative role for a reunited Scottish Presbyterian Church, rather than a state conferred legal status, was acceptable to Denney; but he doubted it would satisfy the Established Church. *LFF*, 158.

[95] See Murray, *Rebuilding,* 62. Murray skilfully disentangles the various motives, concessions and compromises that had to be negotiated in the search for forms of words through which the key principles of both communions could be expressed. Denney's contributions to his own Church General Assembly are found in *UFCAP*, 1911, 276-7; 1913, 265-7; 1914, 291-3.

[96] Murray, *Rebuilding*, 79.

[97] See Denney, *Jesus*, 398ff.

[98] Murray, *Rebuilding*, 81.

[99] Professor of Apologetics and Pastoral Theology at New College, and Principal from 1918-35, he was a major player in the negotiations towards reunion.

generations, overrule any intellectual definition of doctrine, whether in the Westminster or any other form.[100]

So long as any Article was a religious confession of faith, rather than an intellectual definition of doctrine, then spiritual and intellectual freedom, and the fundamental doctrines of the Christian Faith, were adequately preserved. 'The intention of Article 1', according to Denney, 'was to prevent any abuse of liberty in relation to doctrine. The Church claimed the liberty as a Christian Church and in no other way.'[101] This was in accord with his conviction that doctrinal loyalty cannot be secured by the imposition of propositional theology, but by the loyalty of mind and heart to the living historic Christ, testified in Scripture, experienced by faith within the spiritual community, and vitalised by the Spirit of Christ.

Throughout Denney's life, developments had taken place which prepared the ground for fruitful negotiations between the main Presbyterian churches. His own mind had been formed within the rapidly changing context of Scottish theology and intellectual life.[102] The weakening of Westminster Calvinism as the dominant expression of Christian doctrine, examples of denominational co-operation during the Moody and Sankey revivals and the success of more 'seeker friendly' approaches to evangelism, the growth of co-operation in overseas missionary enterprise, each argued the advantages of co-operation and made Church union more thinkable. A more prevalent and progressive openness to biblical criticism encouraged an increasingly relaxed attitude towards fixed doctrinal commitments originally established as primary adjudicators of orthodoxy. This bore fruit during the search for mutually acceptable doctrinal references.

The Kingdom of God, understood as an immanent ethical process with which humanity co-operated by pursuing social change was a dominant liberal theological motif at the turn of the century. By contrast Denney stressed the supernatural and transcendent character of the Kingdom, which was neither the naturalising of Christianity nor the Christianising of natural society; it was something altogether other.[103] Nevertheless, the concentration on the Kingdom of God as a common Christian goal, undergirded the feelings of many, later shared by Denney, that church union was a duty, and the avoidance of needless schism a Christian responsibility.

---

[100] M/17/12/23.

[101] Murray, *Rebuilding*, 91.

[102] S. Sjolinder, *Presbyterian Reunion in Scotland, 1907-1921*, (Edinburgh: T & T Clark, 1962), 58-104. Sjolinder and Murray, together offer a plausible account of the background and realities involved in the complex process of intellectual, theological and spiritual re-alignment required on both sides, if union talks were to succeed.

[103] Denney, *Church*, 95.

It is significant that Denney's *Jesus and the Gospel* is a Christology written as an apologetic statement about the intellectual and spiritual viability of the Christian faith; significant too that it finishes with a conclusion arguing for the union of Christians around a simplified statement of faith. Spiritual unity should now be given tangible expression through an agreed minimal statement of faith, 'a moral integration of all who called Jesus Lord'.[104] It was this moral commitment to Christian union, rooted in a generous recognition of the Christian experience of all for whom Christology is less a metaphysical than a personally experienced reality, and given urgency by the decline of the church's hold on the popular mind, that gradually drove Denney to the conclusion that Church union was now a required expression of Christian unity.

Yet still, during the 1910 Edinburgh Missionary Conference, in a sermon at one of the Conference evening services, Denney expressed ambivalence over moves towards comprehensive institutional union.

> If I thought that all the Christians in Scotland could ever by any kind of arranged basis, theological or ecclesiastical, be brought into one great legal corporation, I should think it an elementary Christian duty to do everything in my power to frustrate such a project.... The Church is one, not as having the same legal constitution which we construct, or the same theological confession, which we draw up; it is one, and it can only be one in this, that all its members represent the same attitude of the soul to Christ.[105]

As late as 1913, he still had mixed feelings, but by then was committed to seeing the process through. 'I dread the consequences of failure, and feel it would be a terrible condemnation of the Churches if there were not wisdom and goodness in them to carry through what has gone so far.'[106] Yet, he felt deeper issues still would determine the future. 'That union with the Church of Scotland, though it seems to me a clear duty to attempt it, will strengthen the Church in our country, I do not see; what it needs is to be spiritually strengthened, not politically or financially, and meanwhile we seem to have lost contact with the source of power.'[107] Then, as the war dragged on, and impatience to resume negotiations increased, Denney wrote in 1917 to the United Free Office Bearer's Union pointing to the positive experience of co-operation the churches had enjoyed through commitment to the common cause provided by the

---

[104] Sjolinder, *Presbyterian Reunion*, 78.

[105] *The World Missionary Conference, 1910. The History and Records of the Conference, Together with Addresses delivered at the Evening Meetings*, (Edinburgh: Oliphant, 1910), 327, 325.

[106] *LWRN*, 204.

[107] Ibid., 220-1.

war effort, and supporting the view that continuing duplication of ministry would be a waste of Kingdom resources; these he felt were causes for optimism.[108]

Involvement in the discussions reflected an important dimension of Denney's life and thought; the Church is a primary sphere where loyalty to Christ is realised in service to His Body, the Church. His later years were enormously busy, perhaps self-exhausting activity had become one way of coping with a growing sense of loneliness. He continued to preach most Sundays, regularly fulfilled his lecture commitments in College, toured North America in 1909,[109] and delivered the Drew Lecture for P. T. Forsyth in 1911.[110] He was Clerk of the Senate in the College from 1907-1914, sat on the Board of Administration for the Glasgow School for Christian Workers, delivering their opening address in 1911 and 1916,[111] and worked to exhaustion to promote the Central Fund.[112]

He continued to contribute leading articles and book reviews to the *British Weekly*. Several series of substantial lecture notes, some of them probably intended for publication,[113] date from this period, including 'The Gospel according to Paul', 'The Christology of Paul', 'The Atonement' and 'The Doctrine of Sin'. His correspondence is peppered with references to non-theological literature he was reading and re-reading, from Cervantes to Boswell, Homer and Goethe, Dante and Burns.[114] There is a distinct impression that Denney was filling the unforgiving minute with more than sixty seconds of distance run.

For the last few years of his life, Denney was Convenor of the Central Fund. The system of pooling financial resources was intended to

---

[108] *Glasgow Herald*, 26 January 1917, 11h.

[109] See DEN10-10, 'Some Impressions of America'. Written in 1906 this refers to his earlier 1905 visit. It is a good natured though critical account of how an Edwardian Scottish Presbyterian theologian, of reserved disposition, reacted to the extrovert 'can do' attitude, the intellectual energy and economic potential of an emerging world power.

[110] Denney, James, *Factors of Faith in Immortality*, (London: Hodder & Stoughton, 1911).

[111] DEN08-76, 'Equipment for Christian Work'; DEN08-83, 'Opening of School for Christian Workers'. Both addresses illustrate Denney's commitment to accessible lay training. Denney's comment on Orr was equally true of himself, ' The traditional Scottish ideal of an intelligent Christian public, before which all Christian causes must be argued out, was deeply rooted in his mind'. Scorgie, *Call for Continuity*, 140.

[112] See below.

[113] *LWRN*, 172.

[114] *The Glasgow Herald*, 26 October 1917, 8d, lists some of the items sold off from Denney's library. His beloved 16 volume Johnson made £3/5/-, the 8 volume Pepys, £2/2/-, and ironically, Frazer's *Golden Bough*, which he disliked intensely, realised £4/4/-. 'Do you expect me to read Frazer's book *through* before I review it?', was his incredulous question to Nicoll, *LWRN*, 155. '*The Golden Bough* has almost killed me', he complained a year later. Ibid., 178.

guarantee a minimum stipend for ministers whose congregations were unable to pay a full and liveable stipend. However, contributions were voluntary, and year to year there was anxiety about whether there would be enough money to pay the full supplement to low paid ministers. This offended Denney's sense of fairness, and compromised the Christian principle of reciprocity amongst those who claim to know the grace of God. He invested enormous amounts of energy and time in visiting churches,[115] he enlisted the support of the *British Weekly*, a modest *quid pro quo* from Nicoll for countless contributions,[116] from 1914-1917 and during his last illness he wrote to the *Glasgow Herald* correcting misunderstandings and misinformation, and he promoted the Fund in long speeches at several successive Assemblies.[117]

The moral and spiritual obligation of mutual congregational support, was an important principle in Denney's ecclesiology. Failure here would have dire consequences for the Church's future. He warned the 1913 Assembly, there must be 'a new sense in the minds of Christian people of the place the Church has in Christian life, of the value of the Church to Christian faith and the indispensableness of the Church...if it were not for the maintenance of the Christian Church the Christian faith itself would not be maintained in our country for two generations'.[118]

War and the Fear of God

On 13 August 1914, Denney published the first of an occasional series of leading articles in the *British Weekly*, exploring the ethical and spiritual issues raised for the Christian Church by the Great War.[119] The previous year Denney had supported an Assembly overture that the country 'should seek peace with Germany, because of most countries in the world, the Germans were close of kin with ourselves, and they had a large interest in common in the spiritual future of mankind'.[120] They were the remarks of one who as a post-graduate student a generation earlier, had studied for one idyllic summer in Germany,[121] later the translator of Delitzsch on Isaiah, and a biblical theologian who owed much of his

---

[115] In one brief period he visited thirty six congregations. *LWRN*, 214.

[116] Ibid., 224.

[117] *UFCAP*, 1912, 212-13; 1915, 253-4; 1916, 308-13. Woven into the statistics, arguments, rebukes and predicted consequences of failure, the usual techniques of the fund-raiser, there are several paragraphs in which the argument is based on an ecclesiology of mutual spiritual obligation under Christ.

[118] *UFCAP*, 1913, 212-13.

[119] These were gathered together in book form. James Denney, *War and the Fear of God*, (London: Hodder & Stoughton, 1916).

[120] *UFCAP*, 1913, 298.

[121] *LFF*, 1-7.

spiritual and intellectual formation to German scholarship. His revised view following the events of 1914, was uncompromising; 'If a Christian cannot take sides in this war and strike with every atom of his energy, then a Christian is a being that, so far as this world is concerned, has committed moral suicide'.[122]

The First World War provoked a profound moral and emotional crisis amongst Christians who, like Denney, felt betrayed by a nation whose culture and spiritual history they had admired and defended, but whose cultural and intellectual values now seemed eclipsed by darker, more destructive purposes.[123] As the war progressed, moral revulsion at German atrocities provoked in Denney new depths of reflection about the moral order of reality. In August 1916 he wrote, 'When we think of Belgium, Serbia, of Scarborough and the Lusitania, of Miss Cavell and Captain Fryatt, we feel that to condone such things would be as infamous as to commit them'.[124]

While moral condemnation was commonplace in pulpits and newspapers,[125] characteristically Denney searched beneath the surface of things, seeking clues and intimations which might suggest to Christian faith that reality is so constructed that national and military atrocities constitute violations of the moral order, and carry within themselves the certainty of retribution. Throughout 1915 and 1916 he expounded the moral realities of war to the readership of the *British Weekly*:

> The mind of man can make no greater mistake than to assume that there is nothing in the world which it cannot master, nothing which it cannot bend and compel to serve the ends of its pride, nothing that will prove refractory to uncompromising force.... The last reality is beyond all these, and it has the last word. It is the moral order established and sustained by God, commanding the instinctive reverence of all who fear Him, and shattering the insolence of the strongest who ignore it.... There is no patience in God which obliterates moral distinctions.[126]

Denney deplored the declared policy of terrorising civilian populations by atrocity. In the context of war he now recalled his pre-war strictures on German arrogance, that as in scholarship so in politics, Germans were 'brusque, peremptory, and occasionally insolent'.[127] Theological responses during the early stages of the war had portrayed it as a religious crusade, even a stimulus to religious revival. But now, as casualties

---

[122] Muir, *John White*, 338.

[123] O'Neill, *The Bible's Authority*, argues the connection between the view of history held by such German theologians as Wellhausen, and support for an aggressive German foreign policy. 198-213.

[124] Denney, *War*, 126.

[125] Peter Matheson, 'Scottish War Sermons, 1914-1919', *RSCHS*, xvii, 1972, 205.

[126] Denney, *War*, 32, 54, 95.

[127] *LFF*, 178-9.

mounted, and the full impact of mechanised warfare by attrition became evident, churches and clergy struggled to offer any pastorally adequate theological account of human loss on such a scale. From 1917 the focus shifted to the sinfulness of pre-war society, as the churches called for national repentance from 'a nation under judgement.'[128]

While many who hoped revival would come through the sacrifice and discipline of conflict were disappointed, Denney never believed such a sanguine outcome. 'War is not a new thing in history, though it may in its present form be a new thing to us; and while its great hours evoke great virtues, it can hardly be questioned that its general effect on men is to harden and degrade.'[129] He was equally unconvinced by widespread expectations that soldiers would return in a new mood, 'with new thoughts, new political, religious and social interests'. And his reasons point to those deeper theological realities which always provided the key to his understanding of the world.

> It is just as true to say that after the war everything will be the same...the centre of gravity will not be too far from the old point. Human nature will be the same. The law of God will be the same. The inconsistencies of a being, conscious of a spiritual calling but with roots descending into the dark places of nature, will be the same. Man's glory and his shame, his hope and his despair, his pride and his need of God, will be the same. What is more, the Gospel with which God comes to meet him will be the same. And the Church, whose special calling it is to represent the changeless interests of eternity in the stream of time, must not be excited too easily by the cry that everything is going to be different. She will have to witness to the same truth, though it may be with a new sense of its scope and a new fidelity to its moral implications.[130]

Much of Denney's writing in these *British Weekly* articles was deliberately pastoral, though with Denney that never meant non-theological. Major themes of death and immortality, of atonement and faith, of hope and realism about the human condition, of the kind of Church and ministry required for the different world that would emerge, were worked through with that combination of hard-headed realism and existential theologising that is a hallmark of Denney's moral spirituality.

His distaste for conscientious objectors;[131] his strong words on behalf of ordinary working people entitled to reasonable income;[132] his defence

---

[128] S. J. Brown, '"A Solemn Purification by Fire": Responses to the Great War in the Scottish Presbyterian Churches, 1914-1919', *Journal of Ecclesiastical History*, 45, 1994, 83, 96.
[129] Denney, *War*, 181-2.
[130] Ibid., 124.
[131] Ibid., 99; *LFF*, 196.
[132] Denney, *War*, 19-20.

of women's role within the home as anchor of the family;[133] his warnings against treating Germany as a pariah in post-war Europe;[134] his passionate hatred for the drinks trade;[135] these reveal a mind independent in judgement, humane in tone, theologically informed, ethically driven, but prepared to make only limited pragmatic allowances in resolving some of the more complex social and moral issues thrown up by war.

Denney's opposition to the drink trade was lifelong and implacable. He was incensed by the diversion of grain from food manufacture to the distilleries.

> The Board of Agriculture is perambulating the country at present urging people to grow vegetables and to rear pigs and poultry, that there may be more food for the people; but what do all the extra patches of cabbage and potatoes, all the additional pigs and fowls mean, compared with the millions of bushels of grain which are destroyed annually for strong drink? The nation is sorely wounded by the war, yet in the liquor trade it opens its own veins, and helps to bleed itself white.[136]

He did his homework and was well equipped with statistics. Glasgow had 1,755 licensed shops, every year £180,000,000 was spent in the country on strong drink. The figure rose by £17.5 million in 1915, and of the overall total the government received £50,000,000.[137] He called for emergency legislation, 'a policy of making drunkenness impossible while the war lasts'.[138] The alternative of State Purchase he dismissed with contempt as 'homeopathy when the one salvation is in surgery'.[139] Anger provoked nationalist sentiment, when in 1916 he complained in a letter to Nicoll, 'it seems to me the most insufferable slavery that what all Scotland wants [prohibition] should be denied to it on the discretion of one obstinate Englishman'.[140] 'If the Government...refuse prohibition they are deliberately prolonging the war; they are deliberately nursing

---

[133] Ibid., 10, 17, 130.

[134] Ibid., 125. 'But I do feel anxious about the wildly anti-Christian way in which people are talking about international relations after the war, as if to boycott Germany, and foster hatred, suspicion and animosity by every political and economic device, were the way to the Kingdom of God. We can surely have a mind above that.' *LFF*, 196. By contrast Nicoll wrote to Professor A. E. Taylor in 1915, 'When the War is over...I should be in strong favour of a heavy tarriff on all German goods.' Darlow, *Nicoll*, 244.

[135] Denney, *War*, 30; 93-5; 105-6; 137-51, 'Prohibition'.

[136] Ibid., 149.

[137] Ibid., 145, 148, 93.

[138] Ibid., 147.

[139] Walker, *Denney*, 128.

[140] Unpublished personal letter to Nicoll, MS 3518/27/10/James Denney/29 July 1916.

inefficiency and waste; they are deliberately working for famine at home and defeat in the field, and deserving it.'[141]

Moral rage combined with rhetorical force in several outspoken public addresses and articles. His 'mastery of detail' and his 'eye for intricacies of argument and motive', proved him 'a match for the journalist and the man of the world'.[142] Like Amos the prophet, the full moral force of his anger, and his instinct for the subterranean motives of political expediency, made him disturbingly outspoken. 'Is there truth in the supposition that the secret party funds, subscribed by the liquor interests, dominate the position - is it graft - hideous graft - that is prolonging the life of this food-destroying monopoly, and that calls the tune the Government shall play?[143] Once again, a secure grasp of hamartiology guided political judgement.

Denney's outrage that the will of the Scottish people on prohibition should be frustrated by decisions made 'by one obstinate Englishman', is consistent with his support for the Irish Home Rule Bill. In 1912 he had warned Nicoll that the Glasgow Presbytery was split over whether or not to discuss a motion sympathising with the Irish Protestants.[144] By 1914, with Europe on the brink of war, he sympathised with Asquith's difficulties and urged unyielding resolve not to be 'coerced into dropping Home Rule, appealing to the country, and sacrificing the Parliament Act and all its natural or possible fruits.'[145] He continued,

> I could not imagine anything which would create a deeper feeling of resentment and disgust in all who have ever supported them. If the House of Lords reject the Amending Bill, as they will no doubt do, I see no recourse for the Government but to pass the Home Rule Bill without it, and take the responsibility of maintaining the King's Government in Ireland meantime, whatever the 'provisional' government may do. If they simply cave in to the tempest of bad passions that has disgraced Christianity in the north of Ireland for two years past, they will never be forgiven...[146]

There was in Denney's political judgements, a combination of pragmatism and moral obstinacy, so that while he wanted solutions, he was unwilling to follow the line of least resistance if the cost was moral capitulation. He believed that if Asquith were defeated, it was due less to the 'strength of the Opposition, [than] to some incurable perversity in the

---

[141] Ibid.
[142] Walker, *Denney*, 122.
[143] Ibid., 132.
[144] *LWRN*, 209.
[145] Limiting to three, the number of times the House of Lords could veto a Government Bill.
[146] *LWRN*, 241.

nature of things'.[147] The years growing up in Greenock with its strong Irish connections, and his lifelong antipathy to the Roman Catholic Church, had not so prejudiced his political opinions that he was unable to see the need for a workable political solution based on the consent and will of the people of Ireland.

Despite efforts to maintain some normality at the College, Denney lamented to Nicoll in 1916, that 'the best of our men have enlisted' and 'the cream of the working classes is in the army, and the relations of those who remain with their employers, were never worse'.[148] Later that same year he found difficulty concentrating because of the cost of the war, his state of mind at least partially explaining why some critics of his last book found it less rigorous in the flow of its argument.

> The Cunningham Lecture is worrying me, and without having written precisely on the same subject before, I seem to have been writing more or less around it and have difficulty in keeping out of my own way. The suction of the war too is so strong that it leaves me little mind free for other purposes. Two of my students have been killed at the Somme and the losses amongst our friends since the first of July have been endless.[149]

At this intensely personal level, thought was deepened by theological reflection on the relation of tragedy to providence. The following passage, written in 1915 for the *British Weekly*, fits closely the psychological profile of a man whose understanding of love and God was shattered and reformed in the experience of personal tragedy. Out of this process of personal sifting, Denney offered hope to others in words laden with autobiographical significance.

> Every day death comes near to some one, and robs him of all that he held dear in the world. His wife or his child is taken away, and there is no value in anything that is left. Death has struck him a fatal blow, has inflicted on him an irreparable defeat. But many a man has had experiences in such a situation which amount to a victory over death. Death if we may put it so, in some wonderful way defeats itself. Though we may not be able to tell how, it makes love more real. It makes all love more real, not only that with which we yearn for the departed, but the very love of God Himself. We are assured in the very presence of death that we can never lose what we have loved in Him. And our love does not die with death. It is made purer and more spiritual.[150]

---

[147] Ibid., 242.
[148] MS 3518/27/10/ James Denney/24 March 1916.
[149] MS 3518/27/10/ James Denney/29 July 1916. See *LFF*, 206-7.
[150] Denney, *War*, 63.

The Christian Doctrine of Reconciliation

The catastrophic scale and consequences of mechanised conflict in World War I, originating in the heart of Western Christendom, inevitably affected the way Christians thought about ultimate questions concerning God, human existence, the nature of evil and of goodness, and the relation of these to the person and work of Jesus Christ. Barth's famous 'bombshell in the theologians' playground', an effective if inappropriate metaphor for his 1919 Romans commentary, announced a theological revolution that would overthrow the hegemony of German-inspired liberal theology. Familiar emphases of twentieth-century theology, including the theology of crisis, the biblical theology movement, the rediscovery of the suffering and crucified God, can plausibly be traced to the aftermath of the Great War. Though he learned much from them, Denney never surrendered to the theological lure of Schleiermacher, Ritschl, Harnack and Weiss. Those who discern a 'change of atmosphere'[151] in Denney's later theology find evidence in *The Christian Doctrine of Reconciliation,* where he emphasised the eternal love of God bearing sin as the originating *objective* source of the atonement, and the experience of being reconciled as the originating *subjective* source of Christian faith.[152]

This posthumously published volume, originally prepared as the Cunningham Lecture, was minimally edited by James Moffatt. Much of it was finalised during his last illness, though it incorporates some material from unpublished lectures.[153] It is doubtful if Denney would have been satisfied with the imbalance in chapter length, and the looseness in organisation and structure. However the decision to leave the manuscript as he wrote it, gives unedited access to his latest theology and thinking. It

---

[151] J. K.. Mozley, *Some Tendencies in British Theology*, (London: SPCK, 1951), 133. Those who discern a change of emphasis include Donald Macleod, 'Atonement', *DSCHT*; B. B. Warfield, *Critical Reviews*, (New York: 1932) 103; A. E. Garvie, '"Christ Crucified" for the Thought and Life of Today', *ExpT*, xxx, 83, 138, 179. Wistar Hodge of Princeton finds 'a progressive watering down of the satisfaction doctrine of the atonement, and a slackening of grip upon such ideas as wrath and imputation, coupled with slighting comments upon the terms 'forensic', and 'legal'.' Noted by Sell, *Defending and Declaring*, 218-9. I. H. Marshall, 'James Denney', in P. E. Hughes (ed.), *Creative Minds in Contemporary Theology*, (Grand Rapids: Eerdmans, 1966), 203-38, suggests ' Denney's basic teaching remained consistent to the end of his life, although, it inevitably underwent rich and deep development.', 225.

[152] G. B. Stevens, *The Christian Doctrine of Salvation*, (Edinburgh: T & T Clark, 1905), 196, discerned a change in 1903, in *Atonement and the Modern Mind*. Mozley, *Some Tendencies*, 132-3, denies significant change either in 1903 or in *Reconciliation* in 1917.

[153] A short series of lectures on the atonement, DEN09-11, DEN09-12, and DEN09-13, are extensively represented verbatim. Compare pp. 68-71 with DEN09-11, pp. 12-14; and pp. 73-4 with DEN09-11 p. 16; compare pp. 246-7 with DEN09-13 p. 7.

is an important touchstone for assessing whether Denney's thought remained consistent but 'underwent rich and deep development', or whether 'he was slackening his grip' on traditional ideas of evangelical orthodoxy.

The Great War raised questions of theodicy in an acute form. Writing to Carnegie Simpson late in 1915, Denney expressed his dissatisfaction with any idea of a 'merely struggling God'. The struggle between good and evil is the Lord's battle, but 'it is essential to believe not only that good is in conflict with evil, but that it is essentially and eternally superior to evil, and destined to be manifestly "all in all"'.[154] Referring to Moffatt's comment on 'They overcame [Satan] by the blood of the Lamb', he insisted, 'it is not merely a struggling goodness with which we co-operate...but a goodness which is on the throne, and which perfects that which concerns us'.[155] Elsewhere he reflected on Psalm 14, 'where God is represented as doing what many people seem to be doing today - looking for indications of His own presence in the world...He is disappointed, just as they are disappointed when they look at the nations trying to strangle each other, and think of Zeppelin raids, and the sinking of passenger ships, and all the nameless and inevitable horrors of battle'.[156] That God struggles in battle, that human suffering impacts on God, is not, for Denney, a sign of weakened omnipotence, but of a living God whose relations to the Creation are moral, intensely personal and intentionally redemptive.

In a less guarded moment, Denney allowed himself a speculative comment to Nicoll, by now implicitly trusted as friend and theological confidante:

> I have often wondered whether we might not say that the Christian doctrine of the Atonement just meant that in Christ God took the responsibility of evil upon Himself and somehow subsumed evil under good.... I fancy it was something like this Calvin had in mind when he said that God did not make His noblest creature *ambiguo fine*, without knowing what for: *i.e.* He was quite prepared to take all the consequences and He took them in Christ.[157]

The idea of disappointed omnipotence, for Denney, refers not to divine weakness but to persistent love. Victory over evil is achieved by the renewal of moral relations through atonement, rather than by the exercise of annihilating fiat. These reflections during war-time indicate a mind apparently less dogmatic, occasionally speculative when dealing with ultimate things, exhibiting less precision but perhaps a more prescient

---

[154] *LWRN*, 187.
[155] Ibid., 188.
[156] Denney, *War*, 88-9.
[157] *LWRN*, 187-8.

awareness that, in the midst of catastrophic conflict, the expression of the Gospel most suited to the moral and theological emergency of the times was the Christian doctrine of reconciliation.

'In the experience of reconciliation to God through Christ is to be found the principle and touchstone of all genuine Christian doctrine: whatever can be derived from this experience and is consistent with it is true and necessary; whatever is incompatible with it lacks the essential Christian character.'[158] What disconcerted the first readers of *Reconciliation* was the way Denney based the argument on experience. Primacy was given not to doctrine or its dogmatic formulation, nor to the biblical text or its critical application, but to these as interpreted by the evangelical experience of being reconciled to God. The first chapter unabashedly asserts the experimental basis of the doctrine of reconciliation, and the final chapter describes its realisation in human life and experience.

Some of Denney's most critical readers, friendly and otherwise,[159] described his treatment as vague, ambiguous, lacking systematic rigour, unfairly dismissive of traditional categories, surrendering far too much ground to the interests of 'the modern mind', too unwilling to learn from the perspectives of others. Almost all reviewers took issue with the authority Denney conferred on experience as a primary datum in theological construction. In his critique of Athanasius he argued 'room has to be made...under the pressure of the New Testament, for ideas more capable of verification in human experience'.[160] Taking issue with the legal categories of Tertullian, he insisted 'the work of Christ...be interpreted on the analogy of human experience in the moral world, experiences in which sin, and satisfaction and reconciliation may be poignantly real. They may not enable us completely to interpret the cross, but...the light they throw on it will be the light by which men actually live'.[161] Anselm is taken to task for deducing satisfaction from rational necessities, a view 'that belongs to the world of metaphysics, not of spiritual experience'.[162]

The real interest here, is in trying to explain why Denney thought as he did. The privileged authority of personal spiritual experience undoubtedly marks a significant shift in his thinking.

---

[158] Denney, *Reconciliation*, 7.

[159] Mackintosh Garvie and Mozley represent the former, Wistar Hodge, Paterson and Macleod the latter. All of them have written critical comment on Denney's theology, details in the bibliography.

[160] Denney, *Reconciliation*, 40.

[161] Ibid., 51.

[162] Ibid., 75.

> The basis of all theological doctrine is experience, and experience is always of the present...it is to the fact and experience of reconciliation, not deductions but *data*, that we owe the very idea that God is love.... We know immediately and at first hand the only things which are of any consequence: that sin is rooted in our nature so deeply, is so congenital and powerful, that we cannot save ourselves; and on the other hand, that God has made us for Himself, and has never left us without a witness in our consciences, so that the possibility and hope of reconciliation are not precluded.[163]

Alongside the emphasis on experience, and partially explaining it, was Denney's concern that in any theory of the atonement, 'personality gets the place, or something like the place, which is its due'. This he believed was one of the great achievements of the Reformation. 'What it did in principle was to expel *things* from religion, and exhibit all its realities as persons and the relations as persons.'[164] The choice of reconciliation as the controlling metaphor for atonement, and the powerful and recurring emphasis on the eternal love of the Father as the fundamental reality of the universe, rendered all abstract, mechanical, legal, that is, impersonal categories, inadequate to the New Testament doctrine and Denney's own experience.

One of the clues to what generates the passion and drives the argument, lies in a hymn couplet quoted three times : 'Thou O Christ, art all I want; more than all in Thee I find.'[165] Paying attention to each context within which these lines are used suggests they had programmatic significance in the book, conveying in concentrated simplicity, the gospel according to the New Testament as it had captivated the emotional and mental life of Denney himself.

> When we really see Him and virtue goes out of Him to heal us, we cry irrepressibly, 'Thou O Christ, art all I want; more than all in Thee I find.' We do not stay to ask what He has done or what He can do for us'; what He is - not according to a doctrine of His person, but in the rich and simple reality we see in the evangelists - is enough for us. *He* is our peace. The whole promise and power of reconciliation is in Him, and we know without proving that He can bring us to God and save to the uttermost.[166]

This was Denney the preacher theologian, preaching his own experience so far as he could grasp it, and in this book he more than once concedes that ultimate realities defy systems of thought - 'we do not stay to ask...we know without proving'. In the far background is Bruce with his emphasis on 'Jesus only! Jesus as opposed to all churches and

---

[163] Ibid., 199, 186, 200.
[164] Ibid., 119, 91.
[165] Ibid., 10, 162, 301. From Wesley's, 'Jesus lover of my soul'.
[166] Ibid., 10.

traditions';[167] in the near foreground Denney's appropriation of Bruce exploited most comprehensively in *Jesus and the Gospel*, and lived out in a spiritual theology radically Christocentric.

> Sin is only forgiven as it is borne. He bore our sins in His own body on the tree: that is the propitiation. It is the satisfaction of divine necessities, and it has value not only for us, but for God. In that sense, though Christ is God's gift to us, the propitiation is objective; it is the voice of God, no less than that of the sinner, which says, 'Thou, O Christ, art all I want; more than all in Thee I find.' And this is our hope towards God. It is not that the love of God has inspired us to repent., but that Christ in the love of God has borne our sins.[168]

Putting such words in the mouth of the Father, addressed to the Son, shows the same quality of imaginative, even speculative, theologising that Denney so admired in McLeod Campbell. Fuelled by his lifelong engagement with the ideas and experiences embedded in the New Testament and realised in his own spiritual experience, much of the writing in this book is homiletic rather than systematic theology. 'A reconciled man, preaching Christ as the way of reconciliation, and preaching Him in the temper and spirit which the experience of reconciliation creates, is the most effective mediator of Christ's reconciling power.'[169] The words are, perhaps unwittingly, self-description.

> Grace is the attitude of God to man which is revealed and made sure in Christ, and the only way in which it becomes effective in us for new life is when it wins for us the response of faith. And just as grace is the whole attitude of God in Christ to sinful men, so faith is the whole attitude of the sinful soul as it surrenders itself to that grace.... To maintain the original attitude of welcoming God's love as it is revealed in Christ bearing our sins - not only to trust it, but to go on trusting - not merely to believe in it as a mode of transition from the old to the new, but to keep on believing - to say with every breath we draw, 'Thou, O Christ, art all I want; more than all in Thee I find' - is not a part of the Christian life, but the whole of it.[170]

Much of the book is a theological articulation of intense spiritual experience passed through the prism of atonement theology. In this book, more than anywhere else in the entire corpus of his writing, Denney sought to explicate his own experience as a Christian man, and what was at stake was not theological clarity and consistency, but such an exposition of the cross as was adequate to an all consuming personal experience which replicated the apostolic testimony. The spirituality of

---

[167] DEN10-02, 3.
[168] Denney, *Reconciliation*, 162.
[169] Ibid., 8.
[170] Ibid., 301.

Denney is absolutely inseparable from, because entirely dependent upon, a theology of the cross which gave to Christ the central place in the eternal love of the Father and in the self-surrendering love of the forgiven. Abstract concepts such as sin, righteousness, satisfaction, imputation, law, penalty and wrath, are only useful to the extent that they are able to bear the meaning of the '*last reality* in the universe'. 'The *last reality* is beyond sin. It is a love which submits to all that sin can do, yet does not deny itself but loves the sinful through it all. It is a love which...bears sin, yet receives and regenerates sinners.'[171]

From the first chapter which bases the doctrine of reconciliation in experience, Denney moved on to survey key thinkers such as Athanasius, Tertullian, Augustine, Anselm, Abelard, and Calvin, identifying as a key shortcoming of traditional formulations that they 'had lost contact with experience.'[172] He then revisited the New Testament evidence, not as in his earlier book which was an exercise in exegetical theology broadly surveying the death of Christ, but as an exploration of the experience of Christ as the One through whom, and in whom, God was reconciling the world. The need of reconciliation he then argued in a chapter heavy with the moral psychology and the theological gravity of sin. Two concluding chapters separate the work of Christ in response to human need into reconciliation as achieved by Christ, the provision of an objective atonement, and reconciliation as realised in human life, the subjective appropriation of atonement.

In this volume Denney interacted with numerous previous and contemporary opinions. None seemed fully capable of satisfying his search for an adequate conceptuality that would persuade the modern mind of the realities that inform the most vital truths of Christian faith. Each time he quoted with approval he went on to point out the shortcoming. His reliance on McLeod Campbell and Bushnell were enough to raise suspicions about the orthodoxy of his conclusions. But he used them selectively, to explain such experimental difficulties as how the believing soul could reconcile the truth that Jesus was sinless with the truth that he bore our sins, and how to retain the penal element in atonement without introducing a bifurcation in the Godhead by suggesting the Sinless One was the subject of the Father's wrath.

Denney realised the attempt to reduce the mystery of the cross would not entirely satisfy, either his readers or his own mind. Like his friend P. T. Forsyth, he discovered, 'words are hard to stretch to the measure of eternal things without breaking under us somewhere'.[173]

---

[171] Ibid., 20. Emphasis mine. The phrase is used regularly throughout the book.
[172] Ibid., 109.
[173] P. T. Forsyth, *The Work of Christ*, (London: Independent Press, 1938). 210.

> But for His death we should have died in our sins: we would have passed into the blackness of darkness with the condemnation of God abiding on us. It is because he died for us, and for no other reason, that the darkness has passed away, and a light shines in which we have peace with God and rejoice in hope of His glory. On the basis of the New Testament, of Christian experience, and of a theistic view of nature…, the writer has done what he can to indicate the rationale of this; but imperfect as all such attempts must be, their imperfection does not shake the conviction that they are attempts to deal with a fact, and that fact the one which is vital to Christianity.[174]

In interpreting the published volume, originally intended for oral delivery, the personal context is not without significance. The Cunningham Lectures were written during the most harrowing days of the Great War. Questions of salvation and sin, eternal life and death, the need for consolation and hope, the meaning of the cross and of human suffering, were far too acute, intense and personal to be dealt with in any way remote from human experience and personal interest. In addition, Denney was under severe pressure himself, overworked on behalf of the Central Fund, at times isolated and missing the support of close colleagues, emotionally shaken by the impact of war casualties, largely exhausted by his moral crusade against the drinks trade, and latterly, seriously ill.

It is not surprising, then, that the book displays such depth and range of human experience - emotional, intellectual, moral, relational and spiritual - each an element which in his own life experience had been transmuted into a radical renewal of personality and intellect through his own encounter with Christ. Reconciliation as he had experienced it in Christ, through which God's love was revealed in Christ, and as he expounded it in Christ's name, was, he believed, 'the greatest regenerative force known to man'. By the time the book was published, Denney had died of pneumonia. The last words of his final manuscript aptly reflect on Christ's reconciliation as victory over sin and death:

> In the sublimest words of the Apostle, 'I am persuaded that neither death, nor life, nor angels, nor principalities, nor powers, nor things present, nor things to come, nor height, nor depth, nor any other creature, shall be able to separate us from the love of God, which is in Christ Jesus our Lord.' The Christian Faith in reconciliation does not find its full expression till it finds it here.[175]

---

[174] Denney, *Reconciliation*, 283.
[175] Ibid., 332.

CHAPTER 8

Conclusion

In 1891, during Denney's ministry at Broughty Ferry, Nicoll had a conversation with Alexander Whyte about the appointment of a colleague for Whyte. Afterwards Nicoll wrote to Marcus Dods, 'I told him that Denney was the true successor of Rainy - a subject on which I am willing to bet a four shilling piece and an apple. As to his being a colleague to Whyte - that is another matter.'[1]

Successor to Rainy – Colleague to Whyte

To link Denney's name with two giants in a denomination not short on intellectual and spiritual stature, raises intriguing questions. The massive influence of Robert Rainy within the spiritual and administrative machinery of the Free Church, owed much to his political leadership in the Assembly, his decisive interventions in the Robertson Smith case, his hostility to Establishment, and at the time of Nicoll's comment, his role as convener of the Confession of Faith Committee which later framed the Declaratory Act. Rainy's desire to preserve the unity and evangelical legacy of the Free Church, and his recognition that to survive in the modern world his Church must adjust to the changing intellectual, cultural and theological climate, created an inner tension easily construed as an ambivalent wanting the best of both worlds.

A similar intellectual tension between firm conviction and honest questioning was evident in Denney, but Rainy's instinctive tact and diplomatic caution were lacking. Admittedly Rainy's openness to biblical criticism, his promotion of spiritual freedom and credal reform, his anti-establishment stance, and his influence in debate and discussion, give the comparison credibility, since Denney largely shared these values, concerns and qualities. But Denney would have found the compromises, the careful word-choosing and theological tip-toeing of church diplomacy required by representative leadership, a severe irritant to a

---

[1] Darlow, *Nicoll*, 102.

personality allergic to ambiguity, and an impossible constraint on a mind that valued truth above tact.[2]

Nicoll's reasons for doubting Denney's suitability as colleague for Whyte are not free of ambiguity either. The warmth of mutual respect and deference evident in their correspondence suggests that two quite different temperaments, a generation apart, had little difficulty finding acres of common ground and a secure basis in shared convictions.[3] Whyte's role as advocate of a believing biblical criticism, his passionate attachment to the gospel according to Paul,[4] the centrality of conscience and moral psychology in his account of Christian spirituality, his disciplined toil in the study 'nailed to his desk', and his self expenditure in applied doctrinal preaching, were each of them mirrored in Denney. In 1911, Whyte wrote to Denney, 'I can honestly say that the writings of no living man restore me and reassure me more than yours, nor so much'.[5]

On the other hand, despite apparent theological sympathy, Whyte was a mystic, and a lover of mystical theology; a catholic-minded evangelical much more hospitable to the oddities and diversities of the entire Christian tradition than Denney ever was. With much that Whyte loved from Teresa of Avila to Jacob Boehme, including his beloved Thomas Goodwin and a host of other Puritan Divines, Denney had little patience.

Even such a summary comparison of Rainy, Whyte and Denney gives a sense of Denney's affinity with the rich breadth and dynamic power of his denomination's best intellectual and spiritual traditions. But, in those areas of human experience open to personal choice, where not all is inherited, accident of circumstance or environmentally determined, selection and assimilation of what becomes intellectually definitive is significantly affected by antecedent influences. These include personal relationships, the context and characteristics of personal experience which shape personality, in home, family, education and life-work, interaction with those sources of knowledge and formation at crucial stages of personal development, and in the case of a theologian, all of these

---

[2] Denney's estimate of Rainy was given in an appreciative obituary. Extolling him as a churchman, he defended Rainy's role in the Robertson Smith case. 'Principal Rainy', *BW*, 3 January 1907, 368.

[3] G. F. Barbour, *The Life of Alexander Whyte*, (London: Hodder & Stoughton, 1923), 507-9.

[4] Denney's treatment of Romans 7 would not entirely satisfy Whyte, who strongly believed that Romans 7 refers to the Christian's post-regeneration experience of spiritual conflict and inner contradiction on the way to sanctification. For Whyte's view see James M. Gordon, *Evangelical Spirituality. From the Wesleys to John Stott*, (London: SPCK, 1991), 243-7. Denney's treatment is in, 'The Gospel According to Paul', DEN08-13-06, 101-5.

[5] Barbour, *Whyte*, 507.

experienced within the specific context of personal and communal religious experience.

As Principal of New College, Whyte had urged students to 'get into some relation of indebtedness to some great authors of past days or of the present day.'[6] Throughout this study of intellectual biography and contextual theology, Denney's 'relations of indebtedness' have been shown to be a complex network of values consciously chosen or unconsciously absorbed, of mental and theological constructions encountered in the stream of books flowing across his desk, of influences which took the form of personal relationships or historical movements, and of particular circumstances which sometimes proved to be decisive critical incidents or defining personal experiences.

The characteristics of Denney's mind, and the theological emphases that compelled his attention and impelled his scholarship, have emerged in this study from his own unique, particular nexus of human experience - intellectual, spiritual, moral, relational, and historical. As intellectual characteristics and spiritual experience combined and developed to maturity, within his personal history and in the context of his times, Denney's mind focused increasingly on several key theological themes which together gave his mind its distinctive cast.

Replying to those who pick and choose from Paul's theology, failing to see the wholeness of his vision and the interrelatedness of the most significant elements of his thought, Denney indicated one way of understanding how his own mind worked.

> A man has to think with the mind he has, with the intellectual resources or implements he has, with the experience he has; and the result of his thinking is what it is, and its value has to be judged by the total result, and by the possibility of assimilating it in our own minds, not by disintegrating it into elements some of which in their isolated condition may be open to depreciation. A living man's thought is not the summation of any constituents or elements; it is rather like a chemical compound which may have quite new, unpredictable, but priceless qualities.[7]

The qualities of his own thought include; the nature of truth and the intellectual obligations and cost of Christian scholarship; the authority of Scripture in its relation both to historical criticism and traditional views of inspiration; the centrality of Jesus as the revelation of God and the content of the Church's message; the necessity of atonement, understood as both propitiation and the gift of sin-bearing love; the absolute significance of Christ as the one who is the reconciliation of all things; these, for Denney, are the essential convictions of New Testament, and

---

[6] Alexander Whyte, *Thirteen Appreciations*, (Edinburgh: Oliphant, 1913), 157.

[7] 'The Gospel According to Paul', DEN08-13-01, 3.

therefore authentic, Christianity. They represent the primary colours of Denney's thought, and in his exposition and defence of them lies much of what was distinctive in his theology.

'Loyalty to truth and obedience to that same truth'

One of Denney's former students, Professor J. A. Robertson, commented on the decisive but limited extent of Denney's debt to the Reformed Presbyterian Church. 'He had been brought up in a strict orthodoxy of religious outlook, the spirit of which he had made his own in his loyalty to truth, and the rigid and cramping trammels of which he had fought through in obedience to that same loyalty.'[8] To Denney's mind, loyalty to truth was a moral and intellectual imperative, taking precedence over all other demands placed on the conscience of the Church's theologians. Orthodoxy was not found in credal fixity, or determined adherence to past articulations of the Faith. These had served the Church well, but the comfort they gave could only be maintained at the cost of fading relevance and loss of intellectual credibility. From his early years at University and College, Denney increasingly abandoned 'the rigid and cramping trammels' which he believed hindered the Church's witness and obscured the central truth to be found in its final form in Jesus and the Gospel.[9]

Insisting on the absolute centrality of Christ as portrayed in the New Testament record of apostolic experience and testimony, Denney placed historically founded and experientially verified knowledge of Christ above all other confessions or articulations of faith. Insisting also on the nature of Scripture as fallible text bearing infallible witness to the One whose reality and authority is final for every Christian conscience, Denney inevitably drew criticism and sparked controversy with those less certain of their theological bearings. In reviewing the distinctive lines of Denney's thought, and trying to understand why he thought as he did, it is worth asking why and how he regularly became embroiled in controversy throughout his theological career.

In 1885, after completion of his studies, he launched his career as trenchant critic by dissecting Drummond's *Natural Law in the Spiritual World*.[10] In 1891 he spoke at the Free Church Assembly against a strong, as he believed, ultra-orthodox interpretation of biblical infallibility and inerrancy, an intervention from a relatively young minister that had a significant afterlife in the long memories of those suspicious of

---

[8] *LWRN*, xxxiv.

[9] Denney, *Way*, 270-3, is Denney's most forthright and passionate statement on intellectual freedom as part of liberty in Christ.

[10] See pp. 91-6 of the present study.

progressive thought.[11] He was on the Committee framing the Declaratory Act of 1892, his views on credal subscription already made public in his preaching ministry. The furore he caused in Chicago in 1894 caused him to rewrite his lecture on 'Holy Scripture' in language much more circumspect, though still unrepentantly refuting the doctrine of textual inerrancy and infallibility.[12] In 1899 A. E. Garvie subjected Denney's treatment of Ritschl in *Studies in Theology* to a Denney-like verbal chastisement, drawing no known response from Denney.[13] Soon after the Union of 1900 Denney was publicly and positively supportive of biblical criticism, and by implication of George Adam Smith, speaking to an audience of United Free Office-Bearers anxious to avoid another looming heresy test-case.[14]

In 1904 Denney was at odds with A. S. Peake, following an exchange of articles in the *Expositor*, on the significance and meaning of union with Christ.[15] That same year in the Glasgow Presbytery he was again embroiled in a public argument, this time about the Davidic authorship of Psalm 110; since Jesus had attributed the Psalm to David, Denney's opinion that it was exilic inevitably offended more conservative minds.[16] The 1906 College Address urging freedom of criticism and extensive doctrinal restatement, elicited an impressive, predominantly hostile correspondence to the *Glasgow Herald*.[17] His 1909 volume, *Jesus and the Gospel*, with its proposal of a radically simplified statement of faith, and its alleged abandonment of 'the three-fold Name', failed to impress those intent upon a more secure receptacle to contain the treasured content of the Faith.[18]

Denney did not court controversy, but neither did he avoid the consequences of plain spoken loyalty to the truth as he perceived it. On each of the occasions recounted, controversy would have been avoidable by silence, or by words more carefully chosen for their negotiating value. Neither came naturally to Denney. Nicoll, recalled with relish, 'Dr Denney loved controversy, and he was one of the most formidable of fighters'.[19]

---

[11] *PDGAFCS*, 1891, 113.
[12] See pp. 139-47 of the present study.
[13] Garvie, *Ritschlian Theology*, 286-96, 360-3.
[14] See pp. 154-58.
[15] See p. 160, note 92 of the present study.
[16] Walker, *Denney*, 89-91.
[17] DEN09-18; and see pp. 168-72 of the present study.
[18] Even Nicoll had some reservations about Denney's truncated confessional statement, and Denney's apparent equivocation about whether Jesus called himself the Son of God. LWRN, 121-2; 126-9.
[19] *LWRN*, xxi.

After Denney's death, Peake wrote from the residual pain of past hurt: 'He had his own point of view very firmly held; and he surveyed the universe so far as it could be seen thence, with a clear and penetrating gaze...what he could see he saw with exceptional lucidity. What he could not see had for him no existence and no right to exist'.[20] On the other hand, a former student saw similar mental characteristics from a more positive perspective:

> The qualities of his mind which impressed us were a precision and exactness of scholarship which could not tolerate looseness or short-cuts or slovenliness; a limpid clarity which glittered like a mountain stream with a kind of fierce impatience of all tangled and confused thinking; a sincerity, a feeling for truth, which was ever scornful of mere futility or irrelevance or trifling finesse; and a passionate intensity which was contemptuous of superficiality or vague imaginative sentiment.[21]

However his love for an argument is interpreted,[22] the importance of controversy as a key to understanding Denney's mind becomes much clearer when the issues on which he chose to fight are identified. The nature and authority of Scripture as means of grace and medium conveying the truth of God in Christ; the inadequacy of credal and confessional statements to secure the core essentials of the Gospel in an age of rapid intellectual change; the supreme place of Jesus as the historical manifestation of God in history, and loyalty to Christ as the defining characteristic of Christian identity; the reconciling death of Christ bearing the sin of the world, expressing the final and supreme revelation of God; the centrality and finality of the exalted Christ as the last reality of the universe and the originating, sustaining source of all things; the necessity of a living encounter with Christ in the personal experience of reconciliation and moral renewal; and each of these as foundational principles providing the parameters for any ongoing restatement of doctrine both relevant to the modern mind and faithful to the original gospel. Denney believed the future of the Church and the

---

[20] A. S. Peake, 'Denney, James (1856-1917)', *DNB, 1912-1921*, 154. In an unpublished paper delivered to the Aberdeenshire Theological Club in August 1971, Professor James McEwen, saw Denney's rationalistic tendencies and dogmatism as a dangerous fault-line running through his theology. See James McEwen, 'The Rationalism of James Denney' unpublished paper delivered to the Aberdeenshire Theological Club, August, 1971, 4, 11.

[21] *LWRN*, xxxiii.

[22] Denney conceded to Nicoll, 'perhaps I have...the intellectual fault of pugnacity.' *LWRN*, 233.

faith to which it bears witness, depended on establishing such core essentials on defensible ground.[23]

For Denney 'the modern mind' was not simply the audience the Church must address. It was the cultural environment the Church must understand, a human questioning of received truth the Church must answer in terms that would bear the scrutiny of an age fascinated by science, history and human intellectual and industrial achievement. Writing to Nicoll in 1903, while contemplating his lectures on *The Atonement and the Modern Mind*, he asked,

> Have you any idea of what the modern mind is? Is it the same as the *Zeitgeist*? or is it something with much more truth and eternity in it than that. It strikes me that the question...is only one phase of the larger question of the relation of reason to revelation, or of human nature to God - a question on which it is easier to say what seem profound philosophical things than to say things which really have power to convince or persuade.

'Loyalty to truth and obedience to that same truth' combined with legitimate spiritual liberty and intellectual freedom to pursue it, were, Denney believed, essential prerequisites if the Church was to be able 'to say things which really have power to convince and persuade'.

'True ideas on the authority of Scripture'

There is a consistent and continuous strain in Denney's thought, traceable to his College days, and publicly exposed in his lectures in Chicago, of resistance to the imposition of *a priori* categories to settle beforehand the nature of biblical authority. He was dismissive of technical terminology used to invest concepts such as inerrancy, infallibility and literal accuracy, with epistemological claims which, he believed, were neither provable nor necessary to secure the proper place for the Bible in the life of the Church. Pushed to defend his views at a Glasgow Presbytery meeting in 1904, he was characteristically blunt:

> It is quite possible for me to profess my faith in the infallibility of Scripture. I believe if a man commits his mind and heart humbly and sincerely to the teaching and guidance of Holy Scripture, it will bring him right with God and give him a

---

[23] A similar apologetic concern to establish the credentials of the Christian message on secure intellectual grounds, and unafraid of honest criticism and scholarship, pushed Bruce, Dods, and George Adam Smith into the arena of controversy. Denney was one of a cluster of believing critics who tried the patience of more circumspect thinkers.

knowledge of God and of eternal life. But literal accuracy and inerrancy are totally different things; and we do not believe in that at all.[24]

The lessons learned in his College days, at the height of the Robertson Smith controversy and during four years as a student of Lindsay, Candlish and Bruce, had instilled in Denney a more radical and dynamic understanding of biblical criticism and interpretation than could comfortably be accommodated by the dogmatic approach to biblical inspiration rooted in Westminster Confessionalism. Throughout his ministry and teaching career he was tireless in defence of the Bible as a means of grace, as the testimony of prophets and apostles to the revelation of God in Christ. Because of the Bible's nature as testimony to the acts of God, he insisted that the biblical documents be accorded their integrity by respecting their historical contingency and context, and seeking to clarify their meaning through critical and exegetical study.

The precision and passion of the exegesis underlying his theological thought grew out of the disciplines he first learned in Jebb's Classics class. A teacher deeply dyed in the values of humanism, Jebb both demonstrated and mediated a historical yet sympathetic thoroughness which combined respect for the ancient text with integrity in textual study. Both qualities underpinned much of Denney's exegetical theology, except that in the case of the New Testament, critical-historical exegesis was carried out by one with a prior commitment to the truth of the experience to which the documents bore witness.

At times Denney appeared to parse experience as if it were simply another language with identifiable rules. However, academic objectivity, even if achievable, would have gone against the grain of one who exploited the gains of historical criticism in the service of a personally appropriated life-changing kerygma. That kerygma, embodied in the deposit of testimony from evangelists and apostles in the New Testament, proclaimed the centrality, finality and absoluteness of Jesus Christ. The peculiar authority Denney accorded to the apostolic testimony exhibits trustfulness of experience, a way of looking at the world without being sceptical of the capacity of the human mind to receive revelation from God through the conduit of divinely touched human experience. The biblical writers portray humanity 'in nature akin to God, capable of fellowship with Him and designed for it, conscious of moral freedom and responsibility, and therefore morally responsible and free'.[25]

A mindset and epistemology rooted in the congenial soil of Scottish realism rather than any kind of Idealism, Denney owed initially to Veitch. Scottish Common-Sense philosophy, described as a way of making

---

[24] *Minute of Glasgow United Free Church Presbytery Meetings*, December 1904, Quoted in Walker, *Denney*, 89-91.

[25] Denney, *Studies*, 75.

human common experience intelligible,[26] sheds light on Denney's passionate engagement with Christian truth as rooted in verifiable historic experience, both in the New Testament and in the succeeding generations of Christian history.

There is an intriguing connection between Denney's lifelong enthusiasm for Boswell's *Life of Dr. Johnson*, and his habit of reading Johnson when he needed a dose of common sense. Johnson several times rooted his own recovery from scepticism to faith in the efficacy of testimony. His words are deeply resonant of Denney's conviction that the testimony of the apostles to their experience of the historical Jesus and Risen Christ, represents a primary datum of Christian evidence.

> The Christian religion has very strong evidences. It, indeed, appears in some degree strange to reason; but in History we have undoubted facts, against which, in reasoning *a priori*, we have more arguments than we have for them; but then testimony has great weight and casts the balance.[27]

In a classic *reductio ad absurdum* Johnson argued in 1763 - at the time of the Peace of Paris - against the truth that Canada had been taken from the French, offering 'pretty good arguments' to support the denial. His performance finished with the disclaimer, 'Yet Sir, notwithstanding all these plausible objections, we have no doubt that Canada is really ours. Such is the weight of common testimony. How much stronger are the evidences of the Christian religion?'[28]

It is easy to see why Denney loved the common-sense reasoning of the Augustan writers, particularly Johnson. In defence of the New Testament writers Denney repeatedly affirmed the validity and 'weight' of apostolic testimony, and its admissibility into any discussion about the historical integrity of Christian faith in Jesus Christ. In an open lecture, he informed students:

> These books have a unity and that unity is a unity of faith, being written, not *ad narrandum* but *ad probandum*, viz., to prove that Jesus is the Christ. They depend upon first hand, original testimony and therefore are not likely to be added to. They were segregated unconsciously, and therefore all the more originally and scientifically, from the floating mass of first century Christian literature.[29]

In his last book he still maintained it is the apostolic experience of the gospel, and the cumulative weight of consistent testimony to it, which

---

[26] Graham, *Scottish Tradition*, 6.
[27] James Boswell, *The Life of Dr. Johnson*, (London: Random, 1992), 151.
[28] Ibid., 269 270. Boswell, 256, comments, 'Johnson had a very philosophical mind, and such a rational respect for testimony, as to make him submit his understanding to what was authentically proved, though he could not comprehend why it was so'.
[29] From a former student's class notes, quoted in Taylor, *God Loves Like That!*, 137.

provides the experimental basis for the Bible's authority over the mind and soul of those who read it and accept its truth.

> When we read the New Testament with susceptible minds, we listen to the voice of those who were once themselves estranged from God, but have been reconciled to Him through Christ, and are letting us into the secret of their new life; it is the nearest approach we can make, and therefore the most vital, to the reconciling power which streamed from Christ Himself...there is certainly no reconciliation but through the historical Christ: there is no other Christ of whom we know anything whatever. But the historical Christ does not belong to the past. The living Spirit of God makes Him present and eternal; and it is not from Palestine, or from the first century of the Christian era, but here and now that his reconciling power is felt.[30]

The familiar tones of Lindsay and Candlish, were early transmuted into settled convictions in Denney's mind, and now after a lifetime defending them, they carried the status of theological assumptions. The Bible is a means of grace, the Spirit inspired medium through which Christ is presented to human intelligence as final and vital truth. That assumption underlies Denney's view of epistemology and the problem of defining what is real. 'Truth is the only thing which has authority for the mind, and the only way in which truth finally evinces its authority is by taking possession of the mind itself.'[31] For Denney, therefore, perceiving truth and receiving the gospel of Christ were near synonyms in Christian experience, and therefore even the Bible was subject to the Christological hermeneutic. The Bible's authority is ultimately derivative from the Gospel of God's redeeming love-bearing sin, which was for Denney that which is really real, the *ens realissimum.*

> We find this truth [of Christ] in the Christian Scriptures undoubtedly, and therefore we prize them; but the truth does not derive its authority from the Scriptures, or from those who penned them. On the contrary, the Scriptures are prized by the Church because through them the soul is brought into contact with this truth.[32]

A fine but clear line was drawn in Denney's mind between the dispensability of historical veracity in incidental details in the New Testament, and the indispensability of historical integrity in the account of Jesus to which the New Testament documents testify. This tension between the gospels and criticism preoccupied him throughout his life as a theological teacher, and at times placed him at the centre of

---

[30] Denney, *Reconciliation*, 9.
[31] Denney, *Atonement*, 8.
[32] Ibid., 9. See also DEN01-125, 2, 'The Completeness of Revelation', a sermon outline which affirms the Bible as the sourcebook for what we know of Christ. 'What is the Christian revelation, in one word, it is Christ...all other authorities are second-hand - and it is not possible to supplement Christ.'

controversy. Sermons from Broughty Ferry, his lectures in Chicago published as *Studies in Theology*, his Opening of Session Lectures in 1902,[33] 1906, and 1912, occasional unpublished papers on 'The Church and the Bible', 'The Authority of Scripture', and 'Christian Faith and the Criticism of the Bible' and lengthy passages in his major books, together constitute a major defence of and exhibition of, believing criticism. In relation to infallibility, Denney reserved the concept if not the word for the finality of Christ as revealed and encountered through Scripture.

Yet Denney never conceded ground on what he considered the essential historical facts of the Gospel, that in Jesus Christ and in his atoning death the righteousness of God has been revealed. 'The Gospel According to St Paul'[34] is a substantial sustained exposition of the historical and spiritual facts of the Gospel; both kinds of 'fact' had equal evidential value for Denney. As early as 1894 he had made this point, and it became axiomatic in his theology of Scripture.

> The Holy Spirit, bearing witness by and with the word of the evangelists in our hearts, gives us, independently of any criticism, a full persuasion and assurance of the infallible truth and divine authority of the revelation of God made in Him...there is a point, viz., the life of the Son of God in our nature, at which the spiritual and the historical coincide, and at which, therefore, as the very purpose of revelation requires, there can be a spiritual guarantee of historical truth.[35]

To his mind, the crucial question concerned the trustworthiness of Scripture as the medium of the Gospel, and the instrument of the Holy Spirit. On what kind of epistemological foundation does the reliability of the Bible rest? What is the relation between Bible, history and truth, so that scripture communicates through the Holy Spirit the reality of that Person whose grace regenerates human experience? In his College Address of 1902, with the George Adam Smith controversy fresh in people's minds, he confidently replied:

> In a theological school like this we study criticism, as we study everything else, in the interests of the Church. I do not mean that we study it in an unscientific spirit, or in unscientific methods, or that we have no interest in the truth for its own sake: I mean rather that the truth with which we are here concerned, and which we wish to see in the clearest light and hold with the surest grasp, is not truth which exists for its own sake; it is the truth of God revealed in His Son for the salvation of the world. We study criticism not that we may dissipate this truth, or get rid of it, but

---

[33] 'The Gospels and the Gospel', *British Weekly*, 6 November 1902, 73-4, and 13 November 1902, 97-8.

[34] 'The Gospel According to Paul', DEN08-13-01 to DEN08-13-06.

[35] Denney, *Studies*, 207.

that we might get as close as we can to it in its historical reality, and know more truly Him in whom we have believed.[36]

'Not Bethlehem, but Calvary is the focus of revelation'

In the same Address, Denney responded to the understandable anxieties of those who feared that criticism of the gospels threatened the very foundations of Christian faith.

> The Christian religion is identical with Jesus Christ; if there is no accessible Christ, there is no Christianity. It is the Church's being to trust in Christ; it is her vocation to bear witness to Christ; if the shadow of uncertainty or of unreality falls upon Christ, her testimony is paralysed, the breath of her life is withdrawn.[37]

Much of Denney's writing on biblical criticism attempted to provide a secure basis for faith, founded on Jesus' estimate of himself as portrayed in the New Testament, particularly the gospels. The value placed on Denney's work on atonement, particularly in its Pauline expression, has tended to eclipse much of his other work on the gospels and Jesus.[38] When Denney wrote to Nicoll, defending Bruce, his old teacher,[39] he was partially discharging a significant debt. From his earliest sermons at East Hill Street, throughout his years at Broughty Ferry, in lectures and articles through to his most mature writings, Denney continued on the road he had first travelled with Bruce, in search of the historical Jesus. But Bruce, far less Denney, was not doing so out of historical scepticism or curiosity, but out of a deep conviction that such a historical search would yield confirmation that the encounter of the first disciples and apostles with Jesus, sifted, reflected on and recorded in the gospels, constituted primary evidence for the historical Jesus, and provided a permanent if contingent textual medium through which Jesus, the eternal truth of God's revelation, was reliably accessible.

In the mind of Denney the historical Jesus and the exalted Christ are one, the point of fusion not dependent upon a metaphysical theory of Christology, but upon an adequate understanding of atonement. The centrality of Jesus for faith is theologically derived from, and experimentally confirmed by, a view of reality in which final truth is discerned in Christ's atoning death, a propitiation necessarily, and for love's sake, willingly offered, for the forgiveness of sins and the

---

[36] 'The Gospels and the Gospel', *BW*, 13 November 1902, 98.

[37] 'The Gospels', *BW*, 6 November 1902, 73.

[38] Surviving sermons on the gospels number: Matthew, 27; Mark, 69; Luke, 77; John 80, a total of 258. The total for Paul, excluding the Pastorals, is 161.

[39] See Appendix 3.

redemption of the world. Like Bruce, Denney devoted long, meticulous and reverent study to the historical documents which bore singular testimony to the revelation of God in Jesus, though not to establish the veracity of this or that detail as a way of strengthening the credibility of the documents. The reality which the gospels attest is eternal treasure in the earthen vessel of human history, and it is understood and appropriated by experience rather than disinterested or hostile historical analysis. Experience of Christ crucified and risen, Denney believed, is the real antidote to historical scepticism.

> Is it inconceivable that historians and critics should have something to learn from the Gospel - something to learn even in criticism and history? The world with Christ in it is another and a greater world, and it is beside the mark for the most gifted of men to measure Christ and the New Testament beforehand as though Christ had never been. The Christian religion came into being through the presence in human history of a Person who gave history a new dimension, and its continuance depends on our power to realise through the history the presence of that great Person still.[40]

'The world with Christ in it is another and a greater world.' In the mind of Denney this was not a reference to the incarnation. He resisted the idea, current in his later years, that the incarnation was the centre of gravity for Christian faith.[41] The significance of the incarnation is that it provided the divine means to God's salvific end, an atonement adequate to the necessities of divine righteousness and human need. To make the incarnation central to Christian theology

> shifts the centre of gravity in the New Testament.... It is not in His being here, but in His being here as a propitiation for the sins of the world, that the love of God is revealed. Not Bethlehem, but Calvary, is the focus of revelation, and any construction of Christianity which ignores or denies this distorts Christianity by putting it out of focus.[42]

It is in making the atonement 'the diamond pivot on which the whole system of Christian truth revolves',[43] that Denney's reputation as a theologian of the cross rests. From his earliest sermons to his final volume he expounded the death of Christ as the 'centre of gravity', 'the diamond pivot', 'the very incredibility of the gospel [that] makes it credible'.[44] Faced with the mystery of sin and the deeper mystery of divine love he resorted to paradox: 'When we look at Christ crucified and risen, the

---

[40] 'The Gospel', *BW*, 6 November 1902, 74.
[41] Denney, *Reconciliation*, 39, 63, 183-4.
[42] Denney, *Death*, 324-5.
[43] Denney, *Studies*, 109
[44] 'Gospel according to Paul', DEN08-13-05, 54.

revelation of God it makes to us is this: God is redeeming love, in power of omnipotence; or God is omnipotent power in the service of redeeming love.'[45]

Denney's reputation as a theologian of the cross rests largely on a received tradition that he is an uncompromising champion of objective atonement understood primarily in terms of penal substitution.[46] But as this study suggests, Denney was resistant to a reduction of the cross, the revelation of the 'last reality of the universe', to the precision terminology of humanly constructed dogmatic confessions. His impatient reply to those who wanted the doctrine of atonement spelt out in unambiguous terms, was that the Apostles' and Nicene creeds followed a sound instinct in not establishing the orthodoxy of any particular formula in relation to atonement.[47] There was a chronic ambivalence in Denney's mind about packaging eternal mystery, revealed in historic events appropriated in human experience, into the restrictive categories of doctrinal articulation, which because human are by nature partial and provisional. 'There is room', he reflected in 1897, at the beginning of his teaching career, 'for a tremendous lot of agnosticism in theology'.[48]

In his later thought, while he remained a proponent of an objective view of atonement, his emphases changed significantly. Concepts he considered abstract, contractual or mechanical were displaced by others more relational, ethical and personal, and latterly his preferred metaphors were those which conveyed the truths of sin as essentially broken relationship and the cross as the effectual and final revelation of divine sin-bearing love. The difference in tone and content between *The Death of Christ* (1902), and *The Christian Doctrine of Reconciliation* (1917), is arguably signalled in the titles. The first deals with facts of history, textually mediated and requiring investigation and interpretation; the second describes an existential reality requiring explanation for purposes of ongoing appropriation.

Denney's unequivocal support cannot therefore be claimed for any single theory of the atonement, nor does he sit comfortably in any one

---

[45] Ibid., 83.

[46] Timothy Gorringe, writing in a contemporary context about violence, punishment and the cross, interestingly selects Denney's *Death of Christ* as a classic presentation of penal substitution. See *God's Just Vengeance*, (Cambridge: Cambrdge University Press, 1996), 214ff. Lesslie Newbigin on the other hand experienced a theological re-orientation after reading Denney's *Romans,* his theology becoming more overtly crucicentric and mission directed. Quoted in G. R. Hunsberger, *Bearing the Witness of the Spirit,* (Grand Rapids: Eerdmans, 1998), 32, 209. Neither of them refer to Denney's later work in *Reconciliation.*

[47] Denney, *Jesus,* 406.

[48] *LFF,* 74.

theological camp.⁴⁹ In his last book he saw merit in the Anselmic emphasis on divine holiness,⁵⁰ and in the Abelardian insistence on love as definitive in God's revelation at the cross.⁵¹ He admired Luther's dynamic understanding of faith as the attitude of the sinful soul to God in Christ,⁵² but also found valid insights in Grotius' governmental understanding of the atonement, 'which directed attention to the effect of Christ's work on men as well as on God, to the new life as well as to the maintenance of God's honour or the satisfaction of His law.'⁵³ In McLeod Campbell he appreciated the insistence on the personal representative nature of Christ's self-offering for sin, 'in our place',⁵⁴ while in Bushnell he found a modern explication of divine love as vicarious self-giving.⁵⁵ With all these writers he agreed, and disagreed. No one treatment could be sufficient to the immensity of the task.

If fundamentally, his theology of atonement remained objective and substitutionary in the portrayal of Christ's work, and it retained albeit in modified form, a strong propitiatory element, nevertheless the increased emphasis on experience in his later writing suggests a position more sympathetic to a subjective relational model, and less comfortable with legal and penal concepts such as satisfaction and imputation.⁵⁶ He never resolved the resultant tension, and in a late lecture indicates why.

---

⁴⁹ In his lecture 'The Atonement I', DEN09-11, Denney notes 'the really original books on the atonement - which have asked new questions, which have suggested new answers, which have introduced considerations or connections hitherto overlooked - are hardly more than three: Anselm's *Cur Deus Homo?*, Grotius' *De Satisfactione Christi*, and McLeod Campbell's *The Nature of the Atonement*, 10.

⁵⁰ Denney, *Reconciliation*, 64-79.

⁵¹ Ibid., 78-82.

⁵² Ibid., 92-3.

⁵³ Ibid., 110-13.

⁵⁴ Ibid., 255-7.

⁵⁵ Ibid., 255-6.

⁵⁶ This ambiguity in Denney helps explain why in the secondary literature some express surprise, even dissatisfaction with his move away from traditional penal substitutionary renderings of atonement theology. Two examples illustrate the point. Donald Macleod in 'The Atonement', *DSCHT*, 42, judges that in *The Christian Doctrine of Reconciliation* 'the dominant impression is one of confusion', and he regrets the loss of such categories as imputation and satisfaction. R. Pitts, in 'James Denney. Evangelical Theologian', *Religion and Life*, 34, 1965, 602, more sympathetically points out the 'Bushnellian' tone of Denney's later writing, the cross being interpreted as vicarious love absorbing and forgiving human sin. Both writers are correct. Denney's emphases, methodology and preferred theological terms had changed from those of his earlier period. That is why it is misleading to categorise Denney too narrowly. It is also important to remember that Denney's last book was not a finished product, and that Denney died relatively early, his mature thought still evolving towards a theological

> The death of Christ is a fact or reality with many aspects, many constituents, many relations, intentions and powers in it, and its reconciling virtue may be dependent on them all... Truths are often dependent on each other for their virtue, even when the interdependence is not perceived; and no doctrine has suffered more than the doctrine of the atonement from exclusive emphasis being laid on this or that element of truth which really ceases to be effective when its connection with others is ignored.[57]

'We may think of the love of God as becoming transcendently or inconceivably loving'

In the lecture series, 'The Gospel According to Paul' Denney anticipated much of what was written in *The Christian Doctrine of Reconciliation*. It is an important late source, because in it many of the most characteristic themes of his theology as they have emerged throughout this study, are refracted through the prism of Paul's letter to the Romans.[58] In this late exposition of Romans 1-8,[59] a high degree of personal investment and intellectual passion are evident. The style of theologising drew inspiration from core convictions evolved through years of exegetical reflection, and from spiritual experiences on the scale of the Pauline rendering of Christ crucified and risen, and only then written preached and declared in the lecture room. Reading these late lectures, it is not difficult to understand why some of his former students recalled the impact of Denney in full flow.

> He set before us the gospel in its grandeur, in its universality, in its freedom from every hampering condition, in its incomparable emotional appeal, in its power to open the sluices of gratitude in the very driest heart. These were days when we came out of class and could not speak to each other. We wandered off into solitary places till we found out what it all meant for us in the privacy of our own hearts.[60]

---

articulation adequate to his own experience of what had become for him the *ens realissimum*, 'eternal love, bearing sin.'

[57] DEN09-11, 'The Atonement I', 6.

[58] The latest fixed date within the text is 1909, a reference to the *Expositor*. DEN08-13-02, 21. A marginal note cites a German article by Weiss, July 1913. DEN08-13-01, 3. This places the work well within Denney's last decade. In 1911 Denney told Nicoll he wanted to write something on Paul. *LWRN*, 172. In 1914 Alexander Whyte asked if the rumour he was writing something on Paul was true. Barbour, *Whyte*, 508.

[59] His third major treatment, supplementing his Romans commentary and the seven articles in the Expositor of ten years earlier. Incidentally, Denney both quotes and corrects his own commentary.

[60] Dr George Johnstone Jeffrey, 'In Praise of James Denney', *The Evening Citizen*, 8 October 1938, quoted by Taylor, *Principal Denney*, 37. The reference is to Denney's lectures on Galatians, DEN12-07.

So while Denney placed Jesus at the centre of his and the Church's faith, it was Jesus as the revelation of a crucicentric Gospel. That Gospel, he was convinced, had never been more faithfully, imaginatively or persuasively presented to the human conscience, heart and mind, than through the mind of Paul. The problem of sin, the reality of the divine righteousness revealed in wrath against sin and in love towards humanity, the foolish wisdom of God revealed in the cross, the vindication and exaltation of Jesus at the resurrection, and the gift of the Spirit who makes the gospel real in the human experience of reconciliation and moral regeneration, these are neither distinctive nor exhaustive in an account of the Christian Gospel. What makes these and all other theological implicates of the Pauline gospel distinctive and utterly convincing for Denney, was his conviction that the *fons et origo* of all Christian theology is a true understanding of what the cross meant to God. Christian theology is indelibly stamped with a cruciform hallmark.

It is this absolutisation of Christ crucified and risen, as the divine answer to the problem of sin as a fundamental rupture in the relations of God to humanity, sin as the moral catastrophe which sets God and the creation against each other, that repeatedly drew Denney's mind to Paul's theology. For Denney the fundamental theological problem of the atonement is the problem of the process and cost to God, and consequently, how the death of Christ is to be construed in such a way as to do justice to law, sin and the condemnation of humanity, and to the righteousness, wrath and love of God. By the early years of the twentieth century influential names such as Rashdall, and Moberley represented a view of atonement very different from that argued by Denney. Ideas such as sin, wrath, substitution and propitiation were either modified or relegated as the obsolete vocabulary of an outmoded theology. Retaining the familiar terminology, Denney subjected these words to a process of refinement by exposing them to the original mind of Paul in such documents as Romans 1–8, so that they emerged in his later writing defined by the apostolic text rather than by the caricature of opponents or the more speculative dogmas of Reformed scholasticism.

By the time Denney wrote *The Christian Doctrine of Reconciliation*, his preferred metaphors were relational. As previously noted this was not new, but the organic development of latent ideas, his own experience and relationship with God becoming a working paradigm as he sought categories adequate to the task of articulating transcendent mystery. These categories he found in the theological masterpieces of Pauline theology.

'Sin is universal...sin is something that belongs to the relations of man and God; if man and God were not related somehow sin would be an impossible idea.'[61] Thus the problem of sin is one of relationship, and the dreadful reality for God is that sin, which God hates, threatens to destroy that which God loves.

> The sin of the world makes a difference to the love of God. Not that it turns it into hatred, or makes it deny itself. It is love still, but it is holy love, challenged by the sin of the world, impelled...in its natural outgoing, obliged to find a way for itself to men through the obstacles which they have placed in its path. Its manifestation...becomes more costly than it would otherwise have been; there is a new element of passion in it because, that it might not deny itself it has been obliged to enter into the new and repellent situation created by the sin of the world. When I say 'obliged', I do not mean that sinners could count on the love which comes to us in Christ, still less that they had any claim on it; it is the wonder of wonders, that such a manifestation of God should be made to men who had done all in their power to wound God's love and forfeit it. The obligation...lies in the love of God itself, and there only. Just as Paul speaks of sin under certain conditions becoming exceeding sinful, so we may think of the love of God as becoming transcendently or inconceivably loving when it does not draw back from the problem sin has created, but advances to resolve it at whatever cost.[62]

Denney saw no conflict between love and propitiation; indeed Christ put forth as the propitiation for sin is the unprecedented proof of love, and gives God a claim on the hearts of all who surrender to that love in the self-abandonment of absolute trust.

> It is possible for God henceforth, without ever seeming to compromise his character as a righteous God, to accept as righteous...those who believe in Jesus. The Jesus in whom they believe is the Christ whom God set forth as a propitiation in his blood. To believe in him means to cast themselves and all their sinful responsibilities on him in this character. It means to take into their hearts God's condemnation of sin - to accept and submit to that annihilating sentence upon it the justice of which was recognised by Christ when he tasted death for every man; the integrity of God is maintained when he receives sinners on this footing - his self consistency, so to speak, in siding with us against himself; the revelation of his mercy does justice to that of his wrath, of his pardon to his holiness.[63]

The role of Christ as propitiation, as Saviour, as crucified and risen Lord, placed Christ at the very centre of Denney's theological world and personal experience. It is a consistent emphasis that survived all the other theological adjustments and intellectual developments which are inevitable in a mind alive to truth, and alert to the claims of new knowledge. When Denney describes the human response of faith in Christ

---

[61] 'Gospel According to Paul', DEN08-13-02, 32.
[62] 'Gospel According to Paul', DEN08-13-05, 61.
[63] Ibid., 68.

in his absolute significance for the world, it is in terms that seem possible only to one who knows the experience he tells:

> Faith has always this absolute character...it is absolute and unreserved abandonment of the soul to that which as divine claims and is entitled to nothing less....Christ on his cross is held up to us as the revelation of God to sinful men. What does it mean? It means (according to Paul) that the absolute reality, the final truth in the world, so far as God's relation to sin is concerned, is this; not that he condones it (he never condones it), nor that he condemns it (though he does condemn it), but that in the very act of condemning it he bears it, takes the weight of it, the pain and shame and death of it upon himself, and shows a redeeming love to the sinful in so doing. Now what are we to do in face of such a revelation of God? What is required of sinful men when faced with this as the last reality of the universe? Simply to let go...to abandon our lives to it without reserve, instantly and for ever.[64]

'Christ at the heart of everything'

In two pages of his article 'Preaching Christ', Denney used the phrase 'absolute significance' with reference to Christ with what amounts to monotonous repetition.[65] The article intentionally presents such an overwhelmingly positive conception of Christ as would inspire Christian preachers to proclaim Christ with unembarrassed confidence, and with a range of imaginative possibility freed from the rationalising intellectual constraints of a culture which privileged history and science as the premier critical disciplines. By exulting in Christ crucified and exalted as the centre and circumference of all things, Denney was expressing one of his most theologically adventurous convictions. Speaking of the impact of Jesus on the author of the Fourth Gospel, he spoke of Jesus as the redefining Reality of a new creation.

> He was a being so great, and had left on the soul of His witness an impression so deep, that the latter felt it could be satisfied by nothing but a reconstitution of his universe in which this wonderful Person was put at the heart of everything - creation, providence, revelation and redemption being all referred to Him...the absolute significance of Christ in the relations of God and man, which is the immediate certainty of Christian experience, stamps Him as a Divine and eternal Person, by relation to whom the world and all that is in it must be described anew.[66]

---

[64] Ibid., 59.

[65] J. Denney, 'Preaching Christ', *Dictionary of Christ and the Gospels*, (Edinburgh: T & T Clark, 1906-8), vol. 2, 396-7

[66] Ibid., 402.

The Johannine Logos and the Colossian Christ were Christological constructs that to Denney's mind, rightly gave to Christ a place that could not be usurped even by the Absolute of the Idealists. His dislike of speculative metaphysics dated back to his University days when he first encountered Idealism in Caird's class. But as a passage like the above shows, he was not entirely averse to some speculative thinking provided it was anchored in New Testament realities.

In the lectures on Paul this speculative strain occasionally surfaced, encouraged by Paul's own example. While Denney was severely critical of speculative mysticism, much in vogue in intellectual circles at the beginning of the twentieth century,[67] and while he argued vehemently that union with Christ was moral rather than mystical or metaphysical,[68] there is some evidence that Denney did not always reduce theological truth to lucid statements of communicable propositions. Indeed in his comment on Romans 8.22-23, he speaks of the redemption of nature, and comments wryly, 'It needs intellectual courage to assent to ideas like these'.[69] Nature and humanity are parts of the same system, he argued. Both are baffled and frustrated by the curse and consequences of human sin, and both have a latent hope of some day fulfilling their destiny in God.

> When man was redeemed by Christ the ban was lifted from nature also and the world born again into a golden age. [At least it has the promise of a new birth just as man has.][70] Perhaps it is not possible to reason about such matters like this; it may be said they belong to the world of imagination rather than of science, that they are poetry, not theology. But however it is to be explained there is something in a passage such as this which appeals to hidden depths in us. Nature is not purely and unqualifiedly natural; it is caught up into and becomes an element in a moral universe.[71]

There is a degree of agnosticism in this, but fused with optimism and a profound sense of the moral nature of reality. In an earlier lecture he had pointed out, 'a conception of nature as a system of things which has its life in itself, and is self-contained and self-explanatory, is quite foreign to the apostle'. Paul did not think of nature, but of 'a creation which is absolutely dependent on God and can therefore be used by him as a medium of communication with man'.[72] It is this conception of the created order as fallen and redeemed through the same process as human

---

[67] Significant personalities include Evelyn Underhill, W. R. Inge and Baron Friedrich Von Hügel.
[68] See letter to Nicoll in Appendix 2.
[69] DEN08-13-06, 110.
[70] The bracketed sentence is added between the lines as a qualifying afterthought
[71] Ibid., 109
[72] DEN08-13-03, 34.

salvation, that gave impetus to Denney's theological imagination as he sought to give content to the absolute significance of Christ, for humanity, for the universe and for the purposes of God on a universal scale. At this late stage in life Denney was still pushing at the limits of his own understanding of the transcendent, tragic but ultimately triumphant mystery of eternal love bearing sin to restore the moral nature of reality.

Reflecting on the Christ of Colossians, he found there a conceptuality approaching his own instinctive sense that Christ can neither be measured by science nor confined to history, neither apprehended by intellect nor comprehended by reason. Christ defies the normal categories simply because He is normative for all things. Christ is, in words which answer to Denney's own as much as Paul's experience,

> the last reality in the universe, the *ens realissimum*, the ultimate truth through which and by relation to which all things must be defined and understood... The presence of God in Christ...is the primary certainty; and that certainty carries with it for him the requirement of a specifically Christian view of the universe. He would not be true to Christ, as Christ had revealed Himself to him in experience, unless he had the courage to Christianise all his thoughts of God and the world.... He is not directly deifying Christ, he is Christianising the universe...he is casting upon all creation and redemption the steadfast and unwavering light of the divine presence of which he was assured in Christ.[73]

The words stand as Denney's own credo.

Throughout this study the aim has been to place Denney in the context of his times in order to gain a more nuanced account of his mind and thought. His story has unfolded, from his early years amongst the Reformed Presbyterians in Greenock, where he imbibed the reverence and moral seriousness that never left him. Then to Glasgow University where he discovered and worked to acquire tools and instruments of thought which opened up new ranges of knowledge and new intellectual possibilities. Immediately afterwards, to Glasgow Free Church College where he was taught by a galaxy of intellectually adventurous but persistently faithful Professors who exemplified believing criticism in the service of the Church, even when the Church resented and resisted such service. Two years in the Gallowgate, then eleven as a minister at Broughty Ferry, instilled pastoral skills and values and taught him to merge scholarship with preaching, and theology with the very human needs of a diverse, growing and demanding congregation.

There followed twenty remarkably fruitful years in Glasgow College, maturing into a respected and increasingly trusted voice on matters as diverse as biblical criticism, church reunion, training and support of ministry, temperance, and latterly the issues raised by the Great War.

---

[73] Denney, *Jesus*, 37.

Woven throughout, a substantial scholarly corpus of writing, from journalism to major monographs, including lecture notes and sermons, a wide-ranging, diverse correspondence, a cache of written thought which cumulatively confirms the humanism and learning of one whose calling was to be a teacher of the Church.

But in the story of a mind, there is a need to weigh also the significance of the events and circumstances which are part of life's contingency and largely beyond control or choice. His upbringing in rapidly changing Greenock, his arrival at Glasgow College during the Robertson Smith affair, experiences of poverty and the challenge of relevance in East Hill Street, his marriage and the deeply satisfying years of ministry, were all humanising experiences. The controversies he sparked, in Chicago and subsequently, the mind-broadening trips to the Continent and America, the death of his wife and its legacy of uncompleted grieving, his friendships with Struthers, Grant, Robertson Nicoll, James Orr, George Adam Smith, each contributed further to the refining of intellectual and emotional capacity. The causes he later fought, including temperance, changes in ministerial training, promotion of the Central Fund, and the impact on faith and theology of the First World War, exposed the ethical urgencies which undergirded his thinking. And suffusing all, forming and informing his personal faith, the theological themes which had fascinated and captivated his mental energies throughout his life.

In studying the mind of a man like Denney, while there has occasionally been an obvious sense of development, of changed perspective, more often there has been a sense that where his mind has changed, it has been by small, perhaps unnoticed increments. What has remained constant throughout this study is the passionate thinking and wide intellectual engagement which gave sub-structure to his faith commitment as absolute personal loyalty to Christ. Whatever changes are discernible in the theological articulations of his faith and experience, the central focus of that faith remained firmly and clearly fixed, as the magnetic North of his mental horizon.

> Very few men, indeed, have reflected on the Gospel with such utter fearlessness.... His mind was always breaking out at a new place. You could not travel over his intelligence and map it out once for all, for a creative evolution went on uninterruptedly. But so deep and strong was his faith that, so far as one could see, these transitions were accomplished without friction.[74]

What has emerged from this study is a clearer portrait of the man and the mind which produced such existentially powerful theology; and a fuller appreciation of how context decisively, if at times elusively, shaped

---

[74] H. R. Mackintosh, 'Principal James Denney as a Theologian', *ExpT*, XXVIII, 1917, 493.

intellectual expression and existential commitment. And as he frequently testified in writings where exegetical precision, intellectual freedom and theological reasoning were woven together and fastened by an experiential faith, the inner dynamic which inspired and fuelled his life of devoted scholarship and theological passion was the One who had for him, as for all things, 'absolute significance'.

> The mind that has been fascinated by Christ Himself, and that has begun to know what He is by its own experience of what He does, must never barter that original quickening and emancipation, and what it learns by them, for any doctrine defined by man.... It does not matter whether it issues from Nicea or Augsburg, from Trent or Westminster.... It is a false progress that is promoted by unbending conformity to creeds and confessions. The only way to become perfect is to cherish the initial liberating impulse, to keep our being open to the whole stimulus of Christ, to grow and still to grow in the grace and the knowledge of our Lord and Saviour.[75]

> It is not open or unanswered questions that paralyse; it is ambiguous or evasive answers, or answers of which we can make no use, because we cannot make them our own. And it is not the acceptance of any theology or Christology, however penetrating or profound, which keeps us Christian; we remain loyal to our Lord and Saviour only because He has apprehended us, and His hand is strong.[76]

---

[75] Denney, *Way*, 273.
[76] Denney, *Jesus*, 411.

APPENDIX 1

Chronology of Early Sermons[1]

East Hill St, July 1883–December 1885

11/5/83	DEN06-76	'This do in remembrance'.
24/6/83	DEN01-44	'God's revelation of himself'.
8/7/83	DEN01-05	'The Call of Abraham'.
7/10/83	DEN04-223	'He was a burning and a shining light'.
28/10/83	DEN03-31	'Haec fecisti et tacui'.
18/11/83	DEN04-132	'The strong man'.
2/12/83	DEN06-02	'Patient continuance in well-doing'.
6/1/84	DEN05-49	'He was a good man'.
10/2/84	DEN04-251	'It is expedient for you'.
9/3/84	DEN03-03	'Meaning of suffering'.
23/3/84	DEN04-175	'The Gospel miracles'.
18/3/84	DEN01-056	'The Sabbath – gift to man'.
27/4/84	DEN03-55	'They that make them are like unto them'.
8/6/84	DEN03-60	'Psalm 119.45'.
15/6/84	DEN06-71	'2 Cor. 7.29-31'.
29/6/84	DEN07-138	'Be clothed with humility'.
7/9/84	DEN06-103	'Every man shall bear his own burden'.
5/10/84	DEN06-102	'Bear ye one another's burdens'.
12/10/84	DEN04-149	'The unjust steward'.
19/10/84	DEN04-150	'He that is faithful'.
26/10/84	DEN02-51	'Promise: the foundation of prayer'.
18/1/85	DEN06-07c	'Sin shall not have dominion'.
22/2/85	DEN06-67	'Let no man glory in men'.
3/5/85	DEN06-99	'Godly sorrow'.
14/6/85	DEN07-27	'In Him dwelleth'.
20/12/85	DEN04-254	'The witness of Jesus to the truth'.

---

[1] Denney dated almost none of his sermons after he left Broughty Ferry in 1897. The following lists identify from the corpus of 951 manuscripts, those which can be dated within his years of pastoral ministry, providing at least a partial chronological survey of Denney's preaching.

Interim Period (December 1885–22 March 1886)

27/12/85	DEN03-62	'Psalm 119.59'.
7/2/86	DEN03-92	'Isaiah 60.5'.
14/2/86	DEN06-15	'Let not your good be evil spoken of'.

Broughty Ferry by Year (22/3/86–1897)

4/4/86	DEN03-80	'Isaiah's consecration'.
11/4/86	DEN04-153	'The kingdom of God cometh'.
18/4/86	DEN07-119	'Whom having not seen'.
15/5/86	DEN07-28	'Raised together with him'.
23/5/86	DEN07-178	'Worship Him that made...'.
6/6/86	DEN04-129	'Lord teach us to pray'.
13/6/86	DEN06-81	'No man can say Jesus is Lord'.
20/6/86	DEN07-134	'Communion: Christ also suffered for our sins'.
24/6/86	DEN07-128	'Temple and priesthood'.
18/7/86	DEN04-220	'Come see a man'.
1/8/86	DEN06-07a	'Dead unto sin'.
19/9/86	DEN06-86	'The grace of our Lord Jesus'.
10/10/86	DEN04-226	'To whom shall we go?'.
17/10/86	DEN06-93	'The light of the gospel'.
26/12/86	DEN04-104	'Nunc Dimittis'.
2/1/87	DEN07-150	'The world passeth away'.
17/4/87	DEN07-154	'The nature and claims of love'.
8/5/87	DEN03-09	'They that know thy name'.
21/8/87	DEN03-87	'Isaiah 33'.
29/1/88	DEN03-32	'The sacrifices of God'.
8/4/88	DEN04-250	'It is expedient for you'.
15/4/88	DEN01-080	'Let them make me a sanctuary'.
22/4/88	DEN07-173	'Unto him that loved us'.
6/5/88	DEN03-27	'The living God'
3/6/88	DEN06-92B	'Paul led in triumph.'
15/7/88	DEN01-014	'Patriarchal religion'.
14/11/88	DEN04-210	'The life was the light of men'.
6/1/89	DEN03-50	'The Lord is good'.
13/1/89	DEN07-142	'God is light'.
27/1/89	DEN07-143	'Friendship with God'.
3/2/89	DEN02-79	'Nehemiah 1.6'.
10/2/89	DEN02-80	'Nehemiah 7.13'.
17/2/89	DEN06-01	'I am debtor'.
24/2/89	DEN04-35	'Peter and Jesus'.
3/3/89	DEN04-36	'The leper'.
4/3/89	DEN03-13	'The world and God'.

10/3/89	DEN04-37	'The Paralytic'.
10/3/89	DEN04-243	'Let not your heart be troubled'.
17/3/89	DEN04-38	'The paralytic'.
31/3/89	DEN01-126	'Thou shalt love the Lord…'.
7/4/89	DEN07-24	'Be careful for nothing'.
14/4/89	DEN06.13b	'Thou shalt love thy neighbour'.
21/4/89	DEN07-75	'Jesus Christ who destroyed death'.
5/5/89	DEN03-111	'Ezekiel 37.1-14'.
5/5/89	DEN03-130	'Joel 2.25 Years the locusts have eaten'.
23/6/89	DEN06-66	'The church's one foundation'.
20/10/89	DEN06-79	'Let a man examine himself'.
27/4/90	DEN03-9	'They that know thy name'.
8/6/90	DEN03-110	'Ezek 33.30-33'.
22/6/90	DEN06-69	'Ye are not your own'.
29/6/90	DEN03-54	'He shall drink of the brook'.
26/6/92	DEN01-128	'He humbled thee'.
??/7/92	DEN02-45	'Saul at Endor'.[2]
23/10/92	DEN06-06c	'Christ died for the ungodly'.
25/12/92	DEN04-101	'Christmas Day: Luke 2.11'.
15/2/93	DEN03-11	'The fool hath said.'[3]
4/11/94	DEN03-53	'They despised the pleasant land'.
11/11/94	DEN02-56	'The god that answers by fire'.
28/4/95	DEN04-255	'Then came Jesus forth'.
??/7/95	DEN06-76	'This do in remembrance of me'.[4]
11/10/96	DEN03-46	'Sermon on the Sabbath'.
25/10/96	DEN04-18	'The necessity of Christ's death'.
20/1/87	DEN03-39	'Queen's diamond Jubilee'.
??/09/97	DEN07-156	We have known and believed the love of God.[5]

---

[2] Denney refers to this sermon in a letter to Struthers, 5 August 1892. *LFF*, 42. It is part of a consecutive series of thirty expositions, placing the series DEN02-17–DEN02-47 during the Broughty Ferry Ministry.

[3] *LFF*, 49. Preached at the prayer meeting.

[4] Struthers, *Life and Letters*, 226.

[5] Farewell sermon to East Free Church, Broughty Ferry.

Major series preached at Broughty Ferry[6]

29/6/86–31/7/87	DEN06-18–DEN06-43	26 sermons on 1 Corinthians
23/10/87–1/6/90	DEN05-01–DEN05-41	40 lectures[7] on Acts
1892-3	DEN02-17–DEN02-47	30 sermons on 1 Samuel[8]
1895-6	DEN01-107–DEN01-119	13 lectures on Deuteronomy[9]
	DEN07-78–DEN07-90	11 studies on 2 Timothy and Titus[10]
	DEN07-106–DEN07-116	11 lectures on James[11]
	DEN01-41–DEN01-60 and DEN01-74–DEN01-93	40 studies on Exodus[12]

---

[6] It is likely that consecutive expository series of sermons, lectures and studies were amongst those Denney burned when he left Broughty Ferry. His ministry would no longer require connected expository preaching. For example, Struthers assured him in November 1888, 'I am sure you will enjoy Joshua. I too was at a loss for a book to lecture on...'. *Life and Letters*, 171. Assuming Denney delivered such a series to his congregation, there is no surviving evidence. Similarly in August 1894 Struthers asked Denney 'How are you getting on with Nehemiah?', *Life and Letters*, 221. Only two survey sermons survive. There is however an undated set of lectures on Judges, DEN02-02 to DEN02-16, and these for reasons given above should also be dated somewhere in the Broughty Ferry ministry.

[7] Lectures to a congregation were sermons with a more didactic approach, and probably longer!

[8] Probably 1892. See note 2.

[9] *LFF*, 70.

[10] Written in note form on A5 sheets similar to other mid-week expository sermons for the Prayer Meeting.

[11] J. P. Struthers, to whom Denney lent his written sermons and lectures, refers to having read these lectures previously, and asked to see them again in June 1900 prior to embarking on a series of his own studies. They are homiletic, and unlikely to be College lectures, therefore probably dating from the Broughty Ferry years.

[12] *LFF*, 70. Again Denney informed Struthers he went through Exodus at the prayer meeting, and the Exodus studies are in the familiar A5 note form. DEN01-61 to DEN01-73 are a series of full manuscript sermons on the Decalogue. The consecutive format points to another series from around the same period.

APPENDIX 2

Transcript of DEN09-17, 'Holy Scripture'

Lecture IX Holy Scripture[1]

The subject of the present lecture is Holy Scripture, its value and its religious authority. Not a step could have been taken in any of our discussions without appeal being made to scripture, and without an authority of some kind being conceded to it, but as yet there has been no explicit consideration of the nature or the limits of that authority. The confessions of the Protestant churches all include a doctrine of Scripture, or of the word of God, but are divided as to where it should come in. Thus the Westminster Confession makes it fundamental; the chapter, 'Of the Holy Scripture' is the first and one of the most elaborate in that document. The original confession of the Scottish Church on the other hand treats it under the heading of means of grace, and in subordination to the doctrine of the Church. This is also the order followed in the Articles of faith drawn up by the Presbyterian Church of England. The article on Holy Scripture is the 18th out of 23, and though there are passing references to Scripture in earlier ones - as in the 2nd which speaks of the mystery of the Holy Trinity as revealed in Scripture, and the 11th which speaks of the Spirit using the truth of God's word as the ordinary means of regeneration - they are no more than incidental; it is only after all the principal doctrines have been defined that the doctrine of Scripture is reached, and we are told that the English Presbyterians 'reverently acknowledge to Holy Spirit speaking in the Scriptures as the Supreme Judge in questions of faith and duty.' These phenomena are significant, I think, in this way. They show that in the use actually made of the Bible, and in the conclusions actually drawn from it, there may be substantial agreement among men who are not agreed historically about the place Scripture should hold in a dogmatic system, or the precise nature of the authority which should be ascribed to it. We must all have seen that this is true in smaller arenas than those represented by Church Confessions. We all ourselves get substantially the same grace from the Bible - the same enrichment about God, and the same inspiration to trust and obedience -

---

[1] The punctuation and syntax are largely left as in the original, except where alterations and deletions require some modification in layout. Long unbroken paragraphs are one of Denney's literary habits.

however we may conceive of the Bible itself. As a means of grace it serves the same purpose, however variously we may define its spiritual authority.

The peculiar form which discussions about Scripture have assumed in the Protestant Churches, and the peculiar interest which attaches to them, are due to historical causes on which it will be convenient to look back. From the end of the second century the Christian Church was in possession of a complete Bible, a canon of sacred Scripture, including both the OT and a New. The documents of the pre-Christian and of the Christian stages of revelation. Its OT scripture was the Septuagint, including the books we now know as Apocryphal; its NT scripture was never precisely determined. There were differences of usage in different quarters; there were churches which used Hebrews, for instance and did not use the Apocalypse; there were churches which did the reverse; there was a broad distinction drawn between books that were homologoumena, universally admitted, and books that were antilogoumena, or contested by some. There were books also, at one time read in churches, like the Ep. of Barnabas and the Shepherd of Hermas, that never succeeded in gaining a footing in the canon, though' as far as one can see, they had as good a chance in their time, as some that actually found admission. It is impossible to tell how, precisely, the canon was formed. There are a great many lists of the sacred books of the NT from the Canon of Muratoria in the end of the 2nd Century downward; but no council sanctioned a list, and made its acceptance an article of faith in the Church, till the Council of Trent did so on the 8th of April 1546. A Christian instinct, guided by historical sense, seems to have led the primitive church in the main; and the area over which all Christendom spread - including as it did the four gospels, Acts, 13 Epistles of Paul the 1st Epistle of Peter and the 1st Epistle of John - was so great, that the hesitations and even the decided differences of opinion on other points, were of comparatively little moment. The Latin church, when Christianity was practically identified with it, was itself one, a living, acting, speaking body; it could answer all its own questions; and as long as there was no one to dispute its authority there was no need, either within it or without, for a more precise doctrine of the limits or the authority of Holy Scripture.

But that need came with the Reformation. The gospel had been corrupted and lost in the church; it had been buried, and made inaccessible neath the vast accumulations of ecclesiastical doctrine and still more of ecclesiastical law. But what had been lost in the Church, Luther found in the Bible. The glad tidings of God's pardoning love freely offered in Christ, for the free acceptance of sinful men - the fundamental truth of Christianity that salvation is of grace, thro' faith - this was rediscovered by Luther, principally thro' the help of St Paul and under the teaching of the Holy Spirit. This doctrine was to him in a quite peculiar sense <u>the word of God</u>. It was the core and kernel of revelation, the very heart of the truth in which God manifested himself to man. It is impossible to exaggerate the significance of this, or to spend too much time or pains in gaining the full comprehension of it. Justification by faith has been discussed in the theological schools till the words have almost ceased to have meaning, or at least till the whole associations which cling to them are of controversy, not of the heart; but what Luther meant by that name was the great and inspiring truth, which is the sum and substance of what we have in Christ - the love of God to sinful men, freely welcoming them, freely bestowed upon them, coming to seek them, winning and subduing their souls for ever. This was what he discovered in the Scripture; this was what he called in a unique, exclusive, emphatic sense, the gospel or the word of God. This it was which God had spoken to him, which God had brought home to his penitent soul as infallibly true and divinely authoritative by the inward working of the Spirit; this it was, which as God's word, was resolutely set in opposition, by Luther, to all ecclesiastical doctrines and practices as merely traditions of men. It will be apparent from this how far Luther himself was from identifying the word of God with the canon of Scripture, received in the Catholic church, or indeed with any Canon of Scripture whatsoever. In point of fact he was the most daring, as occasionally the most arbitrary, of critics. He had an excessive confidence in his own experience, and an unwarranted contempt for that Christian instinct and Christian tradition which in earlier days had roughly defined the Christian writings which should be regarded as normative in the Church. He ejected all the Apocrypha from the OT, and partly with reference to their inadequate historical attestation but far more because they did not contain what he had learned to appreciate as the gospel or the word of God, he treated very freely some of the books of the New. In his translation of the NT he relegated the pp of James and Jude, the Epistle of the Hebrews and the Apocalypse to an appendix. In the list of books at the beginning he numbered the other 23, but did not number these four. He gives in good set terms his reasons for doing so. But he goes further still. He draws distinctions among the books which he receives as canonical, and as containing that word of God which had been made sure by the Spirit to his soul. In the preface to his NT (1552), from all this he says, 'you can now rightly judge among the books and distinguish which are the best. John's Gospel and Paul's epistles especially the one to the Romans, and St Peter's first epistle, are the genuine kernel and marrow among all the books. For in them you find not only the work and miracles of Christ described, but you find also a masterly exposition of how faith in Christ overcomes sin, death and hell, and gives life righteousness and blessedness and this is what the gospel essentially is. John's gospel is the one delicate genuine chief gospel, and to be far preferred to the other three and exalted over them. So also the Epistles of Paul and S Peter are far before the three gospels of Mt, Mk and Lk. In sum, S John's gospel and his first epistle, S Paul's Epistles especially those to the Romans, Gal and Eph and St Peter's first Epistle, these are the books that show you Christ, and teach you all that it is needful and blessed to know, although you should never either see or hear another.' The same principle is stated more rigorously still in the preface to his Epistle. of James. 'The true touchstone of books is this; do they, or do they not *Christum treiben*; what does not teach Christ is not yet apostolic, though Peter or Paul taught it; and on the other hand, what does preach Christ would be apostolic, though it was done by Judas, Annas, Pilate and Herod.'

I have quoted these passages in full, because with all their arbitrariness they exhibit in a clear and unmistakable light the original Protestant attitude to Scripture. The canon of Scripture which was put into Luther's hands by the Church had of course the authority of the church; it was a piece of the common Christian tradition. It was part of what Christendom handed down from generation to generation. But the Church tradition, even in the form of the Bible, could never claim for itself, and could never bestow upon anything else, a divine authority. It could not do so because it was itself human and liable to all the infirmities and errors of humanity. Hence it could not bestow a divine authority on the Canon, either of the OT or the New. Indeed a divine authority for the canon - an authority fixing its limits beforehand and establishing the right of everything within them to be recognised as infallibly true and perpetually binding - neither does nor can exist. God, it is true, speaks to the soul and gives it a sure hold of his grace in Christ, through the Scripture; and the assurance of God, and of one's own relation to him, so gained, is one against which no human authority can plead its rights; but this does not justify us in dogmatic assertions about the authority of Scripture as a whole. It does not bar criticism, either historical or spiritual, but rather gives us the standing ground and the liberty for it. Such is Luther's opinion, and it seems to me the true one. It is represented in as late a Protestant Symbol as the Westminster Confession, where we read that though 'we may be moved and induced by the testimony of the Church to an high and reverend esteem of the holy Scripture...yet, notwithstanding, our sure persuasion and assurance of the infallible truth and divine authority thereof, is from the inward work of the Holy Spirit, bearing witness by and with the word in our hearts.' This, of course, must not be forced, as though any one could claim the '*testimonium Spiritum Sanctum internum*' for his belief that the canon contained so many books and no more, or that every sentence had been spiritually to be true in his experience. This is, in point of fact, impossible. What the testimony of the Spirit does guarantee in our experience is what Luther called <u>the Gospel</u>, or the word of God. That word of God certainly reaches us thro' Scripture; but on the mere ground of the Spirit's testimony to it we cannot say more about Scripture than this. It is the word of God, or Gospel, which lies behind everything; which has created both the Church and the Bible, which is the standard for criticising both, and which gives to both whatever authority they have.[2]

This, which was the original protestant attitude to Scripture, was soon lost in the Prot. Churches, and a more melancholy contrast can hardly be found in history than that which is presented when the religious liberty of the sixteenth century is put side by side with the scholasticism of the 17th. It will be remembered that Luther described the gospel which he found in the Scriptures as the word of God, in opposition to the traditions of men under which it had been lost. But when the controversy with the Romish church had been fairly engaged, and it was necessary to find an authority which could be conveniently opposed to that of the Pope and the great organization of which he was the head, Protestant theologians betook themselves to the Bible. In spite of the fact that the Bible as a collection of books is only a piece of the Christian tradition, they set it in opposition to the tradition. They identified it *simpliciter* with that word of God which had come to Luther through it, which the Spirit had guaranteed to his experience, and which he had freely used to criticise all tradition, including the tradition which fixed the canon itself. They committed themselves to the principle that the canon of scripture *is* the word of God, that these very words, no more and no less and all alike, are the one divine and infallible rule of faith and practice. A dogma of inspiration was formed, and although in its most rigorous form it never received admission to any creed, it gained currency and practical recognition as orthodox in many churches. We can hardly imagine, now that it has been for long in process of dissolution, if not quite dead, to what extremes this doctrine went. God, said Quenstedt, is the sole author of Holy Scripture; it is only in an improper sense that we can affirm the authorship of the prophets and apostles. It is too much even to call them *amanuenses*, they are rather his *calami*; pens. They write at his impulse; he suggests the matter; he dictates the words; even the vowel points of the Hebrew OT are inspired; nothing belongs to the wretched human instruments but, to use Quenstedt's own expression - *externus scribendi deu literas pingendi labor*.[3] A more extraordinary perversion than this of the Reformation doctrine of the word of God no ingenuity could imagine. This Protestant

---

[2] The following is deleted: 'But for that very reason it cannot be identified, off hand, with either. Both the Church and the Canon of Scripture are religious authorities, so far as the word of God to which the Scripture bears witness in our hearts lives in them and works through them. But for that very reason the word of God is not to be identified with either. In the power of that word the Church is to be perpetually undergoing reformation and the scripture to be perpetually the subject of profound and enlightened study, devotional historical and critical.'

[3] Translated as 'mechanical work of writing or embellishment'.

doctrine of inspiration is literally the most stupendous example on record of lying for God; of deliberate shutting of the eyes to the most palpable and obtrusive facts. [4] And the Protestant churches have paid for it, for the last century and a half, and are paying for it at this hour, in internal dissension's, in soul troubles, in unbelief, in the distrust of candid minds. In reality it has been very largely surrendered, but many of its phrases linger, and provoke by the need they bring to be perpetually explained, or explained away. It might be better for us to drop the words 'inspiration' and 'authority' altogether, and try to define the value of the Bible in some other way. But if we wish to clear our minds on the subject, the only simple way is to go to the Bible itself and see what claims it makes in whole or in part, and on what they are founded.

The Bible is a large collection of books, by many authors, of many ages, of many literary forms. Yet in spite of the immense variety which it contains, it has always been felt to possess a certain unity. It is not only a collection of books, but in some true sense a book. In what, then, does its unity consist? In what is it that all the authors and all the books are at one? I should avoid, in answering this question, such a formal answer as that the books constitute an organic whole, and are related to each other as the parts in a living organism are, some of course, being less important than the others, but every one essential as part of a living whole. I do not deny that the conception of an organism, when applied to the Bible, suggests some true ideas; but it is at best and illustration, and illustrations are the bane of science. The real answer is, I believe, twofold. The Bible is one, because it is the record, however difficult it may be to make out the details chronologically, of one series of historical events; and it is one, further, because all its books bear witness to the faith of the writers in one and the same God. According to their place in the series, or to other conditions, the writers may know less or more of God, but what unites them in spite of infinite diversity is that they believe in Him, without exception, and write out of their faith. That outward unity of representing one historical process - may we not say, without assuming too much, one historical purpose and work - and this inward unity of representing one spiritual faith, laying hold of god in and through that history, these together constitute the Bible, not merely a collection of books, but a book. Through the Bible, as such a book, that faith in God which characterises all its authors, has become the possession of the modern world. But what kind of authority does this confer on it? Let us consider this in detail confining ourselves meanwhile to the OT.

Take first the historical books. The time has gone past, one may presume, when it is necessary to argue that supernatural communications of matters of fact were not made to the Bible historians. They had to

---

[4] The following is deleted, 'of deliberate distortion of the most simple and easy truth'.

acquaint themselves with the materials of history in the same way as a modern historian does. They might write of a time for which documents by contemporaries could be referred to; or they might write of a time for which they had no source of information whatever except traditions and legends floating among their own people or strangers. The historical value of their writings therefore, in the scientific sense of the word, may be most various; it may be of the very highest, as in the chapters of Jeremiah which describe the siege and conquest of Jerusalem, or of the very lowest as, e.g. in the first twelve chapters of Genesis. But whether the materials to which the writer had access were meagre or copious, whether they were absolutely trustworthy records, or more popular stories, the Bible presentation of them has this characteristic; it helps them in the light of the writers' faith in God, and as illustrating God's character and dealings with men. It is on this ground, and not because of the literal accuracy of the narratives, that we include them in the Bible as the _documentum_ of revelation. They exhibit to us the manner in which faith in God wrought, when it applied itself to the contemplation of history, in the men to whom God was making himself known. To assume the inerrancy of the history, as such, is perfectly gratuitous. Who that has participated in the intellectual life of the modern world can imagine that he has historical evidence for the innovation of the arts in Genesis iv or for the origin of languages in Genesis xi. What the book of Genesis tells us of these things is in historical value neither of less nor more account than what we are told of similar things elsewhere; the value they do possess as parts of the Bible lies in this – that we see the manner in which the past, so far as it was known or believed to be known, was interpreted by men who were learning to know God. And just as it is gratuitous to assume the infallibility of the history, so is it unnecessary to maintain the infallibility of every interpretation of it which Scripture contains. Religion, as Dr Fairbairn has said, is of God, but it is through man. What we see in these writers is really the attempt to read history thro' religion, and it is in this their value lies. As the Hebrew Bible itself classifies them, they are not historians but prophets. They are important, not as chroniclers but as religious writers. And surely no one need be hurt when it is said that even as religious writers they cannot claim an authority equal to that which belongs to the men who knew God in Christ.

But besides the prophetic historians, the OT contains the writings of those who are called prophets in the stricter sense - men to whom the word of God came with irresistible power, impelling them, often against their will, or at least against their natural inclination, to declare it to their people. One of the results of the modern critical study and reconstruction of the OT has been the restoration of the prophets to their true place and significance in the history. The earlier prophecy from Samuel to Elijah and Elisha, is a subject of extreme difficulty; but from

Amos and Hosea down to the latest writers in the canon, the ground has been thoroughly investigated. One thing has become perfectly clear in the process; that prophecy as it existed in Israel is unique. There is nothing like it in the world. There is nothing like its certain faith in One God, like its continuity, like its consistency, like its ethical riches, like its visions of judgement and its unshaken belief in redemption. When the prophets spoke for God they were conscious of their authority, and we are conscious of it. There is a witness in our hearts that that the God in whom they believe and whose will they declare is, and is the Only One. I say 'the God' in whom they believe, for it is God whom we find in the prophets, God and not merely ideas about God, or things he is going to do. Revelation is personal and so is faith. The precise anticipation of a prophet may not have been verified; the horizon of even the most far-seeing was bounded; but it is nothing to us whether his predictions were destined to receive a literal fulfilment or not; what we have to get from the prophets is not his vision of the future, but his faith in God. And in point of fact that is all we do get; that is all of prophecy that is communicable. The form of every prophecy belongs to his time and is perishable; we never ought to insist on it. What we ought to receive into our souls, and what in our devotional reading of the Bible we do receive, is the prophet's consciousness of God as One, Exalted, the Holy One of Israel, All mighty, All merciful. That conception has its authority in itself, an authority which is brought home to us by the Spirit, bearing witness by and with the word in our hearts; but the maintenance of this authority does not need us to assume that the prophet was in some punctilious sense infallible. Of course he was a wiser man than those who were without the knowledge of God. Of course he saw through much, in virtue of that knowledge through which others could not see; he was able to pronounce sentence on policies of worldly wisdom which ignored God; he was able to vindicate the future of god's cause against the might and violence of a godless world. He was in Him that is true, so far as he knew God, and his great convictions were in agreement with God's mind and will. The fact that the prophets occupy places in that historical line along which God was working toward the final revelation in His Son, attests their significance in another way, at least to those who believe in Christ. It emphasises the unity of the prophetic spirit. It takes away the appearance of isolation from individual prophets. It makes us feel that each one has an importance and an authority which we could not have made out for him had he stood alone. It makes it easier to understand that there should be such a thing as a 'fulfilment' of prophecy - that in the fullness of time that purpose of god, which the prophets were conscious of at one stage, and the future of which they anticipated with such unquenchable faith and courage, should be completely accomplished. But it does not require us to search out material coincidence between the OT and the New, nor to argue from them. It does not require us to assume the infallibility of the prophet, either in his reading of passing events, or in his pictured anticipations of the end. The fulfilment of prophecy is Christ - and this is the only fulfilment of prophecy which the NT recognises went unimaginably beyond any OT vision.

What has just been said of the historical and prophetical books of the OT holds good more obviously still of those which may be designated devotional or speculative. E.g. the psalms and Job. In these also we see how faith in God works in the soul of man. We see how the revelation of God, as it is made to faith, stimulates the soul; how it excites it to praise, prayer, compassion, communion; how it manifests itself, in short, in all the experiences of a religious life. In what sense these books have divine authority we need hardly try to define. They are natural, true, inspiring, full of the life of faith in the living God, and fitted to work responsive faith in those who use them. When such faith is evoked their authority is admitted, but it is impossible to prove it beforehand to an unbeliever. Only he who believes has the witness in himself.

In summing up these considerations on the OT, with traditional concepts of inspiration before the mind, one is apt to lean to the negative side. The negative side, of course, must have its due. We must recognise that dogmatic assertions about the inerrancy of Scripture in matters of fact, and even in the interpretation of fact, are not merely unjustifiable, but beside the mark. We do not need to believe that all the OT narratives are scientific history. We know they are not. We do not need to believe that all the writers had a perfect knowledge of God; We know they had not. But the Scripture is what it is, and it exercises the influence which it exercises when these facts have been fully acknowledged. It is not deposed. It remains the only record we have of the revelation to the souls of men of that God in whom we believe. It is the great _documentum_ of the life of faith. One and all its writers agree in the faith that there is a God, One only, ever present in grace and in judgment; and they are here to communicate that faith to us. The authority of the OT is guaranteed by its power to do this work. We know that it is inspired, because it inspires us. But with what does it inspire us? Not, surely, with a supernatural certainty as to the accuracy of all the facts it records, but with a spiritual conviction that God is, and is what the writers of the OT believed him, and in their experience found him to be - a God merciful and gracious, multiplying pardon yet inexorable to evil, the Creator, redeemer and judge of men. It is this faith with which it inspires us, and this faith is all that our experience of its inspiration covers.

But let us pass from the OT to the New. One of the questions which criticism has raised is whether the gulf between them as bodies of literature is so vast and empty as it was once believed to be. A space of 400 years, it used to be said, elapsed between the last of the prophets and

John; and during that period there was no revelation, and no document attesting it. It does not seem to me matter of regret, but the contrary, if the reconstruction of the OT does something to fill up this gulf. I do not refer to the rehabilitation of the Apocryphal Books, though some of them have certainly significance for our understanding both of the OT religion and of the New; but to the critical reference of many, if not most of the Psalms of parts of the Wisdom literature and something even of the prophetical writings, to the period in question. The faith one only, the living and true God, certainly lived thro' this period, and though it may have been exposed to influences under which it lost something of its earlier rigour and purity we know that it flourished in many souls, and must have given evidence of its vitality in documents not unworthy of a place among the earlier documents of revelation. But however this may be - however the transition may be mediated from the OT to the New, we find ourselves in a new world when we open the gospels. We are face to face with a new potency of Revelation - the man, Christ Jesus.

In the lecture which I gave on Christ's consciousness of himself,[5] I indicated the characteristics of the revelation made in him. Christ stands in a position quite unlike that of even the greatest prophets, quite separate and alone. He is not a prophet but the subject and fulfilment of all prophecy. The word of God comes to the prophets from without; it comes now and again, often at dates which are expressly given; it has reference as a rule to particular situations, and to the hopes and fears of the nation as affected by them; it comes in many parts and in many forms. Even prophets whose whole life was consecrated to their work, like Isaiah, Jeremiah and Ezek., receive the word of the Lord in messages; it is not incorporated in them or identified with them. Their revelation is not co-extensive with their personality. But this is what we find when we come to Jesus. His vocation, as the Revealer of God, and his personality, are one and the same. It is not only what he says, it is he himself who is the word of God. It is a mistake to draw a distinction here, as is sometimes done both by orthodox and rationalistic theologians, between the teaching and the Person of Christ. Occasionally the orthodox emphasise the person at the cost of the teaching; what Christ was, they say, is more than anything he said. Often the rationalists emphasise the teaching at the cost of the Person; the truth Christ revealed, they say, is more important that the Person who happened to reveal it; the eternal must surely take precedence of the historical. But Jesus himself puts the two things simply side by side. Whosoever, he says, shall be ashamed of <u>me and my words</u>.. etc Whosoever shall lose his life <u>for my sake and the gospel's</u>. It is no more than the fairest inference from these utterances of the Lord himself, when John says that in him the Word was made flesh. The whole phenomenon

---

[5] Evidence that this lecture is part of a series. See Lecture 2 *Studies in Theology*.

presented by Jesus in his life, his words, his works, is revelation in its highest power, the word of God in its purest and fullest expression. The faith which receives this revelation is perfect religion.

Now the primary documents of our faith - the *urkunden* - of the word of God - are our gospels, especially in all probability, the first three. They are the work of men who believed in God as God had been revealed in Christ., or if we prefer to put it so, they are the work of men who had believed in Christ and received him as the final revelation of God. It is absurd to say that this diminishes their value as witnesses, and that only disinterested, that is unbelieving men, are capable of giving impartial testimony to facts. When the facts in question are those which constitute a revelation of God, disinterested unbelieving men are simply men who do not see them at all. Plenty of people saw Christ who never saw the revelation in him. Herod and Pilate and Annas and Caiaphas, with all respect to Luther, could not have been the author of gospels. Gospels are the work of men whom the revelation of God in Christ has made its own; such men may write of what they have heard, what they have seen with their eyes, what they have contemplated and what their hands have handled - it is all as historical as one could wish; but it is concerning 'the word', or rather the revelation of life; and it needs religious faith, as well as eyes and ears and hands, to discover, to receive, and to record this word of life in the life of Jesus. The gospels serve their purpose insofar as they put us in communication with Jesus, as the word of God incarnate, and enable us to appropriate by faith, as their authors appropriated, the revelation of God made in him. That the gospels do serve this purpose the experience of the church for 1900 years, and the experience of every Christian man, abundantly testifies. They do put us in communication with one who brings us to God; they enable us to believe in the Son and thro' him in the Father also.

But the gospels remain historical, as well as religious, books, and the same questions recur here which we have already considered in the OT. Must we not have a guarantee of their historicity, before we acknowledge their spiritual authority? Must we not be sure of the infallibility of the writers before we embark life in the Christian faith? Suppose the alleged facts were not true, that the history so called were not historical, what then? The answer to these questions,, is, I think, simply this. Do not suppose anything; read the books with your eye ion Christ. It is by no means necessary that you should know all that is in them to be true, or that you should be bound to believe everything they narrate even before you know what it is. Read the books with your eye on Christ, and of this I am confident; it will be as certain to you as anything is certain to the mind, heart and conscience of man, that the character of Christ as these books exhibit it, is a <u>real</u> character. It is not a fancy character; it is not a work of imagination; the evangelists did not make it out of their own heads. Leaving details on one side, and confining ourselves exclusively to Jesus as a person of such and such a character, a person in whom such and such a relation to God and man is realised, a person who in his moral temper and in all his words and deeds exhibits himself as the Son of God, the brother, friend and saviour of men; leaving, I say, details on one side, and confining ourselves exclusively to this, it is certain with a certainty no doubt can touch that such a one actually lived. But such a one is a supreme and perfect revelation of God, and therefore such a revelation has actually been made. Jesus was such a revelation to the men who wrote the gospels; he is so to us when thro' their work we become partakers of their faith, and believe in God thro' him. He Holy Spirit, bearing witness by and with the word in our hearts, gives us a full persuasion and assurance of the infallible truth and divine authority of the revelation of God made in him, but it is in the fullness of grace and truth, and not the innumerable historical details of the gospels, to whom we give our faith. In other words, the gospels are the means thro' which we become sure of the gospel; and we <u>may become</u> sure of the gospel, while there are details in the evangelic history as to the accuracy of which we know nothing, and may never know anything, and do not need to know.

This, you will observe, brings the gospels as historical books into line with the other historical books in the Bible. The critical questions as to their origins and mutual relations are, as you are aware, among the most perplexing and complicated with which the biblical scholar has to deal, but difficult as they are, patience and candour are gradually mastering them, and the materials are being prepared for the scientific discussion of the relation between revelation and its record. But this much is plain; that it is quite apart from the purpose of God, because quite inconsistent with indubitable facts to put into our hands a Bible that could be used like a table of logarithms. Not even the gospels are inerrant, except in the sense that they truly represent the gospel. But what other inerrancy should we desire? If they truly represent Christ to us, so that we gain the faith in him which their authors had, is not that all we can desire? The evangelists may make mistakes in details, in the order of events, in reporting the occasion of a word of Jesus, or the interpretation of a parable; we may discern here and there the incipient formalism of the second generation in Luke; we may discern everywhere the interpretive power of a great spiritual genius in John; we may distinguish, as a recent analysis of the gospels has done, between a first, a second and a third cycle of oral gospel which preceded our written gospel; and feel more certain on bare historical grounds, of what is confirmed in the Apostolic Source, as Weiss[6] has extracted it from Matt. and Luke than of matter whose authority we cannot define; we may

---

[6] Denney's own gospel criticism can be glimpsed in his annotated copy of Huck's *Synopsis*, DEN10-11. Denney used this from 1907. See *LWRN*, 130.

differ - Christian men do differ - about the correctness of numberless details of this kind; but we ought to say boldly that though all this be left out of view, nay even though' in any number of cases of this kind the evangelists should be proved in error, the gospel is untouched, the word of God, the revelation of God in Christ, attested by the Spirit, live and abides.

In the Protestant controversy with Rome, great stress used to be laid on the attributes of Scripture which adapted it for its controversial use. These attributes, its certainty, its sufficiency, its perspicuity, remain, but are valid only for its religious use. The word of god, or the gospel, is certain. A candid mind cannot escape the conviction that thro' the gospels he is put in communion with a character and life in which a supreme revelation of God is made for the acceptance of faith. The word of god, or the gospel, is sufficient. It does not need supplementing by human traditions. The man who with the evangelists in his hand has come into contact with Christ - the man who has received the Son and the father thro' him - does not need to receive the ecclesiastical tradition - no, nor the Protestant doctrines of the inspiration and infallibility of Scripture either. 'Thou O Christ art all I want.'[7] And again, the word of God, or the gospel, is perspicuous. Scripture is not always perspicuous, but the word of God, or revelation, is. Scripture is sometimes obscure and hard to understand. One wonders sometimes what converted pagans make out of a translation of Romans or Galatians, books the point of which as books only a very expert scholar can understand. Even of simpler books this holds true. The Bible Society in Scotland is a body whose constituted whim binds it to circulate the scripture without note or comment. It does much to aid missions, by giving them gifts of scripture in foreign languages, but in carrying out this work it has lately found it necessary to provide simple annotations for a Chinese version of so plain a book as the gospel of Mark. Of course the annotations are made almost if not altogether on historical points; they explain to the Chinaman ancient Jewish conditions which would otherwise baffle him. But Jesus does not need to be explained. In other words, while the Scriptures are not quite perspicuous to every one, the word of God is. The soul does not understand without more ado about Pharisees and Publicans, temple and synagogue, ancient history and its peculiar conditions; but it does understand whenever it comes near to the Son of God and the Son of man. The best thing we can do for the Bible is to keep it open; but very often it is so jealously defended that the truth is made not only impregnable, but inaccessible. Nobody can reach it over the ramparts of inspiration, infallibility,

---

[7] This line from Wesley featured significantly in Denney's last book, *The Christian Doctrine of Reconciliation*. See 10, 162, 301. Its significance for him therefore spans his entire writing career as a theologian.

inerrancy and so forth. [8] Let Christ have a chance, whatever becomes of the evangelists; let God have leave to speak to the soul, whatever it may think, nay even if it should never think at all, of the writers of the Bible. The word of God to which Scripture bears witness, the gospel which is attested in the gospels, will put forth either victorious and subduing power all the more easily when men are not prejudiced against the books by irrational and untrue claims on their behalf.

In dealing with any one whose mind was confused about the Bible I should always begin at this point. Approach it, I should say, without prejudice; you do not need to believe anything about it but what it itself compels you to believe. You know that the best men in the world have ever thought most highly of it, and that of course, should prevent you from coming to it with any feeling of disrespect or dislike; but you do not require to believe, before you begin to use it, what it will only convince you of in the course of long and patient use. Begin, too, I should say, with the gospel. If the Bible exists for any purpose, it is that it may beget in us that faith in God which inspired its authors, and especially, in the last resort, faith in God as has been revealed through Christ. Begin, then, where Christ is most accessible, in the gospels. There are thousands of questions raised everywhere else which are either answered, or do not need an answer, when we see him. If Christ is once discovered and welcomed by faith, if we believe thro him in one God, the Father, who redeems the lost, gives the Holy Spirit, imparts eternal life and blessedness - we can acknowledge our composure over ignorance of much, and our indifference to much. We have our feet on this rock; we have a fixed point underneath us, and can enlarge the area of certainty as we find opportunity.

If you have to help men, as no doubt you will have, whose minds are at sea as to the authority of Scripture, this is how I should advise you to proceed. Difficulties about Genesis and Leviticus, Judges and Chronicles, difficulties even about the precise degree of historicity which can be vindicated for part of the evangelic narratives themselves, must simply remain in abeyance; it is not assuming anything, it is only recognising a notorious fact, when we say that even with difficulties of all these kinds awake in the mind, a man may have a great and saving certainty of the revelation of God in his Son. All these doubts may be present, while there is no doubt whatever, that in Jesus Christ God has come into the world and is calling men, and calling us, to judgment and mercy. This amounts to saying that in the strict sense of the words, a doctrine of Scripture is not an essential part of the Christian faith. And neither it is. The creeds of the

---

[8] The following is deleted, 'We do a great injury to the gospel, we put an immense stumbling block in the way of faith, when we barricade the approach to Christ with a doctrine of inspiration that no man can defend, not to mention a crude assertion of inerrancy of Scripture which is simply not true.'

oecumenical church do not mention it. We do not believe in the Bible' we believe in Jesus Christ and in God the father, and we can be sure of God - we must be sure of God - while there are many questions connected with the Bible to which we can give no answer. But do not let us lean too much to the negative side. The Bible does us a service - actually does it - in bringing us this certainty, which no other book in the world can do; it is the vehicle of revelation, the instrument used by the Spirit to bring the soul to God, as no other book or agency is. And this must always keep it in a place apart and maintain it in an authority of its own.

The point at which the authority of Scripture is most discussed among theologians is that at which the authority of the apostles come into view. Revelation is summed up in Christ - this is conceded on all hands. But the question at once arises, 'What is meant by Christ?' Is it Christ as he lived and moved among men? Christ as he can be interpreted out of his own express teaching? Christ as he can be preached on the basis, say, of the second gospel alone, or on a narrower basis even than that? There is a large school of theologians who incline to say so more or less dogmatically. For them, our knowledge of Christ ends at the cross. His resurrection is part of the apostolic faith, but incapable of proof as a historical fact. Words ascribed to him after the resurrection may be reminiscences of words he had actually spoken before, only adapted to a new situation; or they may be the product of the loving imagination and reflection of disciples put without misgiving into the Lord's mouth. This is the attitude on the whole of the Ritschlian school. They ignore Christ's exaltation as something belonging rather to the realm of pious imagination than religious revelation. They ignore the recorded giving of the Holy Spirit as a Spirit of truth to enable the apostles to interpret the life and death of Jesus. They ignore, as I had occasion to point out in an earlier lecture, the many things which Jesus could not say to his disciples while he was with them, because they could not bear them, but which the Spirit was to reveal when he was gone. And on the strength of general principles like these, while they accept the apostolic testimony to what Christ said and did, they do not feel bound by the apostolic interpretations of his life and death. Christ they admit to be the perfect revelation, but it does not follow that the apostolic is the final theology. Hence the apostolic theology has no binding authority for us or for the church at large.

I do not think it is worth while to discuss beforehand, in this way, what authority the apostolic theology can have, or ought to have. Where the human mind is concerned, 'the wild living intellect of man', - it is idle to speak of any authority which can simply be imposed. There neither is nor can be any such thing. The real question is whether there is an authority which can impose itself, which can freely win the recognition and surrender of the mind and heart of man. And this is a question not of paper logic, as Newman called it, but of fact. It is a question for the answer to which we can appeal to the intellect and conscience of the church from the beginning. Take, for instance, the great doctrine of apostolic theology - the expiatory significance of the death of Christ. A man may say if he pleases that he is not bound to accept this, merely because it is taught by Peter and Paul and John; his intelligence is in no predestined relation of bondage to theirs. But this is an abstract assertion, with no particular contents. The doctrine of an atonement for sins, made in Christ's death, has never been accepted in the church simply on the ground that it was taught by three carnal men, Peter and Paul and John. The authority it enjoys, and has enjoyed from the beginning, is due to this, that the Holy Spirit has borne witness with that doctrine in man's heart, making sure that in accepting it they were accepting the very soul of God's redeeming love. If there is one truth in the whole Bible which is guaranteed by the *testimonium internum Spiritus Sancti*, and by the consenting witness of Christians in all ages, it is this. It has an authority in it, or along with it, by which it vindicates itself to faith as divinely and infallibly true; it asserts itself irresistibly, and beyond a doubt, as the revelation of God's judgment and mercy to penitent souls. There can be no authority higher than that, nor so far as I can see, can there be any real authority prior to that. But we are bound to remember that the apostles themselves were conscious that their gospels between which and their theology there was no distinction possible, had this authority, and that they preached in the consciousness of it. It had a divine guarantee in their own souls. It was not taught them by man but was received by revelation. It was preached with the Holy Ghost sent down from heaven. It was meant to work in the souls of those who heard it, a faith standing not in the wisdom of man but in the power of God If we consider this consciousness of the apostles themselves, and take it in its NT connexion, with the exaltation of Jesus and the gift of the Spirit, it becomes natural, I think, to concede a far higher importance to the apostolic theology than is done by writers of the school to which I have referred. Of course it cannot possess authority in the sense of being entitled to impose itself beforehand on the mind, in an arbitrary unintelligible fashion; nothing possesses such an authority; it is not claimed even for the word of Jesus. But if the revelation made in Jesus had either to be apprehended or lost; if the apostles themselves claim to have received special spiritual power to interpret and teach it; if the claims they made are attested by the witness of the Spirit finding entrance for their gospel into the souls of men; if they are all at one, as St Paul asserts they are, on what they regard as the very heart of the revelation made in Christ, ought we not to feel that there is something unreal and out of proportion in the claim to reject the central doctrine of the apostolic gospel on the abstract general ground that one man's thought has not authority for another? The action is really

Appendix 2

irrelevant to the premises and the premises leave the real authority of the apostles untouched. The apostles have furnished the standard interpretation of the revelation of God in Christ, and it is not by assuming that on the very heart of the matter they were completely astray that we are likely to grow in the grace and the knowledge of our Lord Jesus Christ.

There will be those to whom such views as I have tried to exhibit in this lecture will appear too indefinite and undogmatic - will crave something more precise, more capable of use as a weapon of war, in attack or defence; perhaps they will crave an easier road to religious certainty than that to which this conception of the Bible offers. But we must take the Bible as we find it, and we need not be more jealous of its honour than it is itself. I think it is a fair question for consideration whether the claims made on its behalf have done more harm than good. If we must assert an infallibility for it, let it be not an infallibility of verbal accuracy, which it does not possess, but an infallibility of saving power, which it does. The man who humbly gives up his mind to the teaching of that Spirit which speaks in the Bible will infallibly be brought to that faith in God which characterizes its writers from first to last; he will infallibly be brought, by the NT, to faith in the God and Father of our Lord Jesus Christ. The Bible has no other infallibility than this; but is not this enough?

APPENDIX 3

Text of letter from Denney to W. R. Nicoll,
MS3518/27/10/James Denney/2 April 1901

21 Lynedoch St,
Glasgow, April 2. 1901.

Dear Dr Nicoll

I am glad you like our new number, and especially Jerdan's article,[1] which I also hailed with joy when it appeared. It would no doubt be very nice to get such things every month, but it is the merest chance what you will get. I never had heard of McMichael before, and could not have asked for an account of him, and this is usually the case. You have to write to people that you believe to be acquainted with the church life of a locality for a considerable period, and there is no saying what they may send. It may be as interesting as McPherson or McCrie.

As to your two questions, I am not sure that I can answer them. What precisely Robinson of Kilmun[2] was deposed for I cannot tell, and therefore don't know whether his position is identical with Moffatt's or not. What makes me anxious about Moffatt's book[3] is that there is an attitude assumed in it to the evangelic history which seems to make it possible and even reasonable to doubt whether at any given point in it we are in direct communication with Jesus. The whole thing has come to us through others, whose faith not only transfigured but expanded it, putting

---

[1] Denney and Orr were editors of the *Union Magazine* from 1900-1904, and had a chronic difficulty obtaining quality copy.

[2] The reference is to Alexander Robinson, minister of the Church of Scotland, Kilmun, Argyll. He was deposed in 1897 for heretical views contained in his book *The Saviour in the Newer Light*. In particular he questioned the divinity, the miracles and the resurrection of Jesus, positions he supported by more basic questions about the authenticity and facticity of the gospels, and the inspiration and integrity of the gospel writers.

[3] In 1901 Moffatt published *The Historical New Testament*. The new translation was accompanied by critical notes and introductory discussions. The content clearly alarmed Nicoll, and Denney's reply indicates considerable anxiety on his part also. Denney reviewed it on 21 February in the *British Weekly*. Taylor says the review was 'detailed and including high praise'. *Principal Denney*, 159. In reality Denney struggled to combine courtesy to a colleague with personal misgivings and significant disagreement.

into the lips of Jesus what their experience of Him had put into their hearts, with a freedom which is simply dumbfounding. The "church" character ascribed by him to many of the most precious words of Christ is what disconcerts one. What his theology is I cannot tell, but the tendency of this construction of the gospels is to merge Christ in the Church and Christianity in the higher life of the world at large, and in this way to deprive Christ of his unique place, and to make the conception of a personal relation, and especially of a personal debt, to Him, in which Christianity has hitherto been supposed to consist, quite illusory. Perhaps that is all I can say about your second question too. I don't know under what restrictions Bruce wrote his article[4] - I mean restrictions imposed by the editors. There are evidently to be articles in the Encyclopaedia Biblica on the resurrection, the nativity narratives etc by other writers and Bruce may have been warned off all these, and restricted to write on the life and teaching and death of Jesus: I don't know. It is open to any one to say that a believer in the deity and resurrection of the Son of God should not have consented to write under restrictions which virtually involved a suppression of his faith: but however much I regret the absence from the article of much that might have been expected, I dare not answer your question in a way which would imply a judgement upon Dr Bruce so severe as it suggests. I would rather say that he wrote this article in a bad week - in one of the times at which he suffered from the temporary eclipse of faith - than that he had ceased to be a believer. There certainly were ups and downs in the fight of faith in him, and he may have done this in one of the downs. But whatever the explanation may be, nothing short of an express statement from his own lips would ever justify me in saying that he did not believe in the deity and resurrection of Christ.[5]

What you say of Cheyne's aim being to obliterate Christ is horrible, but the intention is apparent in much that is written with the pretence of friendship to Christianity.[6] All the neo-Hegelian men - Edward Caird and his pupils - are Christian as they understand it; but as far as Christ is concerned, their whole business is to keep him in his own place. He belongs to history but he does not belong to life, in any other sense than that in which every historical person does. This it seems to me, is to annihilate Christianity at a stroke.[7] Even Harnack, in that much praised book, which is certainly full of intellectual and moral earnestness, *Das Wesen des Christentums*, sets out on the same line. In his chapter on

---

[4] It is widely assumed Bruce's article 'Jesus' proved his capitulation to liberal even radical views about Jesus. This letter was written two years after Bruce's death, showing Denney's concern to affirm Bruce's underlying orthodoxy.

[5] Denney dealt with the matter in an article in the Union Magazine, 1901, 170ff.

[6] The correspondence of George Adam Smith contains letters about *Encyclopaedia Biblica*. ACC9446.

[7] Further evidence of Denney's antipathy to Idealist philosophy.

Christology he says [...][8] How a man can say Jesus has no place in the Gospel, even though he rejects John altogether, it beats me to understand. It is a curious result of "going back to Christ" that in the last resort what we get is only the Christianity of Christ but in a sense Christianity without Christ. I believe one result of all this will be to restore the apostolic testimony to something like its due place in the appreciation of the Church. It is very hard to believe that Christianity took a wrong turn and got fatally on the down grade the very day Peter opened his mouth at Pentecost to preach the resurrection of Jesus and forgiveness and the gift of the Spirit as due to Him.

I will be glad to see Sanday's article, though his opinion of Moberley seems to me quite absurd. It is odd that Moberley's conception of the Holy Spirit as the spirit (as a virtue which)[9] could not be given till Jesus had finished his work as man is the one idea in Milligan's Baird Lecture on the *Ascension and Heavenly Priesthood*. His emphasis on the fact that all the relations involved in atonement are personal relations is quite proper: but the point on which his book turns - that actual displacement of the old 'I', the old personality, by the spirit of the Saviour as a spirit of penitential holiness - is neither more nor less than a renunciation of everything which personality means. It is neither science nor philosophy, nor biology nor even mythology; it is just nonsense - like a great deal that is written about the mystical union.[10] I am going to send you a paper this week on Divine Righteousness in Romans; if you want it to appear in May *Expositor*, you might ask them to send me the proof before April 11, as I go to Germany then for some weeks. If you do not want the *Morning Watches* any more you might return them also before that date; if not, please keep them till the beginning of June.

I hope your influenza is better. I am taking a day in the house myself, which is unusual and uncomfortable, and can so far sympathize,
Ever yours sincerely

James Denney

PS. I suppose 100 people have written to tell you that Struthers' name is not James but John. Probably nobody knows but I that I was not born in Greenock but in Paisley.

---

[8] The following sentence from Harnack is quoted in German by Denney, and has been translated by Isabella Stevenson: 'It is not a paradox, nor is it "rationalism", but the simple expression of "continuance of [illegible word]" as it is found in the Gospel: Not the Son, but only the Father belongs in the Gospel, just as Jesus declared it.'

[9] Writing unclear, meaning uncertain.

[10] One of Denney's clearest statements on what he found unacceptable in a conception of the mystical union within which moral personality is somehow absorbed into the divine, or replaced by something other than redeemed personality.

APPENDIX 4

The Late Dr. Denney[1]

The Kirk session desire to place on record the loss which they and the Congregation have sustained through the death of their former minister, Dr Denney.

Those of our number who had the privilege of membership during Dr Denney's ministry will never forget his wholehearted devotion to the work of the Congregation, he came to us with more than the natural shyness, usually noticeable in a young man starting on his Life's Work, but with a mind stored with the highest ideals of the Work of the Ministry & a heart consecrated to the service of God, and no better evidence of the success of Dr Denney's labours here could be found than in the loving references made to his memory by all who were in any way connected with the Congregation during his residence in Broughty Ferry.

During Dr Denney's ministry here he knew every family in the Congregation & every individual member of every household in it, and by his transparent goodness, his loving sympathy & his genuine interest in Young and Old he was admitted to a place in the affections of his people & regarded as a true friend & his influence on the lives of many will not be fully realised until 'the day breaks & the Shadows flee away.'

During his 20 years residence in Glasgow, in which no one could have led a fuller life, Dr Denney never lost touch with his old Congregation & his annual visits to our April Communion were welcomed by all, & notwithstanding his absorbing duties as Principal and Professor in the College at Glasgow, and as Convenor of the Central Fund Committee he never allowed outstanding events in the lives of his people here to pass unnoticed, & his kindly letters of sympathy or congratulation will remain among the treasured possessions of the recipients & in mourning the loss of our friend, we pray that the memory of his Saintly life may draw us closer to the Source from which he drew his strength & inspiration.

---

[1] Memorial Minute, Broughty Ferry East United Free Church of Scotland, 22 June 1917. CH3/1156/2, 239.

BIBLIOGRAPHY

Primary Sources

1. Unpublished Manuscripts
2. Books
3. Contributions to books
4. Contributions to Dictionaries and Encyclopaedia
5. Contributions to Journals and Newspapers

Secondary Sources

6. Ecclesiastical Records
7. Unpublished Theses and Dissertations
8. Obituaries
9. General Secondary Literature

1. Unpuscripts

Papers of James Denney Located at New College, Edinburgh

DEN01	Sermons: Genesis to Deuteronomy.
DEN02	Sermons: Joshua to Nehemiah.
DEN03	Sermons: Job to Malachi.
DEN04	Sermons: Matthew to John.
DEN05	Sermons: Acts.
DEN06	Sermons: Romans to Galatians.
DEN 07	Sermons: Ephesians to Revelation.
DEN08	Lectures and Papers: Biblical Subjects.
DEN09	Lectures: Theological and Practical Theology.
DEN10	General Lectures and Biographical Papers.
DEN11	Early Essays, Lectures and Extract Notes.
DEN12	Notebooks, Student Notes and Class Lectures.

Papers from the Above Collection Cited in the Present Study

DEN01-44	'God's revelation of himself'.
DEN01-56	'The Sabbath – gift to man'.
DEN01-67	'The Fourth Commandment'.
DEN01-125	'The Completeness of Revelation'.

DEN01-128	'He humbled thee'. (Boxing Day sermon).
DEB03-03	'The meaning of suffering'.
DEN03-31	*'haec fecisti et tacui'*.
DEN03-39	'Queen's Diamond Jubilee'.
DEN03-46	'Sermon on the Sabbath'.
DEN03-55	'They that make them are like unto them'.
DEN04-21	'A ransom for many'.
DEN04-83	'Total Abstinence'.
DEN04-101	'Christmas Day, 1892'.
DEN04-132	'The strong man'.
DEN04-150	'He that is faithful'.
DEN04-152	'Where are the nine'.
DEN04-175	'The Gospel Miracles'.
DEN04-223	'He was a burning and a shining light'.
DEN04-251	'It is expedient for you'.
DEN05-49	'He was a good man'.
DEN06-02	'Patient continuing in welldoing'.
DEN06-07c	'Not under the law but under grace'.
DEN06-18 to DEN 06-43	'Expository Sermons on First Corinthians'.
DEN06-35	'Let a man examine himself.'
DEN06-67	'Let no man glory in men'.
DEN06-71	'Sermon on 1 Cor. 7.29-31'.
DEN06-74	'Sermon on 1 Cor. 10.23-11.1'.
DEN 06 75	'The Lord's Supper'.
DEN06-76	'This do in remembrance'.
DEN06-77	'This do in remembrance'.
DEN06-78	'The Lord's Supper'.
DEN 06 79	'Let a man examine himself'.
DEN06-102	'Bear one another's burdens'.
DEN07-17	'Election of Office-bearers'.
DEN07-27	'In Him dwelleth…'
DEN07-77	'Professor Lindsay's Funeral Sermon'.
DEN07-95	'Death of Professor Orr'.
DEN07-138	'Be clothed with humility'.
DEN07-156	'We have known and believed the love which God has for us'.
DEN07-157	'Communion Address on Love '.
DEN07-177	'These are they'.
DEN08-05	'Present and Future in the Gospels'.
DEN08-10	'Philosophy and the New Testament'.
DEN 08-13-01 to DEN08-13-06	'The Gospel according to Paul'.
DEN08-14	'The Christology of Paul'.

Bibliography

DEN08-16 to	
DEN08-24	'Lectures on the Apostle's Creed'.
DEN08-47 to	
DEN 08-54	'Lectures on various hymn writers'.
DEN08-75	'Church Unity'.
DEN08-76	'Equipment for Christian Work'.
DEN08-77	'Foreign Missions'.
DEN08-83	'Opening of School for Christian Workers'.
DEN08-84	'The Current Aversion to St Paul'.
DEN09-02	'The Bible and the Church'.
DEN09-04	'The Authority of Scripture'.
DEN09-06	'The Restatement of Doctrine'.
DEN09-07	'Christian faith and the Criticism of the Bible'.
DEN09-08	'What a Creed ought to be'.
DEN09-10	'The Church Catholic and Protestant'.
DEN09-11	'The Atonement (I)'.
DEN09-12	'The Atonement (II)'.
DEN09-13	'The Atonement (III)'.
DEN09-14	'The Doctrine of Sin (I)'.
DEN09-15	'The Doctrine of Sin (II)'.
DEN09-16	'The Doctrine of Sin (III)'.
DEN09-17	'IX Holy Scripture'.
DEN09-18	'The Theological College Today'.
DEN09-21	'Preaching and Christian Ethics'.
DEN09-22	'The training of a Minister'.
DEN09-23-01 to	
DEN09-23-15	'Lectures on Practical Theology'.
DEN10-02	'The Work of Dr Bruce'.
DEN10-09	'Reading, Writing and Speaking'.
DEN10-10	'Some Impressions of America'.
DEN11-16	'Free Church Missions'.
DEN11-17	'Missionaries'.
DEN11-18	'Missions in East Africa'.
DEN11-19	'Congo'.
DEN11-20	'West Africa'.
DEN12-01	Student Notebook.

Correspondence

PAPERS OF REVEREND ALEXANDER MARTIN

M/17/7/27	Letter from Denney, dated 12 June 1911.
M/17/7/40	Letter from Denney, dated 9 October 1911.
M/17/12/23	Letter from Denney, dated 15 July 1914.

LETTERS OF JAMES DENNEY LOCATED AT THE UNIVERSITY OF ABERDEEN.
MS 3518/27/10/James Denney Envelope.[1]
MS 3518/27/10/James Denney/2 April 1901.
MS 3518/27/10/James Denney/5 September 1901.
MS 3518/27/10/James Denney/18 November 1907.
MS 3518/27/10/James Denney/3 February 1913.
MS 3518/27/10/James Denney/17 July 1913.
MS 3518/27/10/James Denney/6 September 1913
MS 3518/27/10/James Denney/11 December 1914.
MS 3518/27/10/James Denney/24 March 1916.
MS 3518/27/10/James Denney/25 March 1916.
MS 3518/27/10/James Denney/19 April 1916.
MS 3518/27/10/James Denney/29 July 1916.
MS 3518/27/10/Envelope 6/19 October 1905.[2]

UNIVERSITY OF GLASGOW
GUA 4066, Letter of acceptance of Glasgow D.D., 23 March 1895.

NATIONAL LIBRARY OF SCOTLAND
Acc9446/37, Denney to Mrs George Adam Smith, 21 October 1909.
Acc/9446 No. 142, Denney to George Adam Smith, 20 May 1908.

2. Books

On 'Natural Law in the Spiritual World', by a Brother of the Natural Man, (Paisley: Alex Gardiner, 1885).

Denney, James, T*he Epistles to the Thessalonians*, (London: Hodder & Stoughton, 1892).

Denney, James, *The Second Epistle to the Corinthians*, (London: Hodder & Stoughton, 1894).

Denney, James, *Studies in Theology*, (London: Hodder & Stoughton, 1894).

Denney, James, *Gospel Questions and Answers*, (London: Hodder & Stoughton, London, 1896).

Denney, James, *St. Paul's Epistle to the Romans*, *The Expositor's Greek Testament*, II, W. Robertson Nicoll, (ed.), (London: Hodder & Stoughton, 1900).

---

[1] These letters are unsorted, and contained in an envelope marked 'James Denney Letters, copied and returned by Professor James Moffatt, 1922'. The envelope also notes that they were not included in the published letters. Since they are all addressed to Nicoll, who edited the volume of correspondence between Denney and himself, it is intriguing how they came into the possession of Moffatt. They are identified in this thesis by the MS reference and the date. For convenience they are listed here in chronological order.

[2] This letter is included in a miscellaneous unsorted collection.

Denney, James, *The Death of Christ*, (London: Hodder & Stoughton, 1902).
Denney, James, *The Atonement and the Modern Mind*, (London: Hodder & Stoughton, 1903).
Denney, James, *The Assurance of Faith: a sermon preached on Sunday 13th January, 1907, on the death Rev. Malcolm Donald MacGilvary, M. A., in the East Free U. F. Church, Broughty Ferry*, (Broughty Ferry, 1907).
Denney, James, *Jesus and the Gospel*, (London: Hodder & Stoughton, 1908).
Denney, James, *The Church and the Kingdom*, (London: Hodder & Stoughton, 1910).
Denney, James, *Factors of Faith in Immortality*, (London: Hodder & Stoughton, 1911).
Denney, James, *The Way Everlasting*, (London: Hodder & Stoughton, 1911).
Denney, James, *War and the Fear of God*, (London: Hodder & Stoughton, 1916).
Denney, James, *The Christian Doctrine of Reconciliation*, (London: Hodder & Stoughton, 1917).
Nicoll, W. Robertson, (ed.), *Letters of Principal James Denney to W. Robertson Nicoll, 1893-1917*, (London: Hodder & Stoughton, 1920).
Moffat, James, (ed.), *Letters of Principal James Denney to His Family and Friends*, (London: Hodder & Stoughton, 1921).

3. Contributions to Books

Barry, J. C., *Ideals and Principles of Church Reform*, (Edinburgh: T & T Clark, 1910). Introductory Note by James Denney.
Candlish, J. S., *The Christian Idea of Salvation*, (Edinburgh, 1899). Preface by James Denney.
Delitzsch, Franz, *Biblical Commentary on the Prophecies of Isaiah*, (London, 1891). Authorised translation from the third edition, by the Rev James Denney, B.D.
Denney, James, Dods, Marcus, Moffatt, James, *The Literal Interpretation of the Sermon on the Mount*, (London: Hodder & Stoughton, n.d.).
Missionary Sermons, 1812-1924, (London: Carey Press, 1924). 'The Missionary Motive', 229-40.
Questions of Faith. A Series of Lectures on the Creed etc., 'Can Sin be Forgiven?', James Denney, (London: Hodder & Stoughton, 1904).

4. Contributions to Dictionaries and Encyclopaedia.

Hastings, James, (ed.), *A Dictionary of the Bible*, 5 vols., (Edinburgh: T & T Clark, 1898-1902):
'Adam in the New Testament', vol. I, 37.
'Ascension', vol. I, 101-2.
'Brotherly love', vol. I, 329-30.
'Chastening, Chastisement, Tribulation', vol. I, 374.
'Creed', vol. I, 516-17.
'Curse', vol. I, 534-35.
'Forbearance, Long-suffering', vol. II, 47.
'Gentleness', vol. II, 150.
'Ignorance', vol. II, 449.
'Knowledge', vol. III, 8-10.
'Law (in the New Testament)', vol. III, 73-82.
'Priest in the New Testament', vol. IV, 97-100.
'Promise', vol. IV, 104-6.
'Reprobate', vol. IV, 228.

Hastings, James, (ed.), *A Dictionary of Christ and the Gospels*, (Edinburgh: T & T Clark, 1906-8):
'Anger', vol. I, 60-62.
'Authority of Christ', vol. I, 146-53.
'Holy Spirit', vol. I, 731-44.
'Jealousy', vol. I, 847-48.
'Offence', vol. II, 259-62.
'Preaching Christ', vol. II, 393-403.
'Regeneration', vol. II, 485-89.

Hastings, James, (ed.) *Encyclopaedia of Religion and Ethics*, (Edinburgh: T & T Clark, 1908-26).
'Fall', vol. V, 701-5.
'Mediation', vol. VIII, 515-20.
'Righteousness (in St Paul's Teaching)', vol. X, 786-90.

Jacobus, M.W., with E. E. Nourse and A.C. Zenos, *A Standard Bible Dictionary*, (eds.), (New York and London: Funk and Wagnalls, 1909).
'Church Life and Organisation', 129-36.
'Jesus Christ', 406-23.
'Paul', 645-51.

5. Contributions to Journals and Newspapers

Abbreviations

BW   British Weekly
CWP   Christian World Pulpit
Exp   The Expositor
ExpT   Expository Times
UFCM   United Free Church Magazine
UM   Union Magazine

1886
'The Witness of Peter to the Sufferings of Christ', *The Theological Review and Free Church Quarterly,* 1, 1886, 310-21.

1893
'Questions of Christ', *CWP*, 42, 1893, 250-3.

1894
'The Best Hundred Religious Books', *BW*, 23 August 1894, 290.
'The Life and Letters of Erasmus', *BW*, 4 October 1894, 6.
'The Sadducees and Immortality', *Exp*, Series IV, vol. X, December 1894, 401-9.

1895
'Three Motives to Repentance', *Exp*, Series IV, vol. VII, March 1895, 232-7.

1896
'Caesar and God', *Exp*, Series V, vol. III, January 1896, 61-9.
'The Great Commandment', *Exp*, Series V, vol. III, April 1896, 312-20.
'The Charter of the Church: "I Will Build My Church"', *BW*, 21 May 1896, 65-6.
'David's Son and David's Lord', *Exp*, Series V, vol. III, June 1896, 445-56.
'The Philosophy of Belief', *BW*, 2 July 1896, 198.
'The Dissolution of Religion', *Exp*, Series V, vol. IV, October 1896, 263-76.

1897
'The Growth of the Church, *CWP*, 52, 1897, 312-14.
'Stones of Stumbling', CWP, 52, 1897, 140-2.
'Dogmatic Theology', *Exp*, Series V, vol. VI, December 1897, 422-40.

1898
'The Everlasting Gospel', *BW*, 3 February 1898, 313-4.

'Dr. Dale's Life', *BW*, 1 December 1898, 121-2.

1899
'The Church of the Future', *CWP*, 66, 1899, 198-200.
'The Religious Use of Memory', *CWP*, 61, 1899, 328-30.

1900
'The Apostolic Age: Its Life, Doctrine, Worship and Polity', *Critical Review*, X, No. 3, May, 1900, 253-9.
'Ritschl in English', *ExpT*, vol. XII, December 1900, 135-9.
'The Cross of Christ', *CWP*, 67, 1900, 292-3.

1901
'The True sense of Joy', *CWP*, 59, 1901, 81-3.
The Contemplation of the Cross', *CWP*, 59, 1901, 233-5.
'The Historical New Testament', *BW,* 21 February 1901, 481-2.
'The Theology of the Epistle to the Romans'
I. 'Introductory', *Exp*, Series VI, vol. III, January 1901, 1-14.
II. 'The Doctrine of Sin', *Exp*, Series VI, vol. III, March 1901, 172-81.
III. 'The Doctrine of Sin', *Exp*, Series VI, vol. III, April 1901, 283-95.
IV. 'The Gospel a Divine Righteousness', *Exp*, Series VI, vol. III, June 1901, 433-50.
V. 'Faith and the Righteousness of God', *Exp*, Series VI, vol. IV, August 1901, 81-95.
VI. 'The Righteousness of God and the New Life', *Exp*, Series VI, vol. IV, October 1901, 299-311.
VII. 'The New Life and the Spirit', *Exp*, Series VI, vol. IV, December 1901, 422-36.
'Christ's Teaching on Common Things: Anger', *UM*, I, 1901, 30-3.
'The Propagation of the Gospel in Scotland Today', *UM*, I, 1901, 102-4.
'Christ's teaching on Common Things: On Money', *UM*, I, 1901, 412-14.
'Six Saints of the Covenant', *UM*, I, 1901, 557-9.
'Encyclopaedia Biblica and the Gospels', *UM*, I, 1901, 170-4.

1902
'The Letters of John Richard Green', *UM*, II, January 1902, 20-3.
'Principal Fairbairn's New Book', *BW,* 12 June 1902, 205-6.
'The Letters of a Man of Taste', *UM*, II, June 1902, 259-63.
'The Place of Christianity in Education' (I), *UM*, II, July 1902, 292-6.
'The Place of Christianity in Education', (II), *UM*, II, August 1902, 341-4.
'Offended in Christ', *BW*, 4 September 1902, 467-8.

'The Varieties of Religious Experience', *UM*, II, September 1902, 417-20.
'The Gospels and the Gospel', (I), *BW*, 6 November 1902, 73-4.
'The Gospels and the Gospel', (II), *BW*, 13 November 1902, 97-8.
'The Fact basis of the Christian Religion', *CWP*, 51, 1902, 99-102,

1903
'The Questions of Jesus - I. 'Have Ye Never Read?'", *UM*, III, January 1903, 34-7.
'The Life of Bishop Westcott', *UM*, III, June 1903, 261-4.
'Questions of Jesus. 1 Have Ye Never Read?', *UM, III,* 1903, 34-6.
'Is the Church Losing Her Hold on the Working-classes, especially the Poor?', *UM*, III, September 1903, 389-91.
'The Atonement and the Modern Mind' (I), *Exp*, Series VI, vol. VIII, August 1903, 81-105.
'The Atonement and the Modern Mind' (II), *Exp*, Series VI, vol. VIII, September 1903, 161-82.
'The Atonement and the Modern Mind', (III), *Exp* Series VI, vol. VIII, October 1903, 241-66.

1904
'Can Sin be Forgiven', *CWP*, 65, 1904, 393-6.
'Hard Sayings of Jesus', *UM*, IV, January 1904, 31-3.
'Adam and Christ in St. Paul', *Exp*, Series VI, vol. IX, February 1904, 147-60.
'We Would See Jesus', *BW*, 7 April 1904, 685-6.
'The Wittiest Englishman of his Generation', *UFCM*, April 1904-5, 27-30.
'The Education of a Minister', *The London Quarterly Review*, CII, July 1904, 1-16.
'A State Church Theologian', *BW*, 25 August 1904, 465-6.
'Thomas Chalmers', *The British Monthly*, September 1904, 441-8.
'Mark Rutherford', *UFCM*, November 1904, 20-3.

1905
'New Light on the Apocalypse', *UFCM*, January 1905, 13-16.
'Harnack and Loisy on the Essence of Christianity', *Exp*, Series VI, vol. XI, February 1905, 105-23.
'The Wittiest Englishman of his Generation', *UFCM*, April 1905, 27-30.
'Jesus Christ the Righteous', *BW,* 2 November 1905, 89-90.
'The Latest Word on the Atonement', *BW*, 16 November 1905, 153-4.

1906
'John Wesley on Books', *UFCM*, February 1906, 24-8.

'The Literal Interpretation of the Sermon on the Mount', *BW*, 23 August 1906, 469-70.
'Faith and Freedom', *BW*, 13 December 1906, 289-90.

1907
'Principal Rainy', *BW*, 3 January 1907, 368.
'The Doctrine of the New Birth', *ExpT*, XVIII, January 1907, 182-3.
'The New Theology', *BW,* 21 March 1907, 637-8.
'God, Sin and the Atonement', *BW*, 28 March 1907, 669-70.
'The Gospel According to St. Matthew', *BW,* 18 April 1907, 26.
'Christ in Christian Doctrine', *BW*, 18 July 1907, 353-4.
'Faith and Science', *BW*, 11 April 1907, 717-8.
'Positive Preaching and the Modern Mind', *BW*, 24 October 1907, 57-8.
'The Historical Evidence for the Resurrection of Jesus Christ', *BW,* 21 November 1907, 170-1.
'Speaking Against the Son of Man and Blaspheming the Spirit', *Exp*, Series VII, vol. IV, December 1907, 521-32.
'Women's Work in the Church', *CWP*, 71, 1907, 53-6.

1908
'Taking Away the Lord', *BW*, 9 April 1908, 1-2.
'The Cup of the Lord and the Cup of Demons', *Exp*, Series VII, vol. V, April 1908, 289-304.
'He that Came by Water and Blood', *Exp*, Series VII, vol. V, May 1908, 416-28.
'Jerusalem', *BW,* 28 May 1908, 177-8.
'Principal Hutton', *BW*, 4 June 1908, 202.
'Christ and the World's Women', *CWP*, 74, 1908, 361-4.

1909
'Criticising the Church', *BW*, 4 February 1909, 489-90.
'The Church and Worship', *BW*, 11 February 1909, 513-4.
'The Church and the Gospel', *BW*, 25 February 1909, 561-2.
'The Church and Christian Character', *BW*, 8 April 1909, 1-2.
'Jesus Estimate of John the Baptist', Exp, Series VII, vol. V, May 1909, 60-75.
'The Tests of Life', *BW*, 20 May 1909, 155.
'The Church and the Kingdom of God', *BW*, 20 May 1909, 153-4.
'Why we are not interested in Missions', *Missionary Record of the United Free Church of Scotland*, vol. IX, 1909, 52-3.
'The Church and Legislation', *BW*, 19 August 1909, 457-8.
'Hate', *ExpT*, vol. XXI, October 1909, 41-42.
'Jesus or Christ', *BW*, 18 November 1909, 185-6.
'Love', *ExpT*, XXI, November 1909, 72-6.

1910
'A Jewish View of Christ', *BW*, 27 January 1910, 496.
'Modern Substitutes for Christianity', *BW*, 24 February 1910, 581-2.
'The Quest of the Historical Jesus', *BW*, 7 April 1910, 26.
'Dividing Lines', *BW*, 2 June 1910, 209-10.
'Our Lord's Last Words on Prayer', *BW*, 28 July 1910, 409-10.
'The Christian's Cross', *BW*, 18 August 1910, 473-4.
'The Eschatology of the Gospels', *BW*, 13 October 1910, 33-4.
'The Expositor's Greek Testament', *BW*, 27 October 1910, 121.
'The Work of Christ', *BW*, 10 November 1910, 173.
'Professor H. R. Mackintosh's Sermons', *BW*, 9 December 1910, 282.
'A Great Book', *BW*, 16 December 1910, 344.
'Why was Jesus Sent to the Cross', *BW*, 29 December 1910, 404.
'Young Women and Temperance', *CWP*, 78, 1910, 296-9.

1911
'Factors of Faith in Immortality, (I)', *Exp*, Series VIII, vol. I, January 1911, 1-20.
'Factors of Faith in Immortality, (II)', *Exp*, Series VIII, vol. I, February 1911, 118-28.
'Discipleship and the Church', *BW*, 16 February 1911, 565-6.
'Studies in the Synoptic Problem', *BW*, 23 March 1911, 717.
'The Missionary Motive', *BW*, 27 April 1911, 90.
'Introduction to the Literature of the New Testament', *BW*, 18 May 1911, 177-8.
'St. Paul and Woman', *BW*, 24 August 1911, 505-6.
'The Christian Doctrine of Man', *BW*, 31 August 1911, 532.
'Criticism and the Parables. I. The Transmission of the Parables', *Exp*, Series VIII, vol. II, August 1911, 117-36.
'Criticism of the Parables. II. The Interpretation of the Parables', *Exp*, Series VIII, vol. II, September 1911, 219-39.
'Principal Wm. Patrick', *BW*, 5 October 1911, 3.
'First Corinthians', *BW*, 12 October 1911, 61.
'The Living God', *BW*, 2 November 1911, 129-30.
'Friends of God', *CWP*, 79, 1911, 296-9.
'The Secret of Missionary Enthusiasm', *CWP*, 79, 1911, 273-6.

1912
'Principal Fairbairn', *BW*, 15 February 1912, 574.
'God's Forgiveness and Ours', *BW*, 13 June 1912, 261-2.
'Christian Faith in God', *BW*, 12 September 1912, 561-2.
'Foundations', *BW*, 24 December 1912, 409-10.
'Right and Wrong Ways of Using the Bible', *CWP*, 80, 1912, 367-72.

1913

'Christianity and the Historical Christ', *Exp*, Series VIII, vol. V, January 1913, 12-28.
'The Constructive Task of Protestantism', *The Constructive Quarterly*, 1, June 1913, 213-26.
'There He Spake with Us', *BW*, 14 August 1913, 481-2.
'Religions and the True Religion', *BW*, 21 August 1913, 501-2.
'Professor James Orr', *BW*, 11 September 1913, 576.
'The New Testament and the English Tongue', *BW*, 4 December 1913, 281-2.

1914

'St Paul and the Mystery Religions, *BW*, 29 January 1914, 521-2.
'The Late Rev A. D. Grant', *The Greenock Telegraph and Clyde Shipping Gazette*, 2 February 1914.
'Can Faith Dispense with Facts?', *BW*, 21 May 1914, 201-2.
'The Christian Community and the War', *BW*, 13 August 1914, 505-6.
'The War and the National Conscience', *BW*, 20 August 1914, 521-2.
'A Unique Book on St. Paul', *BW*, 14 December 1914, 257-8.

1915

'War and the Fear of God', *BW*, 21 January 1915, 325-6.
'Men and Money', *BW*, 4 February 1915, 365-6.
'A Commentary on St. Matthew', *Exp*, Series VIII, vol. IX, March 1915, 285-8.
'The War and the Voice of God to the Church', *Record of the Home and Foreign Mission Work of the United Free Church of Scotland*, July 1915, 285-6.
'The Darkness and the Light', *BW*, 12 August 1915, 393-4.
'Victory Over Death', *BW*, 26 August 1915, 425-6.
'Mr Balfour's Gifford Lectures', *BW*, 7 October 1915, 1-2.

1916

'The Constraint of the Cross', *BW*, 30 March 1916.[3]
'Shall He Find Faith?', *BW*, 6 April 1916, 1-2.
'Conscience', *BW*, 13 July 1916, 281-2.
'After the War', *BW*, 17 August 1916, 369-70.

1917

'State Purchase', *BW*, 18 January 1917, 309-10.

---

[3] This article does not appear in the *British Weekly* at the date indicated in *War and the Fear of God*. Having been unable to trace it elsewhere in the *British Weekly* it may be one of the additional chapters not previously published.

'Burns and the Present Distress', *The Glasgow Herald*, 25 January 1917.
'Prohibition', *BW*, 15 February 1917, 381-2.

6. Ecclesiastical and Academic Records, with Location.

Congregational and Session Minutes of Greenock Reformed Presbyterian Congregation, (after July 1876, Greenock Martyrs), held at NAS
CH3 /669/1, Minutes, 1860-83.
CH3/669/2, Congregational Minutes, 1860-76.
Session and Deacons' Minutes of St John's Free Church of Scotland, held at Glasgow City Archives, Mitchell Library
CH3/1162/3, *Session Minutes*.
CH3/1162/8, *Deacons' Minutes*.
Session and Deacon's Minutes of Broughty Ferry East Free Church 1862-1947, held in Dundee Records Office, CH3/1156/1-3
Minutes of Dundee Presbytery of the Free Church of Scotland, 1881-1900, held in Dundee Records Office, CH3/91/5-6.
Minutes of the Free Presbytery of Greenock, held in NAS, CH3/166/4
Free College Church Annual Reports 1897-98, held in Mitchell Library, Glasgow
Annual College Calendar of the Free Church of Scotland, 1880-1900. (Glasgow University Library).
Greek Class Register, University of Glasgow, 1876-77, MSGEN 900/2/2
Minute Books of Senate of the Free Church/ UF/ Trinity College, Glasgow 1857-1977, held at Glasgow University Archives, 84/1/1/1 and 84/1/2/2.
Proceedings and Debates of the General Assembly of the Free Church of Scotland. (Edinburgh: Ballantyne, Hanson and Company, 1890-99).
Proceedings and Debates of the General Assembly of the United Free Church of Scotland, (ed.), G. M. Reith, (Edinburgh: Lorimer and Chalmers, 1900-16).
Church Union Journal, Glasgow, 1911-15. (Glasgow University Library).

7. Unpublished Theses and Dissertations

Campbell, Iain D., 'George Adam Smith, 1856-1942', (Edinburgh PhD, 2001).
Campbell, Keith, 'The Free Church of Scotland and the Territorial Ideal', (Edinburgh PhD, 1999).
Kinnear, Malcolm, 'Scottish New Testament Scholarship and the Atonement', 1845-1920, (Edinburgh PhD, 1996).
Kwon, Moon Sang, 'A Study of Scottish Kenoticism: the Interpretation of the Self-Emptying of Christ in Ethical Categories with particular reference to A. B. Bruce and H. R. Mackintosh', (Aberdeen PhD, 1999).

Mikolaski, Samuel J., 'The Nature of Human Response to the Work of Christ in the Objective Theories of the Atonement advanced in Recent British Theology by R. W. Dale, James Denney and P. T. Forsyth', (Oxford PhD, 1958).

Taylor, John Randolph, 'Principal James Denney: A Survey of his Life and Work and a Critical Analysis and Appraisal of His Contribution to the Field of Biblical Theology', (Aberdeen PhD,1956).

Wilkinson, D. A. ' "We Preach Jesus Christ and Him Crucified": A Comparison and Contrast of P. T. Forsyth and James Denney's Understanding of the Atonement and How They Preached it'. (King's College, London, 1995).

8. Obituaries

James Denney

'Principal Denney, Eminent Theologian', *Glasgow Herald*, 13 June 1917.

'Principal Denney. An Appreciation', W. M. Clow, in *Glasgow Herald*, 13 June 1917.

'Principal Denney', W. Robertson Nicoll, *BW*, 14 June 1917.

'Principal Denney,' James Moffatt, *BW*, 21 June 1917.

'Dr Rendel Harris on Dr. Denney', *BW*, 28 June 1917.

'Professor W. P. Paterson's Tribute to Dr Denney', *BW*, 5 July 1917.

'Principal Denney: Some Tributes', *The Record of the Home and Foreign Mission Work of the United Free Church of Scotland*, August, 1917, 260-64

'Principal Denney as a Theologian', H. R. Mackintosh, in *ET*, vol. xxviii, August, 1917, 488-494.

'Principal James Denney', W. M. Clow, in *Presbyterian Alliance. Quarterly Register*, vol. xi, August 1917, 4.

'Dr James Denney', *The Times*, 13 June 1917, 9d.

Mary Denney

'The Late Mrs Denney', *BW*, 26 December 1907, 341.

'Mrs Denney', *BW*, 2 January 1908, 373.

'Mrs Denney', *Temperance Leader and League Journal*, 28 December 1907, 830.

9. Secondary Literature

Ahlstrom, S. E., 'The Scottish Philosophy and American Theology', *Church History* 24, 1955, 257-72.

Ahlstrom, S. E., *A Religious History of the American People*, (New Haven: Yale University Press, 1972).

Anderson, R. D., *Scottish Education Since the Reformation*, (Dundee: Economic and Social History Society of Scotland, 1997).

Barbour, G. F., *The Life of Alexander Whyte*, (London: Hodder & Stoughton, 1924).

Bebbington, D. W., *Evangelicalism in Modern Britain*, (London: Unwin Hyman, 1989).

Boswell, James, *The Life of Dr. Johnson*, (London: Random House, 1992).

Brackenridge, 'The "Sabbath War" of 1865-66,' *RSCHS*, xvi, 1966, 23-34.

Brown, Callum, *Religion and Society in Scotland Since 1707*, (Edinburgh University Press, 1997).

Brown, Stewart J., 'Thomas Chalmers and the Communal Ideal', in T. C. Smout (ed.), *Victorian Values: A Joint Symposium of the Royal Society of Edinburgh and the British Academy December 1990*, (Oxford: Oxford University Press, 1992), 61-80.

Brown, Stewart J., ' "A Solemn Purification by Fire": Responses to the Great War in the Scottish Presbyterian Churches, 1914-1919', *Journal of Ecclesiastical History*, 45, 1994, 82-104.

Brown, Stewart J., and G. Newlands, *Scottish Christianity in the Modern World*, (Edinburgh: T & T Clark, 2000).

Bryce, Mary R. L., *Memoir of John Veitch, LL.D*, (Edinburgh, 1896).

Cage, R. A., *The Working Class in Glasgow c.1750-c.1914*, (London: Croom Helm, 1987).

Caird, Edward, *Lectures on Literature and Philosophy*, vol. ii, (Glasgow, 1892).

Caird, Edward, *Lay Sermons and Addresses*, (Glasgow: Maclehose and Sons, 1907).

Caird, G.B., 'Biblical Classics, Part 8: James Denney's "The Death of Christ"', *ExpT*, xc, 1979-80, 196-99.

Cairns, David, *The Army and Religion. An Enquiry and its bearing upon the Religious Life of the Nation*, (London: MacMillan, 1919).

Cameron, Nigel M. De S., *Biblical Higher Criticism and the Defence of Infallibilism in Nineteenth Century Britain*, (New York: Mellen Press, 1987).

Cameron, Nigel M. De S. (ed.), *Dictionary of Scottish Church History and Theology*, (Edinburgh: T & T Clark, 1993).

Campbell, Iain D., '"Fact not Dogma": George Adam Smith, Evangelicalism and Biblical Criticism', *Scottish Bulletin of Evangelical Theology*, 18.1, 2000, 3-20.

Campbell, Iain D., *Fixing the Indemnity: The Life and Work of Sir George Adam Smith (1856-1942)* (Carlisle: Paternoster, 2004)
Candlish, J. S., 'Soundness and Freedom in Theology. Can they be Combined?', *BFER*, 1876, 165-76.
Candlish, J. S., *The Authority of Scripture Independent of Criticism*, (Edinburgh, 1877).
Cashdollar, Charles D., *A Spiritual Home. Life in British and American Reformed Congregations, 1830-1915*, (Pennsylvania: Pennsylvania University Press, 2000).
Cheyne, A. C., *The Transforming of the Kirk*, (Edinburgh: St Andrew Press, 1983).
Cheyne, A. C., *Studies in Scottish Church History*, (Edinburgh: T&T Clark, 1999).
Church Union Journal, Glasgow, 1911-15, (Glasgow University Library).
Clow, W. M., *George Reith. A Scottish Ministry*, (London: Hodder & Stoughton, 1928).
Coffey, John, 'Democarcy and Popular Religion: Moody and Sankey's Mission to Britain, 1873-1875', in E. F. Biagini (ed.), *Citizenship and Community. Liberals, Radicals and Cultural Identities in the British Isles, 1865-1931*, (Cambridge: Cambridge University Press, 1996), 93-119.
Corts, Thomas E., *Henry Drummond. A Perpetual Benediction*, (Edinburgh: T & T Clark, 1999).
Couper, W. J., 'The Reformed Presbyterian Church in Scotland', *RSCHS*, ii, 1925, 3-179.
Coutts, J., *History of the University of Glasgow, 1451-1909*, (Glasgow: Glasgow University, 1909).
Currie, D. A., 'Denney, James', in Timothy Larsen (ed.), *Biographical Dictionary of Evangelicals*, (Leicester: IVP, 2003), 185-7.
Darlow, T.H., *William Robertson Nicoll: Life and Letters*, (London: Hodder & Stoughton, 1925).
Davey, Nancy, *Broughty Ferry, Village to Suburb*, (Dundee: City of Dundee District Council, 1976).
Davie, G, *The Democratic Intellect*, (Edinburgh: Edinburgh University Press, 1961).
Davis, H.W.C and J. R. H. Weaver (eds), *Dictionary of National Biography, 1912-1921*, (London: Oxford University Press, 1927).
Devine, Tom, *The Scottish Nation, 1700-2000*, (London: Penguin, 1999).
Dickie, John, *Fifty Years of British Theology*, (Edinburgh: T & T Clark, 1937).
Dillistone, F. W., 'Atonement', in *Christian History and Interpretation. Studies presented to John Knox*, (Cambridge: Cambridge University Press, 1967), 135-56.

Dorrien, Gary, *The Remaking of Evangelical Theology*, (Louisville: Westminster John Knox, 1998).
Dorrien, Gary, *The Making of American Liberal Theology. Imagining Progressive Religion*, (Louisville: Westminster John Knox, 2002).
Douglas, J.D., 'Denney, James', in J. D. Douglas (ed.), *New International Dictionary of the Christian Church*, (Exeter: Paternoster, 1974).
Drummond, Andrew L., and James Bulloch, *The Church in Victorian Scotland, 1843-1874*, (Edinburgh: St Andrew Press, 1975).
Drummond, Andrew L., and James Bulloch, *The Church in Late Victorian Scotland, 1874-1900*, (Edinburgh: St Andrew Press, 1978).
Edwards, D. L., *Leaders of the Church of England*, (Oxford: Oxford University Press, 1971).
Elwell, W. A., and J. D. Weaver (eds.), *Bible Interpreters of the 20th Century. A Selection of Evangelical Voices*, (Grand Rapids: Baker, 1999).
Encyclopaedia Britannica, (11th Ed.), (New York: Encyclopedia Britannica, 1910-11).
Fleischacker, Samuel, 'The Impact on America: The Scottish Philosophy and the American Founding', in Alexander Broadie (ed.), *The Cambridge Companion to the Scottish Enlightenment*, (Cambridge: Cambridge University Press, 2003), 316-27.
Fleming, J. R., *A History of the Church in Scotland, 1875-1929*, (Edinburgh: T & T Clark, 1933).
Franks, R. S., *The Work of Christ. A Historical Study of Christian Doctrine*, (London: Nelson, 1962).
Fraser, Hamish, and Irene Maver, *Glasgow. Volume II: 1830-1912*, (Manchester: Manchester University Press, 1996).
Funk, Robert W, 'The Watershed of the American Biblical Tradition: The Chicago School, First Phase, 1892-1920', *Journal of Biblical Literature*, 95, 1976, 4-22.
Gallagher, T., 'A Tale of Two Cities; Communal Strife in Glasgow and Liverpool before 1914', in R. Swift, and S. Gilley (eds), *The Irish in the Victorian City*, (London: Croom Helm, 1985). 106-29.
Gallagher, T., 'The Protestant Irish in Scotland', in T. M. Devine (ed.), *Irish Immigrants and Scottish Society in the 19th and 20th Centuries*, (Edinburgh: Edinburgh University Press, 1991), 219-43.
Gammie, Alexander, *Preachers I Have Heard*, (London: Hodder & Stoughton, nd).
Garvie, A. E., *The Ritschlian Theology*, (Edinburgh: T & T Clark, 1899).
Garvie, A. E., 'The Influence of Ritschl and His School on Evangelical Theology', *CWP*, 50, 1901, 263-5.
Garvie, A. E., '"Christ Crucified" for the Thought and Life of Today', *ExpT*, xxx, 1918-19, 83-5; 138-41; 179-81.

Garvie, A. E., *The Christian Doctrine of the Godhead*, (London: Hodder & Stoughton, 1925).
Gasque, W. W., 'James Denney', in Walter A. Elwell (ed.), *Evangelical Dictionary of Theology*, (Basingstoke: Baker, 1985).
Gerrish, Brian, *The Old Protestantism and the New. Essays on the Reformation Heritage*, (Edinburgh: T & T Clark, 1982).
Gordon, James M., *Evangelical Spirituality. From the Wesleys to John Stott*, (London: SPCK, 1991).
Gorringe, Timothy, *God's Just Vengeance*, (Cambridge: Cambirdge University Press, 1996).
Graham, Gordon, ' The Scottish Tradition in Philosophy', *The Aberdeen University Review*, LVIII, No. 201, Spring, 1999, 1-12.
Graham, Gordon, 'Morality and Feeling in the Scottish Enlightenment', *Philosophy*, 76, 2001, 271-82.
Graham, Gordon, 'The Nineteenth Century Aftermath', in Alexander Broadie (ed.), *Cambridge Companion to the Scottish Enlightenment*, (Cambridge: Cambridge University Press, 2003), 338-50.
Hart, Trevor, (ed.), *The Dictionary of Historical Theology*, (Grand Rapids: Eerdmans, 2001).
Hayes, John H., *Dictionary of Biblical Interpretation*, 2 vols, (Nashville: Abingdon, 1999).
Hazlett, William Ian P., *Traditions of Theology in Glasgow, 1450-1990. A Miscellany*, (Edinburgh: Scottish Academic Press, 1993).
Helm, Paul, 'Thomas Reid, Common Sense and Calvinism', in Hendrik Hart, et al. (eds.), *Rationality in the Calvinian Tradition*, (Lanham: University Press of America, 1983), 71-89.
Heron, A. I. C., *A Century of Protestant Theology*, (Cambridge: Lutterworth, 1980).
Hetherington, H. J. W., *The Life and Letters of Sir Henry Jones*, (London: Hodder & Stoughton, 1924).
Hinchliff, Peter, *God and History. Aspects of British Theology 1875-1914,* (Oxford: Oxford University Press, 1992).
Hodge, C. Wistar, 'Dr Denney and the Doctrine of the Atonement', *Princeton Theological Review,* xvi, 1918, 623-41.
Hughes, P. E., 'Evangelist-Theologian: An Appreciation of James Denney', *Christianity Today*, 1, 26 November 1967, 196-9.
Hughes, T. H., *The Atonement: Modern Theories of the Doctrine*, (London: Allen & Unwin, 1949),
Humes, W. M., 'Science, Religion and Education: A Study in Cultural Interaction', in Walter M. Humes and Hamish M. Paterson (eds.), *Scottish Culture and Scottish Education, 1800-1980,* (Edinburgh: John Donald, 1983), 115-36.
Hunsberger, G. R., *Bearing the Witness of the Spirit. Lesslie Newbigin's Theology of Cultural Plurality*, (Grand Rapids: Eerdmans, 1998).

Hunter, A. M., 'The Theological Wisdom of James Denney', *ET*, lx, 1949, 238-40.
Hutchison, M., *The Reformed Presbyterian Church in Scotland, its Origin and History, 1680-1876*, (Paisley, 1893).
Iverach, James, 'Edward Caird', *ExpT*, V, 1893-4, 205-9.
Iverach, James, 'Rev. Thomas Martin Lindsay, M.A., D.D.', *UFCM*, January 1906, 6-9.
Jebb, Caroline, *Life and Letters of Sir Richard Claverhouse Jebb, O.M., Litt.D.*, (Cambridge: Cambridge University Press, 1907).
Jebb, R. C., *Humanism in Education*. The Romanes Lecture, (London, 1899).
Jeffrey, George Johnstone, 'In Praise of James Denney', *The Evening Citizen*, Glasgow, 8 October 1938.
Jodock, Darrell, (ed.), *Ritschl in Retrospect. History, Community and Science*, (Minneapolis: Fortress, 1995).
Johnstone, W, (ed.), *William Robertson Smith: Essays in Reassessment*, (Sheffield: Sheffield Academic Press, 1995).
Jones, S. J, *Dundee and District*, (Dundee Local Executive of the British Association for the Advancement of Science, 1968).
Jones, Sir H., and J. H. Muirhead, *The Life and Philosophy of Edward Caird*, (Glasgow: Maclehose, Jackson, 1921).
Jones, Sir Henry, *Old Memories*, (London, 1897).
Kerr, J, *The Higher Criticism: Disastrous Results. Professors Smith, Dods and Denney*, (Glasgow: Bryce, 1903).
Knight, William, *Some Nineteenth Century Scotsmen*, (Edinburgh: Oliphant, 1903).
Leneman, Leah, 'The Scottish Churches and "Votes for Women"', *RSCHS*, xxiv, 1991, 237-52.
Lindsay, T. M., 'The Critical Movement in the Scotch Free Church', *The Contemporary Review*, 33, 1878, 22-34.
Lindsay, T. M., 'Professor W. Robertson Smith's Doctrine of Scripture', *Exp.*, Series IV, vol. X, 1894, 241-64.
Lindsay, T. M., 'The Doctrine of Scripture. The Reformers and the Princeton School', *Exp.*, 1895, 278-93.
Livingstone, David, D. G. Hart and Mark A. Noll (eds), *Evangelicals and Science in Historical Perspective*, (Oxford: Oxford University Press, 1999).
Lynch, J. E. Hazlett, 'James Denney's Doctrine of the Holy Spirit in Relation to the Inspiration of Scripture', *Scottish Bulletin of Evangelical Theology*, 10, 1992, 32-44.
Lyon, John, *Sketch of the History of the Free Church in Broughty Ferry*, (Broughty Ferry, 1884)
MaColl, Dougall, *Among the Masses. Work in the Wynds*, (London, 1867).

MacDonald, H. D., *The Atonement of the Death of Christ*, (Grand Rapids: Baker, 1985).
MacFadyen, J. E., 'Professor A. B. Bruce', *The Biblical World*, February, 1900, 87-104.
Macgregor, William M., *Persons and Ideals*, (Edinburgh: T & T Clark, 1939).
Mackintosh, H. R., 'Dr Denney's New Book: Jesus and the Gospel', *The Scottish Review*, 7, 1908, 748.
Mackintosh, H. R., *The Person of Jesus Christ*, (Edinburgh: T & T Clark, 1912).
Mackintosh, H. R., *Some Aspects of Christian Belief*, (London: Hodder & Stoughton, 1923).
Mackintosh, H. R., *Types of Modern Theology*, (London: Nisbet, 1937).
Mackintosh, Robert, *Historic Theories of the Atonement*, (London: Hodder & Stoughton, 1920).
MacLeod, J. L., *The Second Disruption. The Free Church in Victorian Scotland and the Origins of the Free Presbyterian Church*, (East Linton: Tuckwell Press, 2000).
McN., J. C. W., 'Rev. Professor James Denney, D.D.', *BW*, 11 April 1907, 14.
MacQuarrie, John, *Twentieth Century Religious Thought*, (London: SCM, 1973).
MacQuarrie, John, *Jesus Christ in Modern Thought*, (London: SCM, 1990).
MacRaild, Donald, *Irish Migrants in Modern Britain 1750-1922*, (Basingstoke: MacMillan, 1999).
Marshall, I. H., 'James Denney', in P. E. Hughes (ed.), *Creative Minds in Contemporary Theology*, (Grand Rapids: Eerdmans, 1966), 203-38.
Marshall, I. H., 'They Set us on New Paths, Part 1. The New Testament: Paths Without Destinations', *ExpT*, c, 1988-89, 9-13.
Matheson, Peter C., 'Scottish War Sermons, 1914-1919', *RSCHS*, xvii, 1972, 203-13.
McCosh, James, 'The Scottish Philosophy', *BFER*, 12, 1863, 663-81.
McCosh, James, *The Scottish Philosophy*, (London, 1874).
McCosh, James, 'The Scottish Philosophy as Contrasted with the German', in *BFER*, 32, 1883, 96-114.
McEwen, James, 'The Rationalism of James Denney' unpublished paper delivered to the Aberdeenshire Theological Club, August, 1971. (Author's typescript).
McKim, D., (ed.), *Encyclopaedia of the Reformed Faith*, (Edinburgh: T & T Clark, 1992).
McKim, D., 'Thomas Martin Lindsay', in M. Bauman and M. Klauber (eds.), *Historians of the Christian Tradition. Their Methodology and*

Influence on Western Thought, (Nashville: Broadman and Holman, 1995), 351-75.

McKim, D., (ed.), *Historical Handbook of Major Biblical Interpreters*, (Downers Grove: IVP, 1998).

Mechie, S., *Trinity College Glasgow, 1856-1956*, (London: Collins, 1956).

Mikolaski, Samuel J., 'The Theology of Principal James Denney', *Evangelical Quarterly*, xxxv, 1963, 89-96; 144-8; 209-22.

Miskell, Louise, Christopher Whately and Bob Harris, *Victorian Dundee. Image and Realities*, (East Linton: Tuckwell Press, 2000).

Mozley, J. K., *Some Tendencies in British Theology from the Publication of 'Lux Mundi' to the Present Day*, (London: SPCK, 1951).

Mozley, J. K., *The Doctrine of the Atonement*, (London: Duckworth, 1915).

Muir, Augustus, *John White, CH, DD, LLD*, (London: Hodder & Stoughton, 1958).

Murray, Douglas, *Rebuilding the Kirk. Presbyterian Reunion in Scotland 1909-1929*, (Edinburgh: Scottish Academic Press, 2000).

Neill, Stephen, and Wright, N. T., *The Interpretation of the New Testament, 1861-1986*, rev. ed., (Oxford: Oxford University Press, 1988).

Nicoll, W. Robertson. Scrapbook of letters and clippings relating to Principal Denney.[4]

Noll, Mark A., 'A Brief History of Inerrancy, Mostly in America', *Proceedings of the Conference on Biblical Inerrancy, 1987*, (Nashville: Broadman, 1987), 9-25 and replies, 25-45.

Noll, Mark A., 'Common Sense Traditions and American Evangelical Thought', *American Quarterly*, 37, 1985, 216-38.

---

[4] Consulted by J. R. Taylor in the preparation of his 1956 thesis, courtesy of Lady Robertson Nicoll. In a personal letter the administrator for the family of Lady Robertson Nicoll explained that this item was in a package sent on 28/4/97, while Sir William Robertson Nicoll's papers and the remainder of his library from the Lumsden manse, were being moved in 1997 to the University of Aberdeen. The package never arrived and is presumed lost in transit. The scrapbook was one of a set of 12, 11 of which are as yet uncatalogued but safely held at Aberdeen University. In Scrapbook number one, the Denney scrapbook is itemised as part of the series.

Taylor quoted from this source frequently in his work. Interestingly all his references are to letters written about Denney, by others, after his death, including P. T. Forsyth and P. Carnegie Simpson, George Adam Smith. The absence of any reference to letters written by Denney suggests this was the scrapbook compiled by Nicoll to preserve letters of condolence and appreciation following Denney's death. As such it is an important primary source describing how others estimated Denney's contribution. Its loss is therefore all the more regrettable.

Noll, Mark A., *Between Faith and Criticism. Evangelicals, Scholarship and the Bible*, (Leicester: Apollos, 1991).

O'Neill, J. C., *The Bible's Authority. A Portrait Gallery of Thinkers from Lessing to Bultmann*, (Edinburgh: T & T Clark, 1991.).

Ordnance Gazetteer of Scotland: A Survey of Scottish Topography, 6 vols, (Edinburgh: Thomas Jack, 1882).

Orr, James, *The Ritschlian Theology and the Evangelical Faith*, (London, 1898).

Oulton, J. E. L., 'Books on the Person of Christ. Part 9: James Denney's "Jesus and the Gospel"', *ExpT*, lxiv, 1953, 259-62.

Packer, James I., 'Denney, James', in Sinclair Ferguson and David F. Wright (eds), *New Dictionary of Theology*, (Leicester: IVP, 1988).

Packer, James I., 'What Did the Cross Achieve', in *Celebrating the Saving Work of God*, (Carlisle: Paternoster, 1998), 85-124.

Paterson, W. P., 'Dr Denney's Theology', *Constructive Quarterly*, March, 1919, 69-97.

Paton, D. C., 'Temperance and the Churches in Scotland 1829-1927', *Scottish Records Association Conference Report*, 1987, 22-29.

Paul, R. S., *The Atonement and the Sacraments*, (London: Hodder & Stoughton, 1960), 206-16.

Peake, A. S., 'A Reply to Dr Denney', *Exp.*, January 1904, Series VI, vol. IX, 47-66.

Peake, A. S., *Recollections and Appreciations*, (ed.), W. F. Howard, (London: Epworth, 1938).

Pitts, J, 'James Denney: Evangelical Theologian', *Religion in Life*, 34, 1965, 598-604.

Pritchett, Craig, *Greenock. Housing, Health and Social Conditions 1860-1885*, (Greenock: Local History Archives Project, 1978).

Rashdall, Hastings, *The Idea of Atonement in Christian Theology*, (London: MacMillan, 1919).

Rawlins, Clive, *William Barclay. The Authorised Biography*, (Glasgow: Collins, 1984).

Reardon, B. M. G., *Religious Thought in the Victorian Age*, (London: Longman, 1980).

Reissen, R. A., *Criticism and Faith in Late Victorian Scotland*, (London: UPA, 1985).

Reith, G. M., *Reminiscences of the United Free Church General Assembly, 1900-1929*, (Edinburgh: Moray Press, 1933).

Richmond, James, *Ritschl in Retrospect*, (Glasgow: Collins, 1978).

Robb, J., *Cameronian Fasti. Ministers and Missionaries of the Presbyterian Reformed Church, 1680-1929*, (Edinburgh: Reformed Heritage Press, 1975).

Robertson, C. J. A., 'Early Scottish Railways and the Observance of the Sabbath', *Scottish Historical Review*, 57, 1978, 143-67.

Rogerson, J. W., *The Bible and Criticism in Victorian Britain. Profiles of F. D. Maurice and William Robertson Smith*, (Sheffield: Sheffield Academic Press, 1995).
Ross, K. R, *Church and Creed. The Free Church Case 1900-1904 and its Origins*, (Edinburgh: Rutherford House Books, 1988).
Scorgie, Glen G., *A Call to Continuity: The Theological Contribution of James Orr*, (Macon: Mercer University Press, 1988).
Sell, A. P. F., *Theology in Turmoil. The Roots, Course and Significance of the Conservative-Liberal Debate in Modern Theology*, (Grand Rapids: Eerdmans, 1986).
Sell, A. P. F., *Defending and Declaring the Faith; Some Scottish Examples, 1860-1920*, (Exeter: Paternoster, 1987).
Sell, A. P. F., *The Philosophy of Religion, 1875-1980*, (London: Routledge, 1988).
Sell, A. P. F., *Philosophical Idealism and Christian Belief*, (Cardiff: University of Wales Press, 1995).
Simpson, P. Carnegie, *The Life of Principal Rainy*. 2 vols, (London: Hodder & Stoughton, 1909).
Sjolinder, S, *Presbyterian Reunion in Scotland, 1907-1921*, (Edinburgh: T & T Clark, 1962).
Smout, T. C., *A Century of the Scottish People*, 1830-1950, (London: Collins, 1986).
Stevens, G. B., *The Christian Doctrine of Salvation*, (Edinburgh: T & T Clark, 1905).
Stott, J. R. W., *The Cross of Christ*, (Leicester: IVP, 1986).
Struthers, A.L., *Life and Letters of John Paterson Struthers*, (London: Hodder & Stoughton, 1917).
Taylor, J. R., *God Loves Like That! The Theology of James Denney*, (London: SCM, 1962).
Thomson, Edward A., *The Uncertain Theology in the Colleges of the Free Church*, (Edinburgh, 1880).
Tyler, Colin, 'Spiritual Evolution and the Thought of Edward Caird', in *The Collected Works of Edward Caird*, (www. thoemmes.com/idealism/caird_intro.htm). Last accessed 30/01/04.
Tyler, Colin, 'The Social Liberalism of Edward Caird', in *Collected Works of Edward Caird*, (www.thoemmes.com/idealism/caird_intro2.htm). Last accessed, 30/01/04.
Veitch, John, *Sir William Hamilton. The Man and His Philosophy*, (Edinburgh, 1883).
Walker, T. H., *Principal James Denney, D.D. A Memoir and a Tribute*, (London: Marshall Brothers, 1918).
Warfield, B. B., *Critical Reviews*, (Oxford: Oxford University Press, 1932).
Wells, David, F., 'Introduction', in Denney, James, *Studies in Theology*, (Grand Rapids: Baker, 1976), v-xxvi.

Wells, David, F., *Reformed Theology in America. A History of its Modern Development*, (Grand Rapids: Baker, 1985).

Wilkens, S. and A. Padgett, *Christianity and Western Thought*, vol. 2, (Downers Grove: IVP, 2000).

Witherington, D. J., 'The Church in Scotland, c. 1870-1900: Towards a New Social Conscience?', *RSCHS* 19, 1977, 155-68.

Worrall, B. G., 'Substitutionary Atonement in the Theology of James Denney', *Scottish Journal of Theology*, xxviii, 1975, 341-57.

Wright, D. F., 'Soundings in the Doctrine of Scripture in British Evangelicalism in the First Half of the Twentieth Century', *Tyndale Bulletin*, 31, 1980, 87-106.

Wright, D. F., *The Bible in Scottish Life and Literature*, (Edinburgh: St Andrew Press, 1988).

Wright, D. F., and Badcock, G. D., *Disruption to Diversity, 1846-1996*, (Edinburgh: T & T Clark, 1996).

Wright, R. S., (ed.), *Fathers of the Kirk*, (London: Hodder & Stoughton, 1960).

General Index

Abelardism, 105.
Absolute, The, 59-61,
Ascent of Man, 92, 97.
Atonement, 4, 88, 94, 104-6, 120-1, 132, 145-6, 163-4, 178-9, 202n153, 220-4.
Atonement and the Modern Mind, 61,162-6, 175, 215.
'Authority of Scripture', 155.

Baptists, 115.
Biblical Criticism,3, 35-8, 74-77, 80-5, 140-8, 153-8, 165-6, 174-6, 218-22.
Boswell, *Life of Johnson*, 116, 217.
Briggs, Charles, 141-2.
British and Foreign Evangelical Review, 73, 81.
British Weekly, 1, 3, 5, 7, 148, 184, 196n2.
Broughty Ferry East Free Church of Scotland, 112-14, 149, 189, 220, 257.
Broughty Ferry, Dundee, 3, 11, 88, 112-4, 189, 220.
Bruce, A. B., 66-7, 70, 85-91, 130,
Bushnell, Horace, 207, 223.

Caird, Edward, 4, 5, 40-1, 44-6, 56-61, 64, 65n99, 228.
Cambell, Rev. John McLeod, 131, 206-7, 223.
Candlish, J. S., 71, 80-84.
Carnegie Simpson, P., 203.
Cave, Alfred, 83.
Central Fund, 195-6.
Chicago Theological Seminary, 80, 89, 125-6, 140-8, 181,189.

Christian Doctrine of Reconciliation, 1, 4, 10, 130-1, 202-8, 222-3, 225.'Christian Faith and the Criticism of the Bible', 157-8.
Christological hermeneutic, 175, 176, 218-19.
Christology, 61-7, 88-91, 118-19, 151, 172-3, 206, 221-4, 227-9.
Church unity, 189-96.
Church, 179-81, 185-6, 189-91.
'Church and the Bible', 155-7.
Church and the Kingdom, 184-9.
Classics, 46-48, 167.
College Free Church, Glasgow, 148-9, 152-3.
Cooper, Rev James, 178n36, 191-2.
Covenanters, 17-18.
Creeds, 109, 118-19, 151-2, 173-9, 190-3. *See* Intellectual liberty, Westminster Confession.
Cunningham Lecture, 4, 201, 202, 208.

Darwin, Charles, 35, 91-8, 125, 164-5.
Davidson, A. B., 73.
Davie, George, 41-5.
Death of Christ, 4, 5, 159-162.
Declaratory Acts, 109.
Denney, Elisabeth, 16.
Denney, John, 13-14, 23, 185.
Denney, James
   'Dogmatic Theology'. (Inaugural Lecture, Glasgow), 150-4.
   Appointed Professor at Free Church College, Glasgow, 134-6.
   Awarded Glasgow D.D., 132

Call to Broughty Ferry East Free Church, 112-13.
Call to East Hill Street, Glasgow, 99.
Controversialist, 91-6, 139-47, 154-8, 168-72, 212-15.
Death of Mary Denney, 166-8.
Doctrine of scripture, 8, 140-8, 153-8, 165-6, 174-6, 218-22. *See* biblical criticism, exegetical method, Holy Scripture, inerrancy, infallibility, Reformation and scripture.
Education, 9, 12, 14-15, 22-4, 38-9.
Exegetical method, 48, 109-10, 116-17. See biblical criticism.
Germany, influence of, 12, 30, 35-7, 125, 196-7.
Lectures in Chicago, 125-31, 139-146.
Preacher, 103-12, 117-21.
Reading, 115-16, 195.
Sermons, 3, 103, 117, 123-4.
Theological educator, 10, 72, 153-4, 169-79, 180. *See* pastoral ministry.
Denney, Mary (nee Brown), 103, 114-16, 166-8.
Diamond Jubilee of Queen Victoria, 124-5.
Douglas, Principal George, 71, 73.
Drummond, Professor Henry, 6, 43, 72, 91-98, 212.

East Hill Street Mission, 3, 29, 99-112, 181.
Economic migration, 100-1, 114.
Edinburgh 1910, 194.
Education Act, 1872, 34, 45, 102.
Educational Reform, 40-5, 8.
Ens realissimum, 62, 218, 229.
Evolution of Religion, 61.

Evolution of Theology in the Greek Philosophers, 5.
Experience, 130-2, 163-4, 204-7, 223.

Fraser, Professor, Alexander, 49-50.
Free Church College, Glasgow, 1, 9, 71-2, 127, 148.
Free Church College, Calcutta, 33.
Free St John's, Glasgow, 99-100
Forsyth, P. T., 195, 207.

Garvie, A. E., 128, 213.
Gilmour, Rev. A., 20-21.
Glasgow, 100-2.
Glasgow Herald, 171-2, 196.
Glasgow University, 9, 40-5.
Goold, W. H., 19.
'Gospel according to Paul', 219-22, 224-7.
Great War, 10, 196-201, 203.
Greenock, 12, 15-17, 38.

Hamilton, Sir William, 47, 49, 54-5, 67.
Hegel, G.F., 59, 63-5, 131.
Hodder and Stoughton, 6, 140.
Hodge, Charles, 37, 55.
Holy Scripture, 72-91, 137-9.
Holy Spirit, 145, 177-8.

Irish immigration, 26-28, 201.
Irish Home Rule, 200-1.
Idealism, 59-61, 62, 65, 130-1, 165.
Inerrancy, 125-6, 130, 136, 143-8.
Infallibility, 143-148, 157-8, 212.
Inglis, John, 32-3.
Intellectual development, 2-4, 7-8, 211.
Intellectual liberty, 10-12, 118-9, 139-40, 147, 173-9, 212-15.
Iverach, Principal, 154.

General Index

Jebb, Sir Richard C., 40, 46-9. *See* 'Romanes Lecture', 47-8.
Jesus and the Gospel, 86, 172-3, 176-9, 194, 206, 213.
Jones, Sir Henry, 56, 68.
Justification and Reconciliation, 129.

Kierkegaard, Soren, 162.
Kingdom of God, 184-7, 193.

Labour strikes, 185-6.
'Lecture IX Holy Scripture', 139-146, 237-53.
Lightfoot, J. B., 37, 46.
Lindsay, Professor T. M., 71, 74-80, 166.
Lord's Supper, 110-11, 119-21, 150.
Luther, 37, 144-5.

MacPherson, Rev.James, 135-6.
Martin, Rev Alexander, 191, 192-3.
McCosh, Rev James, 52-4.
Ministerial training, 72, 153-4. *See* pastoral ministry.
Miracles, 169-71.
Missions, 32-4.
Modern Criticism and the Preaching of the Old Testament, 155.
Moody and Sankey, 30, 70, 96, 102, 108, 149.
Moffatt, Professor James, 12, 41, 202.
Mystical union, 160, 228.

Natural Law in the Spiritual World, 43, 91-8, 110, 165, 212.
Nicoll, Sir William Robertson, 1, 5, 6, 64, 97, 114, 156, 166, 167, 191, 201, 203, 209, 213.

On Natural Law in the Spiritual World, 91-5.
Organ music, 121-3.

Orr, Professor James, 1, 4, 56, 57, 153, 166.

Pastoral Ministry, 107-8, 121-5, 132-4, 149.
Paton, John G., 32-3.
Paul, 48-9, 87-8, 106-7, 116-7, 220n38; Colossian Christ, 63-4, 151-2, 229; *See* 'Gospel according to Paul'.
Peake, Professor A. S., 40, 160-1, 214.
'Philosophy and the New Testament', 4-5, 62-7.
Poor, 15-16, 20, 182-3. *See* social concern.
Presbyterian reunion, 19-20, 68, 174, 176-9, 190-1.
Princeton, 24, 36, 140-3.

Rainy, Principal Robert, 209-10.
Rationalism and scripture, 84-5, 128.
Rawlins, Clive, 2.
Reconciliation, 160-2, 202-8.
Reformation and Scripture, 74-6, 141-4.
Reformed Presbyterian Church, 9, 18, 212. Greenock RPC, 20-3.
Reformed Presbyterian Magazine, 17, 21; ethos and content, 24-37.
Reid, Thomas, 50-1, 53.
Reith, Rev George, 148, 153.
Renaissance, 47, 75.
Revival meetings, 30, 96, 102-3, 108.
Ritschl, A, 125, 128-32, 213.
Roman Catholicism, 25-28, 75, 108, 201.
Romans, 6, 137, 210, 224.

Sabbath, 28-30, 113, 124.
Schweitzer, Albert, 3.
Schleiermacher, F., 110, 131.

Science and Christian faith, 43, 91-8, 164-5.
Scottish Common Sense Philosophy, 44, 49-56, 66, 216.
Second Corinthians, 125.
Sin, 136-7, 225-7.
Slavery, 33-4.
Smith, Professor Henry P, 142.
Smith, Sir George Adam, 1, 3, 152, 155-8, 166, 176-7, 213, 219.
Smith, Sir William Robertson, 13, 72-4, 78-80, 81, 83.
Social Concern, 30-1, 33-4, 65, 100, 107-9, 181-4, 184-9. *See* poor, slavery, temperance, women.
Spurgeon, Rev C. H., 115.
Stewart, Professor Dugald, 54, 56.
Struthers, Rev J. P., 110-111, 118, 149.
Studies in Theology, 4, 10, 89, 125-8, 147, 182, 189, 219.
Synoptic Gospels, A. B. Bruce, 90-1.

Taylor, J. R., 1, 6-7, 139, 279.
Temperance and total abstinence, 30-1, 108, 199-201.

Territorial missions, 99, 100-3.
testimonium internum Spiritus Sancti, 83, 141, 145, 159, 219.

Union Magazine, 6, 153.
United Free Church, 3, 157-8, 190. *See* Presbyterian reunion.
United States, 4, 167.

Veitch, Professor John, 40, 46, 49-57, 66, 68.

War and the Fear of God, 196-201.
War, 125, 196-201
Warfield, Professor B. B., 141.
Way Everlasting, 7, 153.
Wesley, Charles, 205.
Wesley, John, 161.
Westminster Confession, 49-50, 70-1, 136, 143, 171, 173-6, 193.
Whyte, Principal Alexander, 209-12.
Women, role of, 187-9, 199.

www.ingramcontent.com/pod-product-compliance
Lightning Source LLC
Chambersburg PA
CBHW061431300426
44114CB00014B/1642